Fatal Fictions

CRIME AND INVESTIGATION IN LAW AND LITERATURE

Edited by Alison L. LaCroix

Richard H. McAdams

and Martha C. Nussbaum

OXFORD
UNIVERSITY PRESS

OXFORD
UNIVERSITY PRESS

Oxford University Press is a department of the University of Oxford. It furthers the University's objective of excellence in research, scholarship, and education by publishing worldwide. Oxford is a registered trade mark of Oxford University Press in the UK and certain other countries.

Published in the United States of America by Oxford University Press
198 Madison Avenue, New York, NY 10016, United States of America.

CIP data is on file at the Library of Congress
ISBN 978-0-19-061078-4

9 8 7 6 5 4 3 2 1
Printed by Sheridan Books, Inc., United States of America

Alison L. LaCroix thanks her parents, Terri and David LaCroix.

Richard H. McAdams thanks his parents, Anne Holt McAdams and Rick McAdams.

Martha C. Nussbaum thanks Saul Levmore and Mike Schill, the two deans who have sponsored our law-literature conferences.

Contents

Contributors

Justin Driver is the Harry N. Wyatt Professor of Law and the Herbert and Marjorie Fried Research Scholar at the University of Chicago. He received his undergraduate degree from Brown University, a master's degree in teaching from Duke University, and a master's degree in modern history from Magdalen College, University of Oxford, where he studied as a Marshall Scholar. In 2004 he graduated from Harvard Law School, where he was an articles editor and book reviews chair of the *Harvard Law Review*. Driver served as a law clerk to Judge Merrick B. Garland, U.S. Court of Appeals for the District of Columbia Circuit, and Justice Sandra Day O'Connor and Justice Stephen Breyer of the Supreme Court of the United States. His principal research interests are constitutional law, constitutional theory, education law, and the intersection of race with legal institutions.

Pamela Foa is a senior fellow at Brown University's Pembroke Center (since 2013). She received a PhD in philosophy from Stanford University in 1974 and a JD from the University of Pittsburgh in 1978, where she also taught philosophy. She served as a clerk to Justice Samuel Roberts of the Pennsylvania Supreme Court and then moved to Chicago, where she was an associate in a large corporate law firm. From there she practiced law in Philadelphia, first civil law as a divisional deputy city solicitor and then criminal law as assistant U.S. attorney for the Eastern District of Pennsylvania. In that capacity she conducted a three-year investigation for the Inspector General of the Department of Justice that uncovered criminal and other misconduct within the Administrative Division of DOJ. She also served in the Eastern District as senior litigation counsel.

Alison L. LaCroix is the Robert Newton Reid Professor of Law and an associate member of the Department of History at the University of Chicago. She is the author of *The Ideological Origins of American Federalism* (Harvard University Press, 2010) and the coeditor, with Martha C. Nussbaum, of *Subversion and Sympathy: Gender, Law, and the British Novel*

(Oxford University Press, 2013). LaCroix holds a BA in history from Yale University, a JD from Yale Law School, and a PhD in history from Harvard University. Her teaching and research interests include legal history, constitutional law, federal jurisdiction, law and linguistics, and law and literature.

Marina Leslie is an associate professor of English at Northeastern University. She is the author of *Renaissance Utopias and the Problem of History* (Cornell University Press, 1999) and coeditor of *Menacing Virgins: Representing Virginity in the Middle Ages and Renaissance* (University of Delaware Press, 1999). She serves on the executive board of the Women Writers Project at Northeastern University and cochairs the Women and Culture in the Early Modern World seminar at the Mahindra Humanities Center at Harvard University. She is currently finishing a book manuscript provisionally entitled "Begetting Crimes," a study of the criminalization of female productive and reproductive labor in seventeenth-century English print culture.

Saul Levmore is the William B. Graham Distinguished Service Professor at the University of Chicago Law School, where he served as dean from 2001 to 2009. His work, often reflecting a law-and-economics approach, has explored topics in public choice and a great many legal subjects, including intellectual property, comparative law, corporate law, criminal law, and inequality. He is currently at work on essays on the challenges of aging and on the timing of lawmaking.

Jonathan Masur is the John P. Wilson Professor of Law and director of the Wachtell, Lipton, Rosen & Katz Program in Behavioral Law, Finance and Economics at the University of Chicago Law School. He holds a BS in physics and an AB in political science from Stanford University and a JD from Harvard Law School. After graduating from law school he clerked for Judge Richard Posner of the U.S. Court of Appeals for the Seventh Circuit and for Chief Judge Marilyn Hall Patel of the U.S. District Court for the Northern District of California. Masur served as deputy dean of the law school from 2012 to 2014 and received the Graduating Students Award for Teaching Excellence in 2014.

Richard H. McAdams is the Bernard D. Meltzer Professor of Law at the University of Chicago. He is the author of *The Expressive Powers of Law* (Harvard University Press, 2015) and coeditor of *Fairness in Law and Economics* (Edward Elgar, 2013). He has served on the National Science Foundation Advisory Panel for Law & Social Sciences, the editorial board of the *Annual Review of Law and Social Science*, and the board of directors of the American Law and Economics Association.

Saira Mohamed is an assistant professor of law at the University of California, Berkeley, School of Law. Her primary interest is the intersection of criminal law and human rights, and her research focuses on responses to mass atrocity and the meanings of responsibility in situations of mass violence. Her most recent articles are in the *Columbia Law Review* and the *Yale Law Journal*. Mohamed previously served as senior adviser in the Office of the U.S. Special Envoy for Sudan and as attorney-adviser for human rights and refugees in the U.S. State Department's Office of the Legal Adviser. She is a graduate of Columbia Law School, Columbia's School of International and Public Affairs, and Yale College.

Melissa Murray is a professor of law at the University of California, Berkeley, School of Law. Her research focuses on the roles that criminal law and family law play in articulating the legal parameters of intimate life and encompasses marriage and its alternatives, the legal regulation of sex and sexuality, reproductive rights and justice, and the marriage equality debate. Her publications have appeared or are forthcoming in the *California Law Review, Columbia Law Review, Michigan Law Review*, and *Yale Law Journal*, among others. Following law school Murray clerked for Sonia Sotomayor, then of the U.S. Court of Appeals for the Second Circuit, and Stefan Underhill of the U.S. District Court for the District of Connecticut. She is a graduate of Yale Law School and the University of Virginia.

Martha C. Nussbaum is the Ernst Freund Distinguished Service Professor of Law and Ethics in the Law School and the Philosophy Department at the University of Chicago. Her most recent book is *Anger and Forgiveness: Resentment, Generosity, Justice* (Oxford University Press, 2016).

Mark Payne is a professor in the Department of Classics, the John U. Nef Committee on Social Thought, and the College at the University of Chicago. His first book, *Theocritus and the Invention of Fiction*, was published by Cambridge University Press in 2007. His second book, *The Animal Part: Human and Other Animals in the Poetic Imagination*, was published by the University of Chicago Press in 2010 and received the 2011 Warren-Brooks Award for Outstanding Literary Criticism. His current book project, "Shared Life," is about ancient ideas of life and the life world, and their viability for the present.

Caleb Smith is professor of English and American studies at Yale University. He is the author of two books on the cultural history of the American criminal justice system, *The Oracle and the Curse* (Harvard University Press, 2013) and *The Prison and the American Imagination* (Yale University Press, 2009), and the editor of *The Life and the Adventures of a Haunted Convict*, an 1858 prison narrative by Austin Reed (Random House, 2016). A contributing editor at *Los Angeles Review of Books*, Smith coedited *No Crisis*, a special series on the state of criticism in the twenty-first century. He has written about contemporary media and the arts for *Avidly, Bomb, Paper Monument*, and other venues.

Richard Strier is the Frank L. Sulzberger Distinguished Service Professor Emeritus in the English Department and the College of the University of Chicago. He is the author of *Love Known: Theology and Experience in George Herbert's Poetry* (University of Chicago Press, 1983), *Resistant Structures: Particularity, Radicalism, and Renaissance Texts* (University of California Press, 1995), and *The Unrepentant Renaissance from Petrarch to Shakespeare to Milton* (University of Chicago Press, 2011), which won the Warren-Brooks Prize for Literary Criticism. He is the coeditor of a number of interdisciplinary collections, including *Shakespeare and the Law: A Conversation among Disciplines and Professions* (University of Chicago Press, 2013), *Writing and Political Engagement in Seventeenth-Century England* (Cambridge University Press, 1999), *Religion, Literature and Politics in Post-Reformation England, 1540–1688* (Cambridge University Press, 1996), *The Theatrical City: Culture, Theatre and Politics in London, 1576–1649* (Cambridge University Press, 1995); and *The Historical Renaissance: New Essays in Tudor and Stuart Literature and Culture* (University of Chicago Press, 1988).

Daniel Telech is a PhD candidate in the Philosophy Department at the University of Chicago and holds a BA from the University of Toronto, Victoria College. He is writing his doctoral thesis on the value and justification of a class of backward-looking emotions, sometimes misleadingly called "moral emotions." In addition to working on issues in moral psychology and ethics, Telech continues to be fascinated by and to pursue research on Nietzsche.

Scott Turow is a former assistant U.S. attorney and the author of ten best-selling works of fiction, including *Innocent* (Grand Central Publishing, 2010), *Presumed Innocent* (Trafalgar Square, 1994), and *The Burden of Proof* (Farrar, Straus and Giroux, 1990), and two nonfiction books, including *One L* (Penguin Publishing, 1977), about his experience as a law student. His books have been translated into more than forty languages, have sold more than 30 million copies worldwide, and have been adapted into a full-length film and two television miniseries. He frequently contributes essays and op-ed pieces to the *New York Times, Washington Post, Vanity Fair*, the *New Yorker*, and the *Atlantic*.

Steven Wilf is the Anthony J. Smits Professor of Global Commerce at the University of Connecticut Law School. A legal historian and an intellectual property law scholar, Wilf is the author of *The Law before the Law* (Lexington Books, 2008) and *Law's Imagined Republic: Popular Politics and Criminal Justice in Revolutionary America* (Cambridge University Press, 2010). He received both his PhD in history and his law degree from Yale University. Prior to teaching law he clerked for the U.S. Court of Appeals for the Second Circuit and was a fellow in comparative legal history at the University of Chicago. He has been the Microsoft Fellow in Law, Property, and the Economic Organization of Society at Princeton University's Program in Law and Public Affairs, a fellow at Harvard University's Radcliffe Institute for Advanced Studies, and a visiting professor at Yale Law School. He is currently completing a history of intellectual property law for Cambridge University Press.

Barry Scott Wimpfheimer is an associate professor of religious studies and law and the director of the Crown Family Center for Jewish and Israel Studies at Northwestern University. Wimpfheimer's first monograph, *Narrating the Law: A Poetics of Talmudic Legal Stories* (University of Pennsylvania Press, 2011), deconstructs a long-standing dichotomy that divides the Talmud into legal and narrative sections. A second monograph, *The Babylonian Talmud: A Biography* (Princeton University Press, forthcoming), charts the reception of the Talmud and demonstrates the impact the work has had over the past millennium as a book, as a central aspect of Jewish intellectual discourse, and as a symbol of Judaism, Jewishness, and Jews. Wimpfheimer received the Salo and Jeanette Baron Prize for his 2005 Columbia University dissertation and has been a fellow at Harvard's Center for Jewish Studies and at Northwestern's Alice Kaplan Institute for the Humanities.

Introduction

THE INTERSECTION OF Western literature and law is perhaps never richer than on the subject of crime. From ancient Greek drama to modern detective fiction, the literary imagination has always focused intensely on the political and psychological causes and consequences of criminal acts, the real or imagined differences in vengeance and justice, and the possibility of mercy, atonement, and reconciliation for those who do criminal wrong. There are at least three reasons for the profound and enduring literary engagement with crime and criminal justice.

First, crime and criminal processes are deeply political and thus an apt subject of political fiction. Defining and punishing crime is one of the fundamental purposes of government, along with the protection of victims by the prevention of crime. And yet criminal punishment remains one of the most abused and terrifying forms of political power, capable of producing grave injustice, preserving repressive regimes, reinforcing social hierarchies, denying fundamental freedoms, convicting the innocent and simply by being excessively harsh and inattentive to the collateral consequences of incarceration. Literary accounts of the struggle against political and social oppression are often focused on the system of criminal punishment.

Second, crime is also—obviously—intensely psychological and therefore an important subject with which a writer can develop and explore character. Although nearly everyone is a criminal in some literal sense (e.g., speeding or jaywalking), the decision to commit certain serious crimes is among the most psychologically difficult and complex that an individual faces in a lifetime, raising questions of moral responsibility and autonomy in the face of extreme deprivation, political injustice, or provocation. The novelist and lawyer Scott Turow describes (in the conference keynote presentation that constitutes the first chapter of this volume) the universal allure of crime fiction as arising from personal struggles with transgression: "It's inherently of interest because we are all battling the impulse to do wrong. . . . People can't help being fascinated by wrongdoing because they are all would-be wrongdoers themselves."

In addition most individuals find themselves involved with crime in other roles at some point in their lives, as victims, witnesses, jurors, or those who are emotionally involved with the recovering victim or ex-con. And as observers of the penal system most of us possess a range of deep, sometimes unexamined, often highly personal beliefs and emotions about what counts as crime, when a person is morally responsible for his or her actions, how the legal system ought to determine guilt, and, given a conviction, what punishment is appropriate. The literary study of character inevitably involves many of these issues, often including the decision whether to cross some criminal line, how to atone for having done so, or how to react to the transgressions or victimization of others.

A third connection between criminal justice and fiction involves the inherently dramatic nature of the legal system itself, particularly the trial. As many critics have noted over the years, the criminal trial in Western culture unfolds as theater. The judge, lawyers, parties, and witnesses all have a ritualized role to perform. The lawyer seeks to adopt a persuasive persona for trial and consciously recognizes the need to "tell a story" with her evidence and argument, a more compelling narrative than the other side will give. Lawyers instruct their clients and witnesses on self-presentation, down to the details of clothing, the costumes of the courtroom. Some lawyers "coach" witnesses in how to perform the testimony in the most convincing way. For a time the jury appears to be the audience of the drama, but it is actually another player, whose verdict provides the climax of the trial.

All of these points might also be said for a civil trial about a real estate contract or accidental slip-and-fall, but there is usually more at stake in the criminal trial, politically and personally, for reasons already stated. The primary focus of fictional trials has always been crime, very often murder, as evidenced by the obsession for film and television shows about police, prosecutors, criminal defense attorneys, forensic pathologists, and crime scene technicians. Turow describes the moment he realized the great theatrical power of a trial: when working as the supervisor of a young prosecutor he observed the prosecutor examine a "star witness" who was "relating most of the tale of how something the community regarded as evil had occurred. And I looked around the courtroom and . . . I realized how spellbound every single person in the courtroom was by this story of what was happening on the witness stand and I suddenly realized: Oh, crime! If you want a universal audience, this is a subject that creates a universal audience."

Because criminal justice touches on so many political and psychological themes essential to literature and comes equipped with a trial process that contains its own dramatic structure, it is no surprise that fiction writers have always engaged crime and punishment. To take an ancient example, the *Eumenides*, the third part of Aeschylus's *Oresteia* trilogy, involves a jury trial of Orestes for the murder of his mother, Clytemnestra, who had murdered his father, Agamemnon. The Furies sought Orestes's death, the next step in a bloody cycle of vengeance. Athena secures an acquittal and then persuades the Furies not to exact vengeance on the citizens of Athens. Thus the play depicts the replacement of retributive vengeance and collective guilt with what we would today recognize as a rule of law. In the February 2014 conference on which this volume is based, we recognized the significance of this ancient trilogy to the enduring themes of the conference by taking a break from the presentation of papers and performing scenes from the trilogy's first and last plays. We are happy to say that one of the first papers we describe below concerns the *Eumenides*.

This volume is the fourth in a series of law-literature investigations emerging from conferences at the University of Chicago Law School. The prior volumes are *Shakespeare and Law: A Conversation among Disciplines and Professions*, edited by Bradin Cormack, Martha C. Nussbaum, and Richard Strier (University of Chicago Press, 2013); *Subversion and Sympathy: Gender, Law, and the British Novel*, edited by Alison L. LaCroix and Martha C. Nussbaum (Oxford University Press, 2013); and *American Guy: Masculinity in American Law and Literature*, edited by Saul Levmore and Martha C. Nussbaum (Oxford University Press, 2014).

We shall not repeat the prior volumes' discussion of the role for law and literature studies, the ways the two fields offer mutual illumination. But the time seems particularly ripe for scholarly investigation of the law and literature of crime. First, in all the prior conferences we observed that crime emerged as a theme even though the organizing topic was not crime, which suggests that criminal fiction deserves some sustained attention of its own.[1] Second, the political themes of crime fiction seem especially pressing in the era of seemingly endless foreign wars and unprecedented domestic surveillance, both addressed to the violent acts of terrorist groups that are, among other things (such as possible acts of war), criminal wrongs. In recent months we have also witnessed greater salience and political protest about troubling aspects of American policing: the militarization of tactics and equipment, racially disproportionate street stops, and racially disproportionate shooting of unarmed suspects.

Finally, it is possible we have arrived at an inflection point for American criminal punishment. The historically unprecedented expansion of incarceration over the past several decades, significantly for the purpose of enforcing the drug war, has slowed, and there are fitful, possibly important efforts to reduce the use of prison. Coincidentally (or not) there is a nascent movement toward the legalization of one drug, marijuana, which is of great significance considering the role that the war on drugs has played in making America a carceral state. And though the future is difficult to predict, it is possible that we are living through the final stages of the American death penalty. With so much activity and controversy about crime and punishment, the time is right for considering the possible collaboration and exchange between law and literature in this troubled domain.

Given the rich potential, we were not disappointed. Our authors wrote essays on literature spanning a wide array of genres, from tragedy to science fiction, lyric poetry, and mystery novels. The literature discussed begins in the age of classical Athens and ends in the current millennium. Most of these works concern the crime of murder, but there is also discussion of perjury, the theft of land, kidnapping, sexual abuse, treason, and the killing of a tree. Within the murders some of the literature focuses intensely on the psychology of individual victims and the search for punishment (Driver on Bigger Thomas; Masur on *The Stranger*; Strier and McAdams on *Othello*; Telech on the *Eumenides*), while others address mass atrocity and systemic political injustice (LaCroix on Thomas Cromwell; Mohamed and Murray on *Omelas*; Nussbaum on *Cry, the Beloved Country*; Smith on antebellum American borderlands). Not all parts of the world are represented, and the dominant original language is English, but the authors analyze texts from Europe, Asia, South Africa, and North America originally written in Aramaic, ancient Greek, French, German, and Hebrew. In sum the essays in this volume are extremely wide-ranging and engaging. The diversity of the collection speaks to the truth of Turow's observation that stories of crime have a "universal audience."

Starting the volume is Turow's "On My Careers in Crime," the keynote speech of the conference, in which he describes his occupations as writer and lawyer. He set out not to be a "crime writer" but simply a novelist, yet he was attracted to stories that included an element of crime, especially after he began working with state prosecutors as a law student and, later, became a federal prosecutor himself. With the unique perspective of a lawyer who has worked on criminal cases weaving narratives for the jury and who has also worked as a writer creating stories about lawyers who weave such narratives, Turow reflects on the deep power that crime stories have for all of us. We have given some flavor of that reflection in the two excerpts already quoted.

The first group of chapters, "Criminal Histories," study history through literature. Daniel Telech focuses, as previously noted, on the third play in the *Oresteia* trilogy. In "Mercy at the Areopagus: A Nietzschean Account of Justice and Joy in the *Eumenides*," Telech provides a compelling reinterpretation of Nietzsche's reading of Aeschylus's masterpiece, saving the reading from the complaint that it oversimplifies and sentimentalizes the *Oresteia* by celebrating the triumph of a modern and liberal understanding of law's rationalist virtues over customary and traditional forms. Telech provides an alternative Nietzschean reading that is consistent with Nietzsche's own, that reintroduces passion and irrationality into the trial and sentencing of Orestes, refrains from romanticizing law, and along the way makes a case for institutionalizing a role for mercy in contemporary legal processes.

Barry Wimpfheimer's essay focuses on the Babylonian Talmud at Makkot 5b, where it records the debate of a hypothetical in which a woman who has already produced two sets of perjuring witnesses attempts to produce a third set of witnesses. One side of the debate believes that the litigant loses the ability to produce a third set of witnesses, while the other contends that witness credibility is unrelated to the litigant and must be evaluated based on the default presumption of witness credibility. In "Suborning Perjury: A Case Study of Narrative Precedent in Talmudic Law," Wimpfheimer connects this legal discussion of perjury to ancient Jewish folk beliefs about women who are twice widowed and are referred to in post-Talmudic literature as *Qatlaniyot*, "killer wives." He argues that the example of the "killer wife" reflects a pattern of rabbinic thought in which the rabbis consistently characterize superstition itself as gendered female. Both stories reflect the absorption of the myth of Pandora's box into rabbinic culture and enrich our understanding of the relationship between rabbinic views of women and the views of their broader culture.

Alison LaCroix discusses the crime of treason as depicted in Hilary Mantel's novels *Wolf Hall* (2009) and *Bring Up the Bodies* (2012). These novels complicate the standard view of Thomas Cromwell as, at best, a Tudor-era fixer and, at worst, a murderer and torturer—a view made famous by Robert Bolt's play *A Man for All Seasons* (1960). In "A Man for All Treasons: Crimes by and against the Tudor State in the Novels of Hilary Mantel," LaCroix claims that Mantel's Cromwell is instead the industrious creator of the modern administrative state. In this characterization Mantel follows the scholarly path of Geoffrey Elton, whose *Tudor Revolution in Government* (1953) rehabilitated Cromwell by arguing that he reformed English government by replacing personal rule with modern bureaucracy and systematizing the royal finances. In different ways both Mantel's and Elton's account rebut the simple image of Cromwell as criminal. But LaCroix argues that Mantel's Cromwell continues to represent two modern species of crime and perpetrator: crimes against the state, in the form of treason, and crimes by the state, in the form of espionage and torture. Because the crimes depicted presuppose the existence of the modern administrative state itself, Mantel's and Elton's modernizing Cromwell may not be as distinct from Bolt's devious Cromwell as the competing accounts would suggest.

Marina Leslie's contribution, "Representing Anne Green: Historical and Literary Form and the Scenes of the Crime in Oxford, 1651," recounts an astonishing tale of crime and punishment. In late November 1650 Anne Green, a twenty-two-year-old Oxfordshire servant, was hanged for the murder of her newborn child. But she did not die. When to everyone's surprise she revived on the anatomist's table at Oxford University, she presented a unique legal, political, and rhetorical problem for the Oxford experimentalists who revived her. Was she guilty or innocent? Subject to the law or saved by God? Leslie explores how these questions were managed in a number of poems in English, French, and Latin by renowned Oxford scholars in 1651 and examines Green's more recent literary legacy in novels by Ian Pears and others.

The historical section concludes with two chapters about Shakespeare. In "Cold-Blooded and High-Minded Murder: The 'Case' of Othello," Richard Strier and Richard McAdams explore the period English law that bears on the crime Othello commits when he kills Desdemona, a matter made complex by his honor motivation and the strange state of mind in which he presents himself. Pointing in one direction, the justice motivation seems to invoke the law of previous centuries that permitted husbands to slay their adulterous wives and lovers. The audience is also made to wonder how the killing would likely appear to a subsequent jury as hot-blooded, done on a sudden affray, and therefore manslaughter rather than murder under the period law. Pointing in the other direction, the English courts at the time Shakespeare wrote *Othello* struggled to contain juries' desire to allow honor killings, and the audience would know that, despite subsequent appearances, Othello's actions were eerily calm at the beginning of the final scene, not obviously hot-blooded manslaughter, but murder. Strier and McAdams argue that, beneath the surface, *Othello* is one of Shakespeare's most legal plays.

By contrast Pamela Foa addresses one of Shakespeare's most overtly legal plays, *Measure for Measure*. There has always been serious disagreement about the motives of the Duke of Vienna, whose odd decisions spur all the action. Foa, a former prosecutor, undertakes to provide a prosecutor's answer—to explore what evidence there is to argue that the duke's motivation is corrupt and criminal. In "What's Love Got to Do with It? Sexual Exploitation in *Measure for Measure*: A Prosecutor's View," Foa shows that the play is at least as much about the corrupting effect of power as the relative virtues or vices of lax or strict enforcement of legal codes prescribing morals and sexual crimes.

The book's second part, "Race and Crime," contains two chapters. In the first Justin Driver explores a connection between Clarence Thomas, associate justice of the Supreme Court of the United States, and Bigger Thomas, the protagonist of Richard Wright's *Native Son*. In his autobiographical account of his life before joining the Court, Justice Thomas includes several striking references to Bigger Thomas. In "Justice Thomas and Bigger Thomas," Driver analyzes Justice Thomas's invocation of Bigger and his reading and apparent misreading of *Native Son*, contrasting that understanding with some of Justice Thomas's more notable opinions in the criminal law realm. The result is a fascinating example of an unusual interplay between literature and law.

Martha C. Nussbaum investigates the connections among anger, injustice, and political change in Alan Paton's *Cry, the Beloved Country*. She argues against the common view that the correction of great injustice requires anger, that is, that anger is a necessary motivation to political mobilization or a necessary creative force for change. The common view includes the idea that political reconciliation requires a process of public atonement on the part of the formerly unjust and public forgiveness by their victims. In "Reconciliation without Anger: Paton's *Cry, the Beloved Country*," Nussbaum describes how the novel shows a personal analogue of the public alternative by which a nation riven by injustice might change. The protagonists are two fathers: a black man whose son has murdered a white man, and a white man whose son is the murder victim. The scenario is a natural one for the classic drama of contrition, apology, and forgiveness, but instead the two fathers turn away from anger to imagine, with generosity, a future of interracial cooperation and constructive work. It is precisely this spirit of generous reconciliation that was eventually instantiated by Nelson Mandela.

The book's third part contains five chapters addressing themes of responsibility and violence. Saul Levmore uses John Fowles's novel *The Collector* to explore the psychology and strategic dynamics of the crime of kidnapping. Kidnapping occurs for many reasons. In *The Collector* the kidnapper seeks emotional control over the victim and hopes for intimacy, while the victim imagines different motives and seeks to gains control of her own, including by faking the trust the kidnapper seeks. The crime shares some of the difficulties of ransom kidnapping, wherein the kidnapper must somehow gain credibility for his promise to harm or kill the victim if he is not paid but also his promise to return the victim alive if he is paid. Levmore concludes that a better understanding of kidnapping would reveal better legal mechanisms for preventing or reacting to it.

In "Premeditation and Responsibility in *The Stranger*," Jonathan Masur examines Albert Camus's use of the French Algerian prosecution, trial, and eventual execution of his protagonist, Meursault, to demonstrate the injustice of French society. Many critics have focused on Meursault's conviction for premeditated murder—actually *assassination*—as the touchstone for this injustice. But Masur argues that Meursault's conviction, and the disquiet Camus means to provoke, can be fully understood only in relation to what might have occurred at a "fairer" trial. Meursault's lawyer suggests that Meursault's act of homicide might have been justified—which would result in Meursault's being acquitted—or that he might face only a short prison sentence for a lesser crime. Yet a close reading of the French Penal Code in effect at the time reveals no such possibility. Even had his trial been conducted fairly, it is implausible that Meursault could have escaped serious punishment for his crime. Whatever sympathy the reader might attach to Meursault, as opposed to his victim, is nurtured by Camus's mischaracterization of French law. A fuller understanding of Meursault's responsibility for the killing, his *mens rea*, and the range of likely carceral outcomes leads to a very different set of conclusions regarding his actions and those of his inquisitors.

Saira Mohamed and Melissa Murray explore Ursula K. Le Guin's famous 1973 science-fiction short story "The Ones Who Walk Away from Omelas," which describes a picturesque utopian paradise and the dystopian bargain necessary to maintain it. The great happiness of the citizens of Omelas is premised on the continuous and abject suffering of a "feebleminded" child who lives alone in a basement. Most Omelans submit to this horrifying bargain with a sense of resignation, but each year a few who can no longer tolerate the bargain walk into the darkness and "do not come back." In "Walking Away: Lessons from Omelas," Mohamed and Murray compare this story to what the criminal law says about those who attempt to walk away from group criminality. The legal defenses of renunciation or abandonment for crimes such as conspiracy require an active thwarting of the crime, which may underestimate the difficulty of extracting oneself from an environment of pervasive wrongdoing.

Mark Payne broadens the focus considerably by discussing crimes with nonhuman victims. In "Before the Law: Imagining Crimes against Trees," he explores the literary depiction of talionic punishments for taking the life of a forest tree. To understand how punishment could have seemed appropriate, he examines a number of fictional examples from antiquity that describe violence against trees in an era before the institution of law as such. In these passages trees are presented as independent beings that require only self-care. As such they provoke violence on the part of human beings who suspect that their own dependence on other humans is akin to the domestication of animals. Talionic punishment for harming a forest tree is thus grounded in the fantasy that the wildness of forest trees stands for the wildness of their human guardians. In conclusion Payne discusses a passage from Nathaniel Hawthorne's *American Notebooks* in which the notion of sacrilege is invoked in relation to harming orchard trees but which grounds this possibility in a different relationship between the lives of trees and human beings: as companion species to one another.

In "Crime Scenes: Fictions of Security in the Antebellum American Borderlands," Caleb Smith moves the focus away from the role of narrative to the role of setting, broadly understood to include spatial claims to jurisprudential standing over allegories of transcendent justice. Opening part 4 of the volume, "Suspicion and Investigation," Smith's case study is the popular literature that emerged from the struggle over Cherokee "removal" between the 1830s and the 1850s: the minister Samuel Worcester's letters from a Georgia prison, the lawyer-novelist William Gilmore Simms's "border romances," and the Cherokee writer John Rollin Ridge's *The Life and Adventures of Joaquín Murieta*, sometimes known as the "first Native American novel." Simms's crime fiction suggested that encounters between antagonistic communities, along the edges of jurisdictions, would produce crime; he argued for the imposition of a single authority to secure the peace. Ridge reworked the same sensational genre to produce the figure of the outlaw as an agent of vengeance in newly annexed California, with its syncretic legal system and its rampant, racist vigilantism. Smith shows how each of these texts attempted, in its way, to coordinate the relations between territories and moral communities in an imperial context.

What we have discussed thus far primarily involves the commission of crime, the trial, and the criminal punishment. But at the end we turn to a genre that focuses on criminal suspicion and investigation: the detective novel. In "Sleuthing toward Bethlehem: Oxford's Tamar, Jerusalem's Ohayon, and Historical Devices in Detective Fiction," Steven Wilf notes that detective novels make it possible to see what often eludes criminal trials: the labyrinth of criminal psychology, a fully developed social context, and the lasting effects of the criminal act as social rupture. Drawing a parallel to legal history—which also situates events—Wilf asks what the gaze of the legal historian might bring to understanding criminality. To answer this question he examines two fictional detectives who are also historians. The Israeli author Batya Gur's protagonist Michael Ohayon is a Sephardic Jew who was trained in history at the largely Western European Hebrew University in Jerusalem. The Ohayon novels revolve around the determination of the social norms of a particular segment of society—and the knowledge that the violation of deeply held norms might lead to murder. The British novelist Sarah Caudwell's quintessential Oxford don, Hilary Tamar, is a fussy and pedantic legal historian. Acutely aware of the interpretive intricacy of medieval English legal documents, Tamar serves as a guide through the uncertain landscape of clues. Wilf examines the contrasting historical methods of Ohayon, who excels at reading social norms, and Tamar, who deftly applies the hermeneutics of legal texts.

The cumulative result of these individual essays is arresting: there are "killer wives" and crimes against trees; a government bureaucrat who sends multiple political adversaries to their death for treason before falling to the same fate himself; a convicted murderer who doesn't die when hanged; a psychopathological collector whose quite sane kidnapping victim nevertheless also collects; Justice Thomas's reading and misreadings of Bigger Thomas; a man who forgives his son's murderer and one who cannot forgive his wife's imagined adultery; and fictional detectives who draw on historical analysis to solve murders. These essays merely begin rather than end a conversation, and they illustrate the great depth and power of crime in literature.

NOTE

1. The volume on Shakespeare—Cormack, Nussbaum & Strier, eds., SHAKESPEARE AND THE LAW: A CONVERSATION AMONG DISCIPLINES AND PROFESSIONS (Univ. of Chicago Press 2013)—involves discussions of murder, adultery, and other crimes in *Macbeth, Othello, Measure for Measure*, and *The Merchant of Venice*. See Daniel Brudney, "Two Differences between Law and Literature," id. at 21 (discussing *Macbeth*); Constance Jordan, "Interpreting Statute in *Measure for Measure*," id. at 101; Richard H. McAdams, "Vengeance, Complicity, and Criminal Law in *Othello*," id. at 121; Richard A. Posner, "Law and Commerce in *The Merchant of Venice*," id. at 147. The volume SUBVERSION AND SYMPATHY: GENDER, LAW, AND THE BRITISH NOVEL, LaCroix & Nussbaum, eds. (Oxford Univ. Press 2013), includes chapters addressing the crimes of infanticide and perjury (see Julia Simon-Kerr, "Pious Perjury in Scott's *The Heart of Midlothian*," id. at 101), and rape (see Marcia Baron, "Rape, Seduction, Purity, and Shame in *Tess of the d'Urbervilles*," id. at 126). In Nussbaum & Levmore, eds., AMERICAN GUY: MASCULINITY IN AMERICAN LAW AND LITERATURE (Oxford Univ. Press 2014), commentators discuss crimes in Faulkner's *Barn Burning*, Fitzgerald's *The Great Gatsby*, and Lee's *To Kill a Mockingbird*. See Saul Levmore, "Snitching, Whistleblowing, and 'Barn Burning': Loyalty in Law, Literature, and Sports," id. at 213; Robin West, "Gatsby and Tort," id. at 86; Richard H. McAdams, "Empathy and Masculinity in Harper Lee's *To Kill a Mockingbird*," id. at 239.

I

On My Careers in Crime

Scott Turow

The keynote address at the Chicago conference on Crime in Law and Literature

---

LET ME START as Rusty Sabich began in *Presumed Innocent*:

> Opening Statement: This is how I always start. I am a prosecutor. I represent the State. I am here to present to you the evidence of a crime. Together you will weigh this evidence; you will deliberate upon it; you will decide if it proves the defendant's guilt. This man . . . and here I point . . . you must always point, Rusty, I was told by John White. That was the day I started in the office. The sheriff took my fingerprints, the Chief Judge swore me in and John White brought me to watch the first jury trial I'd ever seen. New Halsey was making the opening statement for the State and as he gestured across the courtroom, John, in his generous avuncular way with the human scent of alcohol on his breath at 10:00 in the morning, whispered my initial lesson. He was the Chief Deputy Prosecuting Attorney then, a hale Irishman with white hair wild as corn silk. It was almost a dozen years ago, long before I had formed even the most secret ambition to hold John's job myself. "If you don't have the courage to point," John White whispered, "you can't expect them to have the courage to convict." And so I point.
>
> I extend my hand across the courtroom. I hold one finger straight. I seek the defendant's eye. I say "this man has been accused." He turns or blinks or shows nothing at all.

In the beginning I was often preoccupied imaging how it would feel to sit there, held at the focus of scrutiny, ardently denounced before all who cared to listen, knowing that the most ordinary privileges of a decent life: common trust, personal respect and every liberty were now like some cloak you had checked at the door and might never retrieve. I could feel the fear, the hot frustration, the haunted severance.

Now, like ore deposits, the harder stuff of duty and obligation has settled in the veins where those softer feelings moved. I have a job to do. It is not that I have grown uncaring, believe me, but this business of accusing, judging, punishing has gone on always. It is one of the great wheels turning beneath everything we do. I play my part. I am a functionality of our only universally recognized system of telling wrong from right; a bureaucrat of good and evil. This must be prohibited; not that. One would expect that after all of these years of making charges, trying cases, watching defendants come and go it might all have become a jumble. Somehow it has not.

I turn back to face the jury. Today, you, all of you, have taken on one of the most solemn obligations of citizenship. Your job is to find the facts, the truth. It is not an easy task, I know. Memories may fail, recollections may be shaded, the evidence might point in differing directions. You may be forced to decide about things that no one seems to know, or to be willing to say. If you were at home, at work, anywhere in your daily life you might be ready to throw up your hands, you might not want to make the effort. Here you must. You must!

Let me remind you, there was a real crime; no one will dispute that. There was a real victim, real pain. You do not have to tell us why it happened. People's motives after all may be forever locked inside them, but you must at least try to determine what actually occurred.

If you cannot, we will not know if this man deserves to be free or punished. We will have no idea who to blame. If we cannot find the truth, what is our hope of justice?

I want to talk about the very circuitous route that took me to write that, to become a crime novelist and a lawyer. The latter would have come as quite a surprise to me when I left home at the age of seventeen and went to Amherst College in 1966. I was already hungry to become a novelist. That was my great dream and had been born first when I read *The Count of Monte Cristo* and was totally captivated by the novel. I probably was inspired by my mother, whose dream was to be a novelist. But I thought if it was that exciting to read a novel, imagine how much more exciting it must be to write one, to feel the story come to life within you for a longer span of time.

So I went off to Amherst determined to become a novelist and was dashed to discover upon arriving that there was no such thing there as a creative writing class. Of course, if I had spent more time attending to the course catalogue rather than the magnificent landscape that had caused me to want to go to Amherst College, I would have known that. Instead, in a state of bewilderment, I asked the faculty, "Well, why don't you teach creative writing here?" One of them explained to me that creative writing had no more intellectual content than auto shop or basket-weaving. Secondly, he said, you couldn't teach anybody to be a novelist or a poet—those people are born. Of course, if I had wanted to be a concert pianist and I had talked to somebody in the Music Department they would have first mentioned the need to practice.

So I came home that first summer with no instruction in creative writing and determined a couple things. One was that, of course, I had to get a job. I was a college student and, typically, in need of money. The bother was that I was going to try to write a novel on my own since I had no hope of anybody teaching me to do that. What I did that summer was I became a substitute letter carrier in Glencoe, Illinois; I was a mailman. Post office employment, as Herman Melville and Eudora Welty have recorded, has its interesting aspects. In my case it was a pretty steep learning curve. I was overwhelmed at first by the need to sort the mail and then deliver it. But it was one of those tasks that after a number of weeks I had easily mastered, so much so that I discovered that it did not take me the eight hours allotted to deliver all the mail on my route. One time I made the mistake of coming back to the post office early and at that point the chief clerk, a fellow named Walter, who retired only a few years ago, took me down to the basement, to the employees' lunchroom, and explained to me in very colorful terms what might happen if I was unwise enough to come back to the post office early ever again. I was due to appear at 3:15 when I was scheduled to punch out. So that meant I had between an hour and two hours every afternoon to myself.

The only air-conditioned building in downtown Glencoe in those days was the library, so I decided I would cool my heels, as it were, in the library. Once I was there I realized what I should do, namely read what I had learned (during my first year in college while taking English classes) was the greatest novel ever written: James Joyce's *Ulysses*. I had read *Portrait of the Artist as a Young Man* and the stories in *Dubliners* and was beguiled by all of them. So I found *Ulysses* on the shelf, and thereafter every day for the next six weeks, for an hour or two every afternoon, I read Joyce's novel.

When I was done, I had a number of observations. The first was, of course, that I had read many of the most gorgeous sentences I had ever encountered. It was beautiful writing. The second was that this was not a novel as I thought of novels; it wasn't a novel like *The Count of Monte Cristo*; it wasn't even a novel like *Portrait of the Artist as a Young Man*, in the sense that I was not really carried through *Ulysses* by concern for a character and what would happen to him or her. This was at some levels a novel about writing a novel. As a result, it was hard reading. I was not unhappy that the taxpayers of the United States were paying me $2.52 every hour I spent at it.

But the third and perhaps most striking observation was that the library's lone copy of *Ulysses* was always there when I went to look for it. Every day. Here I was in a very affluent community, among people with a very high level of education, and enigmatically, no one else in that town wanted to read the greatest novel ever written. I began a long dialogue with myself about whether *Ulysses* could really be the greatest novel ever written if no one else in town actually wanted to read it.

The one thing that I concluded over many years of further reflection is that, whether I read novels that appealed to a very narrow elite or to a larger but in some ways more humdrum audience, the aspiration of art, as I conceive of it, ought to be to create universals. As I was to express it some years later, when I was a writing fellow at Stanford, a great novel should be enthralling to both a bus driver and an English professor.

Now, back to Glencoe.

When I came home from reading *Ulysses* during the day I did something different at night, which is I wrote a novel. I wrote a novel because, as I said, I realized nobody was going to teach me how to write a novel and that I may as well just plunge in and do it, which, of course, is the only secret there is to becoming a novelist. (Phil Knight, the founder of Nike, is a fancier of my books, and I once wrote him a note saying that Nike had stolen the novelist's slogan, namely, "Just Do It.") What I wrote without training was a novel about two young men from the North Side of Chicago—where I had grown up—who ran away, followed the Mississippi down to New Orleans, and there witnessed the murder of an African American prostitute. It was, in other words, a crime novel, even though I didn't realize that at the time.

It was 1967, and I had spent a little time in the civil rights movement; I thought my book was a civil rights novel about the bad ways of the Old South. I finished the novel over the course of the summer. Martha [Nussbaum] and others will probably find it amusing that I called it *Dithyramb*, and perhaps over dinner Martha will explain to me why I did that because I don't remember exactly what that word means. It's some kind of Bacchic dance, but apparently, Richard [McAdams], I've been invoking classic themes in these novels for a long time.

Dithyramb went the way of many novels that I was to write thereafter, which is to say I sent it to New York with a stamped self-addressed envelope, and after a passage of time it was returned to me in that stamped self-addressed envelope, usually with a form rejection letter.

My three college roommates noticed that this was happening. I'd come trudging back from the mailboxes with the manuscript under my arm every couple of weeks, and, being like young men always, they decided to torment me about it. One way they did that was by reading me statistics that had appeared in *Time* magazine showing that Mickey Spillane, the crime writer, was the best-selling novelist in the world. In those days Mickey Spillane had sold 18 million copies of his books. I had not learned much in a year and a half in college, but certainly I had learned how to be pretentious, so I told my roommates, "Oh, that's just junk. I could write a novel like that in three weeks." My roommates were intrigued. "What kind of junky novel could you write in three weeks?" they asked. It turned out that I actually had an idea for a junky novel that was somehow right in the front of my mind, which again should have told me something about myself. My idea, as a civil rights movement "veteran," was that what the United States needed was a black superhero, and it happened that I had conceived of one. I called him John Henry Steele, The Protector. He was the son of a wealthy white industrial magnate and a famous African American jazz singer—think Lena Horne. John Henry Steele turned his back on his father's business and instead became a protector, that is to say a kind of private secret service man whose job entailed keeping people alive and having sex every twenty pages. To my roommates that sounded like a splendid outline for a novel, and so they made me the following offer: they would go to class for me for the next three weeks, take notes, outline my papers; I would sit at home and write "John Henry Steele, The Protector." Then, when we sent the novel to New York and riches befell me, I would divide them four ways. Two of my roommates went on to become corporate lawyers; the third ended up as the chairman of Northwest Airlines; and I always look back and realize that I was history's first victim of a leveraged buyout.

But, anyway, I did it. I wrote the novel, but history, unfortunately, intervened. Dr. Martin Luther King was killed that spring, an epical event that changed the United States for decades to come and made it totally unacceptable for a young white college student to be writing a book about an African American anything. That didn't keep us from sending the novel out with a colorful cover letter describing how it had been created. One editor wrote back to say that the novel was unpublishable, but the cover letter might make a promising start on a book.

I decided I would give up trashy writing and go back to what I thought were more serious efforts. One night while I was a junior I went to Boston. A friend had introduced me to a young woman and we hit it off. We saw a movie and afterward had a searching personal conversation in which she described having been raped the prior summer. It was a horrifying, deeply unsettling story. (I wish I could say it was the last time an American woman told me a story about being raped, but sadly it's not.) I went back to Amherst and, coincidentally, fell ill. I developed a fever, and in a true fever dream, I got up out of my sick bed about twenty-four hours later and began to write and wrote continuously for a day. That was the first moment I really felt gripped by what I was writing in a way I hoped I would when I had read *The Count of Monte Cristo*. What I wrote was a short story about a rape. It was later published in *Transatlantic Review*, but in the weird way that a writer's imagination transmogrifies the raw materials, my short story was written from the rapist's point of view. I can explain that choice, but the real point is twofold: it was a crime story, and it was the first thing I wrote that I was fortunate enough to publish for pay.

While in college I had dreamt of becoming a creative writing fellow at Stanford. I had realized that many of the American writers I most admired—Larry McMurtry and Robert Stone, and a lesser known name, Tillie Olsen, who was a great icon to me—had been through the writing program at Stanford. I wanted to do that, too, and I was lucky enough to win a writing fellowship there, and I went to Palo Alto in 1970 after I graduated from Amherst. As I like to say, those were good years and bad years. They were good years in the sense that I was surrounded by a number of very talented young writers. Their sheer audacity in being willing to say out loud the same thing that I said, namely, that they wanted to be writers, was encouraging to me and helped confirm me in that identity, which is part of the struggle of every young person in the arts.

They were bad years in other senses. One of the things that characterized the community of young writers at Stanford is that, while they did not all write like Ernest Hemingway, they all drank like Ernest Hemingway and certainly engaged in a number of other related activities, so these were years of some dissipation. But I did of course try my hand yet again at writing a novel.

This time the novel, which was called *The Way Things Are*, was about a rent strike in Chicago, In order to write this novel, I learned about something called the Implied Warranty of Habitability, a doctrine then being incorporated in American law, which set aside the age-old fiction of the common law that a tenant in an apartment is renting the right to occupy the land below the apartment. Instead, U.S. courts were saying that it was the dwelling the tenant was renting, which he or she had every right to expect to be fit to live in.

I was absolutely captivated by the Implied Warranty of Habitability. Many publishers to whom I sent *The Way Things Are* were less captivated by it. The heart of the novel, though, is a kind of massive conspiracy. The book's protagonist is an ex-draft dodger who has come back from Canada sick in spirit and disappointed in himself. The young man who tries to interest the main character in activism again, who, for lack of any other convenient label, is a kind of Catholic Worker type, a socialist

Catholic, keeps digging at the great secret of who owns all the slum property on the North Side of Chicago. This poor activist Catholic finds that most of it is owned by the Catholic Archdiocese of Chicago, a circumstance that was actually proven to be true of Morningside Heights in New York.

Had I looked back at all my writing to that point—the massive conspiracy in *The Way Things Are*, my short story about a rapist, *John Henry Steele, The Protector,* and *Dithyramb*, about the effort of two young men to get justice for the murder of a prostitute—I would have recognized that the common theme in all this writing was crime. Yet I was absolutely blind to it. I thought of myself as Joyce's would-be successor, not as a crime novelist who had any legacy from that junk writer Mickey Spillane.

As a result I was totally unprepared for the degree to which I found myself entranced by the activities of friends who, during the five years I was at Stanford, had graduated from law school. The ones whose careers interested me the most were the ones who were working in criminal law. I remember traveling to Seattle to watch my friend, Jay Reich, one of the roommates who was involved in the creation of *John Henry Steele, The Protector,* who was working as an intern in the Kane County prosecutor's office. He was trying very small traffic cases, but I still thought it was amazing to see my friend involved in the liberty and punishment of other human beings.

Another friend, Jeremy Margolis, who was a little bit ahead of me in school, had gone into the U.S. attorney's office in Chicago. He was involved in major cases, and I would sit there enthralled as he described these trials to me.

I had a friend in San Francisco, Jim Hunt, may he rest in peace, who was a criminal defense lawyer, and I listened to Jim's stories too about trying cases. Jim confessed that every morning when he was on trial he would rush to the bathroom as soon as he woke, bend over the basin, and be sick. I was so enchanted by the world of criminal law that even that part sounded good.

So in there lies the tale. Although it stunned my colleagues in the English Department at Stanford, I decided that I would truly live a life of regret if I did not go to law school. I actually remember sitting in the Green Lounge, trying to talk to students in this law school and get an idea of what it was like to attend here. And I made what seemed to be a dramatic U-turn in my life and headed off for law school.

The only hard part about deciding to go to law school was that writing seemed to hang in the balance. For my whole life I had promised myself that I was going to be a novelist, and I remained unwilling to set that dream aside. But I had no idea how to keep my dream alive. I also found it hard to explain to the literary agent who had been kind enough to represent me for a number of years, including trying unsuccessfully to sell *The Way Things Are* to two dozen publishers in New York, that I was going to law school. I was afraid she'd feel she'd wasted all that work. I could only bring myself to write her a letter in which there was a throwaway line saying something like, "You know, I haven't been able to find a good book by a law student describing what his or her day-to-day experience is like." By then, the novel *Paper Chase* and the movie had appeared, but I didn't think I was likely to fall in love with my professor's daughter, so that didn't seem to describe what I was actually headed for. There were lots of books by faculty members telling students how they ought to think about studying the law. But no book described what it was actually like to be a law student. I made this observation mostly as a sop to my agent, thinking that if she happened to know a nonfiction writer headed to law school—not me, since I was a novelist, an *artist* like Joyce—she could try out the idea on that person.

The way the story goes, my agent, Elizabeth, went out to lunch with an editor, Ned Chase, who was Chevy Chase's father and every bit as zany as his son. It started raining and they got drunk, and Elizabeth found my letter in her purse. Neither one of them noticed that I was not actually proposing to write this book, and Ned signed a contract for it on the spot. In those days, I got lots of mail from Elizabeth, but all of it was brief rejection letters. The next letter from her was more akin to a college acceptance letter, where good news comes in a thick envelope. Inside this fat envelope was a contract to write *One L*. Even though I'd never actually thought about writing that book, I didn't dare turn my back on the opportunity. And so, as I like to say, I signed the contract and went off to Harvard Law School to make new friends and write about them.

I wrote *One L* after my first summer in law school, but at one point I returned to Chicago and visited my friend Jeremy Margolis, who was now the executive assistant U.S. attorney. While we met, the U.S. attorney himself, Sam Skinner, who went on to become the Secretary of Transportation, then chief of staff to President George H. W. Bush, walked in and sat down. He was unhappy. Jeremy was Sam's chief confidante and Sam was distressed because his kingdom was about to diminish. There was a bill in Congress to shrink the Northern District of Illinois and to create a new and separate Western District. Sam read out the list of counties that were going to become part of the new district, then he looked at me and asked, "How many is that?" and I said "Seventeen." Later in the afternoon, after Jeremy and I came back from lunch, Sam told me, "I want you to work in this office next summer." Several years later, after I got to know Sam well, I asked him, "Were there really seventeen counties? Did I actually get it right by accident?" He said, "I had no idea how many counties there were." "Well, why did you hire me?" I asked. He said, "Because you looked so confident when you said 'Seventeen counties,' I thought you would make a good trial lawyer."

I did work in the U.S. attorney's office after my second year in law school. But I'm getting a little ahead of myself.

Ned Chase, who had been drunk when he bought *One L*, called me up after I finished the manuscript and said he had just one question for me: "Why did I ever want to buy this book?" I had no foreknowledge of the great interest Americans were ready to take in the law, but I certainly predicted it full-throatedly to Ned in order to sell him back the book he'd already bought. Because Ned was so dubious about publishing the book and couldn't risk delay, I had to publish it while I was still a law student. I changed the names, of course, to protect the guilty, but it's a work of non-fiction and some people at Harvard Law School who read *One L* understood who they were. Naturally, the people who thought they were favorably portrayed regarded *One L* as a distinguished work. Those who did not think they were favorably portrayed had other opinions, and chief among those with other opinions was one of my first-year professors, who claimed that he was the basis for the heavy in *One L*, a character I called Professor Rudolph Perini. As *One L* came to good fortune and drew excellent notices, this professor grew so agitated that he made a public statement designed to end all the speculation, acknowledging that he in fact was Perini.

I thought that would have been enough to calm him, but I was wrong. At the end of the first semester of my third year of law school, one of my friends came running from this professor's Copyrights final exam with the test book in his hand. The last question was something like this: "You are an associate at a large law firm." (I have to say that I never had an exam question at Harvard Law School that did not begin with that assumption.) "A senior partner has introduced you to his valued client, Professor Rudolph Perini. Professor Perini has undergone the humiliating experience of having a student, Ray Ripoff, write a book based on Professor Perini's daily classroom lectures. Please list all causes of action that Professor Perini can bring against Ray Ripoff."

I concluded that I needed to get away from the Harvard Law School campus, so I went to work as an intern in the Suffolk County district attorney's office, the Boston state prosecutor's office. It was a turbulent time there. I worked for the first assistant, Tim O'Neill, who is a brilliant lawyer and, interestingly, a poet who read his work aloud in the Cambridge tavern Plough and Stars. His boss, District Attorney Garrett Byrne, was approaching eighty and was being challenged for the office by another of his assistants, Newman Flanagan, who had risen to prominence in Boston by an act of what I considered blatant race baiting. He'd prosecuted an African American obstetrician named Kenneth Edelin for the manslaughter of a fetus, breaking Boston's very restrictive abortion laws. Edelin was acquitted, but the case brought Flanagan to prominence and he ended up beating Byrne after I graduated.

By then I was an assistant U.S. attorney in Chicago. Sam was gone, replaced by Tom Sullivan, who was very apprehensive about *One L*, which had been published by then. Before he hired me he brought me in and showed me the Code of Federal Regulations for Department of Justice employees, especially the confidentiality provisions. He said, "I want you to read this and I want you to read every one of these rules and I want you to understand that you can't write a word about this job." And he said, "Besides, you can't write a word about me because I'll kill you." Tom was my principal mentor in the law, and every time I get to introduce him somewhere, I like to tell that story.

I remained faithful to my vow to continue writing fiction, and I tried writing a long literary novella while I was a young AUSA. I had a new agent by then, and there was a young editor in New York, Jonathan Galassi, who was actually interested in this short novel. But when Gail called me in to say Jonathan was intrigued, I said, "Forget about it. I'm working on something better." I was in my second year at the U.S. attorney's office and had begun writing the book that would be *Presumed Innocent*.

I was overcome by what I was experiencing as a prosecutor. It seized me with writhing emotions every day, the battles with defense lawyers, their occasional underhandedness, and the sheer effort that was required to bring to justice somebody who I thought was obviously a crook. The difficulties of discovering the truth were also amazing to me. So were the problems with getting law enforcement agents to understand the way lawyers saw the criminal process. And it was hard to deal with witnesses, getting them to tell the truth or even to know the truth or to recall it.

All of that was in my novel. I set the book in Boston. It's the city I thought I was writing about, an office where the veteran prosecutor was being challenged by one of his assistants who had come to prominence with a race-baiting abortion prosecution of an ob-gyn. I was following the old saw of writing about what I knew.

Even as I started writing *Presumed Innocent*, I did not think that I was becoming a crime novelist. I knew that crime had an immense hold on me, but it wasn't until I became a supervisor in the office, several years along in my writing of *Presumed Innocent*, that my attitude began to change. I went to watch one of the younger lawyers I was supervising try a case. She had called the so-called star witness, the person who was relating most of the tale of how something the community regarded as evil had occurred and I looked around the courtroom and I saw how spellbound every single person in the courtroom was by the witness's story. I suddenly realized: Oh, crime! If you want a universal audience, *this* is the subject.

The *Oresteia* shows us how long crime has been a popular theme in literature. I don't have a lot that's original to say about why that is the case. My fascination with crime is probably rooted in childhood experiences that left me feeling that power was being abused toward me. But I think it's fairly clear that transgression is of enormous interest to all of us because we are all battling the impulse to do wrong. I know that here at the University of Chicago everybody has a cast-iron superego, but anybody who has observed an infant grow up realizes that we are all egocentric savages to start. As Freud taught us, taming these impulses is the great task of civilization and a sad lament, sometimes, of having to live in society. People can't help being fascinated by wrongdoing because we are all would-be wrongdoers ourselves.

In addition there's sometimes a sense in crime literature—and you hear it in the *Oresteia* in some of Clytemnestra's speeches—that the criminal is a more authentic person. Relieved of social restraint, criminals are free to be themselves, whether as someone motivated by a lust for power or for vengeance for the sacrifice of her daughter.

Many in the criminal world are familiar with the phenomenon that in many neighborhoods the criminals and the cops are separable only by who is wearing the uniform. They share a lot of the same interests and the same view of the world. That is also true of criminal defense lawyers. Most of us have a very ambivalent relationship with our clients because at moments we cannot help admiring them. In some ways this admiration is well placed. I always caution people that criminality is one of the greatest expressions of human imagination. This is particularly true in white-collar crimes, although sometimes even murder is committed in an incredibly imaginative way.

The crime story is all about reasserting control over these unruly impulses. Justice, as the *Oresteia* and millions of other crime stories tell us, will ultimately be done.

When I was coming to the end of the first draft of *Presumed Innocent*, I decided that I was going to write a radically new kind of crime novel and not say who committed the crime; it would be the equivalent of "The Lady, or the Tiger?" Yet after a lot of thinking, I realized that I was breaking the rules. The crime novel, the mystery, exists on the assumption that we can reconstruct history and "who done it" with an exactness that the courtroom very often cannot, and, furthermore, that we can even say why the crime was done. In *Presumed Innocent*'s prologue, Rusty says that the criminal process doesn't need to determine motives, but literature does. All narrative works on the convention that motive can be known and understood. Whether that's actually true or not in life I don't know, but the belief that motive can be known and understood helps fulfill the great moral purpose of literature, which is to let us stand in somebody else's shoes, to understand what it is like to be him or her so that we can truly do unto others as we would have them do unto us.

Yet most mysteries teach a far broader lesson, which is that crime does not pay. The wrongdoer will always be brought to justice in the end. When *Presumed Innocent* was in development in Hollywood, Alan Pakula, the director, came to me and said, "The studio heads really don't like the ending of the novel." In the book I wrote the bad guy gets away. The studio types wanted to rewrite the ending so that the person would go to an insane asylum, and that's what they filmed. Fortunately for me, the preview audiences for the movie hated that ending. Alan put it to me, "Well, they didn't seem to like it," and Harrison Ford told me more plainly, "They threw popcorn boxes at the screen." So if you look at *Presumed Innocent* again, you'll notice that the last shot in the movie is actually the first shot, with a new voice-over recorded after the fact by Harrison.

I think I will end there, except to say that I left the U.S. Attorney's office after eight years, when I had what might again seem to be a fairly naïve revelation: I realized that crime was not going to stop. I had been there long enough to see the same defendants come around for a second and even a third time. One lawyer, who had bought suits for the state attorney general in order to get contracts to do state legal work, reappeared in another investigation in the Board of Tax Appeals for bribing hearing officers to reduce real estate taxes for his clients. Even after his death, when I was doing Operation Greylord (a joint federal law enforcement action against judicial corruption in Cook Country, Illinois in the 1980s), I found evidence that the same man had made unrepaid loans to a judge who appointed the lawyer to various paid positions with the court. So I had to drag the representatives of his estate into the grand jury.

Crime is a part of life. There will always be crime, just as surely as there will always be love. Transgression is with us forever.

PART I

Criminal Histories

It conveys an impression of gravity and dignity, and at the same time of grace and attractiveness. The first in its dark deep state, the latter in its light attenuated tint; and thus the dignity of the age and the amiableness of youth may adorn itself with degrees of the same hue.

WOLFGANG VON GOETHE, on red, in *Theory of Colours,* trans. Charles Lock Eastlake (Cambridge, MA: MIT Press, 1970)

2

Mercy at the Areopagus

A NIETZSCHEAN ACCOUNT OF JUSTICE AND JOY IN THE *EUMENIDES*

Daniel Telech

INTRODUCTION

The *Oresteia* ends joyfully: Orestes is acquitted of the crime of matricide; the Furies become honorable; and both of these because Athens initiates the rule of law. According to an intuitively plausible interpretation of the Aeschylean trilogy, this joyful resolution is the result of a coolly rational transition from a primitive cycle of vengeance to a court-centric response to crime.[1] While the House of Atreus was trapped in a net of self-perpetuating vengeance—"the stuff of passion and partiality"—the establishment of the court in the *Eumenides* proceeds via an enlightened grasp of the institutions of punishment, which is subject to robust standards of rationality and impartiality. The prima facie plausibility of this "rationalistic" reading—where "rational" processes are construed as excluding and opposed to the affective—poses a challenge for Nietzschean readings of the *Eumenides*. This is true for two reasons. First, it is incompatible with Nietzsche's view of the value of tragedy, according to which tragic theater psychologically invigorates the audience member by presenting her with a beautiful transfiguration of the agonizing aspects of life. Second, if the rationalistic interpretation of the *Eumenides* were true, this would entail that Nietzsche reveres Aeschylus partly for the same reasons he disdains "Socratic optimism," which he takes to mark the *death of tragedy*.[2]

Fortunately the rationalistic interpretation is largely misguided. This is not to say that the establishment of legal intuitions in the *Eumenides* is the result of *irrational* attitudes; my claim is rather that it involves a joint effort of reason giving, persuasion, and beautiful illusion. Its agents *do* display responsiveness to reasons, but these agents are simultaneously directed by a host of needs and desires, some nobler than others.[3] Furthermore the joyful conclusion of the *Eumenides* depends heavily on the persuasive power of the Olympian gods, sometimes in direct opposition to rules of logical inference. In addition to outlining the partly arbitrary character of the establishment of justice, the first section brings attention to the perseverance in historical Athens of privately inflicted sanctioning practices.[4]

Nevertheless a Nietzschean reading of the *Eumenides* would not point to the arbitrariness present in the (genesis of the) rule of law *in order to discredit it.* Rather, as I argue in the second section, given that it puts an end to the cycle of "senseless resentment," Nietzsche can be read as celebrating the formation of the Areopagus. This event is an instance of what he calls in the *Genealogy* the merciful self-overcoming of justice.

Although justice arrives accompanied by joy in the *Eumenides*, this is not because there exists a constitutive relationship between virtue and happiness, as "the Socratic Optimist" claims. The Socratic Optimist maintains, inter alia, that suffering is inessential for the transformation of individuals and communities. The intellectual apprehension of truths is for him or her sufficient. By contrast, as I argue in the third section, the *Oresteia* evinces commitment to the Nietzschean view that the gates of justice are stubborn and in need of the wisdom of woe to pry open. While suffering *is* essential to this view of tragedy—and to this extent Nietzsche appears to retain a significant kernel of Schopenhauerianism—pessimistic-cum-resignationist it is not. Given that suffering, on the Nietzschean picture, ideally serves as a springboard for a distinctive form of human progress, the view on offer warrants the label *Aeschylean Optimism*.[5]

Why, though, should we care what Nietzsche or Aeschylus might have thought about suffering or justice—not an entirely unfair question. While many aspects of both Aeschylus's and Nietzsche's attitudes toward justice will be foreign to contemporary ears, a goal of this chapter is to turn to progressive voices of centuries past in order to illuminate our debate about the role of mercy in criminal law. Accordingly I conclude with a discussion of the transformative potential of merciful criminal sanctioning.

PRACTICAL REASONABLENESS AND THE APOLLONIAN

The just and joyful conclusion of the *Eumenides* is a result of a transformation of suffering endured in the prior parts of the trilogy. That this is not a coolly rational transformation is evident from consideration of the following three factors: (1) Apollo's arguments and conduct at Orestes's trial; (2) Athena's persuasion of the Furies (*Erinyes*); and (3) historical evidence that motivates the prevalence of passion and partiality in Attic law. I hope to show that Nietzsche's view of the *Apollonian principle* in Greek tragedy bolsters the appeal to each of these factors, which I discuss in turn.

The question of Orestes's punishment is at the core of the *Eumenides*. Having killed his mother, Clytemnestra—in order to avenge his father and to regain the throne from Clytemnestra's adulterer and co-conspirator, Aegisthus—Orestes is now hounded by the Furies, ancient goddesses of (especially familial) vengefulness. Under Apollo's tutelage Orestes requests the counsel of Athena, who, upon the arrival of the Furies in Athens, organizes for Orestes something novel: a trial.

With a jury of twelve Athenians in place, Apollo offers in defense of Orestes's matricide the following "true parent" argument:

> The so-called mother of the child
> isn't the child's begetter, but only a sort
> of nursing soil for the new-born seed.
> The man, the one on top, is the true parent,
> While she, a stranger, fosters a stranger's sprout,
> if no god blights it. And I can prove it to you:
> a father can give birth without a mother.
> And here before us is our witness, child
> of Olympian Zeus, daughter who never fed
> and grew within the darkness of a womb,
> a seedling that no goddess could bring forth.[6]

As *proof* that the mother is inessential to reproduction, and therefore that Orestes cannot have killed a *true* parent, Apollo refers to Athena's divine birth. Suspect though this argument may appear to the contemporary reader, the idea that the mother serves as merely an enabling condition (or "soil") in reproduction is endorsed by Aristotle.[7] In spite of the falsity of its conclusion, then, the "true parent" argument may have been offered (and received) in earnest. We might wonder what evidence could be supplied to justify the argument, but I will not pursue that question here. I put this worry aside because the role of the argument is at least partly undermined by Apollo's lack of consistency about the father's significance as a parent. The Furies criticize Zeus's chaining up of his *own father*, asking Apollo, "How do you square this with your argument?"

Apollo's response? "You stinking, hideous filth, shunned by the gods / We can break bonds, we can slip out of shackles!" (Eu. 748–49).

Apollo's response appears to exploit an ambiguity in what it means to break "bonds": *chains* on the one hand, and contracts on the other. It is no straightforward admission of Olympian dishonesty, but Apollo's illusive nature is not difficult to discern.[8] At a later moment in Orestes's trial, the Furies (who occupy the role of the chorus) accuse Apollo of having once tricked their half-sisters out of exacting due punishment, that time with the power of wine:

CHORUS LEADER: You did the same thing, too, in Pheres' house:
you persuaded the Fates to let men hide from death.
APOLLO: Is it so unjust to treat someone so kindly,
Someone that pious, in his time of need?
CHORUS LEADER: You overturned the age-old covenant
by duping those ancient goddesses with wine.
APOLLO: And when you lose this trial, you'll vomit all
your venom at the ones you hate—quite harmlessly.

(Eu. 842–49)

Apollo's tendency toward pragmatically driven deception is well accounted for on Nietzsche's theory of tragedy. Nietzsche claims that two principles are interwoven in tragic drama: the Dionysian and the Apollonian, where Apollo is the "ruler over the beautiful illusion of the inner world of fantasy . . . the imaged world of dreams" (BT 1, 2). While the Dionysian principle maintains that ours is a world awash with suffering, unconcerned with human happiness, tragic art presents us with this terrible aspect of life *but* wrapped in the "pleasurable illusion of dreams" that the Apollonian affords (BT 4). The logic of dreams permits non sequiturs, and while Apollo never admits to having double standards, he *is* self-conscious about the efficacy of anger in coming to an adequate judgment in the trial. In the course of defending Orestes before Athena, Apollo claims he has "spoken as I have to whip up anger in you who are called to set this matter right" (Eu. 747). Athena continues Apollo's trend insofar as she is unconcerned with nonaffectively convincing the Furies, but her tack is one of spiritedness and persuasion (rather than deceptiveness and insult).

First, Athena prefaces her own vote regarding Orestes's culpability thus: "I acquiesce to the man in all matters [*to d'arsen aino panta*] (except that I choose not to marry) and I take the father's side with my whole *thumos* [*hapanti thumoi*]" (Eu. 855–56).[9] While the spirited element of the soul is sometimes characterized in the *Republic* as irrational and antagonistic to peacemaking,[10] we need only consult Homer for evidence of a conception of *thumos* as politically concerned and responsive to reasons. Consider Odysseus's manner of deciding how to act virtuously: "O woe is me, what am I to endure? It is a great act of cowardice if I should take flight, terrified by the numbers of men; but it will be worse if I am taken alone; the son of Kronos put the other Danaans to flight. But why has my dear θυμός [*thumos*] discussed these things in me? I know that cowards leave the battle, but he who excels in battle must stand his ground strongly, whether he is hit or hits another."[11] Personified as an interlocutor, Odysseus's *thumos* contributes in deliberation over the course of action that he can "stand behind"; "it invigorates him to use his life in a manner that risks life in an honorable way."[12] Similarly, in appealing to *thumos* in casting her ballot for Orestes's acquittal, Athena displays action that is both affective and concerned with political reasons. That is, Athena's action is not "rational" in a narrow, nonaffective sense, nor is it irrational.

There is another way in which Athena's spiritedness is indispensable for the *Oresteia*'s joyful conclusion. After the ballots are counted in Orestes's favor, Athena makes *three* unsuccessful attempts to pacify the Furies. In the final, successful monologue Athena's conciliatory offer is put as follows:

> But if you hold in awe Persuasion's glory,
> the power of my tongue to soothe and enchant,
> you might live here with us. . . .
> The way
> is free for you to be a landholder here,
> enjoying honor justly and forever. (Eu. 1030–38)

Having threatened to express their rage on the entirety of Athens, the Furies are gradually appeased. Like her brother and "spokesman for Zeus" (Eu. 21), Athena is a herald of Apollonian activity. As Martha C. Nussbaum notes, for Nietzsche "Apollonian activity is not detached and coolly contemplative, but a response to an urgent human need, namely the need to demarcate an intrinsically unordered world."[13] The relevant need in the *Eumenides* is the transformation of vengeance—a chain of vengeance that had claimed the lives of Agamemnon, Clytemnestra, Cassandra, arguably all of Troy, Iphigenia, and most of the Argive fleet. The momentousness of this transformation consists in the detail that, in each instance, vengeance had presented itself as a demand and expression of justice (e.g., Clytemnestra and Aegisthus both justify and explain their acts of vengeance by appeal to *justice* [Ag. 1637, 1814, 1847–52]).[14] While the Furies aim to continue indefinitely this "time-honored" retributive cycle and "suck the half-caked gore out of [Orestes's] living flesh" (Eu. 302–303), their vengeful enthusiasm is gradually, very gradually, curbed.

I have been arguing that the transition from the vengeful order to the legal order does not involve the elimination of a passionate response to crime. According to Danielle Allen, the porousness of the boundary between vengeance and punishment is evident too in historical Athens. For example, Athenian democracy permitted "private citizens [to] execute some forms of punishment without passing through the court system at all. For instance, a private citizen was within the bounds of law if he killed a thief or adulterer whom he caught in his house at night."[15] Conversely, as David Cohen argues, the civic institutions of punishment were "developed precisely so as to provide public means of carrying on private wars of vendetta: 'litigation . . . involved the opportunity to contest one's claims to honor with those of one's rivals.'"[16] So, in addition to being absent in the trilogy, we have historical reasons for maintaining that a link between just punishment and the "dispassionate" would have been foreign to Aeschylus.

None of this, it should be emphasized, is meant to discredit the grounds of the joy we find in the *Eumenides*'s conclusion. First, given that Athena's spiritedness is keenly responsive to political reasons, it is only out of misunderstanding that we might demand—as has been demanded in *California v. Brown*, for instance[17]—that deliberation over sentencing be free of sentiment. (I return to this point below.) Second, and more important, against the backdrop of human sacrifice, matricide, patricide, decade-long war, and psychological torture spanning the *Oresteia*, the arbitrariness present in this "Apollonian power of transfiguration" (BT 25) can be no objection to it. How can arbitrariness count as a strike against the Areopagus's worth if its establishment, and *the audience's* appreciation of its establishment, makes "life possible and worth living" (BT 2)? This reference to the lives of the audience is meant to mark Nietzsche's insistence that the transformative power of tragedy be operative on two levels: in its content (the Furies and Athens are transformed) and in the form it takes in the audience's mind; in experiencing an overcoming of extreme suffering, Nietzsche maintains that *we the viewers* will ideally undergo a transformation of consciousness that makes possible not only the endurance of the terribleness of life but a love of it, no longer construed as overwhelmingly terrible.[18] That is, Apollo is representative of rendering beautiful life's dreadful elements, and for this reason "existence under the bright sunshine of such gods is regarded as desirable in itself" (BT 3).

Although the Apollonian principle consists in the beautification of life, which Nietzsche frequently characterizes in terms of "illusion" (BT 3, 7, 16, 18), it is no mere escape from "the real world."[19] "Apollonian art," as Julian Young puts it, "*acknowledges* and does not eliminate from consciousness the terrible in life."[20] For this reason the love of life that the Greeks inspire is no deluded attitude; its ethical significance is manifest in Nietzsche's discussion of justice's relation to mercy and resentment. Apollonian transfiguration *does* alter our view of human action, but as

I argue in the next section, this consists in a correction rather than a mere alteration of the default mode of perceiving human action.

FROM *RESSENTIMENT* TO MERCY

Over the course of the *Eumenides* the Furies undergo an important transformation. This is a transformation from what Nietzsche calls an orientation of *ressentiment* to an orientation of mercy. It thus comprises the "self-overcoming of justice." While discussion of Aeschylus's work in the *Birth of Tragedy* centers on *Prometheus*, Nietzsche there expresses reverence for the "profoundly Aeschylean demand for *justice*" (BT 9),[21] which can be profitably extended to the *Eumenides*. My suggestion is that Nietzsche would welcome the just and joyful end of the *Eumenides* partly because it is put in the service of reshaping (particularly rendering more constructive) attitudes of *ressentiment*. Nietzsche's own view, as Richard Posner aptly puts it, is that there is a "relation of substitution between law and vengeance,"[22] a substitution that is outlined in the *Genealogy*'s second essay, and here it is worth quoting Nietzsche at length:

> Law represents on earth . . . the struggle *against* the reactive feelings . . . to impose measure and bounds upon the excesses of the reactive pathos and to compel it to come to terms. Wherever justice is practiced and maintained one sees a stronger power seeking a means of putting an end to the senseless raging of *ressentiment* among the weaker powers that stand under it (whether they be groups of individuals)—partly by taking the object of *ressentiment* out of the hands of revenge, partly by substituting for revenge the struggle against the enemies of peace and order, partly by devising and in some cases imposing settlements, partly by elevating certain equivalents for injuries into norms to which from then on *ressentiment* is once and for all directed. The most decisive act, however, that the supreme power performs and accomplishes against the predominance of grudges and rancor—it always takes this action as soon as it is in any way strong enough to do so—is the institution of law, the imperative declaration of what in general counts as permitted, as just, in its eyes, and what counts as forbidden, as unjust. . . . From now on the eye is trained to an ever-more *impersonal* evaluation of the deed. (GM II: 11)

The establishment of legal institutions provides the community with means for redirecting and thereby rendering more productive the energy underlying the community members' "senseless raging of *ressentiment*." I follow Nietzsche in his use of the French (*ressentiment*) since the phenomenon of interest differs markedly from what we mean by "resentment."[23] A brief word on this difference will be of use. First, we usually take resentment to be an emotion reflecting the violation of a demand made on members within a single moral community.[24] Nietzschean *ressentiment*, by contrast, is an "emotional *orientation*" and serves as the basis for a range of moral emotions. Second, *ressentiment* involves an asymmetry between classes that resentment need not involve. Jay Wallace captures both of these features when he says that the orientation of *ressentiment* consists in "a kind of focused hatred that grows out of a structural comparative deprivation."[25] Third, part of what Nietzsche finds objectionable about *ressentiment* is that its source in privation is unacknowledged. More specifically this orientation essentially involves self-deception, particularly *repressed vengefulness* (GM I: 7).

This last aspect may sound strange given how vocal the Furies are about their desire to exact revenge on Orestes. Bernard Reginster's elucidation of the connection between self-deception and *ressentiment* is particularly helpful here. As Reginster puts it, "The '[person] of *ressentiment*' is . . . divided between two sets of desires (and values): the apparent desires (and values) which he has as a result of his revaluation, and the real desires (and values) which are 'repressed' but nonetheless covertly motivate his revaluation."[26] In the case of the Furies, it is not difficult to see that a deep longing for recognition underpins much of their vengeful behavior. In complaining about the Olympian gods, the Furies say, "None of them would feast with us at the same table; we have no part in festivals where white robes are worn" (Eu. 415–17). The desire for Olympian recognition that this complaint expresses renders intelligible the warmth with which the Furies *eventually* ease into their crimson robes. At last their wish to be esteemed by the Olympian gods is fulfilled. That their desire for graciousness has been previously repressed is suggested by the following avowals of pride in pettiness:

> Adept at devising,
> Unmatched alike in remembering wrong done
> As in repaying it;
> Awful to men, deaf to their pleas,
> Detested and dishonored we fulfill
> our given office; cut off
> from the gods, we in the dark slime make
> the path rough both for those who live in sunlight
> and for those in sunlessness. (Eu. 462–70)

On the surface the Furies profess that their lowliness is a virtue, a kind of achievement. Yet given the lack of status that this lowliness implies, by postulating a repressed desire for Olympian recognition we can better understand the Furies' pensive though *eventually wholehearted* acceptance of Athena's offers of honor (and its concomitant benefits of friendship, sacrificial offerings, and worship). We need not even rule out that the Furies adjust the relative value they attribute to merciful action partly in virtue of the *sheer difficulty* of maintaining their vengeful resolution in the face of Athena's tempting offer. While it is sometimes rational to develop tendencies to *avoid* reconsidering our resolutions, the mechanism underlying this sort of "judgment-shift" is not by itself irrational.[27]

We might nonetheless worry about the motivation of the Furies. I have claimed that they *become* merciful, but if their vengeful desires are merely overpowered by desire for honor, their change in mind is driven by self-interest. Perhaps they only *appear*, and aim to appear, merciful. Worries of this sort are ill-founded. The fact that the Furies hunger after honor does not rule out their acting mercifully. As Nietzsche claims elsewhere in the *Genealogy*, the very transition from strict retributive justice—and the Furies repeatedly insist that they are motivated by what is "just" (e.g., Eu. 312, 361, 838)—to a model of justice concerned with the well-being of the whole marks a move toward mercy: "The justice which begins with 'everything is dischargeable, everything must be discharged,' ends by winking and letting those incapable of discharging their debt go free: it ends, as does every good thing on earth, by *overcoming itself*. This self-overcoming of justice: one knows the beautiful name it has given itself—*mercy*" (GM II:10). Even if the Furies exercise self-restraint *partly* from self-interest and require a wave of persuasion to adopt a merciful stance, Nietzsche's point is that the contingent factors that contribute to the adoption of the merciful attitude need not discredit its status. Athena's conciliatory power might have been necessary for the Furies to abandon their long-standing retributive resolution, but consider by comparison the young man's being gradually persuaded by his peers to abandon his childhood resolution to never be susceptible to the charm of females. "Surely," as Richard Holton claims, "maintaining that resolution in the face if his later attraction will not be rational."[28] Nor need it be right to construe the contributing role of his peers as *simply* providing a motive from peer pressure when the young man changes his mind.

While the cynical reader of the *Eumenides* may claim that the desire for honor rather than mercy is what *really* motivates the Furies to yield in their plans of seeking retribution, I see no reason to choose one over the other. We should note that even prior to the trial, the Furies claim that they need to exact vengeance in order to preserve their honor (Eu. 379). For this reason the "sweeping denigration of any self-interested or desire-based human motives"—in other words, the insistence on "motivational purity"—is foreign to the world I am considering.[29]

This point furnishes us with tools for responding to a more powerful interpretative objection—namely, that by highlighting discussions of mercy and joy I am presenting an anesthetized Nietzsche, a Nietzsche stripped of his familiar commitment to Thucydidean power politics, a Nietzsche who has forgotten that "justice is thus requital and exchange under the presupposition of an approximately equal power position: revenge therefore belongs originally within the domain of justice, it is an exchange. . . . Justice goes back naturally to the viewpoint of an enlightened self-preservation, thus to the egoism of the reflection: 'to what end should I injure myself uselessly and perhaps even then not achieve my goal?'—so much for the *origin* of justice" (HAH 92). Yet there is no inconsistency in Nietzsche's claiming, on the one hand, that justice has its *origin* in "repayment and exchange," the homeland of revenge, and on other hand, that we are well-served by transfiguring this original condition of justice; this is exactly what the merciful self-overcoming of justice requires. Again the "relation between law and vengeance is roughly one of substitution."[30] Furthermore we can accept this Nietzschean point about justice accepting Nietzsche's undemocratic restriction of the scope of the "we" that would be well-served by the self-overcoming of justice. This is to resist Nietzsche's view—as characterized by Rawls—that the goods of justice and liberty are to be subordinated to those of human excellence in art and culture, the sources of which are "higher types" of individuals.[31] (In other words, we can maintain, as Derek Parfit has recently claimed, that "Nietzsche was a brilliant thinker, who made many claims that are original, important and true," while insisting that "when we encourage people to read Nietzsche's books, we should admit that Nietzsche made some utterly appalling claims."[32])

Given, then, that neither Aeschylus nor Nietzsche has a view of motivation that precludes partly self-interested behavior from being merciful (and so concerned with the civic good), there is no reason not to take the Eumenides at their word when they say:

> Let citizens
> give joy for joy,
> loving the common good,
> hating a common foe:
> they'll cure most ills this way. (Eu. 1132–36)

A way of further resolving the apparent tension between being motivated by both mercy and honor is to look at the level not merely of action but of character: Why not think that being a merciful person *is* a way of being honorable? If we accept this idea, we have a concrete way of describing the longevity of the transformation of the Furies into Eumenides (or "Gracious Ones," as Athena's appellation would have it). Furthermore, given that Nietzsche's "person of *ressentiment*" is self-deceived and so, as Reginster maintains, lacks a trait essential to Nietzsche's view of "nobility" of character—namely *integrity of self*—we have grounds for thinking that mercy and honor are not only compatible but in this case interdependent.[33] It is not just the *decision* of the Furies that changes; in unifying their behavior with a previously repressed and rational desire (namely a desire to cooperate with the Olympian gods), they themselves *become* honorable (de facto and de jure). In subordinating their aggressive drives to their hitherto repressed desire for recognition, the Furies undergo a sublimation that mirrors their newly formed cohesive relationship toward the state. As Ken Gemes maintains, sublimation, which is integral to psychological health on Nietzsche's view, is characterized by "integration or unification, while pathological symptoms involve splitting off or disintegration."[34] Given that the transformation of the Furies consists in a change in *affective orientation*, it is no mystery why, as Nussbaum maintains, the Eumenides come to express a unified range of benevolent sentiments toward the state and its citizens.[35] In coming to view their previous actions as no longer honorable, the Furies undergo a transformation of attitudes that displays the structure of a recently canvassed (and empirically well-supported) honor-based model of moral revolution.[36]

So much for compatibility of mercy with honor; let's now turn briefly to justice. Even if mercy and honor are compatible, this does not by itself render intelligible the compatibility of mercy with justice. The problem is this: if justice demands deserved punishment, and mercy involves punishment that is less than deserved, mercy seems to be unjust. How can the supererogatory nature of mercy be included within the realm of justice while remaining supererogatory? Jeffrie Murphy puts the dilemma thus: "Mercy is either a vice (injustice) or redundant (a part of justice)."[37] Given that the Furies originally seek retribution in the name of justice, how can their leniency be anything other than unjust?

We will be well served by briefly attending to the history of the concepts of justice (*dike*) and mercy (*epiekeia*). On Anaximander's use of the concept (the oldest available to us), justice (*dike*) follows the same sort of regularity that natural processes are taken to exhibit. Like the order of nature, the just judge is not to be moved in the face of ostensible mitigating circumstances. As Nussbaum puts this understanding of justice, "The world of strict *dike* is a harsh and symmetrical world, in which order and design are preserved with exceptionless clarity. After summer comes fall, after fall comes winter, after day comes night; the fact that Agamemnon was not the killer of Thyestes' children is as irrelevant to *dike* as the fact that the night did not deliberately aggress against the day."[38] On the one hand, this natural symmetry guards against discrimination and guarantees treating like cases alike. Yet I cannot help thinking that in at least some cases indiscrimination is tantamount to insensitivity to factors unusually relevant in deciding fair punishment. "Justice as revenge," claims Posner, "has no means of distinguishing between culpable and justifiable injuries or even for developing the distinction. Liability tends therefore to be absolute."[39] This uncompromising character of retribution is especially salient if we put the contrast as one between (1) calculable and unthinking punishment—Anaximander's nature, I take it, does not deliberate; and (2) punishment *informed by* perception of the relevant particulars.

Given the minimal assumption that the judgment of crime, unlike the unfolding of the seasons, ought to be a *cognitive* process, the Aristotelian account of merciful punishment should strike us as attractive: Aristotle "define[s] equity as a kind of justice, but a kind that is superior to and frequently opposed to another sort, namely strict legal justice. . . . Equity [or mercy] may be regarded as a 'correcting' and 'completing' of legal justice."[40] On a model of punishment that takes seriously mercy or equity (*epiekeia*), the "relevant particulars" that the judge is responsive to are broadly those classed as "mitigating circumstances." The merciful attitude to human action recognizes that the stakes in punishment are much higher than night's following day or autumn's following summer—none of these natural events involve parties that *care* about their own well-being or the well-being of society. Nevertheless, since this care is manifest in *intelligent perception*, the judge's verdict will not abandon the demands of impartiality. That is, the cognitive nature of merciful punishment guarantees that there is something for the merciful judge to *get right*.

The Aristotelian view that just punishment sometimes requires *careful perception* of the circumstances is well-captured by Aeschylus's imagery of the Furies' transition from darkness to light. In their default retributive mode the Furies self-identify as "luckless daughters of the Night" (Eu. 921). In this mode they are wholly blind to differences between justifiability and culpability. By contrast, under the tutelage of "All-seeing Zeus" (Eu. 1223) the Eumenides, now dressed in radiant crimson robes, become torchbearers for a humane mode of punishment. It is true that the mitigating factors of Orestes's case are not what *motivate* the Furies' leniency—and this marks an important disanalogy between the Furies and the merciful judge—but once transformed, the Eumenides *are* able to recognize factors of this sort. It is from their new vantage point that they make proclamations like "I ban, too, the untimely killing of young men; and you gods who possess the power to do so, let young girls find husbands" (Eu. 1117–21). Having stepped into new light—the light of the merciful orientation—the Furies bear the responsibility of "oversee[ing] the lives of men" (Eu. 1083–84).

Along with the "perceptual shift" of the Furies comes a newfound ability for expression. As Nussbaum notes, early in the *Eumenides* the Furies make repetitive canine-like utterances: "Their only words are 'get him get him get him get him' (labe labe etc.), as close to a doggy hunting cry as the genre allows."[41] These cries stand in stark contrast to the poetic outpourings of the transformed goddesses.

Metaphors of "entering the light," "seeing with new eyes," "finding grace," and so on have a characteristically optimistic air. This should give us pause. Given, that is, that Nietzsche takes rationalism and optimism to form a union in *Socratic optimism*, the latter must be sufficiently unlike the optimism of the *Oresteia*. In the next and final section I distinguish these two forms of optimism and outline the upshot of my reading for the debate about mercy and criminal law.

VARIETIES OF OPTIMISM

Optimism is for Nietzsche a pejorative term associated with Socratic rationalism. Indeed what Nietzsche calls "Socratic optimism" comprises a set of commitments about happiness, truth, and virtue that he takes to signal the demise of Greek tragedy. In spite of this Nietzsche *is* an optimist of a particular kind, namely an *Aeschylean optimist*. Let me explain.

According to optimism in the Socratic sense, suffering is dispensable for flourishing. "If we had access to the right sort of knowledge," so the Socratic optimist maintains, "the terrible consequences could have been avoided, and we would be better off for it." More generally this is a view according to which knowledge is sufficient for virtue and virtue for happiness. Nietzsche's opposition to Socratic optimism rests on its blindness to the truth of the tragic: "Consider the consequences of the Socratic maxims: 'Virtue is knowledge; man sins only from ignorance; he who is virtuous is happy.' In these three basic forms of optimism lies the death of tragedy. For now the virtuous hero must be a dialectician; now there must be a necessary, visible connection between virtue and knowledge, faith and morality; now the transcendental justice of Aeschylus is degraded to the superficial and insolent principle of 'poetic justice' " (BT 14). Optimism of this sort is antitragic because it aims to eliminate the significance of external contingencies for happiness. If virtue is sufficient for happiness, all unhappiness or suffering must arise from the sufferer's own vice. We need not follow Nietzsche in blaming the disintegration of tragedy on Euripides—whom Nietzsche brands the "poet of aesthetic Socratism" (BT 12)[42]—in order to appreciate his insight that the Socratic view of suffering is only amplified in the modern (quasi-) Christian worldview. In the latter, as a matter of divine fairness regarding desert, one's degree of blameworthiness is construed as proportionate to one's degree of suffering. As Nietzsche puts it in *Daybreak*, "Misfortune and guilt—Christianity has placed these two things on a balance. . . . But this is not *antique*, and that is why Greek tragedy, which speaks so much yet in so different a sense of misfortune and guilt, is a great liberator of the spirit in a way in which the ancients themselves could not feel it.... In antiquity there still existed actual misfortune; only in Christendom did everything become punishment, well-deserved punishment" (78).[43] Indeed it follows that if virtue is sufficient for happiness and vice is blameworthy, then all unhappiness must arise from actions that are blameworthy. What is mistaken about the optimism of the Socratic(-cum-Christian) worldview is the simple and well-known truth that bad things happen to good people and that we sometimes suffer in ways grossly disproportionate to our blameworthiness. In addition to separating happiness from virtue, however, Nietzsche severs virtue from knowledge. That Nietzsche takes happiness, virtue, and knowledge to be mutually dissociable, however, should not surprise us. After all, like Aeschylus, Nietzsche holds that there is knowledge to be had from suffering.

The connection between wisdom and suffering abounds in Nietzsche's corpus. Consider his claim that *everything* that makes life valuable—"for instance: virtue [*Tugend*] art, music, dance, reason, intellect"—arises out of subjection to strict rules, out of "obedience for a long time in a single direction" (BGE 188).[44] Nietzsche's view on the wisdom wrought from suffering is particularly vivid in his discussion of Dionysus, specifically of the "*chorus* of the Greek tragedy, the symbol of the whole excited Dionysian throng": "In its vision this chorus beholds its lord and master Dionysus and is therefore eternally the *serving* chorus: it sees how the god suffers and glorifies himself and therefore does not itself *act*. But while its attitude toward the god is wholly one of service, it is nevertheless the highest, namely the Dionysian, expression of *nature* and therefore pronounces in its rapture, as nature does, oracles and wise-sayings: *sharing his suffering* it also shares something of his *wisdom* and proclaims the truth from the heart of the world" (BT 8). Although Nietzsche posits a deep union between suffering and wisdom, he should not be construed as claiming that suffering is somehow *sufficient* for wisdom. Sympathetic though he is to human impulse to render meaningful one's suffering (GM II: 7), the optimism he endorses is not one according to which suffering inherently *justifies* (or even pushes in the *direction of justifying*) itself through its consequences, by, say, generating "more overall wisdom." Indeed such a view would bear too close a similarity to *Leibnizian* optimism, on which, owing to the rational structure of the universe, every local negative event is a necessary component of a globally maximal positive state of affairs—or, as Voltaire's Pangloss puts it, "All is for the best in this best of all possible worlds."[45]

Apart from its untenability as a reading of Nietzsche, this view displays a deep insensitivity to disproportionate levels of suffering. In the case of the *Eumenides*, is it unimaginable that Athens could have established rule of law without the Argive fleet *entirely* destroying Troy? Or that Nietzsche might have produced great work with one or two fewer "torments that go with an uninterrupted three-day migraine, accompanied by laborious vomiting of phlegm" (EH I: 1)? Tempting though it is to speculate over Nietzsche's *own* redemptive self-narrative and its psychological contributions to his late-career explosion of productivity, this is a topic for another paper.[46]

Leaving aside the question of the sufficient *amount* of suffering needed for "wisdom from woe," it is difficult to deny that Orestes grasps something of significant truth because he has lived through the tumult of the House of Atreus (even if part of it is lived in exile). Seeing what he grasps will help get in view the *kind* of suffering at issue in Aeschylean optimism. Consider Orestes's claim "I have been schooled by my own suffering" (Eu. 319). Orestes's assertion is noteworthy in the context of his predecessors' disavowals of wrongful action. According to E. R. Dodds, Orestes's difference from Clytemnestra and Agamemnon consists in an understanding of a peculiar sort:

> It is not that Orestes is humble where [Clytemnestra] is arrogant, or that his motives are "purer" than hers; he has simple human motives, which he does not conceal (299–304). The deeper difference is that the divine purpose, of which both Agamemnon and Clytemnestra were unconscious and guilty agents, is for Orestes something consciously known and humbly, though not easily, accepted. He is aware that his act is a crime, even before it is committed (903, cf. 106–17 and 1029); but receiving it as a duty, he stands as a type of all those who take upon themselves "the necessary guilt of human action." Orestes has not merely suffered his situation, he has understood it and in a sense mastered it; it is his *learning* which makes him worthy of salvation.[47]

We get a particularly powerful example of Orestes's tragic understanding in his expression of grief over his matricide—grief he feels in spite of taking his act to be inevitable and justified. Shortly after murdering Aegisthus and Clytemnestra, Orestes articulates his sorrow thus:

> Now I am here to mourn,
> Holding this web that killed my father. Still,
> I grieve for what was done, for what was suffered,
> And for all our race, shouldering, as I do,
> A filthy and unenviable triumph. (Lb. 1147–51)

Unlike Agamemnon, who, from the practical necessity of sacrificing Iphigenia, concludes that the act was right, Orestes appreciates that the impossibility of fulfilling two inconsistent ethical demands does not relieve him from the pain of having committed a serious wrong.[48] That is, Orestes understands, as Bernard Williams puts it, "If I eventually choose for one side of the conflict rather than the other, this is a possible ground of regret. . . . These states do not depend . . . on whether I am convinced that in the choice I made I acted for the best; I can be convinced of this, yet have these regrets."[49] Orestes's mourning is especially noteworthy given that he is told in unambiguous terms by Apollo that the god himself is responsible for Clytemnestra's death: "I ordered him to kill his mother. I am responsible" (Eu. 675–76). In spite of Apollo's symbolic alleviation of Orestes's accountability, Orestes does not attempt to disown the fact that his mother died by his own hand.[50]

Why, though, should we take Orestes's anguish to speak in favor of a Nietzschean, in contrast to a Socratic, reading of the *Eumenides*? In answering this question it is important to recognize that for Socrates *too* suffering need not be bad. For example, in Plato's *Gorgias*, Socrates's argument for the powerlessness of tyrants rests on the principle that it is better to suffer injustice than to commit it (469b–474d). There is thus a sense in which Socrates can agree with Nietzsche that suffering may sometimes be painful without being bad. Although agreement on this general point narrows the contrast between Socrates and Nietzsche, the Socratic view of suffering's value is nonetheless substantially different from that evinced in the *Eumenides*. Note that for Socrates suffering is valuable only *comparatively*: given the option to either (1) harm someone or (2) be harmed, Socrates thinks we should accept (2), since (1) is shameful and so must be worse. By contrast suffering's value for Aeschylus cuts across the distinction between committing and suffering harm. Given that Orestes not only undergoes harm but commits it—there is blood on his hands—the value of his suffering cannot be of the narrowly moral sort outlined by Socrates. Rather it consists in bringing about a tragic form of understanding, one that is decidedly anti-Socratic (given the Socratic union of happiness, virtue, and truth).

The importance of Orestes's understanding, however, is secondary to the wisdom wrought from suffering by the Eumenides. It is the latter who enable the longstanding tradition of retribution to be reshaped. The cessation of the Atridae cycle of vengeance acquires the status of political progress in its serving as the occasion for Athens to initiate rule of law. Rule of law provides institutional measures for substantially improving the well-being of Athenian citizens, and it is this presence of human progress that most clearly warrants the name Aeschylean optimism.

Aeschylean optimism differs substantially from its Socratic nephew in that the former places suffering at its center. For all this, however, we should resist pessimistic readings of Nietzsche on tragedy. For example, according to Williams's "Nietzschean" view of tragedy (at least the sort that qualifies as "stark fiction"), tragic theater presents us with the bleak truth of the "inexplicable necessity" of "extreme, undeserved, and uncompensated suffering," for which "there is no justification." Williams is right to hold that Nietzsche thinks life abounds with undeserved suffering, but why should this lead us to accept Williams's suggestion that tragedy's function *consists in* "lay[ing] fictional horrors before us in a way that elicits attitudes we cannot take towards real horrors"?[51]

It is worth appreciating why one might be tempted to endorse, in a Nietzschean spirit, a pessimistic reading of tragic drama's function. Like his educator and exemplar, Arthur Schopenhauer, Nietzsche holds that life is not fundamentally fair; *pace* the Stoics (BGE 9) and other rationalists, the world displays no internal rational structure. It is *we* who justify the sea of suffering that threatens to swallow us, as it has swallowed our friends and forerunners.[52] On Schopenhauer's view, however, we are not simply *vulnerable* to suffering; humans are *essentially* and inevitably sufferers, deserving of contempt as a species, yet *individually* deserving pity.

Nietzsche's indebtedness to Schopenhauer, however, consists not in mimicry but more valuably in his "think[ing] pessimism through to its depths." In immersing himself fully in the pessimistic worldview, Nietzsche eventually endorses the opposite world orientation: "Anyone like me, who has tried for a long time and with some enigmatic desire, to think pessimism through to its depths and to deliver it from the half-Christian, half-German narrowness and naiveté with which it has finally presented itself to this century, namely in the form of the Schopenhauerian philosophy . . . will have inadvertently opened his eyes to the inverse ideal: to the ideal of the most high-spirited, vital, world-affirming individual" (BGE 56). Elsewhere Nietzsche claims that a serious consideration of pessimism results in the position's own "self-refutation" (TI IX: 36). Although he does not say exactly why this is so, part of the reason is plausibly that acceptance of thoroughgoing pessimism undermines one's grounds for issuing prescriptions. According to Schopenhauer, because we are a contemptible species of inevitable sufferers, we ought to "injure no one; on the contrary, help everyone as much as you can."[53] But Schopenhauer's pity-based ethical project is difficult to motivate if we accept the view that humanity is essentially bad.[54] What reason can I possibly have for pitying my neighbor if he is essentially contemptible? In short, the pursuit of caring for and helping others appears to be a lost cause if we adopt Schopenhauerian pessimism.

Pessimism, in other words, provides little basis for avoiding resignation in the face of life's demands. What is essential to the view found in Nietzsche and Aeschylus, by contrast, is the drive for a distinctive kind of improvement. This drive is one for which pessimism cannot adequately account. *Pace* those who take life to be inherently and irredeemably bad, for the Aeschylean optimist there are *things we can do*, within mutable limits, *to make life better*.[55] Here is where the relevance of my discussion of mercy to criminal law surfaces.

We can imagine a version of the *Oresteia* in which Athena, upon reflecting on the nature of the Furies, judges them to be irreparably vicious. If this were Athena's attitude, there would be little reason to think she would endeavor to persuade the Furies to take up the values of Athens as their own. Fortunately, however, Athena's actions are expressive of Aeschylean optimism: in spite of the Furies' formidable track record of malice and blood thirst, Athena recognizes them as beings with whom one can reason. My suggestion is that the "normative hope" that Athena displays toward the Furies ought to serve as a kind of model for merciful sanctioning practices.[56]

What does this suggestion amount to? First, it commends a model of punishment that is psychologically more robust than that of many deterrence-based views. The Aeschylean judge will not view criminals merely in behaviorist terms, "treating them as objects that through their behavior generate either good or bad social consequences,"[57] but as persons with historically rich moral psychological lives. On the level of behavior Orestes differs little from Agamemnon, but when we introduce remorse alongside considerations of Orestes's circumstances, it becomes possible to view him with different eyes. I hasten to add that the merciful judge need not ignore the deterrent function of criminal law. Indeed the formation of the Areopagus *can* be endorsed on purely consequentialist grounds, but a virtue of a hybrid view (i.e., one that takes seriously merciful criminal sanctioning) is its ability to render intelligible the importance of the judge's understanding the inner life of the criminal. In the *Eumenides* an understanding of the nature of the Furies' *ressentiment* is surely vital for, inter alia, appreciating the latent desire for Olympian recognition.

Empirical work gathered by Paul Robinson suggests another possible avenue for defending merciful criminal punishment on consequentialist grounds. Merciful criminal sanctioning might more accurately track lay intuitions about proper punishment, such that it "therefore better enhances the criminal justice system's moral credibility, and thereby its crime-control effectiveness."[58] Thus even if we take the deterrent function of criminal law to be a sole consideration, we should nonetheless pursue merciful sanctioning.

I want to suggest, however, that one lesson of the *Eumenides* consists in its making salient that more matters to us than the deterrent effects of law. This "something more" is captured by the value we perceive in the very transformation that the Furies undergo. To make this point let's focus on another kind of merciful sanctioning that has transformative potential. I have in mind college-in-prison programs. While it is true that programs of this sort drastically reduce recidivism and resultantly cut taxpayer spending on incarcerating prisoners (with an average annual cost of roughly $29,000 per person in the United States, which has a prison population of over 2.3 million),[59] the merciful judge cares about *something more* than these (admittedly nonnegligible) consequences.

This "something more," I think, consists in the merciful judge's *caring* about what "went wrong" in the criminal's civic integration, in the judge's normatively hoping *that* it go better. Furthermore, without such normative hope we have no reason to prefer (1) a world in which the state's citizens care about the civic good to (2) a world in which they don't, provided that the consequences, economic and otherwise, are identical for (1) and (2). "Structural comparative deprivation," recall, was a part of the explanation for the orientation of *ressentiment* that consumed the Furies. Over and above the costs and benefits involved in criminal sanctioning, the merciful judge strives to understand how and under what circumstances citizens feel and think such that they can flourish as responsible and admirable citizens. In other words, the merciful judge acknowledges that the importance of net deterrence effects is parasitic on our experience of the value of another's humanity.

Nietzsche's discussion of the practical significance of the merciful attitude suggests that tragic fiction is well-positioned to teach us about the stakes involved in nurturing certain virtues. For this reason, although Nietzsche *does* claim that tragedy represents some of the immense suffering in human life, his reverence for the "profoundly Aeschylean demand for *justice*" (BT 9) suggests that, in spite of its immensity, this suffering should arouse attitudes other than dismay. This will not surprise us if we keep in mind Nietzsche's many invocations to self-overcoming (D 192; BGE 61, 257; TI X: 38) and self-creating (TI IX: 10; HAH Pref. 3). Indeed reflection on tragedy can provide us with ethical directives for reasonably overcoming some of the default sources of our suffering. There are measures to be taken toward transforming our circumstances. The merciful self-overcoming of retributive justice is just one example.

NOTES

I'm grateful to the participants and attendees of the Crime in Law and Literature Conference held in February 2014 at the University of Chicago Law School—in particular to Emily Buss, Sarah Conly, Brian Leiter, Dhananjay Jagannathan, Jarosław Kuisz, and especially Martha C. Nussbaum, who provided valuable criticism and commentary on earlier versions of this chapter. For fruitful discussion and insight I'm grateful also to Babak Bakhtiarynia, Agnes Callard, James Conant, Joshua Fox, Josh Mendelsohn, Raphael Ng, Skomantas Pocius, Martijn Wallage, and David Wellbery.

1. According to Sommerstein, for instance, the model of punishment at work in Orestes's trial consists in "an independent authority . . . hearing the arguments on both sides and then coming to a rational decision" (introduction to Aeschylus' *Eumenides*, 21).

2. Nietzsche, *The Birth of Tragedy*, 14. References to *Birth* will primarily be to this translation. References to other works by Nietzsche start with translations by Kaufmann, Hollingdale, and Norman, making changes as needed based on Nietzsche, *Sämtliche Werke*. I use the following abbreviations for Nietzsche's works: *Beyond Good and Evil* (BGE); *The Birth of Tragedy* (BT); *Daybreak* (D); *Ecce Homo* (EH); *Genealogy of Morality* (GM); *Human All Too Human* (HAH); *Twilight of the Idols* (TI). Roman numerals refer to major parts or chapters in Nietzsche's works; Arabic numerals refer to sections. So, for example, GM II: 7 refers to section 7 of the *Genealogy*'s second part.

3. It will turn out that the marks of "rationality," as I take Nietzsche to understand them, are inseparable from truths about *human* mindedness, but this is not to endorse a subjectivist view of practical rationality off the bat. Additionally in this paper I speak of both states and processes as rationally governed, leaving aside the related debate over whether rational requirement governs combinations of attitudes. See Kolodny, "State or Process Requirements?," 462.

4. For an argument to the effect that such sanctions are *never* permissible, see Harel "Why Only the State May Inflict Criminal Sanctions."

5. The formation of the Areopagus *can* be esteemed on something like (1) virtue-theoretic or (2) perfectionist grounds—after all, the development of human excellence undergirds Nietzsche's broader project—yet there are difficult issues here regarding (3) Nietzsche's meta-normative commitments (particularly about what makes it the case that those things Nietzsche esteems *are* valuable, if they are), which preclude the straightforward attribution of either view. I must put these issues aside for present purposes. But for (1) see Hunt, *Nietzsche and the Origin of Virtue*. For two very different takes on (2) see Hurka, "Nietzsche: Perfectionist"; Conant, "Nietzsche's Perfectionism." (These readings differ substantially: Hurka's (anti-egalitarian) perfectionism is a version of consequentialism; Conant's Emersonian perfectionism is not.) For (3) see Hussain, "Nietzsche's Metaethical Stance"; Leiter, "Nietzsche's Metaethics."

6. The *Eumenides*, in Aeschylus, *The Oresteia*, 768–79. Unless otherwise noted, references to the *Oresteia* will be to this translation and are abbreviated as follows: Ag. = *Agamemnon*; Lb. = *Libation Bearers*; Eu. = *Eumenides*.

7. Aristotle does not appear to hold that the mother is *eliminable* for procreation, but he does give her contribution the status of passive matter: "If, then, the male stands for the effective and active, and the female, considered as female, for the passive, it follows that what the female would contribute to the semen of the male would not be semen but material for the semen to work upon. This is just what we find to be the case, for the catamenia have in their nature an affinity to the primitive matter" (*Generation of Animals*, 729a).

8. Apollo's line continues thus: "My father made no healing spell for that [i.e., raising the dead], though he can turn all other things, at will, inside and out, and not pant from the effort" (Eu. 759–61).

9. Allen, *The World of Prometheus*, 137. Shapiro and Burian render this "wholeheartedly" [Eu. 856]. Note that Allen refers to the line numbering of the Greek, which differs from the numbering of the translation, which I cite.

10. Plato, *Republic* X 605d, IX 547e.

11. Translated in Caswell, *A Study of Thumos in Early Greek Epic*. See Euripides, *Cyclops; Alcestis; Medea*. Cf. Purviance, "*Thumos* and the Daring Soul."

12. Purviance, "*Thumos* and the Daring Soul," 7.

13. Nussbaum, "Nietzsche, Schopenhauer, and Dionysus," 359.

14. Similarly, upon returning from Troy Agamemnon announces, "Justice has been exacted from Priam's city" (Ag. 931–32).

15. Allen, *The World of Prometheus*, 20–21.

16. Cohen, *Law, Violence, and Community in Classical Athens*, quoted in Allen, *The World of Prometheus*, 21.

17. 479 U.S. 538 (1987). We can maintain that empathy can be put in the service of genuine moral reasoning while holding that, as Nussbaum claims, "it would also be correct to leave aside any mere gut reaction to the defendant's appearance, demeanor, or clothing, anything that could not be made a reasoned part of the 'story' of the case" ("Equity and Mercy," 120). Empathy of the quasi-contagious and mechanical sort is but an immature stage upon which "mutual *moral* empathy" can develop. For a reading of this kind of view in Adam Smith see Carrasco, "From Psychology to Moral Normativity." I cannot argue for this here, but a Smithian sentimentalist account of moral development earns a great deal from empirical work on the topic; cf. Hoffman, *Empathy and Moral Development*, esp. 221–48.

18. Schacht, "Nietzsche on Art in *Birth of Tragedy*," 203. At least this is what tragic theater did for the Greeks; Nietzsche's hopes were invested, at least for a time, in opera.

19. On this point see Young, *Nietzsche's Philosophy of Art*, 42–45.

20. Ibid., 43. Nietzsche's grounds for turning away from historicism—already held by the time of his inaugural lecture at Basel—help explain the peculiar work of poetic-philosophical philology that constitutes *Birth*. See Franks, "Desdemona's Lie," esp. 235–37.

21. The context here is a comparison to Goethe's poem on Prometheus: "But what is most wonderful in this Prometheus poem, which in its basic idea is a veritable hymn of impiety, is the profoundly Aeschylean demand for *justice*. The immeasurable suffering of the bold 'individual' on the one hand and the divine predicament and intimation of a twilight of gods on the other, the way the power of these two worlds of suffering *compels a reconciliation* [italics mine], a metaphysical union—all of this recalls in the strongest possible manner the center and main axiom of the Aeschylean view of the world which envisages Moira enthroned above gods and men as eternal justice" (BT 9).

22. Posner, *Law and Literature*, 149.

23. On Nietzsche's use of the French, see Risse: "Although 'ressentiment' is a French word (and thus missing from the Grimms' dictionary), the German educated elite had used it since the 17th century. The word was presumably adopted because German lacks a good word for the English 'resentment' and the French 'ressentiment.' . . . At the same time, these words serve reasonably well as translations of each other, except that the French word seems to possess a stronger connotation with memory" ("Origins of *Ressentiment* and Sources of Normativity," n11).

24. See Strawson, "Freedom and Resentment."

25. Wallace, "*Ressentiment*, Value, and Self-Vindication," 116, 128.

26. Reginster, "Nietzsche on *Ressentiment* and Valuation," 303.

27. For a discussion of studies of judgment shift in children see Karniol and Miller, "Why Not Wait?"; Holton, *Willing, Wanting, Waiting*, 98–100.

28. Holton, *Willing, Wanting, Waiting*, 140. The example is David Gauthier's.

29. Pippin, "Williams on Nietzsche on the Greeks"; Williams, *Ethics and the Limits of Philosophy*, 175.

30. Posner, *Law and Literature*, 149.

31. See section 50 of Rawls, *A Theory of Justice*. For disagreement based on Nietzsche's use of *exemplar*, see Conant, "Nietzsche's Perfectionism," and for a rejoinder, see Hurka, "Nietzsche: Perfectionist." And see note 5 of this chapter for citations to both.

32. Parfit, *On What Matters*, 578–79.

33. Reginster, "Nietzsche on *Ressentiment* and Valuation," 283.

34. Gemes, "Freud and Nietzsche on Sublimation," 48.

35. Nussbaum, *Anger and Forgiveness*, ch. 1.

36. Appiah, *The Honor Code*. As readers acquainted with Nietzsche's discussion of "revaluation of values" will know, this transition of justice is not Nietzsche's only model for evaluative change.

37. Murphy, *Mercy and Legal Justice*, 169. As Aristotle puts the issue, "When we reason it out, it seems strange if the equitable, being something different from the just, is yet praiseworthy; for either the just or the equitable is not good, if they are different; or, if both are good, they are the same" (*Nicomachean Ethics*, bk. V.1137b1–6).

38. Nussbaum, "Equity and Mercy," 91.

39. Posner, *Law and Literature*, 55.

40. Nussbaum, "Equity and Mercy," 93.

41. Nussbaum, *Anger and Forgiveness*. Thus the Nietzschean reading stands in stark contrast to readings of the *Eumenides* that claim the retributive anger of the Furies is simply shackled beneath the state, their "assimilation" amounting simply to *another* way of repressing the state's aggressive mode. Such views fail to do justice to either the abundance of transformative idioms and imagery in the text or the historical milieu in which Aeschylus produced the *Oresteia*.

42. See Kaufmann's fn. 2 in BT on the inaccuracy of Nietzsche's claim that Euripides is the most optimistic and antitragic of the tragedians (discussed in BT 12–14). See also Nussbaum, introduction to *The Bacchae of Euripides*. It is plausible that Nietzsche's concern with historical accuracy is subordinated to the aim of reinvigorating *our culture* via myth. On the rhetorical function of Nietzsche's historical distortion, see Young, *Nietzsche's Philosophy of Art*, 30–31. Support for this general idea comes from the fact that, in other texts, Nietzsche's relationship to Socrates is far from wholly negative. In a text written a year after the publication of *Birth*, Nietzsche classes Socrates among his favorite pre-Socratic philosophers. See Nietzsche, *Philosophy in the Tragic Age of the Greeks*, 31. On the symbolic function of Socrates in Nietzsche's narrative of tragedy, see chapters 6 and 7 of Silk and Stern, *Nietzsche on Tragedy*.

43. Later in the passage Nietzsche claims that this conceptual connection between suffering and guilt in the Christian moral framework precludes modern Europeans from having a name for what the *Greeks* called "pity."

44. More fully: "Everything there is, or was, of freedom, subtlety, boldness, dance, or masterly assurance on earth, whether in thinking itself, or in ruling, or in speaking and persuading, in artists just as in ethical practices, has only developed by virtue of the 'tyranny of such arbitrary laws.' . . . I will say it again: what seems to be essential 'in heaven and on earth' is that there be *obedience* in one direction for a long time. . . . This always brings and has brought about something that makes life on earth worth living—for instance: virtue, art, music, dance, reason, intellect—something that transfigures, something refined, fantastic and divine" (BGE 188).

45. To be fair, Nietzsche's would be a psychological thesis and so neither known a priori nor a necessary truth.

46. I have in mind social psychological work suggesting that "people who are able to construct a good narrative, particularly one that connects early setbacks and suffering to later triumph, are happier and more productive than those who lack such a 'redemption narrative.'" Haidt, *The Righteous Mind*, 443n24. This point is extracted from McAdams, *The Redemptive Self*, and McAdams and Pals, "A New Big Five."

47. Dodds, "Morals and Politics in the *Oresteia*," 263.

48. Nussbaum, *The Fragility of Goodness*, 36.

49. Williams, "Ethical Consistency," 172.

50. We should not give Orestes *too much* credit, however. Although he expresses remorse over killing his mother, once cleansed by Apollo he silently joins the latter in denying that Clytemnestra was in fact a blood relative.

51. Williams, "*The Women of Trachis*," 58, 59.

52. For an illuminating discussion of Nietzsche's nonstandard use of "*aesthetic* justification," see Leiter, "The Truth Is Terrible."

53. Schopenhauer, *On the Basis of Morality*, 69.

54. I owe this thought to Joshua Fox, who also brings to my attention Schopenhauer's claim that humankind "is not exactly *imperfection*, as has often been said, but rather *distortion*, in everything" (*Parerga and Paralipomena*, 304).

55. There is a risk of making a straw man of Williams here. Williams's students sometimes mean something weaker by pessimism: just that one's well-being is subject to many factors beyond one's control. See, for example, Russell, "Free Will Pessimism." Our abilities and actions are subject to conditions of luck; this observation cannot be denied. But if the belief that I lack full control over my well-being is sufficient for pessimism, the debate over pessimism becomes stale: *everyone* who acknowledges her lack of self-sufficiency or vulnerability on external goods will be a pessimist. Presumably, and in order to avoid the near triviality of being a pessimist, it should be necessary for commitment to pessimism that one at least have a certain *affective and behavioral* orientation toward the world, say, one of "dismay"? Nietzsche appears to think about pessimism. He claims, for instance, that Schopenhauer's entitlement to being a pessimist is undermined by his regular flute playing (BGE 186)! Given that Nietzsche opposes pessimism on the grounds that we ought to "rejoice" in the face of the suffering found in life (TI VIII: 5), we can be confident that he does not endorse an orientation of dismay. Furthermore, given that Williams takes the "morality system" to be a contingent historical product, it appears that dismay would be appropriate only relative to unreasonable expectations about what agency consists in. In this case, if dismay (and so pessimism) is ever appropriate, it will be so only in transition away from the deep-rooted belief in the morality system. I borrow the picture of "dismay" as transitional to the appropriate attitude of "affirmation" from Ted Honderich, whose view is aptly, I think, put forward in a Nietzschean spirit; see his *The Consequences of Determinism*, esp. 146.

56. For an elaborate exposition of normative hope, see Martin, *How We Hope*, esp. 118–40.

57. Nussbaum, "Equity and Mercy," 113.

58. Robinson, "Mercy, Crime Control, and Moral Credibility."

59. These figures are from the Bard Prison Initiative website, http://bpi.bard.edu/faqs/.

WORKS CITED

Aeschylus. *The Oresteia*. Trans. A. Shapiro and P. Burian. New York: Oxford University Press, 2003.

Allen, Danielle. *The World of Prometheus: The Politics of Punishing in Democratic Athens*. Princeton, NJ: Princeton University Press, 2000.

Appiah, Kwame Anthony. *The Honor Code: How Moral Revolutions Happen*. New York: Norton, 2010.

Aristotle. *On the Generation of Animals*. Trans. A. Platt. In *The Basic Works of Aristotle*, ed. Richard McKeon, 665–79. New York: Random House, 2001.

———. *Nicomachean Ethics*. In *The Complete Works of Aristotle*, ed. Jonathan Barnes, 2: 1729–867. Princeton, NJ: Princeton University Press, 1984.

Carrasco, Maria A. "From Psychology to Moral Normativity." In *The Adam Smith Review*, ed. F. Forman-Barzilai, 6: 9–29. New York: Routledge, 2011.

Caswell, Caroline P. *A Study of Thumos in Early Greek Epic*. Leiden: E. J. Brill, 1990.

Cohen, David. *Law, Violence, and Community in Classical Athens*. Cambridge, UK: Cambridge University Press, 1995.

Conant, James. "Nietzsche's Perfectionism: A Reading of *Schopenhauer as Educator*." In *Nietzsche's Postmoralism: Essays on Nietzsche's Prelude to Philosophy's Future*, ed. Richard Schact, 181–257. Cambridge, UK: Cambridge University Press.

Dodds, E. R. "Morals and Politics in the *Oresteia*." In *Oxford Reading in Classical Studies: Aeschylus*, ed. M. Lloyd, 245–65. Oxford: Oxford University Press, 2007.

Euripides. *Cyclops; Alcestis; Medea*. Trans. by David Kovacs. Loeb Classical Library vol. 12. Cambridge, MA: Harvard University Press, 1994.

Franks, Paul. "Desdemona's Lie: Nihilism, Perfectionism, Historicism." *Journal of Nietzsche Studies* 44.2 (2013): 225–45.

Gemes, Ken. "Freud and Nietzsche on Sublimation." *Journal of Nietzsche Studies* 38 (2009): 38–59.

Haidt, Jonathan. *The Righteous Mind: Why Good People Are Divided by Politics and Religion*. New York: Vintage Books, 2012.

Harel, Alon. "Why Only the State May Inflict Criminal Sanctions: The Case against Privately Inflicted Sanctions." *Legal Theory* 14.2 (2008): 113–33.

Hoffman, Martin. *Empathy and Moral Development: Implications for Caring and Justice*. Cambridge, UK: Cambridge University Press, 2001.

Holton, Richard. *Willing, Wanting, Waiting*. New York: Oxford University Press, 2009.

Honderich, Ted. *The Consequences of Determinism*. Oxford: Oxford University Press, 1988.

Hunt, Lester H. *Nietzsche and the Origin of Virtue*. London: Routledge, 1991.

Hurka, Thomas. "Nietzsche: Perfectionist." In *Nietzsche and Morality*, ed. B. Leiter and N. Sinhababu, 9–31. Oxford: Oxford University Press, 2007.

Hussain, Nadeem. "Nietzsche's Metaethical Stance." In *The Oxford Handbook of Nietzsche*, ed. K. Gemes and J. Richardson, 389–414. Oxford: Oxford University Press, 2013.

Karniol, Rachel, and Dale Miller. "Why Not Wait? A Cognitive Model of Self-imposed Delay Termination." *Journal or Personality and Social Psychology* 45 (1983): 935–42.

Kolodny, Niko. "State or Process Requirements?" *Mind* 116 (2007): 371–85.

Leiter, Brian. "Nietzsche's Metaethics: Against the Privilege Readings." *European Journal of Philosophy* 8 (2000): 277–97.

———. "The Truth Is Terrible." In *Nietzsche on Morality and the Affirmation of Life*, ed. Daniel Came. Oxford: Oxford University Press, forthcoming.

Martin, Adrienne. *How We Hope: A Moral Psychology*. Princeton, NJ: Princeton University Press, 2013.

McAdams, Dan. *The Redemptive Self: Stories Americans Live By*. New York: Oxford University Press, 2006.

McAdams, Dan, and Jennifer Pals. "A New Big Five: Fundamental Principles for an Integrative Science of Personality." *American Psychologist* 61 (2006): 204–17.

Murphy, Jeffrie G. "Mercy and Legal Justice". In Jeffrie G. Murphy and Jean Hampton, *Forgiveness and Mercy*, 162–86. Cambridge, UK: Cambridge University Press, 1988.

Nietzsche, Friedrich. *Beyond Good and Evil*. Trans. Judith Norman. Cambridge, UK: Cambridge University Press, 2002.

———. *The Birth of Tragedy*. Trans. W. Kaufmann. New York: Vintage Books, 1967.

———. *Daybreak*. Trans. R. J. Hollingdale. Ed. Maudmarie Clark and Brian Leiter. Cambridge, UK: Cambridge University Press, 1997.

———. *On the Genealogy of Morals*. Trans. W. Kaufmann and R. J. Hollingdale. New York: Vintage Books, 1969.

———. *Philosophy in the Tragic Age of the Greeks*. Trans. Marianne Cowan. Chicago: Henry Regnery, 1962.

———. *Sämtliche Werke: Kritische Studienausgabe in 15 Bänden*. Ed. G. Colli and M. Montinari. Berlin: de Gruyter, 1980.

Nussbaum, Martha C. *Anger and Forgiveness: Resentment, Generosity, Justice*. John Locke Lectures in Philosophy. Oxford: Oxford University Press, forthcoming.

———. "Equity and Mercy." *Philosophy & Public Affairs* 22.2 (1993): 83–125.

———. *The Fragility of Goodness: Luck and Ethics in Greek Tragedy and Philosophy*. New York: Cambridge University Press, 1986.

———. "Introduction." In *The Bacchae of Euripides*, trans. C. K. Williams, vii–xliv. New York, NY: Farrar, Straus, and Giroux, 1990.

———. "Nietzsche, Schopenhauer, and Dionysus." In *The Cambridge Companion to Schopenhauer*, ed. C. Janaway, 344–73. Cambridge, UK: Cambridge University Press, 1999.

———. *Upheavals of Thought: The Intelligence of Emotions*. New York: Cambridge University Press, 2001.

Parfit, Derek. *On What Matters*. Vol. 2. Oxford: Oxford University Press, 2011.

Pippin, Robert. "Williams on Nietzsche on the Greeks." In *Tragedy and the Idea of Modernity*, ed. J. Billings and M. Leonard. Oxford: Oxford University Press, forthcoming.

Posner, Richard. *Law and Literature*. Revised and enlarged edition. Cambridge, MA: Harvard University Press, 1998.

Purviance, Susan M. "*Thumos* and the Daring Soul: Craving Honor and Justice." *Journal of Ancient Philosophy* 2.2 (2008): 1–16.

Reginster, Bernard. "Nietzsche on *Ressentiment* and Valuation." *Philosophy and Phenomenological Research* 57 (1997): 281–305.

Risse, Mathias. "Origins of *Ressentiment* and Sources of Normativity." *Nietzsche-Studien* 32 (2003): 147–70.

Robinson, Paul H. "Mercy, Crime Control, and Moral Credibility." In *Merciful Judgments and Contemporary Society: Legal Problems, Legal Possibilities*, ed. A. Sarat, 99–123. Cambridge, UK: Cambridge University Press, 2011.

Russell, Paul. "Free Will Pessimism." In *Oxford Studies in Agency and Responsibility*, ed. D. Shoemaker. Oxford: Oxford University Press, forthcoming.

Schacht, Richard. "Nietzsche on Art in *Birth of Tragedy*." In *Oxford Readings in Philosophy: Nietzsche*, ed. B. Leiter and J. Richardson, 186–209. Oxford: Oxford University Press, 2001.

Schopenhauer, Arthur. *On the Basis of Morality*. Trans. E. F. J. Payne. Indianapolis: Hackett, 1995.

———. *Parerga and Paralipomena*. Vol. 2. Trans. E. F. J. Payne. New York: Oxford University Press, 1974.

Silk, M. S., and J. P. Stern. *Nietzsche on Tragedy*. Cambridge, UK: Cambridge University Press, 1981.

Sommerstein, Alan. Introduction to *Eumenides*, by Aeschylus, 1–36. Cambridge, UK: Cambridge University Press, 1989.

Strawson, Peter. "Freedom and Resentment." 1962. In *Freedom and Resentment and Other Essays*, 1–25. London: Methuen, 1974.

Wallace, R. Jay. "*Ressentiment*, Value, and Self-Vindication: Making Sense of Nietzsche's Slave Revolt." In *Nietzsche and Morality*, ed. B. Leiter and N. Sinhababu, 110–37. New York: Oxford University Press, 2007.

Williams, Bernard. "Ethical Consistency." In *Problems of the Self*, 166–86. New York: Cambridge University Press, 1973.

———. *Ethics and the Limits of Philosophy*. Cambridge, MA: Harvard University Press, 1985.

———. "*The Women of Trachis:* Fictions, Pessimism, Ethics." In *The Sense of the Past: Essays in the History of Philosophy*, ed. Myles Burnyeat, 49–59. Princeton, NJ: Princeton University Press, 2003.

Young, Julian. *Nietzsche's Philosophy of Art*. New York: Cambridge University Press, 1992.

3

Suborning Perjury

A CASE STUDY OF NARRATIVE PRECEDENT IN TALMUDIC LAW

Barry Scott Wimpfheimer

RABBINIC LAW DOES not consistently separate criminal law from civil or even ritual law. A common feature of talmudic legal analysis is the transition from a topic in one subject area to a topic in an entirely unrelated subject area; this practice highlights the degree to which rabbinic law is not conceptualized as consisting of different subsections. In this chapter I push this idea beyond its basics and demonstrate the ways in which (criminal) law is implicated in cultural discourses of gender and power that become more transparent in the context of the world's unseen forces, whether considered magical or scientific. What follows is an intense literary examination of an unstudied talmudic legal story that reads between the lines to identify a prevalent cultural suspicion of women that emerges in the surprising legal context of suborning perjury. This reading magnifies the sense that one must seek to understand rabbinic society in order to comprehend the nuances of its literature.

Prose narrative (unlike poetic or dramatic narrative) has only recently come to be celebrated as literary art.[1] This fact of Western literature is also true within the parallel universe of Jewish textual discourse about the Jewish canon. The Babylonian Talmud, arguably the most significant text for Judaism and the text that has embodied the tradition for a millennium, contains many prose narratives. For much of the Talmud's reception history, though, readers of the Talmud glossed over such stories, considering them unworthy of the microscopic forms of scrutiny that the Talmud's legal sections have routinely received. While the Talmud engendered sophisticated hermeneutic frames for the processing of talmudic legal matter, it did not similarly develop such frames for talmudic narrative. This point highlights the fact that the age-old distinction between legal (halakhic) and nonlegal (aggadic) rabbinic materials is most significant not as a description of essential texts but in implicating separate hermeneutic frames and concomitant reading practices.[2]

One of the challenges for would-be contemporary readers of talmudic narrative is that they must work without a tradition and produce a robust hermeneutic framework for processing narrative.[3] One of the doyens of the recent turn toward narrative within the study of rabbinic literature, Yonah Fraenkel, adapted a dogmatic New Critical framework and applied it to rabbinic narrative.[4] Fraenkel was attuned to the deep structure of rabbinic stories. This structure came to represent the key to deciphering the encoded didactic messages of the stories. Privileging an aesthetic appreciation for rabbinic narrative, Fraenkel compares narrative structural beauty to the attractiveness of visual art. Aesthetics also encourage Fraenkel to limit the hermeneutic frame to the story itself. This limitation was empowering for Fraenkel, who was gifted at producing deep structural insights within the limited field of the rabbinic story. Other scholars have chafed at such limitations, and even Fraenkel himself could not avoid occasionally defying the boundaries of a story text in pursuit of a particularly rich external fact or framework.[5]

Fraenkel's self-imposed limitations are both artificial and self-serving. They do, however, succeed in producing limitations on the hermeneutic framework for rabbinic narrative. Without such limitations one can be tempted to read a rabbinic story through a seemingly infinite set of lenses. In this chapter I introduce an alternative methodological choice. I attempt to produce for narrative a hermeneutic framework that mirrors the one that exists for the interpretation of talmudic law. Legal precedent is usually considered a discourse of authoritative decision making that allows legists a framework within which to support a legal position. But precedent is also a hermeneutic framework that provides the basic semiotic and linguistic meaning of legal propositions and allows for value judgments that help to limit the semantic range of legal meaning.

Talmudic legal stories draw attention to the starkly different hermeneutic environments that inhere for legal texts on the one hand and narratives on the other. The Talmud's own process of composition produces a framework of statutory precedent that predigests all legal statutory statements by providing them with an address within a legal code and a ready set of comparators, both statutes about the local legal issues and statutes from remote legal issues that overlap structurally or logically. A trained Talmudist (including the later authorities whose interpretations appear already within the Talmud itself) knows instinctually to relate a legal story's statutory content to parallel statutes, relevant biblical sources, and layers of interpretation of both of these canonical corpora. No such instincts exist for handling a story's aesthetic, ethical, or didactic content. Even more starkly, poetic concerns such as character, characterization, plot, and voice have no hermeneutic tradition whatsoever. There is assuredly no traditional reception practice of narratology that would be attuned to the inherently multiple tellings in every narrative.

Literary readers of talmudic stories are challenged by the absence of a prior literary tradition. They are also challenged by the yawning historical and cultural gap that separates the production of these stories and the present. Contemporary readers feel the strain of viewing the past through present lenses. The absence of a reading tradition starkly marks the break between present reading and past composition. This is less true with respect to nonnarrative legal texts read within the framework of legal precedent. While critical legal readers of such texts in the Talmud jump a divide between insider reading and external critique, they nevertheless participate in a fairly continuous tradition. While a critic may determine that a critical reading of a talmudic legal text is preferable to Rashi's commentary on the same, this does not undermine the extent to which Rashi's commentary simultaneously buttresses many of the basic building blocks of the new reading: explaining complicated terms and providing the basic legal context out of which the larger picture of the text emerges. At times the critic will follow Rashi in a violent reading of the text, but the gap between present violence and past text is elided by the gap between Rashi and the present. When one self-consciously seeks to surmount the limitations of having no hermeneutic tradition, the gap is more palpable.

This chapter manufactures a hermeneutic framework for reading a hitherto unexamined talmudic legal narrative by using narratives to read other narratives. Narratives from the Bible and elsewhere in rabbinic literature are employed as a means of teasing out subtle issues from the core story. Narratives are helpful for reading other narratives because the comparator text possesses all of the features of narrative (plot dynamics, characterization, voice, narratological gaps). Furthermore the use of one narrative to read another allows themes that are more explicit in one story to be relevant implicitly for the other.[6]

The narratives I use to read this talmudic story are stories from the Hebrew Bible, Second Temple Jewish writings, and from rabbinic literature. Stories from the Jewish prehistory of the Talmud are relevant because they could reasonably have been known to the talmudic story's composers. Stories from elsewhere in the Talmud are relevant because they allow insight into the culture that produced the core story. Even if the major passage under consideration was complete before the comparative passage was composed, one can use the comparative passage to establish issues in rabbinic culture that are relevant in the first context. In drawing upon biblical and rabbinic stories, moreover, I create a literary hermeneutic out of a preexisting traditional relationship, the one between the Hebrew Bible and rabbinic literature. Rabbinic literature is built upon the canonical Hebrew Bible and its interpretation. Some Second Temple Jewish works were excluded from the canon, but one can often demonstrate the extent to which parallel versions of such stories were known to the rabbis and their sectarian predecessors. The use of ancient Jewish stories helps to transcend the aforementioned gap in tradition since the parallel stories stand as a corrective for the tendency to emphasize present-day concerns.

The core text of this study has not previously received any scholarly attention. The hermeneutic of reading stories with other stories enables this seemingly simple text to reveal rich possibilities.[7]

STORY: BAVLI MAKKOT 5B

That woman[8] who brought witnesses and they were [found to be] lying brought [witnesses][9] and they [too] were [found to be] lying. She went and brought [other][10] witnesses [that were not found to be lying].[11]

Rabbi Simeon ben[12] Laqish said, "she is established."[13]

Rabbi El'azar said to him, "if she is established, is all of Israel established?"[14]

Once, they were sitting before Rabbi Yohanan [and] an episode like this came before them.

Rabbi Simeon[15] ben Laqish said, "she is established."

Rabbi Yohanan said to him, "if she is established, is all of Israel established?"

Thereupon, [Resh Laqish] fixed Rabbi El'azar with an evil look. He said to him, "You heard something from *Bar Nafha* and did not say it to me in his name?"

Two episodes of false testimony appear in this story. The first is a hypothetical scenario discussed by two Palestinian rabbis active in the early third century CE.[16] A woman who had produced two sets of witnesses who were established as liars seeks to produce a third set in her civil matter. Rabbi Simeon ben Laqish asserts that a pattern of lying has been established, and the third set is automatically disqualified even if no evidence is produced to establish them as lying. Rabbi El'azar responds with a rhetorical question that communicates his disagreeing position; while she may be established, the pattern attaches to her but cannot discredit the new witnesses who come in off the street.

As a legal disagreement the debate between these two authorities centers around the relationship between witnesses and parties. Contemporary U.S. law routinely considers witnesses as testifying on behalf of one of the parties. As such, they are "witnesses for" these parties. Ancient Greek law similarly understood witnesses in this fashion.[17] But biblical law considers testimony an Israelite religious duty.[18] As such, witnesses may be considered witnesses to the truth rather than witnesses for a party even though the facts of testimony may benefit one of the two parties. The view that does not disqualify the third set of witnesses on the basis of the established pattern severs the relationship between the witness and the party and refuses to allow the party's pattern to determine credibility.

The hypothetical scenario is potentially complicated by the gender of the party in question. Is the fact that this party is female relevant either for establishing a pattern of lying or for refusing to extend that pattern from the party to the witnesses? If gender is not relevant to these theoretical matters, why would the debate have transpired specifically about a case in which the party was female when the default subject of rabbinic theoretical discussion is always male?

The second episode of false testimony in the story transpires when an actual case resembling the hypothetical materializes in front of these same two rabbis and their mentor or colleague Rab Yohanan. Rab Yohanan is the most oft-cited authority in the Palestinian Talmud and an important tradent within the Babylonian as well. When the second episode transpires, Reish Laqish again asserts that a pattern of lying has been established, and Rab Yohanan responds with the same rhetorical question that Rabbi El'azar had used to reply in the hypothetical scenario. The repeated use of the identical question tips Resh Laqish off to the fact that Rabbi El'azar had heard this stated by Rab Yohanan. Resh Laqish confronts Rabbi El'azar with his own rhetorical question: "You heard something from *Bar Nafha* [a nickname for Rab Yohanan] and did not say it to me in his name?"

Nearly all talmudic legal texts are recorded in the name of their authors. As such, nearly every talmudic passage has an implicit narrative of composition. Readers often imagine a room full of rabbis discussing the issues in a scholastic manner. In the present text, though, the implicit narrative of scholastic discussion becomes both explicit and more robust. Attention is directed away from the potentially lying witnesses and their related party toward a different set of actors: the rabbis in the study hall. The real world intrudes upon the hypothetical scholastic activity in the form of the case, and we read of the realpolitik of the study hall itself. The villainess who conspired with lying witnesses gives way to the villain who neglected to credit his teacher for a creative (and winning) turn of phrase.

The text contain two stories: the story of the woman producing the lying witnesses and the story of the rabbis in their scholastic (and real-life) conversation. To argue against a naïve view that the frame story of the rabbis is merely reportage, it should be noted that the identical frame story is employed elsewhere in the Talmud, in a section that discusses the pattern of establishing someone as having a priestly lineage.[19] A source critical approach to these two parallel texts would attempt to determine which one is the original and which the derivative copy. For literary purposes, though, it is merely necessary to note that one of these is a derivative copy. Talmudic composers in one of these contexts understood the frame narrative of the three rabbis as a formal feature that could be adapted to a new context and redeployed. This suggests that analysis should productively consider the purpose of such a frame story and its relationship to the content it frames. On a basic level both the present text and its parallel usage at Ketubot 25b are interested in personal credibility. In that context there is concern over someone who claims to be a priest and may not be one. In this context there is concern that a set of witnesses is lying. The frame story is also about credibility. Rabbi El'azar plagiarized his teacher's rhetorical question during his debate with Resh Laqish. The story closes with Resh Laqish's fixing Rabbi El'azar with an evil stare while chastising him for not citing their teacher. The very rabbi who refuses to establish a pattern of lying and insists on the credibility of Israel is engaging in an act of unethical borrowing. Read in this way the frame story serves to undermine the finality of the rhetorical question. While the rhetorical question is literally given the last word in the debate about the hypothetical scenario, it is undermined by Resh Laqish's response in the second scenario.

In the Talmud's collage-like composition style source texts sometimes already receive interpretation within the text itself. The treatment of the present text in the talmudic passage does not engage the existence of multiple overlapping stories or the way the frame story undermines the definite character of the rhetorical question. Rather the Talmud's anonymous later voice reduces the two-narrative text to a statutory version of itself in which all that exists are the propositional legal positions of the two rabbis (one saying a pattern is established and one saying that the witnesses are credible). In *Narrating the Law* I noted the tendency of the Talmud's later anonymous voice to flatten legal stories into statutes and highlighted a proclivity for reducing the complex multiple meaning of a legal story to a simple legal position that coheres with parallel such positions elsewhere in the Talmud.[20] The present example provides further instantiation of this theory. All talmudic passages appear as comments on the second-century Mishnah, a statutory code. The story passage appears as a comment on a Mishnah in a chapter about perjury that deals with a scenario in which multiple sets of witnesses, as many as one hundred, were found to be conspiratorial and punishable with a talionic quid pro quo. The anonymous majority position in the Mishnah is that each of these sets of witnesses is treated independently and receives the criminal punishment even of death. Rabbi Judah, though, resists this absurdity and says that only the first convicted set of perjuring witnesses could be executed in such a scenario. The mishnaic text and the story are interested in different matters of law: the Mishnah is concerned with an ad absurdum possibility that could emerge from the rules of perjury punishment, while the story is interested in the question of witness credibility. The two texts share an element of multiple lying witnesses, and this allows the Talmud's anonymous voice to attempt to collapse the two arguments upon each other, suggesting that Resh Laqish's disqualification of the third set of witnesses maps onto Rabbi Judah's refusal to punish the second set of lying witnesses and Rab Yohanan/Rabbi El'azar's insistence upon the independence of each set of witnesses onto the majority's decision to prosecute each set of witnesses as if they were on their own, ignoring the obvious conspiracy. The Talmud's anonymous voice, in typical fashion, severs the two arguments by showing that the mapping is imprecise.

The Talmud's own treatment flattens the story into the statutory debate. None of the traditional commentators attends to the gender of the party or to the relationship between the core story and its frame. Maimonides conflates the story with the Mishnah, learning from both that even though witnesses have materialized who were established as lying, each new set of witnesses retains its own credibility. So while the Mishnah's issue was punishment and not credibility, Maimonides takes the Talmud's comparison of Mishnah with story as an opportunity to rewrite the Mishnah's position as a matter of credibility.

NARRATIVE PRECEDENT

In what follows I employ four (Judah/Tamar, Eldad/Meidad, Susannah, Yevamot) external texts to produce a narrative framework for further fleshing out both the matters of gender and the significance of what transpires in the frame story of the rabbis. The purpose of these materials is to suggest a richer literary understanding of the story text that is a responsible contextual reading of this text.

Judah/Tamar

Genesis 38 interrupts the novella of Joseph with another tale of patriarchy. Joseph's brother Judah has three sons. The first two marry Tamar and die. While the third one is destined by levirate law to marry his brothers' widow, Judah is reluctant and doesn't arrange the marriage, claiming to wait for his son Shelah to mature. The rejected Tamar disguises herself as a prostitute and seduces Judah. After the seduction Tamar asks for her payment in Judah's property and retreats home pregnant with twin sons. When Judah discovers his daughter-in-law's pregnancy, she is tried for adultery. Tamar does not mount a formal defense but presents the identifying objects. Judah recognizes his items and exonerates his daughter-in-law because Judah had not provided Shelah for levirate marriage, as expected. Twin sons are born, including the ancestor of the Davidic genealogy.

Tamar is the archetype of the biblical trickster.[21] A trickster is a person limited by social position who uses trickery to manipulate the scenario to his or her benefit. The trickster is a criminal whose crime is contextualized within a larger frame that authorizes and justifies the transgression. The regular manifestation of tricksterhood in biblical narrative marks the manifestation of the trickster as a site for understanding God's intervention in the normal social order. Biblical tricksterism is female-gendered. Most of the trickster characters in the Hebrew Bible are female. Even biologically male tricksters, such as Jacob and even Samson, exhibit characteristics of female gender. Since female gender is a mark of powerlessness within the dynamics of gender in the ancient world, it makes sense for tricksterhood, a strategy for circumventing powerlessness, to go hand in hand with gender.

Jerome Bruner has coined the terms *canonicity* and *breech* to collect the views of literary theorists who argue that stories become stories by virtue of a violation of some expectation.[22] In this sense the trickster is not only a common hero of biblical literature but also a specific manifestation of a ubiquitous narrative phenomenon. The trickster does not just mark grand narrative but is the basis for narrativity itself.

Tamar participates in the legal process without acting as an active participant. She does not speak at the trial but allows the evidence to speak for itself. This models a quietistic form of femininity that buttresses an image of martyrial saintliness. In this way the trickster participates in the dominance that her trick attempts to subvert. The voiceless Tamar doesn't demand a voice but works within the limitations of her society to have something speak on her behalf.

The Tamar episode is a clear model for the biblical book of Ruth, which tells the story of a Judean widow with no fraternal levirate options who seduces a cousin (and potential levir) and eventually receives the social and financial support intended by the levirate system and to which she would have been otherwise denied. A close reading of Ruth demonstrates how an author can create an active female heroine while continuing to encode a preference of female passivity and voicelessness. The character of Noemi, Ruth's mother-in-law, forces the docile Ruth to act. Like Rebekkah's pushing of Jacob to trick his father, Isaac, the crime of Ruth's seduction is not one for which she takes ultimate responsibility.

The female protagonist of the talmudic story is also quiet. She attempts to win her case through the agency of false testimony. Testimony, it should be noted, is a legal realm from which women are largely excluded. Women are occasionally considered reliable witnesses for limited purposes in rabbinic law. In most ritual or litigation circumstances in which witnesses are procedurally necessary, women are not considered eligible. This was not surprising in a contemporaneous world in which women were ineligible to act as witness in certain areas of Roman law.[23] Though this fact is basic to rabbinic jurisprudence, the rabbis are hard-pressed to find either biblical or logical justification for it.

Susannah is another work that illustrates the gap between male and female voices in the Jewish court. The book of Susannah is a chapter of the book of Daniel that appears in certain biblical canons and not others. The beautiful Susannah engenders strong male desire, and two would-be rapists conspire to blackmail her into a sexual relationship. When these men follow through on a threat and testify that Susannah is guilty of a capital sexual offense, Daniel discovers through interrogation that they are liars, and they receive the capital punishment as a quid pro quo for the intent of their testimony. Unlike Tamar and Ruth, Susannah speaks twice in the story. But the speech is self-deconstructing. Her first words are in response to the blackmail threat and indicate a refusal to accede; the effect is an acceptance of the ramifications of her plight. The second words are a vocal prayer to God, who knows that the men are liars and she is innocent. These words underscore the fact that the human tribunal provides her with no license to defend herself against the charges. The story asserts that the two witnesses, as elders, are especially credible, but they are also more credible than she because they are male. The prayer to God is a trickster's method of transcending the limitations of voicelessness. Susannah cannot testify, so she prays loudly enough to influence Daniel to take up her case and denounce the lying witnesses.

The female protagonist of the talmudic story is not celebrated even if she is victorious. She is unnamed, and while she may ultimately succeed in the present case (i.e., the third set of witnesses is allowed to qualify, and she wins her case), hers is not a case in which the particulars of her treachery are overlooked while being recontextualized in a grand narrative (like Tamar and Ruth). Such a narrative might have taken advantage of her powerlessness in a courtroom (she cannot testify herself) to demonstrate how she nevertheless succeeded in this space. The author of the talmudic story does not sympathize with the female protagonist as the authors of Tamar's, Ruth's, and Susannah's stories do. While Tamar, Ruth, and Susannah are undoubtedly heroes from their author's perspective, the woman in this story is not considered heroic at any point. One way of understanding this is to recognize that the author of a trickster narrative is critically aware of the power dynamic that suppresses the powerless and employs the narrative to undermine and reverse that dynamic and its telos. The author of the talmudic narrative, though, does not sympathize with the female protagonist and neither shows recognition of the power dynamic nor critiques it.

There may be a deeper connection between the talmudic story and Susannah. The plot of Susannah involves a conspiracy of men to besmirch a pious woman. The talmudic story inverts this plot by imagining a conspiracy of a single woman who is trying to take advantage of a number of men. One specific feature of our talmudic story suggests that this connection is not farfetched. The mishnaic context for our story is a discussion of the quid pro quo punishment for perjury. The term used for this kind of false testimony is *Hazamah*, which derives from the biblical verse describing the malicious intent of a lying witness. The Mishnah develops a protocol for this kind of witness, and the first chapter of tractate Makkot in Mishnah and Talmuds is about this protocol and employs this terminology. The story, on the other hand, refers to the witnesses not using the term *zomemin* or the like, but using verbs off the root sh/q/r, meaning "to lie." This type of lying witness is understood by the rabbis to be established not according to the protocol of the punished false witnesses of this chapter but on the basis of inconsistent or contradictory testimony among the respective witnesses. It is this kind of lying that Daniel demonstrates in Susannah.

When dealing with the Talmud, especially text critically, one deals with predigested matter. The reader encounters the legal scenario of the putative heroine as it is already being considered by the frame story's rabbis. More so than in a common talmudic pattern of an anonymous text's framing a legal statute, the effect veils the female protagonist and occludes the gender dynamics that stand at the heart of the legal case. One could even suggest that the frame story purposefully shifts attention away from the primary case and toward the rabbinic interactions. This shift might be fairly innocent and reflect the editor's greater interest in rabbinic sociopolitics. It might also represent a more sinister refusal to consider the story's underlying gender dynamics. Most likely a combination of the two is at play. This suppression of the gender dynamic may be entirely unaware but still reflects something about gender in rabbinic society. It is fair to suggest that (unlike those responsible for Tamar, Ruth, and Susannah) the redactors of this talmudic passage do not exploit the inherent opportunity for subverting or otherwise highlighting the gender dynamic that the episode represents. And so, rather than celebrating the female protagonist, the frame story accepts the episode's dynamics as unremarkable by shifting into the more narratable issue of rabbinic plagiarism. In this move, though, the redactors create an opportunity for readers to seize upon two questions of credibility and compare them to each other.

When scholars began employing feminist perspectives in the study of women and gender in rabbinic literature there was an initial tendency to characterize the rabbis who produced this work as misogynistic and anti-women.[24] As gender scholarship by Miriam Beth Peskowitz, Daniel Boyarin, and others became more sophisticated, there was a greater appreciation both for the multiplicity of approaches to women and gender in rabbinic literature and for a reevaluation of the rabbis on the basis of a comparison with either biblical or more contemporaneous Greco-Roman materials.[25] Tikva Frymer-Kensky argues that Greek misogyny was introduced into the Judean world during the Hellenistic period and eventually led to a rabbinic mindset in which women were considered more dangerous because of their sexuality and that there developed a more polarized binary opposition of men and women.[26] Boyarin argues that rabbinic gender discourse must be differentiated from Greco-Roman culture because it routinely demonstrates a unifying focus on the body in its corporeality that distances it from the common dichotomization in Greco-Roman culture of woman as body and man as soul.[27] There is little disagreement that rabbinic texts evidence a highly polarized discourse of gender. This fact marks as significant the gender of our story's protagonist (surprising) and the lack of sympathy from the story's author (not surprising).

R' Elazar's homiletical rhetoric is not typical for rabbinic legal debate. On a basic level this text rejects Resh Laqish's idea and respects the natural credibility of all witnesses. But the rhetoric suggests more. Notice the contrast between the protasis and the apodosis. It compares the lying woman with "all of Israel." But "all of Israel" is a gendered statement including only eligible witnesses—namely males. The rhetorical format of the homiletical statement is a nice contrast with a similarly pithy comparison that turns the tide in the Tamar story. As Tamar is taken to be executed she loudly connects paternity to the meretricious currency of Judah's property; Judah recognizes his own items and announces, "She is more righteous than I." While Genesis 38 reinscribes righteous gender performance (Tamar does not officially speak and never lies with Judah again), it unequivocally vindicates Tamar as the story's heroine and the mother of the Judean monarchy. Our talmudic story, in contrast, creates an outcome that favors the female protagonist, but it does so without vindicating her behavior. If she is to win the case it is because the witnesses are not being manipulated and are independent agents. Resh Laqish had been suspicious of a woman who brings multiple sets of lying witnesses. The homiletical flourish dismisses her entirely, recapitulating the gendered dynamic that excludes women from testifying in the courtroom at all. And it does so in a statement that extols the credibility of "all of Israel."

In the frame story R' Elazar uses R' Yohanan's homiletical question without citation. The uniqueness of the question—not its content, but its form—testifies against R' Elazar and makes Resh Laqish instantly aware of the breech of ethics. The notion of entities' speaking for themselves is nearly identical to the evidence in Tamar's story. Tamar produces Judah's personal effects and allows them to speak on her behalf. The implicit testimony persuades Judah to take responsibility for his actions and vindicate Tamar. Where Tamar's items exonerate her, the question accuses R' Elazar of plagiarism.

Plagiarism is uniquely sordid in a scholastic community such as that of the rabbis. Elsewhere rabbinic literature incentivizes citation with homiletical promises of heavenly reward and apocalyptic redemption.[28] The immorality of plagiarism is further tinged in this story by the relationship between the content of the plagiarism and its form. R' Elazar contrasts the lying female protagonist with the meritorious "all of Israel" to sing the praises of Israelite (male) honesty—while engaged in an act of plagiarism. The rhetorical question establishes a presumption of credibility while engaging in a dishonest act.

Eldad/Meidad

To further appreciate the stakes of rabbinic plagiarism and the frame story's themes, it is sensible for the hermeneutic frame of narrative precedent to introduce the biblical story of Eldad and Meidad, two Israelites who prophesy in the camp at Numbers 11. At a time of crisis Moses asks God for assistance with the burden of leadership. God encourages Moses to appoint seventy elders who will be graced with some of Moses's divine charisma and will assist him in governance. The transfer of charisma happens as planned, except that two men, Eldad and Meidad, who were not part of the select group of seventy who were to receive a charismatic transfer begin to prophesy in the camp. When a messenger runs to the tabernacle and informs Moses (and the elders) of these figures, Moses's apprentice Joshua reacts harshly and says, "My master Moses, restrain them!" Moses responds, "Are you wrought up on my account? Would that all the Lord's people were prophets, that the Lord put His spirit upon them."

Charisma in the form of biblical prophecy was both a form of communication with the divine and the basis for communal authority. Unauthorized charisma can be viewed suspiciously, as a threat to the authority structure. The threat of such charisma has been one of the major sources of tension over Jewish mysticism for two millennia. Joshua's violent reaction represents a narrative foil for Moses's gracious position. Joshua wants to restrain (or destroy) the threat to Moses's authority. Implicit in this story is the notion that Joshua, as heir apparent, cannot tolerate unbridled charisma. Moses, on the other hand, has no anxiety about his own authority. Unlike his unstable apprentice, Moses views the two charismatics not with suspicion but with generosity. The rash reaction of Joshua allows the story to contribute to an image of Moses's humility that places him above petty squabbles and restores charisma to its spiritual (rather than political) place. Moses is eager to share charisma with whomever the Lord is willing to bestow it upon.

By the time of the rabbis the notion of charismatic prophecy had long abated. (It actually faded during the Babylonian Exile after the destruction of the first Jerusalem temple in 587 BCE.) The rabbinic world was a scholastic one in which authority derived from legalistic prowess. In this pre-institutional educational system in which small groups of students gravitated toward great intellectuals, figures gained charismatic authority (in a Weberian sense) from their reputation as legal scholars. Scholars who were creative and subtle thinkers attracted students. This form of charisma is possibly even less stable than one connected with divine grace. Within this environment the frame story reads as an analogue of the Eldad/Meidad biblical antecedent.

Resh Laqish introduces the legal question of a woman's suborning perjury and claims that new witnesses are not credible. R' Elazar's rhetorical flourish pedantically recapitulates Moses's response to Joshua by embracing a more generous and less suspicious perspective. While the question's content (there is no inherent legal connection between a witness and a party) has no obvious advantage over that of Resh Laqish (a party with two false sets of witnesses has established a conspiratorial pattern), the form of the question dismisses Resh Laqish for his suspicion and diminishes him. The great merit of Israel mocks Resh Laqish's suspicion.

It is unclear which rabbinic texts can be used to read which other texts. This has challenged a field that used to produce biographies of rabbis by piecing together all of their vignettes and citations.[29] With some caution, then, I introduce into my reading the idea (implicit in the story itself) that Resh Laqish and R' Elazar are contemporaries and rivals who both function, at times, as Rav Yohanan's star pupils. The benefits of plagiarism here become magnified when we consider the rivalry and the value of scholarly reputation. Talmudic stories such as this one frequently present rabbis as engaged in single combat, dueling with words as if each substantive encounter would singularly establish their standing within the rabbinic arena. R' Elazar asks the rhetorical question that transforms him into Moses to Resh Laqish's Joshua. If R' Elazar had cited their teacher, the question would not have had the same sociopolitical effect.

In Resh Laqish's accusation he refers to R' Yohanan as *Bar Nafha*, a not uncommon nickname for the great teacher. The use of this nickname here, though, may not be random. *Bar Nafha* means "the son of coal: and reflects Yohanan's humble origins within a fairly aristocratic rabbinic society. Rabbinic rhetoric touts inclusion and claims to promote a meritocracy even as the community in reality consisted of a disproportionate number of elites (priests, royals, wealthy). Referencing the nickname reminds R' Elazar (and the reader) of Rav Yohanan's hard-won reputation and further shames R' Elazar for attempting to usurp his master's position as Resh Laqish's superior.

Yevamot 64b

The last text I will use to flesh out the story at Makkot 5b about the woman accused of suborning perjury is a talmudic discussion found at Yevamot 64b. Talmudic passages defy summary because of the nonlinear manner in which they connect disparate types of text and intersperse these with framing questions and justifying answers. A source critic is trained to read from the primary canonical text outward even when such a reading comes at the expense of the order of the redacted text. In this reading I first introduce a set of stories about patterned behavior, then describe an early fourth-century layer of interpretation, and finally discuss a later fourth-century layer of interpretation.

Yevamot 64b contains three stories about patterned behavior. Story 1 is about sisters whose infant boys die as a result of circumcision (the specific cause of death is not delineated in the text). After three of the sisters experience this tragedy, the fourth sister approaches Rabban Gamaliel, who tells her not to circumcise her son. Story 2 is about a mother of triplets whose first two infants die from circumcision; she approaches Rav Yohanan for dispensation on the third son, but he orders her to circumcise. Story 3 is about the famous rabbi Abaye's marrying Homa, daughter of a distinguished rabbi, despite the fact that she had already buried two husbands; Abaye marries her anyway and also dies.

It is necessary to say a word about talmudic composition and method. The Talmud is a work that presents canonical traditions within a framework in which such traditions are framed, debated, interpreted, and commented upon. One of the hallmarks of text criticism of the Talmud has been a source criticism that differentiates between the source traditions and the layers of interpretation, both explicit and implicit, that they engender within the talmudic text. In the context of talmudic law the source critical method has been employed both to provide new interpretations within a somewhat traditional discourse of talmudic reception and to create a strong chronological paradigm for describing legal evolution within the rabbinic period. My own work differs in attending to sources and their interpretation within the Talmud for primarily literary rather than historical purposes. The gaps between the sources understood on their own and their framing interpretations within the talmudic text become opportunities for mining a range of meanings within the text. Unlike historical source criticism that aims to produce a single coherent paradigm within which the text makes sense, the literary source criticism I employ highlights a plurality of meanings that the text enables.

I have dealt with Yevamot 64b more extensively elsewhere.[30] In this context I want to think about these stories in light of both pattern and gender. The issue of pattern is simultaneously a legal predictor, a result of folk cultural practices, and a staple of literary composition. As a legal predictor in rabbinic statute, the pattern is usually established on the basis of three instances, though there are cases in which the pattern is established on the basis of two instances and applies in the third instance. Similarly literary analysis of ancient literatures, including specifically Jewish ones, evidences both a pattern of three and a pattern of three-and-one. Ancient mystical and magical texts also place emphasis on patterned repetition.

The first two stories establish definitively that the legal pattern is established by three instances and behavior can be changed at the fourth instance. Both stories rise to the level of narrativity by producing something unexpected. Rabban Gamaliel's dispensation is shocking because circumcision is a basic feature of (male) Jewish identity. Rav Yohanan's imperative is equally shocking, particularly because the prior story of Rabban Gamaliel prepares the reader to expect a dispensation. As a result Rav Yohanan's imperative to circumcise registers as callous. The legal message of the two stories seems unequivocally that a pattern is established only after three instances.

The third story undermines this clear message of the first two. Abaye ignores the pattern of Homa's two dead husbands and becomes the third Mr. Homa. That a rabbi would ignore a killer-wife pattern established by two dead husbands is entirely in keeping with the legal content of the two prior stories. But while Rav Yohanan's imperative-to-circumcise story does not tell the reader whether the infant was circumcised and whether he died, Abaye's story concludes with his death. The implicit message is that one ignores a pattern of two instances at one's own risk. While the legal authorities may determine that a pattern requires three occurrences, the forces that stand behind the pattern are more fickle and harsh.

These three stories appear in a passage that functions as commentary to a legal statute from Mishnah; they are interrupted by framing questions and commented upon by editorial rabbis within the text. Some of these comments are attributed to named rabbis, and one can create a chronology on this basis that also potentially affects one's reading of the material.

One of the key comments in the passage is a sentence linking the second story with the third. Abaye, the protagonist of the third story, comments upon the second story. The comment has generally been understood in light of the commentary of Rashi, the influential eleventh-century commentator. Rashi understands Abaye's comment as an observation that Rav Yohanan's imperative not only asks the mother to endanger her child but also licenses the violation of the Sabbath under questionable circumstances. This reading makes use of the story's claim that the woman approaches Rav Yohanan on Yom Kippur, that fell in that year on a Saturday. In my opinion, though, this calendrical detail is there for literary effect, to heighten the sanctity of the story's context, and has no bearing on the content.[31] In place of Rashi's understanding I would like to suggest that Abaye's comment notes that Rav Yohanan extrapolates from legal patterns even to scenarios involving mortal, real-world danger.[32]

I earlier noted that Jewish law does not distinguish between subsections. But law was not the only discourse of rabbinic society. And it was not the only one in which patterned behavior could be considered meaningful. Abaye astutely notes that patterns exist in multiple registers and that the choice of a legist to apply the necessity of three instances to a case of health risk implies contiguity between the discourse of legal constructs and those of the natural world. This is not the only instance in which talmudic authorities take note of the discourse of health risks.

In a passage at Hullin 10a the Talmud addresses a statute that creates laws about exposed water in light of the cultural notion that an exposed receptacle is susceptible not only to ritual impurity but also to hazardous animal defilement that could be fatal. The Talmud concludes that "[health] danger is more severe than ritual prohibition." This pithy characterization has been invoked many times in subsequent Jewish jurisprudence. Abaye's comment on the second story at Yevamot 64b notes that Rav Yohanan makes no such distinction; on the contrary Rav Yohanan insists on the standard of three instances to produce a pattern even in the face of a potentially dying infant. Abaye's comment is a moment in which a rabbi punctures the constructed nature of Jewish law and notes that the implication of Rav Yohanan's action in the story is to presume that patterns are established in the realm of health risk in the same manner as they are established in areas of ritual law.

This reading is buttressed by the editorial linkage between stories 2 and 3, which asserts that Abaye learned from Rav Yohanan's precedent and relied upon it when he married Homa. The linking text establishes that Abaye was aware of the pattern created by the deaths of Homa's first two husbands and aware that this pattern was potentially a risk to his own health. Abaye married Homa anyway and died. Abaye's death in the story stands as a counterpoint to his interpretation of Rav Yohanan's action. Abaye relied on legal precedent for a health risk and suffered the consequences.

But even in the early fourth-century layer of the text—the layer contemporaneous with Abaye—this textual turn toward a pattern established after two incidents is directly undermined by Abaye's contemporary Rava. For after reporting the story of Abaye's death, the text cites Rava as questioning the story. Would Abaye have relied for his own life on Rav Yohanan's action, Rava asks, when he was generally suspicious of the person who told that story? There are a range of meanings for this question. It may be that Rava is expressing incredulity about a story that he believes to have happened. But it also could be that Rava's question rejects the content of this story and its implicit claim that patterns are established in the natural world on the basis of two incidents alone. The latter reading undermines the implicit claim of Abaye's story and reestablishes the idea that three episodes are required.

To review, then: The first two stories argue that one needs three instances to establish a pattern. The third story suggests that one who acts that way on the basis of legal patterns may be putting his or her life at risk. Rava's comment on Abaye's story dismisses the story as an unfounded rumor and rejects the idea of a pattern established by two incidents.[33]

By starting with the three stories I began this discussion in medias res. The Talmud opens its commentary to the local Mishnah by citing a statute in which the debate over establishing a pattern is explicit. In speaking about the circumcision scenario, Rebbe and Rabbi Simeon ben Gamaliel debate the number of cases that produce an actionable pattern. Rebbe says that two infant deaths exempt a third son from circumcision; Rabbi Simon ben Gamaliel says that the third son is circumcised, but the fourth would not be. This debate is attested in a number of other instances as well. While the statutes seem to have a balanced debate between these two positions, the stories seem to push in the direction of requiring three episodes. Even the one story with an implicit critique of that requirement (the story of Abaye's death) is rejected by Rava for being unlikely. This is important to mention because the story of the woman's suborning perjury at Makkot 5b seeks to establish a pattern on the basis of just two sets of witnesses.

The third story of the killer wife causes the Talmud to veer into a discussion of patterns and the killer wife. Within this subsection the Talmud introduces a statute about the killer wife identical to the one on circumcision. Again Rebbe says that a woman with two dead husbands cannot remarry, and Rabbi Simon ben Gamaliel says that she would have to have three dead husbands. The introduction of the statute allows the Talmud's editorial voice to question the similarity of the two cases. Dying siblings, the Talmud notes, create a pattern on the basis of a shared medical condition. How, though, do a woman's dead husbands create a pattern? In this line the Talmud seeks to probe that which stands behind the pattern.

The editorial question is connected with two potential answers—possible ways in which a woman is responsible for her husbands' death—attributed to rabbis who were active in the late fourth century. One answer points to the woman's astrological sign. This approach suggests that the proper discourse for understanding the killer-wife pattern is not the law as much as popular belief about astrology and its influence on the world. The second answer points not to her astrological sign but to "her source." The woman causes the pattern because she has a uterus that kills. While a woman's uterus is usually thought of as the source of life, in this case it is a source of death.

The notion of the source of life embodying the source of death brings to mind the myth of Pandora's box. This myth's most famous version is found in Hesiod's *Works and Days*.[34] In this myth Pandora is created and presented, along with a box of evils, to Epimetheus. Stirred on by her curiosity, Pandora opens the box and unleashes evil in the world. Froma Zeitlin, in a reading popularized by Boyarin's *Carnal Israel*, draws upon the confusion of the adjectival description of evil in Hesiod's account to suggest that Pandora's box is anatomical—that the opening of the box is a sexual encounter that unleashes female sexuality upon the world.[35] This reading suggests an ancient worldview that begins by labeling sexuality as evil and ends by applying this label to women in general. For Boyarin the myth of Pandora's box becomes a crux with which to establish the relationship between rabbinic notions of gender and those of Hellenistic Judaism and biblical literature. Boyarin argues that the sharp gender dualism that characterizes women as evil is ever present in Hellenistic sources but absent in biblical and rabbinic literature. This move allows for a sharp divide between misogynistic Greek sources and homosocial Jewish sources that resist the misogyny and gynecophobia of the Greeks. Boyarin is familiar with rabbinic misogynistic sources, but he allows the variety of rabbinic views and the regular rabbinic practice of including later commentary on earlier materials as a way of downplaying such sources. If a classic misogynistic midrash would seem to place the rabbis firmly within Greek dualistic notions of gender, the fact that this midrash is rejected in the Talmud grants the opportunity to claim that the Talmud rejects this hostile organ donation from Greek culture.[36]

It is difficult to make broad arguments of the sort Boyarin does for a corpus as large as rabbinic literature. And yet his argument was a necessary corrective to the unnuanced critiques of misogyny that were the first feminist assessments of rabbinic literature. Boyarin's work alerted the field to the variety of possible discourses about gender and the body and the ways the rabbis (and this is one of the most fascinating things about them) manage to somewhat insulate themselves from the dominant imperial culture of their day.

The notion of the killer wife's power coming from her uterus follows Judith Butler in deconstructing the sex/gender dichotomy.[37] Cultural notions of the feminine are attached to a woman's sexual anatomy. Boyarin asserts that rabbinic literature was less prone to the gynecophobic impulse one finds in Greek and Greek-influenced sources.[38] It is hard to contest this argument from frequency. But the text at Yevamot 64b is not alone in thinking of women's bodies as a potential source of bodily danger. The Talmud at Sanhedrin 21a cites the view of Rabbi Isaac that the biblical Tamar of II Samuel 13 (not the Tamar of Genesis discussed above) castrated her rapist half-brother, Amnon, with her pubic hair. There can be no more explicit example of the *vagina dentata* (the vagina with teeth) made famous by Freud than castrating genitals.

To be clear, I do not mean to argue that every rabbinic text that confirms the notion of the killer wife understands the underlying basis for this notion as the physiological danger of female genitalia or the death emerging from a woman's uterus. Even within this specific passage this idea is only one of two possible late fourth-century understandings of that basis; there is little reason to presume either as the historical basis for earlier positions. For my purposes, though, both the answer of the astrological sign and the answer of the killer uterus contribute to the sense that the rabbis functioned within a society in which multiple extralegal discourses considered women to be more suspicious than men. It is not surprising that these cultural biases contribute to a greater suspicion of women in the legal discourse as well.

Astrology and myth-centered folk belief constitute, from our perspective as moderns, pseudo-intellectual discourses predicated on received wisdom and not subject to tests of falsifiability that establish scientific truth today. But in the ancient world astrology and myth were not far removed from science.[39] The inhabitant of rabbinic culture believed in the cause and effect of a killer wife no less than someone in our own day subscribes to the efficacy of prescription medication without an understanding of the underlying molecular biology. The Talmud is replete with remedies that can be understood on either magical or scientific terms. Faced with the ubiquity of beliefs about such cause-and-effect realities, the rabbis sometimes absorb such cultural constructs into the law. For example, the rabbis prohibit consuming meat with fish because of the cultural notion that this practice was dangerous to health. And following up on the idea mentioned earlier, the rabbis treat this prohibition on meat and fish more severely than the prohibition on meat and milk since the former is a health risk and the latter a spiritual legal construct. The killer wife is a cultural construct who poses a health risk to potential husbands. The legal absorption of such a concept brings along the heightened suspicion of health risk and leads to the idea that a pattern of killing can be established after the deaths of merely two husbands, an easy bar to cross in a premodern world of intergenerational marriage and low life expectancy.[40] While the legal discourse has other cases in which a pattern of behavior is argued to be established after two incidents, it is fair to suggest that the prevalence of cultural beliefs about women in other discourses leads to the increased suspicion within the legal realm and the idea that patterns can be established more easily.

Along these lines consider the stories of the infants dying from circumcision. In its statutory expression rabbinic law unequivocally places the obligation for circumcision on an infant's father. To this day traditional Jewish liturgy and practice maintains this focus. Even the statute with which the Talmud opens its discussion introduces the debate about patterns between Rebbe and Rabbi Simeon ben Gamaliel with a statute that uses third-person *male* singular forms, expecting that it is the father who circumcises his son. Why, then, do both stories about patterns invoke the mothers?

Scholarship on ancient magic has noted that while men seem to have been better represented within the actual discourse of magic, women were more likely to be accused of witchcraft, and the magical was routinely demonized through a female characterization.[41] If this is true of ancient cultures in general, the rabbis—particularly in Babylonia—were prone to this form of othering that displaced women through an association with magic.[42] This kind of thinking explains why a woman with two dead husbands can be considered to have caused their death because of her astrological sign even as the text makes no such allowances for Jewish men to be similarly treated.[43]

Scholars interested in medicine in the Talmud have looked to the circumcision scenario as an example of talmudic awareness of disease. The pattern of three dying infants becomes a talmudic diagnosis of hemophilia.[44] This is certainly defensible within the passage; the Talmud explicitly comments on the notion that there are families who bleed excessively. But it is also possible that the pattern is a derivative of the suspicion of women and their bodies. It should be noted that one of the areas in which the notion of a legal pattern (*hazaqah*) is most prevalent is in the context of the laws on menstrual purity. Within those laws all menstruating women permanently reside within a pattern that establishes the days of their menstrual cycle. Such patterns can be positive (e.g., a woman who has begun her period on the thirtieth day three times in a row) or negative (e.g., a woman who does not have a consistent pattern of days between periods). And they are related to both blood and female sex organs. I would like to suggest that the choice of the mother in the circumcision stories is both to increase pathos within the drama and because of the notion that women are somehow subject to invisible forces that underlie the accuracy of such signifying patterns. The infant who recently emerged from the "source of life" is subject to the pattern of this potential "source of death."

The story of Judah and Tamar utilizes the killer-wife motif.[45] Mordechai Friedman has argued that the story effectively eliminates a pagan notion of the killer wife from an enlightened Jewish religious culture. In order to do so, Friedman claims, the story of Judah and Tamar includes the killer-wife motif within the erroneous character position of Judah.[46] Thus when the narrator sympathizes with Tamar and she is victorious, her victory also eliminates the notion of the killer wife as mere superstition. Friedman's reading is reductionist and fails to appreciate the multiplicity inherent in the Bible as a reflection of ancient culture, the textual production of a specific group of writers within that culture, and as the basis for multiple and variegated forms of canonical interpretation. One could read as Friedman does and eliminate the killer wife. Alternatively one could say that the text provides evidence for the cultural prevalence of the killer-wife concept while preserving such a concept to be applied by later readers. Indeed the story of Judah and Tamar might also stand as the reason why women are under suspicion after only the second incident. That pattern might also be supported in the context of circumcision through a reading of the highly ambiguous passage in Exodus in which a woman, Zipporah wife of Moses, performs a roadside circumcision of her second son to save someone from demonic danger.[47]

The story of the woman suborning perjury at Makkot 5b gains texture from this line of reasoning. It is possible that Resh Laqish seeks to disqualify the third set of witnesses specifically because the litigant is female. Sexual difference leads to a suspicion of women and the attempt to use the tools of male rabbinic hegemony (legislation and adjudication) to deny women even those activities to which they are legally entitled.

The Mishnah that forms the basis for the story at Makkot 5b considers whether the ordinary rules of punishing a malicious witness can be applied in cases of conspiracy.[48] I would like to argue that in rabbinic culture women were inherently under conspiratorial suspicion. As such, a woman for whom two sets of lying witnesses have testified raises the possibility of eliminating witness credibility altogether. In other words, women's lack of credibility connects with their suspicion of mythic and supernatural connections to negative energy sources and produces a legal possibility. That possibility is rejected, but only by severing the male witnesses from the female litigant. In this context, I have shown, female criminality is easier to prove and the consequences are produced more swiftly because of cultural ideas operant in other parallel discourses in rabbinic society.

The use of multiple narratives from the Bible and rabbinic literature has provided fertile ground for a close examination of the story at Makkot 5b. As this reading demonstrates, it is possible to employ such texts as narrative precedents to produce a thick hermeneutic context in which to unpack the meaning of a talmudic story.

NOTES

1. O'Neill, *Fictions of Discourse*, 12. I developed this idea within the context of Mikhail Bakhtin's thought in Wimpfheimer, *Narrating the Law*, 13–14.

2. This is a major thesis of my first monograph: Wimpfheimer, *Narrating the Law*.

3. Here I intend tradition in its Gadamerian sense as a set of inherited assumptions and hermeneutic tools within which a contemporary reader encounters older canonical texts. See Gadamer, *Truth and Method*.

4. Frenḳel, *Sipur ha-agadah*, 32ff.

5. For example, ibid., 44. For a critique of Fraenkel, see Rubenstein, *Talmudic Stories*, 12.

6. As the proverb found at PT Rosh Hashanah 3:5; 58d says, "The words of Torah are poor in their own contexts but rich in another."

7. Unless otherwise specified, translations are mine.

8. Munich and Bazzano have "she the woman." This might be the original formulation, which was modified to the more common "that."

9. The absence of the implicit term in Bazzano suggests that this was explicated in a later source and was not originally present.

10. The implicit word is added in the margins of Herzog and is explicated in the three other textual witnesses.

11. The implicit words are explicated in Herzog and Venice. Venice confuses the matter and reads "brought other witnesses *that* they were not lying." This does not fit well with the story.

12. Herzog, Munich, and Venice have the common nickname "Reish" instead of his full name.

13. Herzog has a homoioteleuton that accidentally deletes much of this line.

14. Herzog has a third-person pronoun as the end of this question. This is possibly the original text or the result of an erroneous extended abbreviation.

15. Herzog, Munich, and Venice again have "Reish."

16. One cannot demonstrate definitively that the case is a hypothetical. The analysis is unchanged if you take the story seriously as a transpired event.

17. Thur, "The Role of the Witness in Athenian Law."

18. Leviticus 5:1.

19. Bavli Ketubot 25b.

20. Wimpfheimer, *Narrating the Law*, 27–30.

21. Niditch, *Underdogs and Tricksters*.

22. Bruner, "The Narrative Construction of Reality," 11ff.

23. Grubbs, *Women and the Law in the Roman Empire*, 70–71.

24. See, e.g., Wegner, *Chattel or Person?*

25. Peskowitz, *Spinning Fantasies*; Boyarin, *Carnal Israel*.

26. Frymer-Kensky, *In the Wake of the Goddesses*, 203–12.

27. Boyarin, *Carnal Israel*.

28. Mishnah Abot 6:6; *Sifre Aggadah al Esther* B:2.

29. See, e.g., Finkelstein, *Akiba*.

30. Wimpfheimer, "Footnotes to *Carnal Israel*."

31. Even for Rashi there is little advantage to the fact that it is both Saturday and Yom Kippur.

32. My reading relies on a shift from one verbal root to another.

33. This approach potentially makes Rava a precursor of Maimonides, who struggled to eradicate the killer-wife principle from law but could do so only via a legal fiction because of the strongly held cultural notion of the killer wife.

34. Hesiod, *The Poems of Hesiod*, 99.

35. Zeitlin, *Playing the Other*, 64ff; Boyarin, *Carnal Israel*, 85.

36. Boyarin, *Carnal Israel*, 105–6, 90–94.

37. Butler, *Gender Trouble.*

38. Boyarin, *Carnal Israel*, 206.

39. Stratton, *Naming the Witch*; Goldin, "The Magic of Magic and Superstition," 344ff.

40. This point is well developed for the medieval period in Grossman, *Pious and Rebellious.* Tal Ilan cites the ethnographic work of Hilma Granqvist, who found the killer-wife belief active among Palestinians in the 1920s and established by as few as one dead husband ("Babatha the Killer Wife," 268).

41. Stratton, *Naming the Witch.*

42. Aubin, "Gendering Magic in Late Antique Judaism," 122–59.

43. The lack of parallel cases of Jewish men is noted in Ilan, "Babatha the Killer Wife," 274–76.

44. Preuss, *Biblical and Talmudic Medicine.*

45. Tobit is also relevant, though in Tobit the pattern is established only on the seventh episode and the underlying cause is an external demon.

46. Friedman, "Tamar, a Symbol of Life."

47. For a detailed account of this episode, its ambiguity, and its connections to Ancient Near Eastern mythology, see Pardes, *Countertraditions in the Bible.*

48. Valuable new scholarship on this material can be found in Naeh, "Shtay Parshiyot Shehen Ahat"; Friedman, " 'Lo Hargo Neheragin.' "

WORKS CITED

Aubin, Melissa M. "Gendering Magic in Late Antique Judaism." PhD dissertation, Duke University, 1998.

Boyarin, Daniel. *Carnal Israel: Reading Sex in Talmudic Culture.* The New Historicism. Berkeley: University of California Press, 1993.

Bruner, Jerome. "The Narrative Construction of Reality." *Critical Inquiry* 18.1 (1991): 1–21.

Butler, Judith. *Gender Trouble: Feminism and the Subversion of Identity.* Thinking Gender. New York: Routledge, 1990.

Finkelstein, Louis. *Akiba: Scholar, Saint and Martyr.* Cleveland, OH: Meridian Books, World Pub. Co., Jewish Publication Society of America, 1962.

Frenḳel, Yonah. *Sipur ha-Agadah, Aḥdut Shel Tokhen ve-Tsurah: Ḳovets Meḥkarim.* Sifriyat "Hillel Ben-Ḥayim." Tel Aviv: ha-Ḳibuts ha-me'uḥad, 2001.

Friedman, Mordechai A. "Tamar, a Symbol of Life: The 'Killer Wife' Superstition in the Bible and Jewish Tradition." *Association for Jewish Studies Review* 15 (1990): 23–61.

Friedman, Shamma Yehuda. "'Lo Hargo Neheragin' (Bavli Makkot 5b): Mispah O Mishpat?" *Sidra* 20 (2005): 171–94.

Frymer-Kensky, Tikva. *In the Wake of the Goddesses: Women, Culture, and the Biblical Transformation of Pagan Myth.* New York: Free Press, 1992.

Gadamer, Hans-Georg. *Truth and Method.* 2nd edition. New York: Crossroad, 1989.

Goldin, Judah. "The Magic of Magic and Superstition." In *Studies in Midrash and Related Literature*, ed. Judah Goldin, 337–57. Philadelphia: JPS, 1988.

Grossman, Avraham. *Pious and Rebellious: Jewish Women in Medieval Europe.* Waltham, MA: Brandeis University Press, 2004.

Grubbs, Judith Evans. *Women and the Law in the Roman Empire: A Sourcebook on Marriage, Divorce and Widowhood*. London: Routledge, 2002.

Hesiod. *The Poems of Hesiod*. Trans. R. M. Frazer. Norman: University of Oklahoma Press, 1983.

Ilan, Tal. "Babatha the Killer Wife: Literature, Folk Religion and Documentary Papyri." In *Law and Narrative in the Bible and in Neighboring Ancient Cultures*, ed. Klaus-Peter Adam et al., 263–78. Tübingen: Mohr Siebeck, 2012.

Naeh, Shlomo. "Shtay Parshiyot Shehen Ahat: Iyyun Bemishnat Makkot 1:4–6 Uvetalmud Shealeha." In *Netiot Ledavid: Festschrift for David Halivni*, ed. Yaakov Elman et al., 109–25. Jerusalem: Orhot Press, 2005.

Niditch, Susan. *Underdogs and Tricksters: A Prelude to Biblical Folklore*. New Voices in Biblical Studies. San Francisco: Harper & Row, 1987.

O'Neill, Patrick. *Fictions of Discourse: Reading Narrative Theory*. Theory/Culture. Toronto: University of Toronto Press, 1994.

Pardes, Ilana. *Countertraditions in the Bible: A Feminist Approach*. Cambridge, MA: Harvard University Press, 1993.

Peskowitz, Miriam. *Spinning Fantasies: Rabbis, Gender, and History*. Contraversions. Berkeley: University of California Press, 1997.

Preuss, Julius. *Biblical and Talmudic Medicine*. Trans. Fred Rosner. Northvale: Jason Aronson, 2004.

Rubenstein, Jeffrey L. *Talmudic Stories: Narrative Art, Composition, and Culture*. Baltimore: Johns Hopkins University Press, 1999.

Stratton, Kimberly. *Naming the Witch: Magic, Ideology and Stereotype in the Ancient World*. New York: Columbia University Press, 2007.

Thur, Gerhard. "The Role of the Witness in Athenian Law." In *The Cambridge Companion to Ancient Greek Law*, ed. Michael Gagarin and David Cohen, 146–69. Cambridge, UK: Cambridge University Press, 2005.

Wegner, Judith Romney. *Chattel or Person? The Status of Women in the Mishnah*. New York: Oxford University Press, 1988.

Wimpfheimer, Barry S. "Footnotes to *Carnal Israel*: Folk Belief and Jewish Law." In *Daniel Boyarin Festschrift*, ed. Charlotte Fonrobert et al. Supplements to the Study of Judaism. Tübingen: Brill, forthcoming.

———. *Narrating the Law: A Poetics of Talmudic Legal Stories*. Divinations, Rereading Late Ancient Religion. Philadelphia: University of Pennsylvania Press, 2011.

Zeitlin, Froma I. *Playing the Other: Gender and Society in Classical Greek Literature*. Women in Culture and Society. Chicago: University of Chicago Press, 1996.

Statements, indictments, bills are circulated, shuffled between judges, prosecutors, the Attorney General, the Lord Chancellor's office; each step in the process clear, logical, and designed to create corpses by due process of law. George Rochford will be tried apart, as a peer; the commoners will be tried first. The order goes to the Tower, "Bring up the bodies." Deliver, that is, the accused men, by name Weston, Brereton, Smeaton and Norris, to Westminster Hall for trial.[1]

The Justices' precept to the Constable of the Tower, commanding him to bring up the bodies of Sir Francis Weston, knt. Henry Noreys, esq. William Brereton, esq. and Mark Smeton, gent. at Westminster, on Friday next after three weeks of Easter. The Constable returns that before the receipt of the precept the persons within-mentioned had been committed by the King's Council for high treason, but that he nevertheless would bring them up as he is required.[2]

4

A Man for All Treasons

CRIMES BY AND AGAINST THE TUDOR STATE IN THE NOVELS OF HILARY MANTEL

Alison L. LaCroix

THE TUDOR NOVELS of Hilary Mantel—*Wolf Hall* (2009) and *Bring Up the Bodies* (2012), with a third installment still to come—depict two species of crime: crimes against the state and crimes by the state. The crimes against the state are variations on the obvious one in the context of the court of Henry VIII: treason. The crimes by the state, in contrast, are more inchoate and subjective; indeed, they are portrayed by Mantel as perhaps only potential crimes. Torture, or merely aggressive questioning? Blackmail, or simply shrewd intelligence gathering? The reader cannot be certain whether a crime has in fact been committed, or whether she simply expects that a crime will be committed, given that Mantel's protagonist is Henry's notorious *consigliere* Thomas Cromwell. Cromwell is described in Mantel's "Cast of Characters" as "a blacksmith's son: now Secretary to the King, Master of the Rolls, Chancellor of Cambridge University, and deputy to the king as head of the church in England."[3]

Throughout the novels, Mantel plays with her readers' expectations of Cromwell, whose notorious posterity stems from at least two sources, only one of which was contemporary: his brooding, massy, black-clad portrait by Hans Holbein the Younger from 1532–33, and Robert Bolt's 1960 play *A Man for All Seasons*, in which Henry describes Cromwell as one of his "jackals with sharp teeth and I am their lion," and another character calls him "a coming man" (surely a faint-hearted euphemism for the man whom Bolt depicts as holding Cromwellian protégé Richard Riche's hand in the flame of a candle).[4]

As I will demonstrate, Mantel gives readers a Cromwell famous in his own time as a formidable enforcer of the royal will, a man tutored in the armies, alleys, and countinghouses of continental Europe. Mantel's Cromwell is fluent in, inter alia, Flemish, ancient Greek mnemonic tools, knife fighting, silks and woolens, and canon and common law. Cromwell's reputation in his own time made his contemporaries fear him, Mantel suggests, permitting him to prosecute his work as the king's servant efficiently and with a minimum of actual violence. By 1536, the year he helped to bring down Anne Boleyn, Mantel's Cromwell is such a terrifying figure that his presence leads the targets of his inquiries to talk themselves into believing that they have been tortured.

Yet Mantel also presents a richer picture of Cromwell. To be sure, her Cromwell possesses some qualities of the Machiavellian henchman (indeed, one personally acquainted with, if unimpressed by, that author and seised of an early version of *The Prince*[5]) and all-around fixer. But the portrait that emerges here is more complex. As Mantel wrote in an essay in the *Guardian*, "If a villain, an interesting villain, yes?"[6]

Mantel thus gives us a complex and interesting villain who is less thoroughly villainous than the petulant, narcissistic king he serves and more far-sighted and committed to building the nascent English state than any of the courtiers and councilors surrounding him. Mantel's Cromwell is nothing less than the industrious creator of the modern administrative state. In this characterization, Mantel follows in the scholarly path of G. R. Elton, whose *Tudor Revolution in Government* (1953) and subsequent decades of work sought to rehabilitate Cromwell by arguing that he systematized the royal finances, replaced personal rule with modern bureaucracy, and reformed English government. Mantel's novels also sound in the tradition begun by Josephine Tey, whose novel *The Daughter of Time* (1951) acquits Richard III of the charge of murdering his nephews. Mantel's project is less explicitly rehabilitative, but she does redeem Cromwell from Bolt's characterization. Her Cromwell is always thinking of the future. "Cold-blooded and ruthless though he was," Elton writes, Cromwell "was also a constitutionalist who realized the potentialities of common law and parliament, and who elaborated and employed the equipment of constitutional monarchy."[7]

In different ways, both Mantel's and Elton's accounts rebut the image of Cromwell as a criminal. I argue that Mantel's Cromwell should in fact be seen as something subtler: not exactly a criminal himself, but a representative of the many aspects of crimes committed by and against the state. The novels depict both types of crime as occurring at the same historical moment in which the modern state was being formed. Because crimes against the state and by the state both presuppose the existence of the state itself, Mantel's and Elton's modernizing, list-making Cromwell may not be as distinct from Bolt's devious Cromwell as the competing accounts would suggest. Mantel has expressly disclaimed the suggestion that her novels are intended to repair Cromwell's image. "It wasn't that I wanted to rehabilitate him," she notes. "I do not run a Priory clinic for the dead. Rather, I was driven by a powerful curiosity."[8]

Mantel's chronicle thus gives us four Cromwells. The first is Cromwell the political operative, the monarch's faithful counselor conducting an internal, civil war that requires harsh interrogations amid claims of exigency and crisis. Closely related is the second Cromwell, the prosecutor who zealously brings charges, proffers (some) evidence, and presses for a conviction. The third is Cromwell the modern bureaucrat, always thinking of reforms (even just hours after Anne Boleyn's execution on May 19, 1536); in modern constitutional terms this Cromwell is also an arm of the executive. The fourth is the potentially evil Cromwell: his reputation as torturer is apparently undeserved, at least in the scenes shown to readers, but we still see occasional glimpses of cruelty that hint at the hidden sources of that reputation.

Questions of crime, law, and the relationship between them permeate Mantel's novels. Connecting these themes is their corporeal consequence: the collision among state power, law (both statutory and judge-made), and human bodies that the late medieval, early modern Tudor state produced and consumed.

CROMWELL THE POLITICAL OPERATIVE

In order to understand Cromwell's role as an early modern political counselor, one must situate him in his own legal and political landscape. Scholars of Cromwell, whether critics, apologists, or something in between, have focused on his key role in developing the English law of treason. Cromwell ably deployed the treason prosecution as a weapon against Henry's enemies, until that weapon was turned against him, leading to his own trip to the block on Tower Hill and his ensuing execution for treason and heresy in 1540.

The Tudor law of treason comprised both statutory and judge-made law. Before 1534, the textual basis of the law of treason was the Treason Act of 1351, a parliamentary statute that defined treason as follows:

> When a Man doth compass or imagine the Death of our Lord the King, or of our Lady his Queen or of their eldest Son and Heir; or if a Man do violate the King's Companion or the King's eldest Daughter unmarried, or the Wife [of]

> the King's eldest Son and Heir; or if a Man do levy War against our Lord the King in his Realm, or be adherent to the King's Enemies in his Realm, giving to them Aid and Comfort in the Realm, or elsewhere, and thereof be probably attainted of open Deed by the People of their Condition . . . that ought to be judged Treason which extends to our Lord the King, and his Royal Majesty.[9]

In addition to defining treason, the statute thus also established an evidentiary standard. Proving treason required an overt act—an "open deed."[10] Moreover, the statute contained open-ended language that invited Parliament, acting in its judicial capacity, to expand the definition of treason to cover particular cases as they arose.[11]

Between 1351 and Anne Boleyn's execution in 1536, however, the penumbra of the statute gradually extended to include new categories of treason. Much of this expansion occurred at the hands of judges. In 1554 Serjeant-at-Law Stanford, one of the prosecutors in Nicholas Throckmorton's treason trial, chided the *pro se* Throckmorton for relying too heavily on the language of the Treason Act. "You are deceived, to conclude all Treasons by the statute of the 25th of Edw. the 3rd; for that Statute is but a Declaration of certain Treasons, which were Treason before at the common law," Stanford informed Throckmorton, who had attempted to parse the statutory language as part of his defense. Stanford, for his part, maintained that the Treason Act was merely declaratory of a broader, more diffuse set of conditions that judges had the power to identify as treason. "Even so there doth remain divers other treasons at this day at the common law, which be not expressed by that statute, as the Judges can declare," Stanford insisted.[12] Against the background of the 1351 statute, treason had evolved through judicial construction to become a common law doctrine. This fact reflected the sixteenth-century conception of a permeable boundary between statutes and judge-made law. Both were regarded as emanations from an overarching body of law, sometimes termed "the common law" and sometimes "the laws of England."[13]

The crucial language of the Treason Act was that making it a crime to "compass or imagine the Death of our Lord the King." In the cases in which Cromwell was involved, particularly that of Anne Boleyn, this charge formed the basis of the indictment. Anne and her alleged lovers were accused of compassing the death of Henry on specific occasions. The indictment returned by the grand jury for Middlesex stated, "And further, the said Queen and these other traitors, 31 Oct. 27 Hen. VIII., at Westminster, conspired the death and destruction of the King, the Queen often saying she would marry one of them as soon as the King died."[14] The wording comported with the language of the statute: according to the indictment, Anne and her lovers had gone well beyond imagining Henry's death; they had actually conspired to bring it about.

But the indictments against Anne and her alleged confederates (Henry Norris, William Brereton, Francis Weston, Mark Smeaton, and her own brother George Boleyn, Lord Rochford) listed no overt act in furtherance of the conspiracy. On the contrary, the charges against Anne rested on reports of words: "the Queen often saying she would marry one of them as soon as the King died." The open deed, to the extent that one existed, was at most an indirect contemplation of the possibility that Henry might die. Contemporary accounts of Anne's conduct told a similar story, in which her comment about the king's death appears to have been merely a dependent clause to her main outburst during a quarrel with the courtier Norris a few days before her arrest. The historian Eric Ives describes the scene with such color as to merit a lengthy quotation:

> It had begun by Anne asking Norris, till then a close ally, why he was postponing his proposed marriage to her cousin, Margaret Shelton, the king's old flame. She obviously suspected that Norris was reluctant to complete the match in view of the current pressure on the Boleyns, so the noncommittal reply he made ["I would tarry a while"] provoked Anne into a shocking imprudence. Flinging away the safety of courtly convention, she said, "You look for dead men's shoes; for if ought came to the king but good you would look to have me." Norris's horrified response to this totally unfair and improper shift in the basis of their relationship was to stammer that if he had any such thought, "he would his head were off," but the queen would not let him escape. She could, she said, undo him if she wanted to. A right royal quarrel about their relationship had then ensued.[15]

The centrality of this episode to the case against Anne, a case largely constructed by Cromwell in his role as Henry's loyal servant, illustrates the power of the species of treason termed "treason by words." Here, too, the extension beyond the precise terms of the 1351 statute initially took place at the hands of courts, through the vehicle of judge-made common law. But the expansion predated Cromwell, for Elton notes that words had been used as evidence of treason at least as early as the fifteenth century.[16]

Two years before Anne's downfall, however, Parliament had passed another treason statute, which codified the common law doctrine of treason by words. The Treasons Act of 1534, under which Thomas More was prosecuted and sentenced to death in that year, supported the Succession to the Crown Act of 1533 and the Act of Supremacy of 1534.[17] The succession act made the offspring of Anne and Henry, who had married the previous year, the legal successors to the Crown and required all subjects to swear an oath upholding the succession and the supremacy. The supremacy act declared that the king was and always had been the "supreme head of the Church of England." (The statute was characterized as "corroboration and confirmation" of this recognition.) The third piece of this legislative package was the Treasons Act, which made it treason to "maliciously wish, will or desire by words or writing, or by craft imagine, invent, practice or attempt any bodily harm to be done or committed to the King's most royal person."[18] Even under this expanded definition, however, Anne's conduct did not clearly fall within the scope of treason. If the accounts of Anne's statements to Norris are to be believed, she had used words contemplating the king's death, but it is not clear that she maliciously wished, willed, or desired any harm to befall him. Under the 1351 act, moreover, Anne could be understood as compassing the death of the king, but she had arguably not engaged in an overt act, or "open deed," connected with that possibility.

Mantel depicts Cromwell as the originator of these political and dynastic developments. He propels the passage of the succession, supremacy, and treason acts in 1533 and 1534 in order to support Anne's position as queen, and he then uses those statutes to build the case against her in 1536. As Mantel draws him, Cromwell has an ambivalent relationship toward statutes as a legal form, and toward legislative power more broadly. On one hand, she shows him perpetually drawing up new legislation and contemplating the activities of Parliament. He is therefore not simply a spokesman for raw, unchanneled executive power. On the other hand, when Mantel's Cromwell uses Parliament, he is always using it for a reason: in a cynical reading, to bolster the legitimacy of an already chosen course of action; in a reading more in line with modern sympathies, to make progress toward what would become the post–Glorious Revolution belief that the king-in-Parliament was the true locus of English sovereignty.[19] But even according to this more sympathetic view, Cromwell employs Parliament as a tool of executive power, albeit a new and improved version of executive power.[20]

Not surprisingly, Mantel's Cromwell is a keen drafter and promoter of statutes to aid Henry's campaign to replace Katherine of Aragon with Anne, including not only the act of succession but also the enhanced treason act. Elton argues that the Tudors "reli[ed] on statute" to "expand or contract treason."[21] In a similar vein, John Guy notes that the Reformation was "declared by parliamentary statutes and enforced by common law procedures."[22] Mantel's account goes even further: her Cromwell relies on statutes as one more tool in the arsenal of promoting the king's interests. Thus, in *Wolf Hall*, the narrative voice of Cromwell describes the Act of Supremacy as "an act which draws together all the powers and dignities assumed by the king in the last two years." In Cromwell's view, the act is a shorthand or a stand-in for a set of (presumably expanded) powers that Henry had recently claimed and exercised. The act is simply a restatement of already extant royal authority. "It doesn't, as some say, make the king head of the church. It states that he is head of the church, and always has been. If people don't like new ideas, let them have old ones. If they want precedents, he has precedents."[23] The statute, then, is a neat encapsulation of preexisting law, and that law stems from royal practice met with acquiescence. As Guy puts it, "Treason, not heresy, became the penalty for denying the royal supremacy."[24]

When Mantel's Cromwell discusses the Treason Act of 1534, his words exemplify the view that statutes are codification mechanisms for the benefit of the executive rather than avenues for popular will. Cromwell-the-narrator describes the act, focusing on its treason by words provision, in this way:

> A second enactment, which will come into force in the new year, defines the scope of treason. It will be a treasonable offense to deny Henry's titles or jurisdiction, to speak or write maliciously against him, to call him a heretic or a schismatic. This law will catch the friars who spread panic and say the Spanish are landing with the next tide to seize the throne for the Lady Mary. It will catch the priests who in their sermons rant against the king's authority and say he is dragging his subjects after him to Hell. Is it too much for a monarch to ask, that a subject keep a civil tongue in his head? *This is new, people say to him, this treason by words, and he says, no, be assured, it is old. It casts into statute law what the judges in their wisdom have already defined as common law.* It is a measure for clarification. I am all for clarity.[25]

In *Wolf Hall*, Cromwell deploys this clarified treason statute against Thomas More, who had refused to swear the oath of supremacy. In *Bring Up the Bodies*, it is the combination of the new statute's treason by words provision and the 1351 statute's prohibition on compassing the death of the king that destroys Anne, again wielded by Cromwell.[26]

Mantel depicts in careful detail the process by which Cromwell investigated Anne's "light ways" and assembled the case against her. As in the historical account, Anne's interactions with certain of Henry's male courtiers, and in particular her exchange with Norris, become the crucial evidence against her. Mantel's description of Anne's fatal exchange with Norris follows the historical account closely. Following Anne's statement that Norris "look[s] for dead men's shoes" in hoping to marry her if Henry were to die, Mantel has Norris ask Anne, "Will you spill all your secrets or only some?" Anne then becomes "frantic," in Mary Shelton's retelling: "She said a priest must be fetched, she said Harry must take an oath that he knew her to be chaste, a faithful good wife. She said he must take back everything said, and she would take it back too, and they would put their hands on the Bible in her chamber, and then everybody would know that it was idle talk."[27]

In a pivotal interview with Norris shortly thereafter, Cromwell tells Norris, "The king knows what to think. He does not ask for eyewitnesses. He knows your treason and the queen's." Norris replies, "I am not ashamed of any dealings I have had with Anne. . . . And if I am, Cromwell, even if I am . . . you cannot make my thoughts a crime." Cromwell, however, follows the logic of the new treason act—his new treason act—to rebut Norris: "If thoughts are intentions, if intentions are malign . . . if you did not have her unlawfully, and you say you did not, did you intend to have her lawfully, after the king's death?"[28]

Although treason by words had been a common law doctrine for many decades, Cromwell's statutes transformed it into a weapon to be wielded by the king's closest counselor. In an exchange with the poet and courtier Thomas Wyatt—a friend of Cromwell and another of Anne's suspected lovers, although he escaped charges—Mantel's Cromwell carefully explains the connection between Anne's adultery and treason. The conversation also illustrates Cromwell in his mode of skepticism toward law:

> [WYATT:] "As I understand the law, a queen's adultery is no treason."
> [CROMWELL:] "No, but the man who violates her, he commits treason."
> "You think they used force?" Wyatt says drily.
> "No, it is just the legal term. It is a pretence, that allows us to think well of any disgraced queen. But as for her, she is a traitor too, she has said so out of her own mouth. To intend the king's death, that is treason."
> "But again," Wyatt says, "forgive my poor understanding. I thought Anne had said, 'If he dies,' or some such words. So let me put a case to you. If I say 'All men must die,' is that a forecast of the king's death?"
> "It would be well not to put cases," he says pleasantly. "Thomas More was putting cases when he tipped into treason."[29]

The treason act gave a veneer of parliamentary authority to the silencing of those who would speak against the king, even if such speech consisted in little more than a secondhand report of a conversation in which the king's mortality was discussed. It is therefore possible to view the treason act as nothing more than a fig leaf for personal rule and royal prerogative.

Yet even if the act of Parliament was mere show, intended to cover might with a thin coating of right, that fact must mean that at least a few legal formalities were necessary to convince some important audience that the exercise of royal will was also lawful. In other words, even if the impetus for the statute came from Cromwell, the fact that he went to the effort of shaping a common law doctrine into legislation demonstrates something important about the nature of legal authority in the period.[30] The legislature was the arm of the executive, but legislative power itself clearly had some ideological *puissance* independent of the executive.

CROMWELL THE PROSECUTOR

The trial procedures, as Mantel depicts them, show a similar blend: legal forms and process are tools of the prince, but they nevertheless are adhered to because they serve crucial legitimizing purposes. Following the interrogations of Anne's alleged co-conspirators, which I discuss below, Cromwell directs his own retinue of young lawyers and courtiers to begin drafting indictments. Indictments are necessary for Cromwell, for although Anne is at this point held captive in the Tower of London, she has not yet been formally charged.[31] "Her judicial status uncertain, the charges not yet framed, it is hard to describe Anne. If she is a traitor she is, pending the verdict of the court, technically dead; though at the Tower . . . she eats heartily enough, and giggles."[32]

But first Cromwell and his company must deal with the fact that the case against Anne still rests on weak evidence. As Cromwell emerges from an interview with Francis Weston, one of Anne's alleged lovers, his young associates press for news: "Are we finished?" Thomas Wriothesley, clerk of the signet and nicknamed "Call-Me Risley" by his colleagues, asks.[33] "He has confessed?" Cromwell shakes his head in the negative: "Each man will give a good account of himself, but he will not absolve his fellows. Also, they will all say 'I am innocent,' but they do not say, 'She is innocent.' They are not able. It may be she is, but none of them will give his word on it." The pressure to get an indictment then leads Wriothesley to hint that force might be necessary to obtain a confession:

> "Well, you have no confessions," Wriothesley says. "Do you want us to get them?"
>
> He gives Call-Me a look that knocks him back, so he steps on the foot of [Solicitor General] Richard Riche. "What, Wriothesley, do you think I am too soft to the young?"
>
> Riche rubs his foot. "Shall we draw up specimen charges?"[34]

Indictments are necessary, but in order to get indictments, one must be willing to contemplate violence. Throughout the novels, Mantel's Cromwell alternates between his two imperatives of law and force. Here again Mantel gives us Tudor politics as a case study in the transition between medieval kingship based on notions of royal prerogative and the early modern conception of the monarch as bound by law, or at least by legal forms. When the indictments are finally produced, Cromwell views them as documents embodying the king's emotions for consumption by the key audience anticipating and attending Anne's trial. Cromwell reads them as artificial narratives, polemics written in order to shock and persuade. The language in the indictments carries "the king's voice in every line: his outrage, jealousy, fear." It is "more like a conversation" with a "scandal-loving woman, than it is like a document one carries into court; but all the same it has its merits, it makes a story, and it puts into the heads of those who will hear it certain pictures that will not easily be got out again."[35]

In addition to the lurid descriptions of Anne's alleged conduct, including her incestuous relationship with her brother, Cromwell tells his clerks to add boilerplate language that will lend a coating of legal authority to what a later generation of Britons would call a "sexed up" document.[36] Cromwell instructs the clerks to "add at every point, and to every offence, 'and several days before and after.' Or a similar phrase, that makes it clear the offences are numerous, perhaps more numerous than even the parties themselves recollect." In so doing, Cromwell says, "if there is specific denial of one date, one place, it will not be enough to injure the whole."[37] Cromwell is the master of all his crafts here: the judge of salacious rhetoric that will sway the audience for the political theater of the trials, and the canny lawyer who knows how to draft an impregnable document.

On Mantel's account, the trials of Anne and her co-conspirators proceed according to Cromwell's plans. Following the order to "bring up the bodies," the alleged lovers who are commoners—Weston, Brereton, Smeaton, and Norris—are conveyed from the Tower to Westminster Hall on Friday, May 12, 1536. The four are brought before a commission of oyer and terminer, a special court of investigation that appears to have been summoned by Cromwell and Lord Chancellor Thomas Audley.[38] Weston, Brereton, and Norris plead not guilty; Smeaton pleads guilty. Mantel describes the process as "clear, logical, and designed to create corpses by due process of law." Watching the scene, Cromwell notes, "There is only one penalty for high treason: for a man, to be hanged, cut down alive and eviscerated, or for a woman, to be burned. The king may vary the sentence to decapitation." All four are found guilty and sentenced to drawing, hanging, and quartering. Mantel's Cromwell, watching the convicted men leave the courtroom, notes that the guards have turned the axe edge of their halberds toward them, who "push through the uproar, dead men."[39]

As peers, Anne and her brother George are brought three days later before the court of the lord high steward (their uncle Thomas Howard, 3rd Duke of Norfolk), in the great hall of the Tower. Anne is tried first; she is "tainted now, she is dead meat," Cromwell thinks. Cromwell acts as prosecutor. Then "the dizzying catalogue" of charges against Anne is read, "and then the loose words and taunts, the jealous quarrels and twisted intentions, the declaration, by the queen, that when her husband is dead, she will choose some one of them to be her husband, but she cannot yet say which." Cromwell: "Did you say that?" Anne, shaking her head, in an "icy little voice: 'No.'" Anne pleads guilty; she "disdains to enlarge, to excuse, extenuate: to mitigate. And there is no one to do it for her."[40] She is convicted. The Duke of Norfolk reads the sentence: "Thou shalt be burned here, within the Tower, or else to have thy head smitten off, as the king's pleasure shall be further known." An outcry arises in response to this sentencing in the alternative, but Cromwell pushes Norfolk to ignore the protest from the judges.[41]

Anne is taken out; George is brought in. George plays to the crowd, reading aloud a statement about Henry's alleged lack of potency despite Cromwell's order not to do so. But George quickly realizes that his gambit has led him to repeat the words in court, and thereby to own them. "In one moment of bravado, to get the applause of the crowd, he has impugned the succession, derogated the king's heirs, even though he was cautioned not to do it." But then Cromwell thinks, "It is hard on George that he cannot even mention the charges against them without becoming guilty of them."[42] George, too, is condemned, sentenced to drawing, hanging, and quartering.

Mantel's account of the trials is well supported by the historical evidence. But her narrative emphasizes a particular theme: Cromwell as the ultimate servant of the king, a counselor and politician able to use legal forms and processes to further the monarch's will. He achieves this by transforming mundane, gossip-fodder causes of action such as adultery into the subject of statecraft and by using the institutions of the courts and Parliament to process the private intricacies and disappointments of one marriage. While making his final arguments in Anne's case, Cromwell's attention momentarily drifts, and he sees "the Attorney General stifle a yawn." Cromwell then muses, "I have done what I thought I could never achieve, I have taken adultery, incest, conspiracy and treason, and I have made them routine. We do not need any false excitement. After all, it is a law court, not the Roman circus."[43]

Cromwell's state of mind here is difficult to discern from the text. Is he congratulating himself, a blacksmith's son from Putney, for bringing about the execution of the queen of England, a queen he himself had helped to ascend the throne? Or does his pride spring from a more workmanlike source, from the attorney's pride in the craft of corralling unruly, unsavory facts into the forms of pleading?[44] The key appears to lie in the final phrase: "it is a law court, not the Roman circus." He, Cromwell (to borrow Mantel's phrasing), has shepherded the bloody bodies of the traitors into their graves in a way that satisfies the emotional and the procedural needs of both the sovereign and the broader court, and perhaps even the populace.

The desire to avoid the Roman circus drives Cromwell the prosecutor, but because he serves a would-be emperor, the rule of law remains an elusive goal.

CROMWELL THE BUREAUCRAT

Despite Mantel's statement that she did not set out to rehabilitate Cromwell, a consistent theme in the novels is his dedication to modernizing and rationalizing the institutions of government. In a 2012 interview, Mantel appears to endorse Elton's characterization of Cromwell as "the man who created a bureaucracy and parliamentary structure as bulwark[s] against kingly incompetence," a view that she contrasted with Bolt's depiction of Cromwell in *A Man for All Seasons*.[45]

In the final chapters of *Bring Up the Bodies*, we see Cromwell, newly created Baron Cromwell of Wimbledon, preparing to extend his power while ever more aware of his own vulnerability to the sudden political shifts of Henry's court. Amid the giddiness of some of his supporters following the executions of Anne and the others, the still-wary Cromwell sees opportunities for progress and reform ("useful wreckage"). Despite a needling sense of unease about his own future, Cromwell's grasp of realpolitik—and his desire to triumph over his growing number of enemies—emboldens him to seize the king's favor while he can. His goals are only partly personal, for Mantel depicts him as energized by new plans to reform the laws and administration of the realm, which in turn fills him with defiance: "Let them try to pull him down. They will find him armoured, they will find him entrenched, they will find him stuck like a limpet to the future. He has laws to write, measures to take, the good of the commonwealth to serve, and his king; he has titles and honours still to attain, houses to build, books to read, and who knows, perhaps children to father."[46]

Cromwell's desire to bring modernity to England is so irrepressible that it breaks in upon him at unlikely moments. Within the space of a half page in *Wolf Hall*, he moves from musing about Thomas More's horsehair jerkin and habitual scourging to contemplating the economy behind such tools of self-humiliation: "Are simple villagers paid—how, by the dozen?—for making flails with waxed knots?" Cromwell the man of business then thinks, "People ought to be found better jobs."[47] Similarly, in the aftermath of Anne's execution, during an interview with the king's illegitimate son Henry Fitzroy, Duke of Richmond, Cromwell the record keeper begins planning for a registry of births.[48] With these ironic juxtapositions between Tudor court intrigue and modern bureaucratic rationalization, Mantel creates a dynamic account of a polity in transition. Her account of Cromwell depends on the rise of the state, and her account of the early modern English state depends on Cromwell's vision.

Scholars of Cromwell have taken different views of his role in the development of the modern state. The principal points of controversy have been two: first, whether Tudor government did indeed witness a transformation from medieval personal rule to something approaching a modern, systematized, bureaucratic state; second, to the extent that such a shift took place, how significant Cromwell's role was.

As the title suggests, Elton's book *The Tudor Revolution in Government*, published in 1953, argues both for transformation and Cromwell's centrality. In a series of books and articles spanning more than two decades, Elton rehabilitates Cromwell, calling him the "most remarkable English statesman of the sixteenth century."[49] Viewing Cromwell as at heart a moderate who nonetheless embraced radical strategies, Elton argues that at the time of his execution in 1540, Cromwell had more to give: he was "cut off in the middle of vigorous activity and yet full of plans for the better organizing of the realm." For Elton, Cromwell was a "constitutionalist."[50] He did not merely use Parliament as a mouthpiece of the executive branch or its statutes as vessels for royal prerogative. Rather he was a creative legal and political thinker who developed what became the early modern theory of the king-in-Parliament: a mixed executive-legislative entity in which sovereignty resided and which was the first genuine institution of English government independent of the personal rule of the monarch.

On Elton's view, the key elements of the Tudor revolution in government were (1) the establishment of the Court of Augmentations and the Court of First Fruits and Tenths, which grew out of the dissolution of the monasteries and formalized the Crown's control of its lands and revenues; (2) the emergence of the office of the principal secretary, which Cromwell occupied and which would evolve into the secretary of state, "the prime agency through which king and council administered the realm"; and (3) the development of the Privy Council.[51] Moreover, Elton attributes the motive force for this transformation to Cromwell rather than to Henry.[52] Elton thus emphasizes Cromwell's zeal for reform. "Cold-blooded and ruthless though he was," Cromwell also "realized the potentialities of common law and parliament" and consequently "elaborated and employed the equipment of constitutional monarchy."[53] Elton, like Mantel, portrays Cromwell as a thoughtful political theorist, not just the henchman of unconstrained royal power.

Critics of Elton's view, chief among them R. B. Wernham and Brendan Bradshaw, have attacked this Cromwell-centric view of things, while Guy has tended to support many of Elton's conclusions. A lively debate has been conducted in the pages of historical journals among these and other scholars over just how novel Cromwell's reforms were and whether those changes came about as a result of Cromwell's initiative or Henry's. The main counterclaim to Elton's thesis is captured by Wernham's observation that although "the routine work of collecting and administering the new revenues from the monastic lands, even the revenues from the other Crown lands and feudal rights, had to be delegated more than ever to organizations that could run on their own . . . that was administration, not government."[54] If claims that Cromwell brought about a revolution in government—meaning the state—rely on the expansion of the offices that oversaw the royal fisc, those claims may founder if the fisc was still seen as the property of the king rather than of the state.

A similar point can be made with respect to what Bradshaw terms "the hotly debated issue of king or minister."[55] Even if one allows that Henry's reign witnessed an increase in the revenues available to the king following the dissolution of the monasteries, and a consequent increase in the number of officials collecting those revenues, the question remains to what degree those policies and offices had any independence of the king. Did Cromwell's work lead to the replacement of what Elton terms "government by the king" with "government under the king," carried out by bodies such as the Privy Council?[56] Wernham's response is that although Cromwell's policies may have created more offices and officeholders, that bureaucracy was simply an arm of the executive and so "dependent for its strength and effectiveness upon the strength and effectiveness of the monarch's personal action."[57] In other words, bureaucratic growth was evidence of Cromwell's power at the center; it therefore represented a tool of executive administration rather than the rise of a distinct institution.

Mantel clearly sides with Elton in this debate. In the novels, Cromwell's desire to make England work better extends beyond greasing the wheels of royal revenue collection. Not only does he seek a "single coinage," but he also hopes for "just one method of weighing and measuring, and above all one language that everybody owns," and he plans a roads bill that would "give employment to men without work."[58] It is Cromwell alone who grasps the extent of the commercial, political, and legal webs connecting subjects to each other and to their king. Her Cromwell seizes the opportunity to transform the king's marital problems, dynastic anxieties, and diplomatic negotiations into the impetus toward self-conscious progress.

And some essential element in Cromwell's character makes him regard these reforms as a test of his own strength. Consider this passage from *Wolf Hall*:

> Business always increases. . . . A number of noblemen are indebted to him, not just for arranging loans, but for making their estates pay better. It is not a matter of exactions from tenants, but, in the first place, giving the landowner an accurate survey of land values, crop yield, water supply, built assets, and then assessing the potential of all these; next, putting in bright people as estate managers, and with them setting up an accounting system that makes yearly sense and can be audited. Among the city merchants, he is in demand for his

> advice on trading partners overseas. He has a sideline in arbitration, commercial disputes mostly, as his ability to assess the facts of a case and give a swift impartial decision is trusted here, in Calais and in Antwerp. If you and your opponent can at least concur on the need to save the costs and delays of a court hearing, then Cromwell is, for a fee, your man; and he has the pleasant privilege, often enough, of sending away both sides happy. These are good days for him: every day a fight he can win.[59]

We can hear a similar tone of energetic ambition, albeit with a vaguely sinister undercurrent, in the historical Cromwell's 1538 prayer "God gyue me no longer lyfe than I shall be gladde to vuse myn office in ediciatione, and not in destruction."[60]

Perhaps one way to reconcile the historiographical debates about Cromwell and the growth of the state is to consider the developments of Henry's reign as a prelude to the development of England's overseas empire under Henry's daughter Elizabeth. In 1533 Parliament passed the Statute in Restraint of Appeals, which was drafted by Cromwell and contained the distilled constitutional essence of the English Reformation. The statute provided that the king, and not the pope, was the ultimate legal authority in the realm. The "one supreme head and king" possessed "plenary, whole and entire power, preeminence, authority, prerogative and jurisdiction to render and yield justice and final determination to all manners of folk resiants [*sic*] or subjects within this realm, in all causes, matters, debates and contentions happening to occur, insurge or begin within the limits thereof, without restraint or provocation to any foreign princes or potentates of the world."[61]

The statute thus made the king the supreme source of jurisdiction within the realm and prohibited as unlawful appeals to other sovereigns. It also amplified the Tudor practice of passing statutes that codified and strengthened older common law precedents. Since the fourteenth century, the writ of praemunire had been used to "protect the king's rights against interference by foreign courts," especially the papacy.[62] The praemunire had been wielded against Cardinal Wolsey in 1529, when he failed to obtain Henry's divorce from Katherine of Aragon, leading to Wolsey's downfall; Mantel uses it in her plot as well. Of course the immediate imperative behind the Statute in Restraint of Appeals was to bring jurisdiction over the divorce within the ambit of English courts rather than those in Rome.

Yet the authority behind the Statute in Restraint of Appeals rested on a particular claim about England's global status. The act began with the statement "This realm of England is an empire, and so hath been accepted in the world"—and therefore Henry was an emperor over whom no superior authority existed.[63] This was one of the first recorded characterizations of England as an empire, and it would give rise to extensive debates centuries later, as British North Americans reshaped the constitutional relationship between the colonies and the imperial center.[64] In 1533 those controversies lay far in the future, but the act unquestionably announced a new view of the nature of the polity.[65] Even if Cromwell's contributions to the rise of the English state were subject to dispute, the act was a significant initial assertion of the English empire. Moreover that empire would be launched into the New World by Elizabeth, the offspring of Henry's union with Anne—the very union that had occasioned the act's passage.

CROMWELL THE EVIL

Locked in the room with these mixed characterizations of Cromwell as executive agent, prosecutor, and administrator, there is also Cromwell the torturer, the evil enforcer of the king's will. Here Mantel uses her readers' expectations of Cromwell to create a multilayered narrative in which the reader is never certain whether Cromwell did or did not use torture to extract information and confessions from his opponents. We do know, however, that Cromwell's contemporaries believed that he used torture; moreover, Mantel's Cromwell makes us aware that he knows that his contemporaries believe this of him.

The locus of reports, then and now, of Cromwell's use of torture is the interrogation of Mark Smeaton, Anne's musician and alleged lover. Most historians view Smeaton as a bystander to the intrigues among the Boleyns, the Seymours, and Cromwell, but he was swept up in the conflict because he was widely viewed as part of the circle of licentiousness and immorality that surrounded Anne. Unlike Norris, Brereton, Weston, and Rochford, however, Smeaton's status as a musician, and likely a foreigner, made him a relative outsider with few allies at court. Smeaton was the only one of Anne's alleged lovers and co-conspirators to confess.[66] Over the same weekend as Anne's quarrel with Norris, which was followed by her exchange with Henry in the window of Greenwich Palace while she was carrying Elizabeth, word reached Cromwell that Smeaton was suspected as the queen's lover. Cromwell had Smeaton taken to Cromwell's house in Stepney, where he was questioned for twenty-four hours before confessing to adultery with the queen. On Monday Smeaton was dispatched to the Tower. Cromwell, and even Henry, then began to press the others to confess. Ives observes that Smeaton's confession "turned the denials of Anne, Norris, and later Rochford into evidence of guilt" because it suggested that they were all implicated in the clandestine events taking place in Anne's rooms.[67]

Mantel's account of these events takes full advantage of the ambiguities surrounding both sixteenth- and twenty-first-century beliefs about Cromwell's activities. In a scene of excruciating detail and suspense—even though the reader knows how it will end—Mantel shows Cromwell's careful psychological torture of Smeaton. A request for a fire from Cromwell, whom Mantel calls "Master Secretary," as though to emphasize that he is in his official role as the king's servant, leads the nervous Smeaton to panic: "Just an ordinary household request, and yet Mark thinks they mean to burn him. He jumps off his stool and makes for the door."[68] Master Secretary then builds the pressure by asking Smeaton whether he would like to be left alone with Cromwell's burly French servant Christophe, who is lurking at the door. Cromwell continues to build the threats, locking Smeaton in a dark closet overnight with Christmas decorations covered in feathers and points so that Smeaton's mind creates a scene of torture for himself. The following morning, Smeaton confesses to adultery with Anne and also names dozens of other courtiers as her lovers.

Throughout the scene, Cromwell is acutely aware of his reputation as a rough brute,[69] even a torturer. He was not unique in his association with the practice; during the early modern period, torture was considered a permissible tool for obtaining confessions, especially from political criminals who were alleged to have conspired against the monarch.[70] But other characters repeatedly mention Cromwell's reputation. After passing incriminating rumors to Cromwell, Jane Rochford—wife of George Boleyn—notes, "You are what you are, a man of resource who spares no one. It will be thought that you drew the truth out of me, whether I was willing or no." After hearing news of Smeaton's confession, Anne's uncle, the Duke of Norfolk, greets Cromwell, "Now, Cromwell! I hear the singer has sung to your tune. What did you do to him? I wish I had been there." While Anne and the others await their fate, Cromwell reflects on his power: "None of the men except Mark have been properly interrogated: that is to say, interrogated by him."[71]

Only during his interrogation of Norris does Cromwell appear to lose control, but only briefly, in response to Norris's challenge—and only to threaten:

> "You will not put gentlemen to the torture, the king would not permit it."
>
> "There don't have to be formal arrangements." He is on his feet, he slams his hand down on the table. "I could put my thumbs in your eyes, and then you would sing 'Green Grows the Holly' if I asked you to." He sits down, resumes his former easy tone. "Put yourself in my place. People will say I have tortured you anyway. They will say I have tortured Mark, they are already putting the word about. Though not a gossamer threat of him is snapped, I swear. I have Mark's free confession."[72]

Such scenes are the apotheosis of Mantel's meta-Cromwell: aware of himself, aware of his own reputation, and able to use that reputation in order to compel others to do his will.

Mantel thus presents Cromwell as always stepping back from the precipice: using threats of torture, but not torture itself, to extract the admissions he needs.[73] Cromwell pursues this course partly because he is the king's loyal servant and enforcer. But Mantel gives him an additional motive for punishing Brereton, Norris, Weston, and Boleyn: at a masque several years before, they performed a humiliating impersonation of Cromwell's former patron, Cardinal Wolsey. As he finishes his interrogation of Norris, Cromwell sees the scene in his mind: "Four men, who for a joke turned the cardinal into a beast; who took away his wit, his kindness and his grace, and made him a howling animal, groveling on the boards and scrabbling with his paws." Throughout *Bring Up the Bodies* we become increasingly aware of the depth of Cromwell's feeling for Wolsey, which leads him to merge his own revenge against the four courtiers with Henry's quest to be rid of Anne. "He needs guilty men. So he has found men who are guilty. Though perhaps not guilty as charged."[74] The theme of Cromwell's loyalty to Wolsey emerges slowly, and it appears to provide an emotional justification for many of Cromwell's other actions. Perhaps, then, Mantel's Cromwell does have a heart after all?

But Mantel appears unwilling to give her readers that solace. Instead, in a few key scenes she portrays a different kind of Cromwell: an almost comic-book–style evil villain. The most telling such exchange comes during the interrogation of Smeaton while he is being held at Cromwell's home. Besides Smeaton and Cromwell, also present are Cromwell's protégé Thomas Wriothesley and Cromwell's nephew Richard Cromwell (great-grandfather of Oliver). "I explained to you, Mark, that Mr. Wriothesley will write down what we say. But he will not necessarily write down what we do. You follow me? That will be just between us." Mark's reply: "Mother Mary, help me."[75] Then follows this exchange:

> Mr Wriothesley says, "We can take you to the Tower where there is a rack."
>
> "Wriothesley, may I have a word with you aside?" He [Cromwell] waves Call-Me out of the room and on the threshold speaks in an undertone. "It is better not to specify the nature of the pain. As Juvenal says, the mind is its own best torturer. Besides, you should not make empty threats. I will not rack him. I do not want him carried to his trial in a chair. And if I needed to rack a sad little fellow like this . . . what next? Stamping on dormice?"
>
> "I am reproved," Mr Wriothesley says.
>
> He puts his hand on Wriothesley's arm. "Never mind. You are doing very well."[76]

This exchange shows us yet another Cromwell: not the political operative, not the prosecutor, and not the administrator. This Cromwell is coldly cruel, calculating the precise measure of suggestion needed to make his victim become the victim's own torturer. Most striking is Cromwell's tone in the final statement to Wriothesley. His display of concern for Wriothesley is chilling in its detachment. He rushes to reassure Wriothesley that he is "doing very well" at interrogating a political prisoner whose confession he knows to be coerced and, even more important, false.[77] Smeaton's confession is the key to the entire case against Anne and her alleged lovers. But the real targets are the four men whose complicity in the Wolsey parody so enraged Cromwell. "He has spun his enemies to face him, to join him: as in a dance. He means to spin them away again, so they look down the long cold vista of their years . . . so they bed down in ruins, and wake up cold."[78] The enemies here are the four from the Wolsey masque, and perhaps also the extended Boleyn family, with their open scorn for Cromwell and Wolsey.

Anne is therefore a pawn even in Cromwell's crusade against her. She is a casualty of what Mantel suggests may be Cromwell's sole noble deed: his campaign to avenge Wolsey. This cruelty is apparent in the thoughts that Mantel puts in Cromwell's voice as he helps Anne make her way to the Tower after her arrest. Anne falls to the ground, "her head thrown back, wailing." Cromwell "takes hold of her—since no one else will do it—and sets her back on her feet." As in the later scene with Wriothesley, we see Cromwell acting in an apparently sympathetic manner. But then the inhumanly cold observation: "Silent, she steadies herself against his shoulder, leans into him: intent, complicit, ready for the next thing they will do together, which is kill her."

Mantel redeems Cromwell from the charges of torture, at least with respect to Smeaton; readers are not confronted with the events that gave rise to his contemporary reputation for roughness. But Mantel also—relentlessly—exposes a different ugly side of her creation. In Cromwell's moments of utter coldness Mantel gives us not just a devoted servant but a hollowed-out, guilt-conjuring machine. As Wriothesley observes admiringly, "It is not so much, who is guilty, as whose guilt is of service to you."[79]

Cromwell's desire to avenge Wolsey initially appears to invest him with a degree of humanity. By the end of *Bring Up the Bodies*, however, his clinical interactions with Wriothesley and Anne suggest that he has started to become the dead-eyed figure pictured in Holbein's portrait. The bodies are brought up for punishment, just as those bodies once brought up the sham body of Wolsey for the entertainment of the court. Eventually, we know, Cromwell's body will also be on the pile.

NOTES

I thank William Birdthistle, Richard Helmholz, and Richard McAdams for helpful comments and discussion. I am pleased to acknowledge the support of the Mayer Brown Faculty Research Fund.

1. Hilary Mantel, *Bring Up the Bodies* (New York: Henry Holt, 2012).

2. Charles Wriothesley, *A Chronicle of England During the Reigns of the Tudors, from A.D. 1485 to 1559*, vol. 1, ed. William Douglas Hamilton (London: Camden Society, New Series XI, 1875).

3. Mantel, *Bring Up the Bodies*, ix.

4. Robert Bolt, *A Man for All Seasons* (New York: Vintage Books, 1962), 44.

5. Hilary Mantel, *Wolf Hall* (New York: Picador, 2009), 97 ("He has got Niccolò Machiavelli's book *Principalities*: it is a Latin edition, shoddily printed in Naples, which seems to have passed through many hands. He thinks of Niccolò on the battlefield; of Niccolò in the torture chamber. . . . Someone says to him, what is in your little book? and he says, a few aphorisms, a few truisms, nothing we didn't know before.").

6. Hilary Mantel, "How I Came to Write Wolf Hall," *Guardian*, December 7, 2012.

7. G. R. Elton, "The Political Creed of Thomas Cromwell," *Transactions of the Royal Historical Society*, 5th ser., 6 (1956): 92.

8. Mantel, "How I Came to Write *Wolf Hall*."

9. Treason Act 1351, 1351 Ch. 2, 25 Edw. 3 Stat 5, c. II. The date of the statute is sometimes given as 1352 because the act was passed during the Hilary Term of 1351, which ran from January to March. Because in the old style, or Julian calendar, the new year began on March 25 (Lady Day), the year of the statute depended on which dating system was used. England, and later Great Britain, used the Julian calendar until 1752, when Parliament adopted the new style, or Gregorian calendar.

10. G. R. Elton, *The Tudor Constitution: Documents and Commentary*, 2d edition (Cambridge: Cambridge University Press, 1982), 59; see also Throckmorton's Case (State Trials, 1 Mary 1554), in *Cobbett's Complete Collection of State Trials and Proceedings for High Treason and Other Crimes and Misdemeanors from the Earliest Period to Present Time* (London: T.C. Hansard, 1809), 1:889 ("for thereby the law doth understand the discovering of your treasons") (Bromley, C. J).

11. "And because that many other like cases of treason may happen in time to come, which a man cannot think nor declare at this present time, it is accorded, That if any other case supposed treason which is not above specified doth happen before any Justices, the Justices shall tarry without any going to judgment of the treason till the case be shewed and declared before the King and his Parliament, whether it ought to be judged treason or other felony" (25 Edw. 3 Stat. 5).

12. Id. at 389.

13. See John Guy, "The Henrician Age," in *The Varieties of British Political Thought, 1500–1800*, ed. J. G. A. Pocock (Cambridge: Cambridge University Press, 1993), 29 ("The common lawyers' achievement was therefore to ensure that the word 'law' in Tudor political practice meant 'the laws and customs of England.' ").

14. Middlesex Indictment of Anne Boleyn, May 10, 1536.

15. Eric Ives, *The Life and Death of Anne Boleyn* (Malden, MA: Blackwell Publishing, 2004), 335. Ives and other historians regard this quarrel, which took place before several witnesses, as a key turning point leading to Anne's downfall. Immediately following the exchange, Anne "tried to forestall gossip by instructing Henry Norris to go to her almoner on the Sunday morning and volunteer to take his oath that the queen 'was a good woman.' " This desperate ploy seems to have raised suspicions in the opposite direction, leading to a public confrontation between Anne and Henry in the window of Greenwich Palace a few days later, in which onlookers saw

Anne producing the two-year-old Elizabeth as she appeared to implore Henry (325). In Mantel's depiction of the scene Cromwell notes that no observer could have heard the words that passed between Anne and Henry (*Bring Up the Bodies*, 262).

16. Elton, *The Tudor Constitution*, 59–60.

17. 26 Hen. 8 c. 13; 25 Hen. 8 c. 22 (another product of the Hilary Term and so sometimes dated 1534); 26 Hen. 8 c. 1.

18. 26 Hen. 8 c. 13. By the end of the sixteenth century the charge of treason by words was waning. Most of the statutes that recognized the crime had been repealed because their moment of exigency had passed, and the common law version of the offense was no longer recognized (Elton, *The Tudor Constitution*, 60).

19. In a conversation with Mary Tudor, daughter of Henry and Katherine of Aragon, during her period out of favor because of Anne's rise, Mantel's Cromwell uses a positivist account of Parliament's power to justify Henry's, and therefore his own, decision to remove Mary from the succession by statute. Mary asks Cromwell, "How is it I am put out of the succession, Master Cromwell? How is it lawful?" Cromwell responds, "It is lawful if Parliament makes it so." Mary replies, "There is a law above Parliament. It is the law of God. Ask Bishop Fisher." Cromwell: "I find God's purposes obscure, and God knows I find Fisher no fit elucidator. By contrast, I find the will of Parliament plain" (Mantel, *Wolf Hall*, 515).

"Where does the prince get this power, and his power to enforce the law? He gets it though a legislative body, which acts on behalf of the citizens. It is from the will of the people, expressed in Parliament, that a king derives his kingship" (id. at 494). See also Elton, "The Political Creed of Thomas Cromwell," 6 (arguing that Cromwell's political creed "centred on the legal supremacy of the king in Parliament and included no ambitions for a purely royal despotism").

20. In the early period of Anne's reign, Mantel depicts both Henry and Cromwell using Parliament to cement the legitimacy of the marriage and its issue. "The king calls him in, with [Bishop] Gardiner, to look through the bill he proposes to put into Parliament to secure the succession of Anne's children," Mantel's Cromwell notes. (The "he" in "the bill he proposes" is most likely Cromwell; the ambiguity of the first-person male pronoun is a hallmark of Mantel's style in *Wolf Hall*.) When Anne objects that the draft bill contains provisions concerning Anne's possible death ("she looks up, shocked: it mentions my death!"), Cromwell replies, "I can't exclude the event. . . . Parliament can do anything, madam, except what is against nature" (Mantel, *Wolf Hall*, 498–99).

21. Elton, *The Tudor Constitution*, 60.

22. Guy, "The Henrician Age," 22.

23. Mantel, *Wolf Hall*, 546.

24. Guy, "The Henrician Age," 22.

25. Mantel, *Wolf Hall*, 546 (emphasis added).

26. Mantel, *Bring Up the Bodies*, 260 ("It is treason. Possibly. To envisage the death of the king. The law recognizes it; how short the step, from dreaming to desiring to encompassing. We call it 'imagining' his death: the thought is father to the deed, and the deed is born raw, ugly, premature.").

27. Id. at 259–60.

28. Id. at 326, 327, 328.

29. Id. at 353–54.

30. Cf. Margery S. Schauer and Frederick Schauer, "Law as the Engine of State: The Trial of Anne Boleyn," William & Mary Law Review 22: 49, 50 (1980) ("When law is used as 'an engine of state,' it explains as much about law as about the state." (paraphrasing T. F. Plucknett's observation that "the forms of law became the engines for the perpetration of judicial murders")).

31. See Ives, *The Life and Death of Anne Boleyn*, 320 ("The Tudor rule was arrest first, interrogate later; no need to wait to collect evidence; delay spelled danger, particularly for Thomas Cromwell.").

32. Mantel, *Bring Up the Bodies*, 310.

33. Thomas Wriothesley was a cousin of Charles Wriothesley, who wrote the *Chronicle of England During the Reign of the Tudors* quoted in the epigraph.

34. Mantel, *Bring Up the Bodies*, 341.

35. Id. at 349.

36. "10 Ways to Sex Up a Dossier," *Guardian*, September 23, 2003 (describing allegations that the British government "sexed up" a dossier dealing with Iraq's weapons as a prelude to the 2002 invasion of Iraq).

37. Mantel, *Bring Up the Bodies*, 349.

38. See Ives, *The Life and Death of Anne Boleyn*, 322–23 (discussing the rationale for and procedure leading to the commission).

39. Mantel, *Bring Up the Bodies*, 364–65, 366.

40. Id. at 373, 374. Ives notes, "Defendants in a Tudor criminal trial—even more, a state trial—were at an enormous disadvantage. They had no advance warning of the evidence to be put, and since defence counsel was not allowed, they were reduced to attempting to rebut a public interrogation by hostile and well-prepared Crown prosecutors determined not so much to present the government case as to secure a conviction by fair questions or foul" (*The Life and Death of Anne Boleyn*, 340).

41. Mantel, *Bring Up the Bodies*, 374, 375 ("There is a yelp from one of the justices. . . . Norfolk says, 'These fellows tell me I have not done it right, I cannot say burning or beheading, I have to say one, and they say it must be burning, that is how a woman suffers when she is a traitor."). See also Ives, *The Life and Death of Anne Boleyn*, 341 ("An angry rustle went round the judges; such an either/or judgment was most improper!").

42. Mantel, *Bring Up the Bodies*, 377. See also *Ives, The Life and Death of Anne Boleyn*, 342 ("Rochford showed his contempt by reading out what Cromwell wanted kept secret.").

43. Mantel, *Bring Up the Bodies*, 374.

44. At least one spoken delivery of the words, by Simon Vance, conveys a clearly self-congratulatory state of mind. Hear *Bring Up the Bodies*, Audible.com, ch. 16, 7:00, Macmillan Audio (2012).

45. "Hilary Mantel: 'If I'm Suffering, I Can Make That Pay," *Guardian*, October 17, 2012.

46. Mantel, *Bring Up the Bodies*, 399, 406.

47. Mantel, *Wolf Hall*, 80.

48. Mantel, *Bring Up the Bodies*, 323 ("He means to begin, when he has time to plan it, some form of registration, documentation to record baptisms so he can count the king's subjects and know who they are, or at least, who their mothers say they are.").

49. G. R. Elton, "Thomas Cromwell Redivivus," in *Studies in Tudor and Stuart Politics and Government*, ed. G. R. Elton (Cambridge: Cambridge University Press), 3:373.

50. Elton, "The Political Creed of Thomas Cromwell," 76, 92.

51. R. B. Wernham, review of *The Tudor Revolution in Government*, *English Historical Review* 71: 92, 93 (1956).

52. Elton, "The Political Creed of Thomas Cromwell," 70 (arguing that "the ideas underlying the Reformation emanated from Cromwell rather than the king, and that the Reformation legislation embodies his views of Church and State").

53. Id. at 92.

54. Wernham, review, 94.

55. Brendan Bradshaw, "The Tudor Commonwealth: Reform and Revision," *Historical Journal* 22: 455, 461 (1979).

56. Elton, *The Tudor Revolution in Government: Administrative Changes in the Reign of Henry VIII* (Cambridge: Cambridge University Press, 1967), 94.

57. Wernham, review, 94.

58. Mantel, *Bring Up the Bodies*, 70, 43.

59. Mantel, *Wolf Hall*, 83.

60. *Life and Letters of Thomas Cromwell*, ed. R. B. Merriman (Oxford: Clarendon Press, 1902), 2:129.

61. Statute in Restraint of Appeals, 24 Henry VIII c. 12 (1533).

62. Elton, *The Tudor Constitution*, 25 n.61. See also Mantel, *Wolf Hall*, 153 ("The law of praemunire dates from another century. No one who is alive now quite knows what it means. From day to day it seems to mean what the king says it means.").

63. 24 Henry VIII c. 12.

64. See Alison L. LaCroix, *The Ideological Origins of American Federalism* (Cambridge, MA: Harvard University Press, 2010), 12.

65. See Elton, *The Tudor Constitution*, 341.

66. Anne's chamberlain, Sir Edward Baynton, who helped collect evidence against her, wrote, "Here is much communication that no man will confess anything against her, but all-only Mark of any actual thing" (quoted in Ives, *The Life and Death of Anne Boleyn*, 326).

67. Id.

68. Mantel, *Bring Up the Bodies*, 276.

69. This scene, which takes place on a 1535 visit to Katherine of Aragon in exile, is illustrative:

> "How do we know you?" a sentry bellows. "Show your colours."
>
> "Tell him show a light and let me in," he says, " or I'll show his backside my boot."
>
> He has to say these things, when he's up-country; it's expected of him, the king's common adviser. (Id. at 83)

70. Elton, *The Tudor Constitution*, 172 (noting that while the Court of Star Chamber did not torture, the Privy Council did use the rack, and that confusion about which institution conducted torture stems from "a total confusion between this court of law [Star Chamber] and the security services of the state [the Privy Council]"). Elton also observes that "all governments of the day" used torture to extract the details of treason (172n28).

71. Mantel, *Bring Up the Bodies*, 268, 293, 323.

72. Id. at 325–26.

73. Ives concludes that Cromwell likely did not torture Smeaton, other than through "psychological pressure," perhaps including a promise of a pardon if he confessed, or perhaps a promise to avoid death by drawing, hanging, and quartering. Cromwell also had Smeaton (and none of the other prisoners) held in irons, which Ives speculates was "an earnest of what worse might befall if he changed his story" (*The Life and Death of Anne Boleyn*, 327).

74. Mantel, *Bring Up the Bodies*, 329, 330.

75. Id. at 277.

76. Id.

77. Cromwell asks Smeaton, " 'You have had to do with the queen how many times?' Mark says, 'A thousand.' [Cromwell's servant] gives him a little slap. 'Three times or four.' " Cromwell replies, "Thank you." (id. at 284).

78. Id. at 352.

79. Id. at 299, 285.

5

Representing Anne Green

HISTORICAL AND LITERARY FORM AND THE SCENES OF THE CRIME IN OXFORD, 1651

Marina Leslie

IN DECEMBER 1650, during an Assize Court session in Oxford, a twenty-two-year-old unwed house servant named Anne Green was sentenced to hang for the murder of her illegitimate newborn child. There was nothing remarkable about the jury's guilty verdict nor unexpected in the capital punishment meted out to her. Public attitudes toward unmarried mothers for much of the seventeenth century were neither generous nor forgiving, and the Infanticide Act of 1624, under which she was convicted, represented a particularly aggressive legislative response to the public perception that alarming numbers of unmarried women—particularly women in service—were not only concealing their pregnancies but actually killing off their illegitimate offspring in order to hide their misdeeds.[1] Yet despite her low social standing, the ignominy of the crime with which she was charged, and even her guilty verdict, Green became a public cause célèbre. She was a supremely unlikely hero for still unlikelier causes because of a remarkable turn of events—her failure to die.

This essay sets out to revisit and recover the scene(s) of Green's crime and to examine her enduring textual remains in two principal locations: the archive and the historical novel. The archive is represented by the surviving contemporary pamphlets that sensationalize and memorialize her case.[2] The historical novel in evidence is Iain Pears's *An Instance of the Fingerpost*, a historical "whodunit" in which a character based upon Green plays a pivotal role.[3] Rather than treat these as discrete repositories of fact *or* fiction, law *or* literature, respectively, I want to consider each in turn as a source of highly mediated representations of Green, in which her status as a potent but limited exemplar is shaped and deployed in the service of a variety of narratives whose motives and morals have almost nothing to do with Green herself.

I argue that it is only by connecting the sometimes incongruent, sometimes overlapping legal and historical representations of Green to her more literary representations that we can arrive at a coherent account of her situation. To demonstrate the strangely mixed evidence, I turn first to the surviving contemporary pamphlets upon which any reconstruction of actual events must rest. Their documentary value notwithstanding, these early modern news accounts include conspicuously featured literary elements that have excited virtually no discussion. The most often cited of the pamphlets, *Newes from the Dead*, includes forty-four poems in English, Latin, and French written to commemorate the occasion.[4] The two other surviving pamphlets, *A Wonder of Wonders* and *A Declaration from Oxford*, have no poetry but place at their literal and literary center the device of the dream vision, which, while offered as part of a factual account, shares generic features with literary texts having genealogies reaching back to classical times. It is important not to mistake these literary elements as decorative or superfluous to the news accounts in which they were printed. Indeed precisely those features that we would identify as literary, and therefore most suspect in offering "evidence," presented for early modern readers the rhetorical and aesthetic features and exegetical conventions that made heightened claims on credibility. Finally, I will argue that in both the archive and the novel the historical Green is ultimately legible only as a fiction (legal as well as literary) and that fully comprehending her historical situation is, paradoxically, to watch her disappear as a material and autonomous historical subject. However, before we can evaluate Green's literary effects, it is necessary to return to the scene of the crime and to review what were reported to be the facts of Anne Green's case and the situation of Oxford in the wake of the civil wars.

RECONSTRUCTING ANNE GREEN

It was in late November 1650 that Green, then a servant at Duns Tew, the Oxfordshire estate of Sir Thomas Read, was taken into custody for the murder of her newborn child. The child would have been as much of a scandal living as dead, not only because Green was unmarried but because she had publicly declared that Sir Thomas's teenage grandson, Jeffery, was the child's father.[5] The child did not live, however, and when its body was discovered hidden in a dung heap in the "house of office," or privy, Sir Thomas demanded justice.[6] As Green's master and chief prosecutor, a former sheriff of Oxfordshire, Berkshire, and Hertfordshire, and the largest landowner in the area, Sir Thomas was in a powerfully privileged position to make the claim against her. Her admission to bearing the child and her claim that it was Sir Thomas's illegitimate grandchild would not have aided in her defense, which she would have presented herself without legal representation.[7]

What exactly was said during her trial we do not know. Unfortunately no court record of her case survives.[8] What happened after Green climbed the scaffold on Saturday, December 15, 1650, is necessarily a matter for historical reconstruction and speculation based on the surviving published testimonies and representations of events. Yet ironically in Green's case, as we shall see, it is not so much the dearth of documentation but its surplus that makes the historical reconstruction of actual events such a vexed matter. Although the surviving accounts of her experience vary significantly on important details I discuss below, all accounts more or less agree on the following sequence of events: Anne Green prayed and spoke briefly to those assembled. The executioner then turned her from the ladder and she hung by her neck for approximately half an hour while her friends attempted to hasten her end—and thus relieve her suffering—by hanging onto her legs and pounding on her chest. A soldier from the local Oxford garrison aided in this humanitarian effort by landing five or six powerful blows to her chest with his musket. After about half an hour, when no further signs of life were detected in her, she was cut down, placed in a coffin, and delivered to the lodgings of William Petty, where Petty and a group of Oxford physicians and experimentalists were gathered for the purpose of an anatomy demonstration.

This should have been the end of Anne Green and, given the lack of surviving court documents, the last ephemeral record of her sad fate as well. However, to the astonishment of the Oxford physicians, and no doubt to her own as well, Green revived on the table even as she was being prepared for dissection.[9] Her celebrity was immediate and widespread, generating a number of accounts and commentaries in news pamphlets, letters, diary entries, and poems. Green, the lowborn house servant and convicted infanticide, whom Petty inauspiciously described as "of a middle stature, strong, fleshie, and of indifferent good feature," was suddenly regarded as a wonder of the world.[10] There was even a sudden influx of what might be called resurrection tourism as thousands were reported to be flooding into Oxford for a chance to see this "miracle." Indeed this was likely the first occasion that brought civilians in any number back into Oxford, a city that had recently been ravaged by battle, famine, and disease as the site of Charles I's final failed attempt to regain power against parliamentary forces. Green's seeming return from the dead excited curiosity and inspired wonder, but it also required interpretive intervention. For as extraordinary as this turn of events may have been, Green's survival of her hanging was not unprecedented, whereas her subsequent exoneration for the infanticide was. Moreover the counterintuitiveness of the seeming unanimity in the surviving print record regarding Green's blamelessness is all the more striking given (1) the contemporary assumption that single women in service were contributing to an epidemic of infanticides; (2) the unlikely constituencies and interests convinced of her innocence despite the verdict of her trial; and (3) the very different conclusions drawn from a shared conclusion that Green suffered rather than committed a terrible injustice.

While all accounts of Green's revivification mention the evident hand of Providence in the matter, divine intervention in defense of injured innocence was not the only interpretation available for her failure to die.[11] First, the law was clear that her sentence was to hang until dead, and it should not be assumed that the law had any predisposition to show tenderness to a woman who survived hanging. Robert Plot in his *Natural History of Oxford-shire* (1676) describes Green's miraculous revival in a section entitled, inauspiciously enough, "Concerning the death of women," alongside a case from 1658 (just seven years later), with which it shares any number of uncanny parallels.[12] In this second case a young serving girl, whom Plot calls only "Elizabeth,"[13] was accused and convicted of murdering a bastard child and subsequently hanged; her body was given to anatomists, who revived her, following medical protocols similar to those used on Green. However, unlike Green, in whose case Plot sees the workings of "the Justice of Heaven," Elizabeth, as he recounts the story, "having no friends to appear for her . . . was barbarously dragg'd the Night following . . . and drawn up over one of the Arms of the Trees and hanged a second time 'till she was dead." Although Plot and other contemporary commentators are quick to note God's intercession on Green's behalf, they are not at all clear why such a similar case would not have similarly manifested God's will. Plot cites Pliny's observations that women "much more frequently revive after they have been reputed dead, than males do," adding wryly that this is "doubtless" the source of the proverb "Mulieri ne credas, ne mortuae quidem [Never trust a woman, even when she's dead]."[14] Plot's inclusion of this witticism in his account, his stated sympathy for Green notwithstanding, suggests the generic instability of Green's exemplarity. Plot asserts Green's revival as a self-evident miracle, while at the same time she offers him an irresistible occasion for a misogynist aphorism. In either representation the verification of miracles does not and cannot rest on the truthfulness of the evidence provided by women—even when that evidence is provided by their silenced and mangled bodies. An examination of the language of the Infanticide Act of 1624 provides a window on the profound early modern suspicion of female "shamming" and thus what Green's ultimate vindication required in public and in print. For although admittedly Green's physical resuscitation was supremely unlikely, her legal and literary recuperation were without question unlikelier still.

MISCARRIAGES OF JUSTICE

Single women in service in seventeenth-century England were particularly vulnerable when they found themselves pregnant, and dismissal was not the worst thing they had to fear. Parishes responsible for the care of unwed mothers and their children responded to this burden by pushing desperate women out of their jurisdiction to avoid the drain on their resources. The Poor Act of 1601 responded to the distress of parishes required to provide poor relief for illegitimate children whose mothers could not provide for them by incarcerating the mothers. Since mothers escaped such sentences only in cases where the fathers acknowledged the child and provided for its support, the law in essence criminalized female poverty while creating perverse incentives for attributing or acknowledging paternity.[15] Working women with illegitimate offspring therefore found themselves in the double bind of being unable to work and yet criminalized for being unable to support their offspring. Therefore the motivation for and pressures on unwed mothers of illegitimate children to take alternative steps, that is, to disguise the pregnancy and abandon or even murder the child, were eventually perceived so great as to require additional legislative action. The Act of 1624 targeted "lewd women" so as "to prevent the destroying and murthering of bastard children."[16] However, since murder was already a capital offense and women were already subject to incarceration for producing illegitimate offspring, what, it might fairly be asked, was the intent or impact of this legislation that wasn't legally redundant?

At the least the Act of 1624 pointed to a political consensus that current law was not sufficiently effective to address the perceived problem. More significantly it demonstrated that Parliament was willing to pass legislation that singularly shifted the burden of evidence to a presumption of guilt in the infanticide of bastards, despite the presumed protections of common law. Although married women could also be suspected of producing illegitimate offspring, the framing of the law explicitly focused on unmarried mothers whose bastard children were obviously and by definition the illegitimate products of illicit sexual behavior. In such cases the law required that the mother be *presumed guilty* for the death of her offspring unless she was able to provide convincing evidence of her innocence in the form of a witness.[17] The language of the statute made this assumption of guilt and women's deadly motives clear: "Lewd women that have been delivered of bastard children, to avoid their shame and escape punishment, do secretly bury or conceal the death of their children and after if the child be found dead the same women do allege that the said child was born dead; whereas it falleth out sometimes (although hardly is it to be proved) that the said child or children were murdered by the said women their lewd mothers or by their assent or procurement."[18] In other words, in order to escape detection and prosecution for murder, the demonstrably "lewd" mothers of illegitimate children were declared to be taking advantage of the relatively common occurrence of stillbirth and the difficulty of determining after the fact whether a child was born alive or dead or, for that matter, whether a child alive at birth subsequently died of natural causes or perished through an act of violence. Despite or rather because of the acknowledged difficulty of demonstrating the cause of infant mortality, the statute placed the burden of proof entirely upon the accused.

Policing women's behavior is at the center of the law's concerns, and female secrecy, perjury, and conspiracy are underscored as the primary problems. Focusing specifically on the behavior of hiding the dead child rather than the child's death per se, the law supplements the provisions against murder. The child is less the victim under this statute than the irrefutable evidence of his mother's lewdness and therefore, it was reasoned, her murderous motives to hide her shame. The statute aimed to fill in where both common law and natural law were seen to have failed, expressing a powerful discomfort with women who eluded the regulations provided under the laws of coverture. The presumptive culprits, unmarried adult women in service were already regarded as dangerously mobile, unconstrained in their ability to act on their desires, unsupervised by husbands, and beyond the control of (and with at least a degree of financial independence from) their fathers. Even aside from the crimes of which they were accused, these women were suspected of exceeding and evading the social and legal codes of conduct regulating feminine decorum. As the 1624 statute makes explicit, they were also believed to be—quite literally—getting away with murder.

Given the legislative, social, and historical responses to unmarried mothers I've just outlined it would seem anything but obvious that Anne Green would find herself exemplifying wronged innocence and the miscarriage of justice. I therefore want to consider what has quite strikingly passed without mention in accounts of her fate in recent scholarship, that is, the unexpectedness and downright peculiarity of the sympathetic representations of her survival and the general agreement about the injustice of the judgment against her. Indeed there was nothing about her situation, *including her revivification*, that made obvious the role she was to play and the attentions she was to receive. It is therefore important to bear in mind the full weight of the legal narratives available to contain and dispatch even a revivified infanticide if we are to assess the peculiar forces at work in Green's restoration to life, retroactive innocence, and unexpected exemplarity in the popular literature, poetry, and contemporary novels she inspired.

ANNE GREEN'S AFTERLIFE IN PRINT

The principal architect of Green's reputation was William Petty, a brilliant polymath, inventor, and entrepreneur. While employed as physician general to the Commonwealth forces in Ireland, Petty developed the statistical and surveying techniques that allowed him to greatly enrich the Protectorate (and himself) by mapping out the transfer of huge tracts of confiscated lands. After the Restoration he would go on to become a founding member of the Royal Society. His many successful ventures under both commonwealth and royalist governments offered ample proof he was in practice as well as theory an adept political strategist.[19] In 1650 Petty was twenty-seven, an ambitious young man with a new appointment to an anatomy lectureship at Brasenose College at Oxford. Petty wrote a letter to his mentor Samuel Hartlib two days after the hanging in which he recounts the "miracle" of Green's revival, concluding that "my endeavors in this business have bettered my reputation."[20] Two days after that an unattributed letter dated 18 December 1650 that contained a very similar and in places identical account found its way into print in the highly partisan parliamentary news weekly *Mercurius Politicus*. The anonymous "Letter from Oxford" recounts how Green was "gotten with child" by Sir Thomas's grandson and how Green, "near the fourth month of her time" and "over-working her self about her ordinary employment of turning Malt, fell in travel, [with] (neither herself nor her fellow servants well-knowing what the matter might be)."[21] Green's "overworking" is as notable in this description as the abortive birth of a child who was "not above a span long" and whose sex could be "scarce distinguished." Her hard work combined with the alleged paternity of the child relies on the partisan parliamentarian sympathies of the publication's readership to shift the moral fault from the unfortunate servant to her royalist gentry master and his intemperate grandson. The fact that the birth is so premature that both Green and the other servants are described as ignorant of the cause of her pains addresses the presumed concerns about her murderous intentions and a conspiracy to evade discovery. Finally, and most important, the descriptions of the newborn as insufficiently developed to survive serves to marshal the necessary material evidence to establish it as stillborn and not a victim of foul play. In the "Letter from Oxford" the evident hero of the day is Dr. Petty himself, who, along with Henry Clerke and Thomas Willis, is credited with bringing Green back to life. Their collective skills as physicians notwithstanding, establishing Green's innocence is as important to their fame as it is to her continued survival as a convicted felon. For his efforts with respect to the latter, the governor of the parliamentary garrison at Oxford is also praised for his wisdom in securing her reprieve. The "Letter from Oxford" goes so far as to declare, that of the "thousands of people come from all parts to see her," "all seeme to be satisfied of the wenches innocency to the murther" (469).

This epistolary entry in *Mercurius Politicus* was not simply a sensational news report; it was also a brilliant piece of media management. Petty was a newcomer to Oxford, brought in as part of Oliver Cromwell's concerted effort to discipline and reform the university that had served as Charles I's court in exile. Petty, however, was anything but a doctrinaire puritan, and the group of experimentalists with whom he collaborated was diverse in its composition. Henry Clerke, described in the letter as another principal in Green's recovery, was a former royalist who submitted to the examination of the parliament visitors to Oxford in 1648, while Thomas Willis, the future father of cognitive neuroscience and endocrinology, remained a steadfast and unapologetic royalist, refusing to take the oath of conformity demanded by the visitors. Petty saw in Green's resurrection an opportunity to bring attention and admiration, from both within and beyond Oxford, to the extracurricular and largely marginalized activities of the Oxford Experimentalist Club and at the same time to ease tensions between the largely royalist faculty and the influx of Parliament-sanctioned scholars who were in many cases replacing them. By refocusing attention on the bipartisan and cross-sectarian success represented by Green's revival, Petty could bring good press to Oxford generally, while shining a particularly flattering light on his own and his co-experimentalists' efforts.

However, it was at this point that Petty lost some control over his careful management of Green's fame and thus her symbolic power, when she became an equally unwitting standard-bearer for another faction and another narrative, in this case for the dissenting sectarians known as Levellers.[22] Oxford's garrison of soldiers was known to harbor some of the last remnants of Leveller sympathizers after Cromwell and Fairfax just the year before had brutally crushed the so-called Banbury Mutiny in Burford, only twenty miles west of Oxford. In two very similar pamphlets published in swift succession in 1651, *A Wonder of Wonders and A Declaration from Oxford*, Green is represented as the eloquent defender of the oppressed and exploited. In both pamphlets she gives a conventional enough scaffold speech, acknowledging herself a sinner, though steadfastly maintaining her innocence of infanticide. However, after her hanging she opens her eyes and delivers a vatic speech from beyond the grave with all the authority of a heavenly vision: "Behold Gods providence, and his wonder of wonders, which indeed, is a deliverance so remarkable, since the ceasing of Miracles, that it cannot be parallel'd in all Ages for the space of 300 years, and withal it may remain upon record, for a precedent to all Magistrates, and courts of Judicature, to take a special care in denouncing a sentence, without due and legal process, according to the known Laws of the Land by an impartial and uncorrupted Jury, either of men or women &c."[23] Her postmortem clarion call to reform jury trials and due process has unmistakable resonance with the complaints of the Banbury mutineers and the show trials of Leveller leaders in London, as well as the well-documented discontent of the local Oxford garrison. In "A Declaration from Oxford," Green goes on to describe seeing in her vision ". . . 4 little boyes with wings, being four Angels, saying, Woe unto them that decree unrighteous Decrees, and take away the right from the Judges, that the innocent may be their prey" (4). The odd specificity of this vision I take as an oblique but pointed reference to the four young men whom Cromwell had summarily executed in the field as leaders of the Burford Mutiny.[24]

Although the topical focus was on Green's revivification, both *A Wonder of Wonders* and *A Declaration from Oxford* embrace a familiar and inflammatory political rhetoric that targets both the royalist abuse of privilege, represented in this case by Sir Thomas, and the injustice of the parliamentarian courts. Green's rapturous vision and hortatory voice convey a providential warning to those corrupt authorities who overstep their bounds and abrogate the natural rights of men.

The Oxford experimentalists, doubtless guided by Petty's canny political instincts, responded to these expressions of political discontent and even possible insurrection with *Newes from the Dead.* This pamphlet is strikingly different in tone and content, even as it relates the same basic sequence of events and shares an unequivocal assumption of Green's innocence. *Newes from the Dead* is the only surviving pamphlet discussing the case that does not include the cover woodcut illustration featuring Green. There is no vision, graphic, or narrative of the afterlife, and Green is represented with no voice or even memory from the time she was brought to the scaffold to fourteen hours after she awakened on the anatomy table. The pamphlet describes her with the mechanist metaphor of a clock whose hands have been stopped and then set in motion again.[25] Green is thus transformed from a righteous angelic voice to a voiceless automaton. God is not absent from *Newes from the Dead*, but his intervention is cited mainly to confirm the right action and moral seriousness of the Oxford physicians.

Most of *Newes from the Dead* is taken up with a minutely detailed account of the remedies administered, in what amounts and at what intervals, and her responses to them. She is put to bed with a "good woman," who is instructed to rub her limbs, presumably to improve her circulation, and offer her services as a human bed warmer. Despite the importance of Green's remarkable recovery to the future fame of the Oxford physicians, the medical treatment she receives at their hands seems neither remarkable nor particularly experimental. The pamphlet details a sequence of remedies that include tickling her throat with a feather, forcing her to drink strong spirits, applying warm poultices, giving her numerous enemas, and bleeding her repeatedly. The few iatrochemical treatments they administer seem designed to cover all bases more than to feature medically advanced treatments, and with ingredients like "preserved mummy" even they seem to be presented as much for their magical as their scientific properties. Where the other two pamphlets represent the soldiers as the protectors of Green, willing and ready to stand against those in power determined to hang her again, *Newes from the Dead* bases its legal defense on forensic evidence and the medical diagnosis of spontaneous abortion that had already been published in the "Letter from Oxford." Thus *Newes from the Dead* takes a decidedly less politically inflammatory approach to exonerating Green than the Dissenter accounts to focus importantly on the intersection of medical and legal discourse. The Oxford physicians' defense of Green's innocence is careful not to impeach legal authority even as it contests the outcome of her trial. Instead Petty, adhering to the requirements of the 1624 Infanticide Law, provides the required witness, a midwife who is described as having examined the child's remains. It is unclear if her testimony was presented at trial, but it provides both the medical evidence and the necessary witness to exonerate Green. Somewhat paradoxically, Petty's relation of the midwife's conclusions (that may have been either overlooked or overruled at trial) invests them with the medical, rhetorical, and political clout that the midwife alone would not have enjoyed; and yet her first-hand testimony offers him the forensic evidence that satisfies both the experimental and legal protocols necessary for Green's exoneration.

THE UNBEARABLE LIGHTNESS OF ANNE GREEN

Among all of the accounts of Green's revivification, *Newes from the Dead* is the pamphlet that is most often cited from the seventeenth century through the present, and it has found a small but secure perch in the history of science.[26] There is a second tradition for discussing Green's case that spans the centuries and focuses on the legal implications of her case, for which a recent entry is Randall Martin's study of Green as an important figure in changing attitudes about equity.[27] But what neither scientific nor legal histories have registered or discussed about this document beyond a cursory mention is the inclusion of a number of prefatory poems in English, Latin, and French produced by a variety of Oxford scholars, which praise Green in classically inflected verse that is far more mock than epic. Although a few poems take a serious and genuinely commendatory tone, these generally direct their praise to the success of the physicians, whereas the poems that are most heavily leavened with sardonic and cynical witticisms, which is to say the vast majority of them, invoke the dubiousness of Green's character to exploit the satirical and comic potential of her survival.

The inclusion of these poems has most likely been ignored because they seem strangely discordant with the account that follows them, which insists on Green's innocence of the charges of infanticide and asserts that a miracle was evident in her salvation. My own reading of this strange hybrid document is that it brilliantly served multiple purposes and that both the occasional poems and the prose account were, in their own ways, designed to be read against—and to help discredit—the Dissenter pamphlets that preceded it. In this two-part program the experimentalist physicians save Green and clear her of infanticide through forensic evidence designed to uphold the law, while the scholar poets satirically disqualify her as a divinely inspired voice in support of political dissent in images that dislodge her from heaven to consign her mythographically to the morally ambiguous classical underworld. Although framed as poems of praise, they are with few exceptions misogynist in tone and by design. By taking a "low" subject (female, servant, unmarried mother) and raising her up with exalted comparisons (Orpheus and Eurydice, Virbius and Virbia, et al.), the Oxford scholars conform to Aristotle's requirements for comedy in his *Poetics*, where genre is aligned with class distinctions and defined by the trajectory of their violation: the tragic fall of the great one brought low or the comic rise of one brought above his (or her) proper station. Comic in both mode and effect, these poems about Green fall more specifically into the genre of the *paradoxical encomium*, a popular humanist genre in which a poet undertook to commend a subject that seemingly defied praise. Indeed praising Green would have been for the Oxford scholars analogous to the most famous early modern paradoxical encomia addressed to topics such as folly, baldness, or a fly, that is, a patently absurd object and therefore a worthy challenge to and test of their poetic virtuosity.[28] It is only in reading the poems with and against the prose account of Green in *Newes from the Dead* that we can find both the origin and the motives for the divided representation that Plot gave her case in his *Natural History of Oxford-shire*, when he accounts her revival a miracle and with no evident sense of the irony or incongruity follows by citing the Latin tag about never trusting a dead woman.

Among the epideictic versifiers of *Newes from the Dead* Henry Perin of Trinity College can serve as a useful example of the several poets who invoke the story of Orpheus and Eurydice. His verse takes the same form as Herrick's "Upon Julia's Clothes" (published two years before and also written in tercets of iambic tetrameter) to offer a strikingly different effect in the following untitled poem:

Orpheus, to fetch his wife, did go
A Voyage to the Shades below
('Twas more than many a man would do)

The blood-less Ghosts did weepe (they say)
And Pluto groan'd, as He did play;
Yet She came back but Halfe the way.

Now we have seen a stranger sight;
Whether it was by Physick's might,
Or that (it seems) the Wench was Light.

But sure 'twill Spoyle her Marriage-day,
For who so hardy to assay
Such an Immortal *Virbia*!

Wives may deceive; and do their best
To counterfeit in all the rest;
Only let them not Dye in jest. (3–4)[29]

As in Plot's later account, we see the same mix of mythic exaltation and misogynistic degradation, and that is not by chance. Plot is referring back to his sources when he writes his account of Green in 1677, and he is not confused by this seeming conflation or, more aptly, deflation. This is indeed the work of satire, a genre with a long tradition of misogyny going back to Juvenal, among other classical practitioners, and in which Plot, himself an Oxford scholar, was as well versed as Perin and the other faux panegyrists. The fact that these poems uniformly fail to name Green as their satiric target, choosing instead to allude to her by her mythological counterparts or, more often, to substitute the generic "Woman" or "Wench," confirms that their interest is not ultimately in Anne Green at all. There is no poetic counterpart to the very specific forensic evidence that exonerates her in the prose account. Instead her revival is rendered again and again as a humorous and familiar cliché in the service of the unyielding paternalistic logic of class and gender. One of several poems attributed to HB of New College makes the case this way:

On the Shee that was Hang'd, but not Executed.
Rare Innocence! A Wench re-woman'd
See what the small Sophs say to this Fallacy.
Up to the eares in death, and scape! No kind
Was thought more fit then to tye up her wind.

Woman in this with Cats agree, I think,
Both Live and Scratch after they have tip't the Wink.
Henceforth take head of trusting Females. Shee
That Scapes Welch Parsly, Souldiers take for mee. (3)

The author opens with "rare innocence" but concludes with a clear disavowal of either the rarity or the innocence of female deception in life or death. "Welsh Parley" here refers to hemp and metonymically to the halter or rope into which it is fashioned. By escaping the noose, Green, the unnamed "Shee" of the poem, is transformed from a victim to a menace. Bidding the soldiers to "take [her] for mee," the poet reconceives the political and polemical contest between the university and the Oxford garrison soldiers as a tug-of-war over a wench not really worth fighting over, thus rhetorically and preemptively robbing the Levellers or their sympathizers of any advantage they might take in linking their cause to Green's fate. In a somewhat more elevated classical register, the same author supplies an additional poem in Latin in which Green gets as far as the ferry to the underworld but then looks back with one eye and winks with the other, a double-faced image of woman's duplicity even in (and as) the face of death.

More than one poem jokes about the difficulties in Green's legal situation, but predictably they do so in a different register than the prose account of her false accusation and wrongful conviction. In one example, a poem entitled "A Woman's Case to the Lawyers," John Watkins of Queen's College explores the possibility that Green's revivification might allow her to overcome her dubious morals but then he undercuts the same fantasy by depicting her paying a fee in the suspended and presumably comical hope that lawyers could or would make the case for her retroactive virginity:

Mother, or Maid, I pray you whether?
One, or both, or am I neither?
The Mother dyed: may't not be said
That the Surviver is a Maid?
Here, take your Fee, declare your sense;
And free me from this New Suspense.

Because this is the only poem in *Newes From the Dead* to give Green a voice and present her in the first person, it offers a particularly pointed comparison to the vatic utterances attributed to her in the Dissenter pamphlets. As Frances Dolan points out, the title of the Oxford pamphlet is ironic insofar as Green in fact brings "very little news from the dead."[30] At least she doesn't do so in the medical prose narrative. However, the title seems less strange if we allow the poems their critical due in shaping Green's story and its reception, and particularly in responding to and containing Green as a Leveller prophet. Her poetic journey through the underworld and back is designed to make abundantly clear the myriad problems that can result in letting women be the bearers of any news whatsoever, let alone news from the beyond.

Taken together the poems constitute more than half the document, and the second edition of *Newes from the Dead* greatly expands the number of poems included in the first edition, as every would-be versifier at Oxford seemed eager to get in on the joke.[31] As the production of a second edition suggests and any number of contemporary accounts make clear, Oxford University as an institution clearly benefited from the sensation that Green had created. However, the poems belie an uneasiness not only with the Dissenter hijacking of Green as a spokesmodel but also with the problems inherent in linking Oxford's institutional prestige with a woman of such low class and compromised morals, conditions that her retroactive legal vindication could not erase. The mixed genre of misogynist verse wedded to forensic evidentiary prose achieved in print what had eluded the university in recent times. Within the university *Newes from the Dead* dramatized the harmony of royalist and parliamentary voices; moreover it could paper over differences between the old guard and the new by simultaneously demonstrating the technical expertise of the experimentalists while asserting and preserving the academic privileges and disciplines that many feared were being overthrown. *Newes from the Dead* also offered a politically expedient one-two punch from the formerly royalist (and still politically and religiously divided) university in service of an urgent parliamentary political problem by attempting to contain and neutralize the populist Leveller and other Dissenter efforts to make Green a potent symbol for their cause.[32]

Taking seriously the centrality of the poetry to the political and institutional work of *Newes from the Dead* also allows us to go back to the prose representations and note a witty and knowing snicker or two that might otherwise have escaped notice. One interesting example of the doubt cast upon the Dissenter account is the very different treatment of an event mentioned in *A Declaration from Oxford*. Sir Thomas, Green's former master and prosecutor, died three days after she was revived. In the Dissenter pamphlet this was taken as yet more evidence of God's design in preserving Green and striking down her oppressors. The same evidence is given a more equivocal review in *Newes from the Dead*: "There is yet one thing more which hath been taken notice of by some, as to the Maid's defence; That her Grand Prosecutor Sir Thomas Read died with three daies after her Execution; even almost as soon as the probability of her reviving could be well confirmed to him. But because hee was an old man, and such Events are not too rashly to be commented on, I shall not make use of that observation" (7). With scientific detachment and political discretion *Newes from the Dead* brackets the death of Sir Thomas as evidence of God's will even as it casts doubt on the Dissenter pamphlet's providentialist account. By asserting that its own truth value is not in the least linked to this "observation" about the "old man's" life or death, *Newes from the Dead* ultimately frees itself from the business of divine exegesis. Green's innocence is established as a legal and medical fact, and her cure is documented as the concerted effort of professional men practicing empirical science. The poetry paradoxically erases Green with praise by never naming her as the heroine of her story, while the prose account represents Green as the inert and dreamless woman who awakens only to express her preference of warm beer to the other remedies offered by the physicians.

Newes from the Dead deals its final blow to the credibility of the Leveller pamphlets in lines that deliberately echo the themes brought up in the poems:

> I may perhaps be expected by some (and 'tis a pity I can give them no better satisfaction) that I should here relate some story (like those of Orpheus or Aeneus in the Poets) of what fine visions this maid saw in the otherworld; what celestial musick, or hellish howling she heard; what spirits she conversed with; and what Revelations she brought back with her, concerning the Present Times, or the Events of things to come. But, for such matters the Ballad-makers must rest contented: since shee (as you have heard) was so far from knowing any thing whilst shee was dead, that she remembered not what had happened to her even when shee was yet alive.

This is an odd passage insofar as it seems to disavow precisely the sort of poetic conceits about Orpheus that the document begins with; however, the difference it establishes here is telling. *Newes from the Dead* acknowledges the comical fancifulness of such efforts and thus has power over its representations. The poems are thus revealed to be less about Anne Green per se and more a means for mocking the Leveller's efforts to establish her as a messenger from God. *Newes from the Dead* draws attention to genre precisely to make its own claims to legal, scientific *and* literary authority. Conversely the Dissenter pamphlets are compared to the lowest form of sensational broadside ballads because they do not know the difference between truth and fiction and are therefore consigned to a popular genre that does not make such distinctions. Paradoxically perhaps to us, but not so for early modern audiences, *Newes from the Dead* uses its classical poetics as well as its scientific prose to establish itself as the vehicle of truth, while the serious political message of the Leveller pamphlets is reduced to the cheap, populist genre of verse ballad, even though they contain no verse at all.

THE COLD CASE OF ANNE GREEN AND THE NOVEL AS FORENSIC LAB

In 2006 the Oxford art historian and novelist Iain Pears published *An Instance of the Fingerpost*, a historical novel in which a character named Sarah Blundy, explicitly modeled on Green, figures importantly.[33] Although the novel is set a few years later, during the Restoration, and involves an entirely different set of principal characters, the central mystery of the narrative revolves around Blundy, her guilt or innocence, unlikely resurrection, and mysterious fate. The novel is divided into four chapters, each narrated by a different character, beginning with Marco de Cola, a Venetian gentleman merchant-scholar and would-be experimentalist who offers an outsider's view of Oxford in 1663. While de Cola seems to be an imagined or composite character, the novel's other three narrators are all named for or based on historical figures: Jack Prescott, whose character and situation is inspired by the mentally ill son of the royalist traitor Sir Richard Willys; Dr. John Wallis, the noted mathematician and code breaker; and Anthony Wood, the noted Oxford scholar and antiquarian.

Each of these narrators—the fictional and the historical—is grounded in minutely detailed historical research, and yet, significantly, none of them is reliable. Pears's project and plot offer a kind of romance of the archive, which is to say that he brings the archive alive as a series of interested misrepresentations, inconclusive facts, half-truths, and outright lies recovered in a series of documents: letters, wills, coded communications, and personal papers. His stories are drawn from history, not to verify but to dramatize and elaborate what gets left out of historical accounts. He takes pains to reveal that the narrative structure of history, that which gives it coherence and makes it persuasive, is precisely that which is least reliable about it. Again and again in the novel we are given narratives that make sense of the fragmented accounts that can be cobbled together by our narrators, only to discover again and again how incomplete and misleading they were. Our ability to put together a more complete story is, in the end, based on our ability to direct our skeptical analysis not only to the courts, under new management with the Restoration, and the New Science, still under construction at Oxford in the 1660s, but to flawed humans who literally and figuratively made and recorded that history. That the romantic hero of the story, so far as it has one, is the naïve, passionate, and charming Anthony Wood, whose indispensible and comprehensive (which is to say long, boring, and tedious) institutional history of Oxford has never struck anyone as remotely romantic, is both a delicious irony and a serious commentary on the inevitable gap between the historian and his history.

Sarah Blundy is not given a chance to tell her own story; it is an important feature of the novel that her description by each of the four key narrators provides a fractured, kaleidoscopic portrait of her. While Blundy is not identical to Green in biography or characterization, perhaps her most important similarity is the problematic and unreliable nature of our knowledge of her. Indeed Blundy is not identical to herself in any of the four portraits of her, which suggests Pears's sensitive and historically informed reading of Green's situation in the masculine academic culture of the time, as well as the volatile and often violent sectarian politics of the civil wars and their aftermath. For example, although we do not learn this for much of the novel, Blundy's parents are revealed to be active in the Leveller cause, and her father, presumed dead, has been living in hiding. During her furtive visits to the secret meetings of the surviving Levellers Blundy reveals a mysterious talent that further ties her to Green. She preaches sermons that do not seem to come from her or be "of" her. Blundy is in fact "a prophetess," and consistent with the representation of contemporary female prophets, she draws her authority and her language from God and scripture. Indeed, her sermons also seem to conflate her voice with God's in ways that attribute Christ's power, grace, and sacrifice to her: "My grace and my peace and my mercy and my blessing are upon you. Few see my coming, and fewer still will see my going. This evening the last days begin, and men move to entrap me, the same men as before, the same as always. I forgive them now, for I will remember sins and iniquities no longer; I am come to give absolution in my blood. I must die and all must die, and will keep on dying to the end in every generation" (606–7). Whoever is understood to be speaking here, woman or God, these mystical and messianic lines represent the rare occasion when, Blundy is directly quoted. Nonetheless, even her prophetic voice is entirely mediated by the descriptions of Wood who follows and observes her. Significantly she herself has no memory of what she says during her vatic trances. "I do not know what it is," she says to Wood. "There is no point wondering, as I am sure you do. I have no recollection of what I say or why I say it" (608). In fact she does not want to be a prophet and she has no explanation for her gift. Pears manages both to echo and to realign the values of the Green pamphlets, asserting Blundy's gifts as real and yet demonstrating her lack of control over her story or even her own voice.

The questions raised by the novel's partial and unraveling stories about Blundy explore many of the same issues raised by the incompatible seventeenth-century representations of Green. As in the early modern descriptions of Green, the contradictions tend to exist within rather than divide between clear points of view. Whether

Blundy is a whore and a murderer or a young innocent working in an unwholesome house, whether she is a seducer or a victim of seduction, and even whether she is a vessel for dangerous sectarian dissidents, or a spiritual medium for a divine message are all questions that are drawn from the historical narratives surrounding Green. And, as in Green's story, the answers depend not only on who is telling the story but on what their particular interests and motives are at the moment of the telling, as well as the interests and motives of those to whom they are telling the story. Within the novel the "truth"—at least as far as Wood is able to tell it—is the least satisfying story of all, and it moves no one to mercy or action to have it told. It does not save Blundy, and it is rebutted, suppressed, and ultimately burned with Wood's papers at the end. The multiple narratives of the novel lay out such possibilities not to make us choose between them but rather to dramatize the multiple ways in which the "truth" of Blundy's story (and, by extension, Green's) is both less and more than the sum of its representations.

In this respect Blundy does not represent the only version of Green's story to appear in the novel. In Book 1, chapter 15, Richard Lower, one of the Oxford experimental scientists whose professional activities and personal rivalries are a central interest of the novel, attends a hanging in hopes of bringing home a body for dissection. The woman whose execution he witnesses was charged with killing a man who was said to have raped her, and "the town was by no means convinced of her guilt." However, the jury judged this a lie since she had conceived a child, "which cannot occur without the woman taking pleasure in the act" (146). When she miscarries the child, she loses her last chance to forestall her execution by "pleading the belly" and thus securing a reprieve. What her defenders viewed as "an unfortunate outcome," "those who believed in her guilt considered divine providence." But in the end the public contest between the town and the jury comes to nothing. The poor woman bungles her scaffold speech "and quite lost the sympathy of the crowd" (146). Her failure of rhetoric comes before and ends with her hanging. This of course is neither a true nor a mirror image of Green's case, but an alternative fictional universe where successful rhetoric, revivification, and redemption are not on offer. Ironically this imagined account is far more realistic and typical than the unlikely story recovered from history. Pears's novel underscores in his representation of these multiple female felons both their literal and figurative fungability. The body that Lower carries off with him for the benefit of science comes to play a critical role in saving Blundy by offering a cadaver to substitute for hers when she herself is brought to Lower's laboratory after her hanging and revives, like Green, on the table.

In Pears's double image of Green's story we see one redeemed Green proxy who is saved by masculine intervention and an unredeemable Green who is not. Although the novel suggests sympathies for both women's stories, the version of Green whose physical labors are menial and whose reproductive labors are abortive—that is, the one who is most like Green—is obliterated from the novel and from history. She is never even offered a fictional name. Although Blundy is saved from death, whether this was due to luck (be it the unnamed woman's bad luck or Blundy's good luck), science, or divine intervention is left radically ambiguous. Blundy's survival depends now on her disappearance to protect her from those who wished her, and now believe her to be, dead. At the end of the novel she leaves Oxford and takes passage to America. Inexplicably she never arrives: "It was the last anyone ever heard of her. She never arrived in America and it was assumed she had fallen overboard. But the boat was becalmed at the time and was in any case so crowded it was difficult to imagine anyone coming to grief without being noticed. Yet she simply disappeared one day in full sunlight and without any sound, as though she had been taken up bodily into the heavens" (672). As was true of the historical Anne Green, Sarah Blundy's final act is represented as her ability to disappear in plain sight. As Green and Blundy are both the cynosure and cypher of their respective narratives, their stories do not belong to them. The fantasy of a complete archive is shown to be just that, as Pears dramatizes the limits of preserved documents, their authors, and their archivists. His novel reveals how the records of history that survive and those that are never written are as problematic to the dream of a complete historical record as those documents that vanish or burn. Inevitably *both* Green and her fictional shadows leave only ventriloquized textual remains, which ultimately can only reveal those who attempt to tell their stories, however imperfectly.

NOTES

1. The Act of 1624 remained in effect until 1803, when proof of murder became the requirement in infanticide cases. Infanticide studies that have focused on the eighteenth century (for which there is also a more complete record of cases) have noted that juries were increasingly reluctant to convict under the law, especially if the mother could present any evidence that she had prepared for the pregnancy, known as "the defense of linens." However, the extant evidence suggests that in the period from the act's origins to the Restoration the law was enforced—and juries were willing to convict. The noted historian of crime James A. Sharpe argues, "It seems likely that, taking Europe as a whole, more women were executed for infanticide than for the more familiar offence of witchcraft." Sharpe further notes that convictions were linked to the social class of the accused and that "the typical infanticidal mother was an unmarried servant girl" James A. Sharpe, *Crime in Early Modern England, 1550–1750*, 2nd edition (New York: Longman, 1999), 158.

2. The pamphlets I examine are Richard Watkins, *Newes from the Dead* (Oxford: printed by Leonard Lichfield and H. Hall for Tho. Robinson, 1651), copy from the British Library; the second edition of *Newes from the Dead,* was printed in the same year and by the same publishers, and is preserved in a copy in the Bodleian Library; W. Burdet, *A Wonder of Wonders* (London: John

Clowes, 1651), copy from The British Library; and the anonymous *A Declaration from* Oxford (London: John Clowes, 1651), copy from the Henry E. Huntington Library and Art Gallery. All of these editions are available electronically on Early English Books Online (EEBO).

3. Iain Pears, *An Instance of the Fingerpost* (New York: Random House, 1997).

4. Although *Newes from the Dead* is attributed to Richard Watkins, it seems likely that Watkins served more as scribe than as sole author, given the similarity of the language of this pamphlet to a letter from William Petty to Samuel Hartlib written days after the event and the account recorded in Petty's private papers.

5. Jeffrey (or Geoffrey, as it is alternatively spelled) remains an obscure figure in the Reade family genealogy. Burke's Peerage mentions a Goeffrey, who is a brother of Sir Thomas said to have died by December 10, 1649, but mentions no other Geoffrey Reade A second Geoffrey is noted in *A Record of the Redes of Barton Court, Berks, With a Short Précis of Other Lines of the Name* (Hereford: Jakeman and Carver, High Town, 1899); he was baptized on April 20, 1634, at St. Mary's Burford, Salop, making him sixteen in 1650, when Anne Green was impregnated (47). He is identified as the fifth son of Thomas Read (1606–34), Sir Thomas's second son, named for George Boleyn, an ancestor of his mother, Mary Cornwall. He is also mentioned in Sir Thomas's will, dated June 28, 1650: "A farm called Holditches farm in Denford, co. Northampton, to my grandchild Gefferie Read, son of my deceased son Thomas" (22). Born the same year his father died, Geoffrey is not mentioned in his father's will. *A Record of the Redes* cites the manuscript *History of the Reade Family* by Edward A. Reade, C.B., of Ipsden House, where Geoffrey is speculated "to have become estranged from his family in consequence of a divergence in political views, and to have gone over to Ireland or to America." There is no information suggesting he either married or had children. *A Record of the Redes* relegates Green to a footnote beginning, "In the year 1650 Anne Green was gotten with child by some servant, or as she affirmed, a member of the family" (21). The note cites Plot's *Natural History of Oxford-shire* and follows its wording, while omitting at the end the phrase "as she constantly affirmed when she had little reason to lye" (197).

6. This justice, it scarcely needs noting, would not have focused Sir Thomas's particular interest in or dismay over the loss of his alleged great-grandchild, and it is unlikely he accepted Green's assertion that Jeffrey was the father. This situation and others like it suggest why the preciousness of the life of a bastard was not at the center of charges for infanticide.

7. The rule against defense counsel in capital cases held until around the mid-1730s. See John H. Langbein, "The Prosecutorial Origins of Defense Counsel in the Eighteenth Century: The Appearance of Solicitors," *Cambridge Law Journal* 58.2 (1999): 314–65.

8. Cases of bastardy, including those involving infanticide suspects, were seen first in quarter sessions, overseen by county justices of the peace. They had the power to examine and hold suspects for the assize courts, which had jurisdiction over infanticide trials. The courts of assize met semi-annually in circuits held in major market towns across England. See Peter C. Hoffer and N. E. H. Hull, *Murdering Mothers: Infanticide in England and New England 1558–1803* (New York: New York University Press, 1981), xiv–xv, who also note that the mobility and extensive caseload of the courts of assize did not "conduce to extensive trial record keeping."

9. Before the 1860s hanging involved being turned from a ladder or having a stool or other support knocked out from beneath the feet of the convicted felon, whose death was produced by suffocation as the ligature tightened over the trachea.

10. Quoted in J. Trevor Hughes, "Miraculous deliverance of Anne Green: an Oxford case of resuscitation in the seventeenth century," *British Medical Journal*, vol. 285 (December 18, 1982): 1792–1793.

11. Several accounts that focus on the medical representation of Green oppose the Oxford physicians' version of events to those pamphlets most often described as providentialist, which focus on Green's visions, but it is important to note that *all* accounts assume and describe the hand of God in her revival.

12. Robert Plot, *Natural History of Oxford-shire, being an essay toward the natural history of England* (Oxford, 1676), 197–200. Plot organizes his book into three sections: "Natural Things"; "Extravagancies and Defects" "occasioned either by exuberancy of matter or obstinencey of impediments, as in monsters"; and "Artificial Operations." Although in Plot Green is clearly accounted innocent of the legal charges, her place in his natural history seems to hover ambiguously between the exuberance and obstinacy of female nature to defy even death. The book, printed by Oxford University's press, bears the imprimatur of Ralph Bathhurst, vice chancellor and one of the original experimentalists attending Green's revivification. The frontispiece features an engraving of Athena with her arm partially obscuring the snaky visage of Medusa on her aegis. This classical feminine symbol of knowledge and horror captures nicely the symbolic work of Green's story in the Oxfordian narrative.

13. This was Elizabeth Russell, who on April 22, 1658, was brought before the Sessions of the Peace in Oxford.

14. Plot, *Natural History of Oxford-shire*, 199–200. Erasmus offered a variation on this common classical tag in Adage 21: "So essential is it to put no trust in a woman that even if you were to see her on her deathbed, you should assume she's shamming." Desiderius Erasmus, *Collected Works*, vol. 34: *Adages*, ed. R. A. B. Minors (Toronto: University of Toronto Press, 2005), 136.

15. 43 Eliz 1 c 2.

16. Statutes of the Realm, "An Acte to prevent the murthering of Bastard Children" (1624), 21 Jac. I. ch. 28.

17. An unmarried mother's innocence being a relative thing, of course, since she would still have been universally regarded as guilty of, if not criminally charged with, fornication and adultery.

18. 21 James I c 27 1624.

19. Marx called Petty the father of English political economy, maintaining that he was unjustly neglected as an important and foundational economic theorist. His evident admiration notwithstanding, he goes on to, describe him as "The keen-witted but cynical army surgeon who was as ready to plunder in Ireland under the shield of Cromwell as to crawl before Charles II . . ." Karl Marx, *A Contribution to the Critique of Political Economy*, trans. N. I. Stone (Chicago: C.H. Kerr, 1904): 57–60 note 1.

20. William Petty to Samuel Hartlib, 16, December, 1650, Beineke Library, Osborn Manuscript Files (#16601–16817).

21. *Mercurius Politicus* No 28, December 18, 1650: 468–69.

22. Because neither *Newes from the Dead* or *A Declaration from Oxford* are dated more specifically than by year, the order of their publication with respect to the other documents discussed in this essay is necessarily a matter of speculation. My own argument asserts but does not depend upon a settled sequence of publication. Oxford was not a large city and the views represented

in the pamphlets would have been widely discussed both before and after the publication of specific documents.

23. "A Declaration from Oxford," 4; "Wonder of Wonders," 5.

24. This passage in particular aligns the interests of the anonymous author of *A Declaration from Oxford* with the Leveller cause. The author of *A Wonder of Wonders,* is identified as W. Burdet, identified by some as William Burdet, a Baptist who held religious meetings in his home in Mowbry. While not a Leveller, Burdet would have shared many of the Leveller's dissenting views with respect to both royalist and parliamentary abuses of power. He was arrested in 1685 for participating in Monmouth's Rebellion. See Alan Betteridge, "Early Baptists in Leicestershire and Rutland," Part 3 *Baptist Quarterly* (1974): 367.

25. For an important and compelling account of the medical response to Green, see Frances Dolan, *Dangerous Familiars: Representations of Domestic Crime in England, 1500–1700* (Ithaca, NY: Cornell University Press, 1994), 133–35, 138–39.

26. Green's story even serves as the epigraph to the current fourth edition of Michael S. Gazzaniga, Richard B. Ivry, and George R. Mangun, eds., *Cognitive Neuroscience: The Biology of the Mind* (New York: Norton, 2013), where it serves as a parable of the miracle of science, or at least a remarkable instance in the development of Thomas Willis's groundbreaking work in neurology, despite, as I have suggested, the fact that it is quite unclear what, if anything, the doctors did was responsible for reviving Green, and some that might well have impeded her recovery.

27. Randall Martin, *Women, Murder, and Equity in Early Modern England* (New York: Routledge, 2007).

28. Erasmus famously practiced the form in "The Praise of Folly." Synesius of Cyrene was widely admired for his praise of baldness, as Lucian was for his praise of the fly. The art form was only ostensibly humble, as the fame of its practitioners would indicate.

29. This poem, placed fourth in the first edition, is relocated to appear first in the second edition, presumably to set the desired tone for the whole collection.

30. *Dangerous Familiars*, 138.

31. Fourteen new poems are added in the second edition to the original thirty. While the second edition relocates the poems to follow the prose account, this should not be construed as minimizing their importance given that the poems comprise almost three fourths of the total pamphlet.

32. Green's symbolic value may well have been further enhanced by the coincidence that sea green was the emblematic color of the Levellers.

33. See "Dramatis Personae," 687. Pears names Blundy's mother "Anne," presumably to establish a familial connection to the name of her historical forebear.

6

Cold-Blooded and High-Minded Murder

THE "CASE" OF OTHELLO

Richard Strier and Richard H. McAdams

THE LEGAL FRAMING OF THE PLAY

Legal terminology pervades *Othello*. Throughout the play terms that can carry both legal and nonlegal meanings appear in context to invoke, at least in part, their legal meaning. A "suit" can refer to any kind of appeal but obviously includes a lawsuit; "suitor" had its own legal meaning.[1] Right at the beginning of the play, when Iago is using his missed promotion to convince Roderigo of his hatred for Othello, Iago claims that three "great ones of the city" went to Othello in "personal suit to make me [Iago] his lieutenant" (1.1.8).[2] This is not clearly a legal usage, but then Iago says that Othello "Nonsuit[ed] my mediators" (1.1.15). A nonsuit was a legal judgment against a plaintiff for some form of default.[3] In promising to present Cassio's suit to Othello, Desdemona states, "For thy solicitor shall rather die / Than give thy cause away" (3.3.27–28). English lawyers are either barristers or "solicitors." And "cause," as in this speech, is another word like *suit*. A *cause of action* was the basis of a valid lawsuit.[4] As we shall see, this meaning of the term, as in Desdemona's description of her advocacy, resounds throughout the play. "Proof" is obviously central to legal cases and to this play, in which the term appears ten times.

The pattern of "complex words" with legal meanings is striking enough, but what is even more so is that legal references often appear in the play in contexts that would not seem to demand them.[5] This is particularly true with regard to descriptions of complex mental states or processes. For instance, in explaining her willingness to find excuses for Othello's weird behavior to her with regard to the missing handkerchief, Desdemona employs a remarkably clear and detailed legal analogy; she had been, she tells Emilia,

> Arraigning his unkindness with my soul,
> But now I find I had suborned the witness
> And he's indicted falsely. (3.4.153–55)

Shakespeare certainly did not need to give her this sort of language to describe her shifting attitudes toward Othello's behavior. The legal terms are used here for their emotional power. They suggest how deeply she feels that she has acted badly in (so to speak) mentally prosecuting Othello with the thought that he had actually intended "unkindness" toward her. The use of the ideas of subornation and false witnessing suggests how intensely she feels that this view of Othello's behavior was wrong, even ethically wrong. The legal language provides for an extraordinary precision in presenting a complex state of mind, or the transition from one state of mind to another.

An even more spectacular example occurs early on in the great central temptation scene of the play.[6] It also has to do with states of mind or soul. When Iago is pretending to be unwilling to be coerced into revealing the content of his private thoughts, he asks this question, which is clearly intended to be, as we say, "rhetorical":

> Who has a breast so pure
> But some uncleanly apprehensions
> Keep leets and law-days and in session sit
> With meditations lawful? (3.3.141–44)

By the end of this sentence "uncleanly" has turned into unlawful. Leets were "special courts, held by some lords of the manor once or twice a year."[7] The world of the psyche suddenly emerges as an ethically compromised English legal landscape. "Uncleanly apprehensions" are corrupt but established judges. "Sit" takes on a strangely disturbing and uncanny quality, suggesting comfort, power, and authority. Again the legal reference adds force and precision to the evocation of a mental state.

To move from words to larger structures, the play is bookended by contrasting major scenes that call our attention to law. In the first, something akin to legal process allows Othello to refute a false charge (Act 1, scene 3); in the other, the lack of such process prevents Desdemona from refuting a false charge (Act 5, scene 2).[8] When Brabantio brings Othello before the duke and council to accuse Othello of manipulating her through the use of witchcraft and related drugs—serious

English crimes at the time—the scene unfolds like a legal proceeding. Initially, after Brabantio had Othello (essentially) arrested, Othello asks, "Where will you that I go / To answer this your charge?" Brabantio answers, "To prison, till fit time / Of law and course of direct session / Call thee to answer" (1.2.84–86). Brabantio expresses optimism at the thought of presenting his charge to the duke and council, saying, "Mine's not an idle cause" (1.2.95). The duke tells Brabantio that, if his charges are true, he may "read in the letter" from "the bloody book of law," and that he may do so "though our proper son / Stood in your *action*" (1.3.70–71). Representing himself, Othello claims that he will not be adept at putting forth "my cause" (1.3.89). When Brabantio then states his charges against Othello, the duke says, "To vouch this is no proof / Without more certain or more overt test" (1.3.107–8). At Othello's request, the duke sends for Desdemona to serve as a "witness" (1.3.171) before he will pass "a sentence" (1.3.120). This law-like process serves to exonerate Othello from the false charge.

In contrast, Desdemona receives no such process when she is accused of adultery, a legal "cause" that was an ecclesiastical crime and a basis for legal separation.[9] In Act 3, Iago and Desdemona each refer to Othello's suspicion of Desdemona as a "cause" (3.3.414, 3.4.158). In the great speech that we analyze later, Othello claims, at least partially in the legal sense, "It is the cause" (5.2.1). Characters in the play repeatedly speak of adultery in legal terms. In Act 4 Desdemona mingles legal with religious language in denying being a "strumpet" when she tells Othello that she preserved her "vessel" from any "hated foul *unlawful* touch" (4.2.86, emphasis added). Again in Act 5, when Othello charges her with being "used" by Cassio, she clarifies by asking, "How? unlawfully?" and Othello answers, "Ay" (5.2.70). Even Roderigo refers to his solicitation of Desdemona as "unlawful" (4.2.201). Yet Othello denies Desdemona the kind of process by which he was able to refute a false charge, not allowing her an opportunity to rebut the "evidence" against her, lest she be guilty of "perjury" (5.2.51). He twice refuses her demand to call a witness in her defense (5.2.50, 67). So while *Othello* is not overtly a "legal" play—as is, for instance, *Measure for Measure*—*Othello* is permeated by thoughts about legal processes, about evidence, and about what constitutes a crime.

THE ANATOMY OF A KILLING

Three of Shakespeare's four "mature" or "great" tragedies (*Hamlet, Othello, King Lear,* and *Macbeth*) involve plot-determining murders.[10] But in thinking about these plays, it matters a great deal not only who commits the crucial murder but *where in the structure of the play* that murder occurs. In *Hamlet* the murderer is not the protagonist, and the plot-determining murder (as opposed to the other killings) takes place before the play begins—though through the bizarre narrative supposedly spoken by the victim, we have something like a sense of having witnessed it.[11] In *Othello* and *Macbeth* the protagonists are the murderers. But in *Macbeth* the plot-determining murder (there are many others) takes place early, at the beginning of the second act, and, though we see a good deal of the preparation for it and a great deal of the aftermath, the murder itself is not dramatized. We are told that Macbeth is "about it," and then told, ten lines later, that he has "done the deed," but "the deed" is not presented (2.2.4, 14). Only in *Othello* is the crucial murder presented on stage, and only in *Othello* is that murder the culmination of the action, occurring at the beginning of the final scene of the play (Act 5, scene 2).[12]

The matter of *how* the killing of Desdemona was going to be presented was clearly a major one for Shakespeare. His decision about this was, as we shall see, quite remarkable. But what must have been clear to him from the outset, or very close to it, is that he could not follow his source text with regard to this. Up until the murder of Disdemona/Desdemona, Shakespeare follows his narrative source—story 7 of the Third Decade of Giraldi Cinthio's *Hecatommithi* (*A Hundred-Ten Stories*, 1565; French translation, 1584)—fairly closely. But the murders in the two works could hardly be more different. In Cinthio the (unnamed) Moor and the (unnamed) ensign have some discussion about how to kill Disdemona (poison or dagger), but the ensign comes up with a plan that, as he tells the Moor, "will satisfy you and that nobody will suspect." The idea is to "beat Disdemona with a stocking filled with sand" and then arrange for the ceiling of the bedroom to fall on her, so that it will look as if she had been killed by a falling rafter. This is the plan that is executed, though the ensign does all the actual dirty work; he is the one who beats her to death with the stuffed stocking. In the short run the plan succeeds, though in the finale both the Moor and the ensign come to bad ends: the Moor, after being exiled, is killed by Disdemona's relatives ("as he richly deserved"), and the ensign is "tortured so fiercely that his inner organs were ruptured," and he dies miserably shortly thereafter.[13]

Clearly this version of the wife's murder will not do. But it leaves Shakespeare with the problem of how he will present it. Until he does, we are not sure how he will. But that he will is never in doubt. The possibility of Othello forgiving or simply divorcing Desdemona is never imagined. Yet an exactly contemporary English play, Thomas Heywood's *A Woman Killed with Kindness* (1603), dramatizes a version of both separation *menso et thoro* and forgiveness.[14] When Iago finally succeeds in introducing his "poison" (3.3.328) into Othello's psychosocial system and uses the vivid *narratio* of how Cassio (supposedly) enacted on

Iago's body Cassio's (supposed) sexual relation with Desdemona (3.3.416–28) to "thicken other proofs," Othello reacts in what was legally and medically called "hot blood," crying "I'll tear her all to pieces" (3.3.434).[15] When Othello hears about Cassio's supposed possession of the handkerchief—again "with the other proofs"—he seems to have fixed on his role as a revenger, using typical Senecan rant: "Arise, black vengeance, from the hollow hell" (3.3.450).[16] Cassio is his focus (though when Othello says, typically beautifully, "Yield up, O love, thy crown and hearted throne," he is surely referring to Desdemona). Othello calls for "blood, blood, blood" (3.3.454)—though it is not clear whether he says this in a "hot" or "cold" mode. He comes to proclaim his own resoluteness, shifting into grand and controlled rhetoric and adapting the idea of relentlessness to his normal self-presentational role as a world-encompassing military adventurer.[17] He uses an epic simile for his resolution, drawing on specialized knowledge from his travels; the image is of something cold and "compulsive":

> Like to the Pontic sea, whose icy current and compulsive course
> Ne'er keeps retiring ebb but keeps due on
> To the Propontic and the Hellespont:
> Even so my bloody thoughts. (3.3.456–60)

He presents his resolution to "swallow them up" in his revenge as "a sacred vow" to be guaranteed by a strangely solid "marble heaven" (perhaps connected to the solidity and "hardness" that he likes to imagine in himself).[18] We are now in the world of planning. Iago, always the brilliant improviser, picks up the high cosmological mode ("Witness," he says, "you ever-burning lights above") and vows to carry out, with conscientiousness and devotion, any order that Othello gives him. So Othello commands him to kill Cassio—not, it should be noted, that hour but "[w]ithin these three days" (3.3.475). Iago has to remind Othello to kill Desdemona. With typical manipulative cleverness, Iago advises, "But let her live." Othello then says that he will "withdraw" to plan "some swift means of death / For the fair devil" (3.3.48–81). The method is still undetermined, though poison seems to be implied. We are no longer in the world of "hot blood."

When Othello tried, sensibly, to demand "ocular proof" of Desdemona's infidelity (3.3.363), Iago had to convince him that such was "impossible" (3.3.405), and that Othello didn't really want to see this. Then Iago could build on the suggestion that seeing Cassio with the handkerchief was equivalent to such proof.[19] The text becomes focused on the handkerchief. Othello allows himself to use his grand rhetoric to tell Desdemona what Iago had earlier called "fantastical lies" (2.1.221) about the creation of the handkerchief and what the loss of it would mean (the story of the Egyptian charmer, the sybil, the hallowed worms, etc. [3.4.58–77]).[20] In the next scene Othello receives the "ocular proof"—of the handkerchief. Again, Cassio is the focus, and Othello's fantasy is of physically marking the face of the malefactor, symbolically castrating him and associating his genitalia with an unclean animal: "I see that nose of yours, but not that dog I shall throw it to" (4.1.141–42).[21] Again, Iago has to work to get Othello to think about Desdemona as well as Cassio—or rather, he has to work to get Othello to think murderously about her.

With Cassio, Othello has no problem—"I would have him nine years a-killing" (4.1.175)—but in the next sentence Othello finds himself thinking of Desdemona with admiration and erotic appreciation: "A fine woman, a fair woman, a sweet woman!" Iago admonishes him to "forget that." Othello tries to remind himself of the "hardness" of his heart, but he cannot keep from admiring and prizing Desdemona ("[T]he world hath not a sweeter creature; she might lie by an emperor's side"). Again, Iago says, "[T]hat's not your way." But Othello will not or cannot stop. He is deeply aware not only of Desdemona's physical beauty but of her womanly accomplishments, her skill at sewing and music, and also of her mental and verbal gifts—"of so high and plenteous wit and invention" (4.1.185–87). She, as we (and he) would say, "has it all." But Iago has the answer. Earlier Othello had observed of her talents, qualities, and enjoyment of life that "[w]here virtue is, these are more virtuous" (3.3.189). Iago now notes that since she is corrupt, "[s]he's the worse for all this" (4.1.188), for the misuse of such gifts. Othello sees the destruction or corruption of such a creature as profoundly sad—"the pity of it," he says twice (4.1.192–93)—but Iago reminds him of honor and of shame. If, he tells Othello, her iniquity "touch not you it comes near nobody." This produces a predictably "hot-blooded" response: "I will chop her into messes! Cuckold me!" (4.1.197). But that is an exclamation, not a plan. Othello reverts to the poison idea and likes it because he can use it from a distance; he knows himself and his susceptibilities well enough to be worried "lest her body and her beauty unprovide my mind again." But Iago comes up with an alternative plan: "[S]trangle her in her bed—even the bed she hath contaminated." Othello assents to the talionic beauty of it: "[T]he justice of it pleases" (4.1.206).[22]

So now there is a plan. After an episode in which Othello cannot maintain decorum and strikes Desdemona in public (4.1.239), he confronts her in private, though since her lady-in-waiting, Iago's wife Emilia is there (or just outside the door), he only verbally abuses Desdemona. She defends herself in a sensible way, demanding specifics of her supposed unfaithfulness—"[W]ith whom, how am I false?" (4.2.41)—but her question about what supposed sin she has "committed" leads Othello into an aria on the word. He plays on the phrase "committing adultery," as if by using the word she were admitting to the act, and his cosmological mode becomes oddly comic and prudish:

> What committed!
> Heaven stops the nose at it and the moon winks,
> The bawdy wind that kisses all it meets
> Is hushed within the hollow mine of earth
> And will not hear it. (4.2.77–81)

He seems oddly unwilling to say what "it" is. But he directly calls her a whore and adopts Iago's view of her beauty and accomplishments. Venice was famous for its high-class courtesans, and so all Desdemona's acknowledged charms and skills only serve to make her, in Othello's mind, a "cunning whore of Venice" (4.2.91).[23]

Othello leaves early in 4.2 (at line 96 of 246) and does not appear in the next scene. He makes only a brief appearance in the first scene of Act 5, which is mainly devoted to another "brawl" arranged by Iago in which Iago wounds Cassio and then kills Roderigo in "revenge" for the wounding of Cassio. Othello enters only to hear Cassio crying out that he has been attacked, which leads Othello to praise Iago's "noble" sense of mission (5.1.22) and to focus Othello on his own task: the killing of Desdemona. Still aware of the erotic power she holds over him, Othello tries to use this (as Iago did) as the basis for a plan: "Thy bed, lust-stained, shall with lust's blood be spotted" (5.1.36). We will refrain from going into the matter of whose "lust" has "stained" the bed, but it may well be that Stanley Cavell has this right and that it is Othello's sexual success that torments him.[24] But that is another essay. We are now ready to examine the actual killing.

The final scene opens with Othello carrying a torch into his own bedchamber and soliloquizing over the sleeping Desdemona. We are both prepared and unprepared for this speech. It is entirely Shakespeare's invention and is one of his strangest and most wonderful pieces of writing. It is just as abrupt and just as detached from its immediate context as Hamlet's great central soliloquy is. The first line is unintelligible: "It is the cause, it is the cause, my soul!" What is the cause? All we know is that Othello is claiming to be driven by some abstract reason and that he is addressing his "soul"—something with which he has been continuously concerned.[25] Again, a kind of cosmic delicacy or prudery comes in—"Let me not name it to you, you chaste stars"—but the line clarifies for us what the "cause" is, namely, as we have seen, adultery, an offense against (married) chastity. When Othello repeats "It is the cause" at the beginning of the third line of the soliloquy, we now understand it. He is acting for a cause, and he is also specifying his cause of action—legal as well as psychological and ethical—against Desdemona. But it seems that the plan has changed since Othello's appearance in the previous scene in which the bed "shall with lust's blood be spotted." Blood is now to be avoided rather than shed. In *A Woman Killed with Kindness*, the adulterous wife fully expects to be killed by her husband, but she requests that he do it without marking her face or hacking her with his sword, so that she may go, as she says, "Perfect and undeformèd to my tomb" (xiii: 98–100). Othello has taken such a resolution on his own. And he makes a great point of it; he will punctiliously respect Desdemona's bodily integrity and her erotic appeal (the tactile is added to the visual here):

> I'll not shed her blood
> Nor scar that whiter skin of hers than snow
> And smooth as monumental alabaster. (5.2.3b–5)

This is a kind of reverse Pygmalion moment. It is as if Desdemona were dead already and has been transformed into a statue of herself, the kind of statue that one might find on a grand family tomb for a couple.[26] But this is a fantasy; she is still alive. Othello reminds himself that "she must die" and adds another "cause": "lest she betray more men" (5.2.6).

As the Arden editor notes, this is completely absurd; Othello cannot care about this.[27] But the point may be seen to reside in his odd and extreme unwillingness here to make the matter personal. Recall Iago's "[I]f it touch not you it comes near nobody" (4.1.195–96). Othello is here, in a sense, acting as "nobody."[28] The fantasy is that he will be doing a sort of public service in killing Desdemona. He then begins to think about what killing her will actually mean, that it cannot be undone. He turns eloquent, witty, and philosophical; she is no longer a (supposedly) sinning person but a kind of living archetype. Instead of being a "cunning whore," she is now "the cunning'st pattern of excelling nature" (5.2.11).[29] This is all very grand and fancy. Othello is using his whole range of learned reference, classical and biblical: "pattern" of nature, "flaming minister," "Promethean heat." His Latinate vocabulary is on full display: he cannot her "light relume" (5.2.13). It seems that he could not be calmer. He moves from physics to biology, now seeing her animate being not as a light that cannot be relit but as a "rose" than can be plucked but not regrown. This leads him to the erotic realm, focusing on the function that signifies life and that he is planning on removing; he decides to smell "the rose," which means her breath. The first-person becomes personal here ("I'll smell thee"), though her body remains strangely metaphorical: "I'll smell thee on the tree," as if he were Eve in the Garden about to touch the forbidden fruit. The personal quickly disappears. He states that "balmy breath," addressed generally, almost leads him to change his mind about the killing, but this is not put in personal terms and is clearly not a serious possibility;

the "almost" looms large. The breath, he says to her (or rather to it), "dost almost persuade / Justice to break her sword" (5.2.16–17).

Othello is, of course, imagining himself as occupying the position of Justice, but this is (again) not only bizarrely abstract but also weirdly self-deconstructing, since Justice is marked as feminine here, and Othello has not displayed a sword. He is entranced by smelling the breath—"Once more, once more"[30]—and he says, "Be thus when thou are dead and I will kill thee / And love thee after" (5.2.18–19). In this necrophiliac fantasy, Othello seems to be imagining that, as in the stories of various saints, Desdemona will continue to smell sweet after death.[31] He takes another whiff and then concludes by commending himself for the purity of his motive; he is acting out of love and therefore like the biblical God: "This sorrow's heavenly, / It strikes where it doth love."[32] There is still nothing personal in all this, except perhaps the olfactory emphasis, which is itself treated as if it were an act of detached connoisseurship. The "I" here does not seem to have any characteristics except care ("I'll not scar"), appreciation ("O balmy breath"), and love. It is as if Othello is viewing the whole scene from the outside, as a commentator ("So sweet was ne'er so fatal"). His own emotion is treated as a kind of impersonal necessity ("I must weep") and then commented on ("But these are cruel tears"). The last line of the speech echoes the first, with a double "it." But now, in Othello's self-apotheosis, the "its" are agent rather than motive: "It strikes where it doth love" (5.2.22).

But then "[s]he wakes." Othello continues to insist that he is playing a "heavenly" role, allowing her to confess her "sins" before she dies. He is being pious ("I would not kill thy soul") and spiritually careful. He repeatedly calls her "perjured," as if he were a judge as well as a priest (a confessor was both, and perjury was not limited to a courtroom.)[33] Othello is trying to maintain his calm, but Desdemona notices physical manifestations of emotion that Othello cannot control ("[Y]our eyes roll . . . why gnaw you so your nether lip?"). Attending to his body rather than his words, she sees something like "hot blood": "Some bloody passion shakes your very frame" (5.2.44). He comes to see himself now as in the grip of a process that is both intellectual and visceral: "the strong conception / That I do groan withal."[34] He is thrown from his composure by the vehemence of her protestations of innocence. In responding to her with anything other than love and care, he is disturbed by the idea that what Desdemona is doing is forcing him to commit a crime. He has a clear idea of what constitutes murder and what does not. He experiences Desdemona's protestations of innocence as interfering with his love; "Thou dost stone my heart," he says, and "makest me call what I intend to do / A murder, which I thought a sacrifice" (5.2.64–65). A murder, it seems, requires anger and especially malice, and cannot be done out of love. (In the "malice aforethought" formula, Othello focuses only on the first component.)[35] The alternative, in his mind, is not, as one might think, an execution but "a sacrifice." Othello's thought seems to be that he is giving up something in killing Desdemona, that he is making a sacrifice of the woman he loves, or (and?) the idea seems to be that she is a sacrifice to Justice, and he is obliged to carry it out despite his love for her. In this moment he does not want to imagine himself as stony-hearted, as not loving her in doing this act, since, as we said, in his mind that would make the act "a murder." He resorts to his view of himself as Justice, urging his "proofs" and seeing Desdemona's distress over Cassio's (apparent) death as proof of her status as a "strumpet." Her resistance serves as an irritant. He was much happier when she was asleep. He is on the edge of anger when he finally does smother her, but he recovers his high view of his actions and feelings, and once again commends himself—this time for killing her quickly so that she does not "linger in her pain" (5.2.87).

For many more lines Othello continues to believe that he proceeded "upon just grounds" (5.2.136). When the truth about Iago's role in the events is finally revealed, a Venetian nobleman says to Othello in genuine puzzlement:

> O thou Othello that was once so good,
> Fallen in the practice of a cursed slave,
> What shall be said to thee?

Othello at first refuses to answer, saying, "Why, anything," but then specifies, "An honorable murderer, if you will, / For nought I did in hate, but all in honour" (5.2.291–92). This is the position that he clings to. His motive was pure. He acted out of honor, even out of love. When he is pleading to have his story told objectively—"Nothing extenuate / Nor set down aught in malice" (5.2.340–41)—he insists that the reporter "must speak," that is, cannot do otherwise than speak, of Othello as "one that loved not wisely, but too well" (5.2.342). He insists on his basically good character; he was "wrought," like a piece of metal by a craftsman. But to him the important point is "nought I did in hate" (5.2.292).

Othello's killing of Desdemona was, in his eyes, an honor killing, and even more so in that he insists—probably in some sense rightly—that he continued to love her throughout. The essential feature of an honor killing is the (theoretical) purity of its motive. It is not a matter of hatred but of restoring a previous state of wholeness or purity through a necessary act of violence. In Othello's case, the focus seems to be on restoring Desdemona's rather than his own purity through the murder; her corpse will be perfect. He seems less concerned with his own shame than with the project of restoring her to purity (monumental alabaster). Othello seems to have committed what the French in the nineteenth century would have called a *crime passionel*, which one scholar sees as a "spiritualized" version of honor killing. Othello seems to know that "the act itself did not restore a man's honor" but what did so was "his good reputation, according to spiritualized notions of honor, along with proof that he had shown loyalty, devotion, or romantic attachment to his partner beforehand."[36] In societies in which honor killings currently have legal standing, "the commission of an offence with honorable motives" is considered mitigating or even exculpatory (see the Iraqi Penal Code); the (convincing) allegation of an honorable motive "fully exempts or further mitigates the penalty of killers" (under Syrian law).[37]

The seventh story in Cinthio's Third Decade, the source for *Othello*, is preceded by a story in which a man "discovers his wife committing adultery and revenges himself in arranging her 'accidental' death." Story 7 begins by describing the reaction to the prior story of the Italian ladies who constitute the fictional audience for the stories. The ladies express the view that the adulterous wife in the prior story "appear[ed] worthy of the severest punishment" and "that it would be hard to find any other man who, discovering his wife in such a compromising situation, would not have slain both of the sinners outright." Indeed, "[t]he more they thought about it, the more prudently they considered him [the murderous cuckolded husband] to have behaved." The storyteller then moves to the tale of the Moor who slays his wife out of jealousy, though she is without fault. The problem was that the Moor was wrong. If he had not been so, there would apparently have been no problem.

The late fifteenth century *Book of the Knight of the Tower*, translated from the French by Caxton, contains a similar story, "A Roper's False Wife."[38] A roper tried to prevent his wife from meeting her adulterous lover by breaking both of her legs, but he awoke one night to discover the lover had come to his house and was *in flagrante* with his wife. In response, "he hastely toke oute a long kniff and persed hem bothe thorugh into the bedde." Having slain them both in the act, the roper called in his neighbors and "officres of the lawe" and showed them what he had done. The neighbors and officers all declare that it was "well done" to punish them in this manner.

The Spanish theater contemporary with Shakespeare treated the issue of honor killings repeatedly. But it may have only seemed to support the logic of them. *Othello* may have been a clearer instance of a true honor killing than any of the comedia, since, as Melveena McKendrick states, there is little sense in the Spanish plays that the outraged husbands actually loved their supposedly erring wives.[39] Would the early modern English audience have thought that Othello's sentence on himself (execution as if he were a traitor) was, as in Cinthio, "richly deserved" or, rather, too harsh?[40]

Near the end of the play, when Othello has fully admitted that he killed Desdemona (and conspired to kill Cassio), the Venetian leader Lodovico is oddly vague about what Othello has done. He tells Othello that he is to be detained "[t]ill that the nature of your fault be known / To the Venetian state" (5.2.334–35). Lodovico does not say until "your murder" or "the nature of your murder" or even "the nature of your crime" is known to the state, but the less specific "nature of *your fault*." Perhaps it was still not clear to those present that what occurred was a murder. What could possibly account for this uncertainty?

DESDEMONA'S KILLING AND THE ENGLISH LAW OF HOMICIDE

We shall begin our answer with some formal legal materials, the kind that an Elizabethan-era lawyer might consult, and then consider how a period jury might have reacted to the case and what verdict it might have given (or wanted to), whatever the law.

As we shall see, the law in Shakespeare's England did not formally recognize honor as a legal defense for a killing. This refusal represented a change from earlier centuries in which English law had recognized a husband's right to kill an adulterous wife and her lover. The tenth-century laws of King Alfred the Great, included this rule: "A man may fight, without becoming liable to vendetta, if he finds another [man] with his wedded wife, within closed doors or under the same blanket; or [if he finds another man] with his legitimate daughter [or sister]; or with his mother, if she has been given in lawful wedlock to his father."[41] Interestingly, the eleventh-century laws of William the Conqueror state only that a man may slay his daughter or mother found "in adultery."[42] The omission of the wife (and sister) from the rule might indicate either that those killings were no longer authorized or (more probably) that they were so obviously authorized as not to merit mention in the written law. In any event, the entire rule was eventually abandoned. Maitland and Pollock, in their survey of early medieval English law, report that by the thirteenth century "[t]here are signs that the outraged husband who found his wife in the act of adultery might no longer [legally] slay the guilty pair or either of them." However, the husband "might [legally] emasculate the adulterer" (!).[43]

In the Maitland-Pollack formulation, the occasion for sanctioned revenge, whether killing or castrating, was limited to the husband's discovery of the wife or other female relative "in the act." If a husband learned of the adultery in some other way, he presumably had no right to use violence directly but had to rely on a legal process. Yet by the thirteenth century, adultery was an ecclesiastical offense, so the lawful punishment was left to church authorities, whose sanctions were relatively mild.[44] This mildness created tension between church authorities and the popular sense of justice. Maitland and Pollock explain, "Some [sexual] crimes [including adultery] which old law had treated with great severity were appropriated by the church and so escaped from lay justice. . . . If the church had left the matter to laymen, it is probable that some of these crimes would have been sternly, if not savagely, punished."[45] As an instance, the authors cite for this claim the castration of adulterers. However, it is important to note that if the husband were to kill the adulterer, the common law courts, not the ecclesiastical courts, would have jurisdiction over the homicide prosecution, leaving the possibility that lay justice could, via the jury, still have some say. This is a point to which we will return.

By the early seventeenth century, English legal treatises give no recognition to the old rights to kill or to maim an adulterer that a husband discovers "in the act." The treatises do not even refer to the old law for the purpose of rejecting it, at least not in specific terms. Yet one murder case from 1616, *Roy v. Taverner*,[46] does consider the justification of honor (though not in a sexual context). On account of an unpaid debt Birde challenged Taverner to a duel, and the two men had mutually agreed on a time, place, and set of weapons. In the meantime, Taverner attempted to pay off the debt and to reconcile with Birde, but Birde "denied him." So Taverner fought "for the preservation of his reputation, not to be accounted a coward," and killed Birde. The court upheld the indictment for murder, strongly stating that "If this were not murder, nothing would be murder, if men could fight by appointment in an open field *under the pretense of defending their supposed honor*."[47] "Pretense" here did not mean the court doubted that Taverner thought his honor was at stake. The court simply saw no way to accommodate the motive of honor within the law of murder. There were, as we shall see, circumstances in the law when intentional killing was not murder, but the defense of honor was simply not, as a formal matter, one of those. Indeed, the court referred to the King's proclamation against dueling, which it described as "only the common law."[48]

By the nineteenth century we have something close to an explicit denial of the right to an honor killing in the context of a sex crime. In *Regina v. Fisher* (1837),[49] a father killed a man who had taken "unnatural liberties" with his son, some form of sodomy. The court states, "There would be exceedingly wild work taking place in the world if every man were to be allowed to judge in his own case. The law of England has laid it down positively and clearly, that every killing of another is itself murder, unless the party killing can shew by evidence that it is a less offence; or unless circumstances arise in the case which will either reduce the killing to manslaughter, or reduce it to no crime at all." The court here refers to specific grounds like misadventure (accident) or self-defense, which might excuse or justify the defendant or lower the crime to manslaughter.[50]

In Shakespeare's time, a manslaughter conviction left the convict eligible for the benefit of clergy and therefore a sentence other than death, frequently just a branding on the thumb (the brand serving the purpose of preventing an individual from claiming benefit of clergy a second time).[51] Honor provided no defense to murder, but in the discussion below we show that honor is indirectly relevant to manslaughter, and we show that, despite the absence of a formal recognition of honor killings, Shakespeare's play engages some legal doctrines that might excuse Othello's killing or render it a less severe form of homicide.

Taking Literally Othello's Claim to Justice

We should briefly consider the unlikely possibility that Othello possesses the legal authority to carry out the execution of Desdemona. At least we should not overlook the fact that Othello exercises some governmental powers on Cyprus. He has a "commission" (1.3.282) from the duke to replace the duke's "substitute" there, most likely the governor (1.3.224, n), which is how Cassio is designated when he replaces Othello (4.1.236, 5.2.365). Othello certainly feels free to threaten to execute anyone who continues to fight when he discovers the Cassio-Roderigo brawl (2.3.161, 170). He is acting as a military commander enforcing discipline in "a town of war" (2.3.209). There does not seem to be any Venetian civilian authority in Cyprus at this time, although Montano has held that position. As the highest governmental authority, Othello may take himself to be authorized to hand out death sentences.

In the English legal commentary attributed to Bracton, written in the thirteenth century, there is the following discussion of killing by the administration of justice: "[I]t is homicide if done out of malice or from pleasure in the shedding of human blood [and] though the accused is lawfully slain, he who does the act commits a mortal sin because of his evil purpose. But if it is done from a love of justice, the judge does not sin in condemning him to death, nor in ordering an officer to slay him, nor does the officer sin if when sent by the judge he kills the condemned man. But both sin if they act in this way when proper legal procedures have not been observed."[52] The commentator Lambard states the same idea circa 1581: "Not everie Manslaughter deserveth punishment (saith M. Bracton) for in expressing that Homicidium corporale facto committitur quatuor modis s. Iusticia, necessitate, casu vel voluntate, therewithall he addeth that the firste of these is no sin at all, if it been done sincerely, and without delight in shedding of bloud."[53] This is exactly what Othello saw himself doing. He acted "sincerely"—that is, "purely"—without malice, without "delight in shedding of blood" and with no "evil purpose."[54] There is, however, a serious question of whether "proper legal procedures" have been observed.

The Mitigation to Manslaughter for Provoked, Hot-Blooded Killings

The closest the law came to a defense for honor killing was one of the grounds for reducing the evaluation of a homicide from murder to manslaughter: "provocation."

Some background here is necessary. The difference between murder and manslaughter was still being worked out by Elizabethan courts; it involved the distinction between killing by malice prepensed or forethought (murder) and killing without such malice (manslaughter). Malice at the time had the nontechnical meaning of "general malevolence or cold-blooded desire to injure."[55] The law would frequently infer malice from the circumstances of a killing. But one case where it would not infer malice was when the killing occurred on a sudden quarrel or "chance-medley."[56] A prominent example is where *A* assaults *B*, or a member of *B*'s family, in such a way that *B* is not legally justified in responding with deadly force (because the attack is not serious or has clearly ended, and *A* is leaving the scene) but *B* nonetheless immediately kills *A*. Another possibility is that *A* and *B* "fall out" and engage in combat, each delivering or attempting blows before *B* kills *A*. These situations might qualify for manslaughter. By contrast, if *A* provokes *B* merely with words, however insulting, *B*'s killing of *A* is murder. This point was established by 1661 in *Raven's Case*: "No words, be they what they will," were such a provocation in law, as, "if upon them one kills another, would diminish or lessen the offence from being murder, to be but manslaughter."[57]

This distinction would become operative if two instances of near violence in the play became lethal. Iago's first speech to Othello concerns different kinds of killing. First, Iago dismisses killings done in the normal course ("trade") of war as not worth discussing; he then claims a special abhorrence for "contrived murder" ("I hold it very stuff o'th' conscience / To do no contrived murder" [1.2.2–3]). But he then asserts that had he (supposedly) not been deficient in useful iniquity ("I lack iniquity / Sometimes to do me service"), he would have been provoked to kill Brabantio because Brabantio "spoke such scurvy and provoking terms / Against [Othello's] honour" (1.2.7–8). Iago claims to think that if a killing is not "contrived" (that is, premeditated), is verbally provoked, and involves "honour," it is an "iniquity"—but not a murder. As we have seen, legally this is incorrect. No matter how much Brabantio "prated" (1.2.6), no matter how insulting his words had been to Iago or to Othello, and no matter that Iago's response was not "contrived," it would have been murder had Iago had sufficient proper iniquity to have "yerked [Brabantio] . . . under the ribs."

A second instance of potential verbal provocation to a killing involves Iago and Othello. When Othello commands Iago to provide proof of the adultery he alleges, lest Othello's "waked wrath" wreak "woe upon [Iago's] life" (3.3.369), here too had Othello killed Iago for the insult to Desdemona and himself, the mere words would not legally have been sufficient provocation to lower the crime from murder to manslaughter.

Yet physical assault was not the only type of legally recognized "provocation." Another type, potentially helpful to Othello, was the discovery of adultery. In 1706 the court in *Mawgridge's Case* described the rule: "Where a man is taken in adultery with another man's wife, if the husband shall stab the adulterer, or knock out his brains, this is bare manslaughter; for adultery is the highest invasion of property, and there cannot be a greater provocation."[58] We have found a published expression of this rule as far back as a 1670 opinion. When John Manning "found [a man] committing adultery with his wife in the very act" and immediately beat him to death with a stool, it was held to be manslaughter rather than murder.[59] The penalty was a branding on the hand, and the trial court "directed the executioner to burn him gently, because there could not be greater provocation than this." There are strong grounds to believe that the rule existed well before 1670: because written opinions are rare in the period; because the law evolved from the twelfth-century rule treating the killing of adulterers caught in the act as no crime; and because the opinion cited here does not consider the issue at hand to be novel or difficult. If the seventeenth-century court felt comfortable stating "there could not be greater provocation than this," it seems extremely likely that prior courts had reached the same result, including sixteenth-century cases—which must have existed[60]—of wife killing after the discovery of adultery.

Nonetheless, it requires speculation to know how the law of provocation would have applied to Othello, given that the rule is so undeveloped in the formal materials at the time Shakespeare wrote the play.[61] We should also note that there is less than perfect consistency between cases from the same time period. Intriguing, however, are two apparent barriers to Othello's use of the doctrine, judging by later judicial precedent. First, Othello doesn't (of course) find Cassio and Desdemona *in flagrante. Mawgridge's Case* refers to the decedent being "taken in adultery," and John Manning found the man he killed "in the very act." These defendants had the "ocular proof" that Othello tried to demand (and that Frankford, in *A Woman Killed with Kindness*, had). We have found no English case before 1800 where the discovery of adultery mitigated murder to manslaughter where the adulterers were not caught *in flagrante*. In the nineteenth-century *Fisher* case mentioned above (the case of the allegedly sodomized son), the defendant tried to rely on an analogy to the precedents involving the discovery of adultery. But the court rejected his provocation claim, stating:

> If this man had *seen* the thing happen, and had at that moment inflicted the injury, I should have rather inclined to think that it would have been within the [adultery-as-provocation] rule in [the cited] case. . . . *In all [such] cases the party must see the act done.* What a state should we be in if a man, *on hearing* that something had been done to his child, should be at liberty to take the

law into his own hands, and inflict vengeance on the offender. In this case the father only heard of what had been done from others.[62]

There is another, more fundamental doctrinal limitation (from which the above may be derived): the necessity of "hot-blooded" motivation—that one kills immediately after the provocation while in the "transport of passion."[63] After the passage of "cooling time," the mitigation was lost, and the killing would be murder, despite legally adequate provocation. For example, if two individuals fell into an argument and agreed to meet to fight the next day (or possibly even hours later on the same day), any resulting death would be murder rather than manslaughter because the court would not believe that the passions remained sufficiently inflamed after the interval. As Justice Coke explained in a 1610 case, only if the challenge was sent "and then instantly, *upon hot blood*, they met and fought, and one of them kills the other," is it manslaughter.[64]

However, the rule about "hot blood" and "cooling time" might conceivably allow the mitigation even if one did not discover the adultery in progress. When *Fisher* says "*In all cases* the party must see the act done," this seems to be an exaggeration of the case law, although a useful approximation. *Usually*, if one is not close enough to the provoker to witness the act of provocation, there is cooling time before one can find and kill the provoker. But if this is the reason for what we might call *Fisher*'s ocular rule, then it must admit of exceptions. There is at least one period case involving assault of a family member where the killer doesn't see the assault but acts quickly enough still to be in the "transport of passion," meriting manslaughter instead of murder. In *Royley's Case*, a father killed a boy who had bloodied his son and the father successfully argued provocation even though he had to walk "about a mile" to find and kill the attacker.[65] The court emphasized that the defendant set out immediately from his home upon discovering his son's injuries. The point is that the requirement of an *immediate* response to the provocation is ambiguous. There are no early cases like this involving adultery, but one could imagine the courts granting someone a defense for killing within a very limited time-span after learning of the adultery.

It should now be clear that if a court knew all that the audience of *Othello* knows, Othello would have no legal ground for claiming that his killing Desdemona was manslaughter. The play has some notorious issues of timing, one possibility being that the events occur in a single day, which might shorten the time from Othello's "discovery" of adultery.[66] But the argument still seems implausible. First, Othello believes in Desdemona's adultery from some time in Act 3, scene 3 to Act 5, scene 2, and during that time he manages to restrain himself from lethal violence on the two occasions in which he confronts Desdemona (4.1.214–60, 4.2.24–96), though he does strike her on the first occasion. Second, as detailed above, Othello begins Act 5, scene 2 with an unexpected, eerie calmness, the very opposite of "hot blood." He has reflected on what he is about to do and continues to delay while he contemplates Desdemona, smells her, provides her time to pray, and so on.

Yet the audience might recognize that a real-world jury would not know all the facts. Lorna Hutson argues that Shakespeare and contemporary writers elicited from legally conscious audiences the dual perspectives of one who knows all that the play reveals and of one who, like a jury, knows only what can be subsequently proven.[67] The perspective of Lodovico is informative here since he has no prior knowledge of the events and is struggling to understand them. He refers to Othello as a "rash and most unfortunate man" (5.2.280), whereas Iago is a "viper" and "villain" (282). "Rash" might suggest hot blood. And Othello, as we have noted, characterizes himself as "[a]n honourable murderer" (290). Someone who is distraught from having killed in the heat of passion might call his killing "murder" (and himself a "murderer"), though his action were legally manslaughter. Thus, just as Lodovico, Venice's representative, expresses uncertainty about "the nature of [Othello's] fault," so might an English jury have done.

One uncertainty for the Venetians (or a later jury) would arise from the means of killing Desdemona. Where poison quintessentially implies malice, the act of smothering does not.[68] It might appear to have been the spontaneous act of a man whose wife just confessed her adultery. The Venetians and the jury would know that Othello had recently struck Desdemona in public, although they might suppose, as Lodovico did at the time, that it was the letters from Venice recalling Othello from Cyprus that served, in that instance, to "work upon his blood" (4.1.275). Moreover, with the deaths of Desdemona, Emilia, and Othello, and if Iago keeps his vow "from this time forth" never to speak a word (5.2.301), would it even be clear to the jury or the Venetians that Desdemona did *not* commit adultery? Cassio will deny it, of course, but that is not proof. The dual perspectives of actual audience and imagined jury create considerable cognitive dissonance. It is easy to imagine the jury seeing Othello's action as a classic instance of hot-blooded rage, although the audience has experienced his eloquent, witty, and philosophical soliloquy, his very cool and high-minded version of his action.

There is no early case where a confession of adultery rather than "ocular proof" mitigates murder to manslaughter. Yet what is relevant to the Shakespearean audience is the difference between the formal law and its application "on the ground." Despite the legal doctrine reviewed above, juries at the time of Shakespeare (and before, and after) were considerably more indulgent to provocation claims. This happened in the nineteenth-century *Fisher* case (with the allegedly sodomized son).

As we have already indicated, the court instructed the jury that "in all cases the defendant must see the act done." The defendant in that case had not seen and did not claim to have seen the decedent take "unnatural liberties" with his son, so the case should have been a simple one. Yet the jury ignored the judicial instruction; it convicted the defendant of manslaughter rather than murder, and, moreover, recommended leniency in the sentencing for manslaughter.

That was in 1837. But juries in Shakespeare's time and before were also in conflict with the judiciary about the legal significance of adultery and the evolving murder/manslaughter divide. As the historian Sara Butler explains, "Medieval [English] juries were notorious for fabricating judgements of self-defence . . . when they believed a death was excusable even though it did not meet the parameters of contemporary legal requirements. Nowhere is the jury's manipulation of the self-defence plea more in evidence than in cases of the slaying of an adulterer."[69] We have found no such adultery case contemporaneous with Shakespeare, but two legal sources reveal a more general judge-jury conflict regarding honor killings. One is a judicial decision immediately before Shakespeare wrote *Othello*; the other is a statute enacted just after.

In *Watts v. Brain* (1599), the plaintiff was the wife of the deceased Watts.[70] The relevant story began with a fight between Brain and Watts in which Brain was injured but both sides survived. Had Watts's death occurred during this fight, Brain would probably have been guilty only of manslaughter since the death would have occurred on a sudden occasion. However, the fatal incident occurred three days later when Watts walked by Brain's shop and, according to Brain, "smiled upon him, and wryed his mouth at him." "[F]or this mocking of him," Brain pursued Watts and "struck him upon the calf of his leg, whereof he [Watts] instantly died."[71]

The court thought this killing was obviously murder, not manslaughter. The jury was instructed that "a wry or distorted mouth, or the like countenance upon another" is "such a slight provocation" that it "was not sufficient ground or pretence for a quarrel." The reporter's abstract to the opinion states the general rule: "*No words or gestures, however provoking, will justify homicide from the crime of murder.*" So, as the judges told the jury (following normal procedure at the time), the crime was murder even if "what the defendant pretended had been true." Yet the jury returned a verdict of acquittal. This did not sit well with the judges. "The Court much misliking thereof, being contrary to their direction, examined every one of them by the poll, whether that was his verdict." Two jurors said they thought the defendant was guilty but, being outvoted, had agreed to report out an acquittal, "whereupon [the jurors] were sent back again, and returned, and found the defendant guilty."[72] For their initial misbehavior several jurors were imprisoned and fined. Brain was hanged.

The point for us is that juries resisted the legal limitations on the provocation doctrine. They were inclined to apply the logic of mitigation even when the provocation was merely a verbal or nonverbal slight. If a "wryed" mouth could so motivate a jury, imagine what a jury would think of the provocation that Othello endured in thinking that Desdemona had committed adultery with Cassio and then wept for the death of Cassio "to [Othello's] face" (5.2.76).

Now to the relevant statute. The one that reveals the resistance of Elizabethan juries to the formal law of homicide was enacted by Parliament in 1604, and came to be known as the Statute of Stabbing. It declares that even if "malice aforethought cannot be proved," it is murder, not manslaughter, for a person to "stabbe or thruste" another person who has not struck a prior blow nor drawn a weapon.[73] The stated aim of the statute is to restrain "stabbinge and killinge men on the sudaine." But preexisting law already required some kind of mutual combat to justify manslaughter. If insulting words are insufficient provocation, how would it *not* be murder to stab a person who has not struck a blow or drawn a weapon? The answer is that the statute's purpose was not to change the law but rather to compel juries to follow it. As in *Watts v. Brain*, juries clearly were resisting the law's formulation, so the statute attempts to identify a common class of cases—men reacting with swords to provocations that were not physical attacks—and to create a bright line rule: a killing that occurs in such a case is murder, without any further proof of malice. Parliament clearly thought the statute was needed because juries were overly receptive to certain kinds of things—like honor killings.

This understanding of the Statute of Stabbings was affirmed by a distinguished group of judges prior to the trial of Lord Morley for murder in 1661. The Lord Chief Justice of the King's Bench stated, "[W]e were all of opinion that the statute of 1 Jac. for stabbing a man not having first struck, nor having any weapon drawn, *was only a declaration of the common law*, and made *to prevent the inconveniencies of juries*, who were apt to believe that to be a provocation to extenuate a murder, which in law was not."[74]

Taken together *Watts v. Brain* and the Statute of Stabbings demonstrate that the historian Thomas Green's generalization of an earlier period also applied to the time of Shakespeare: "The jury's most important factual inquiry, and the one that most often led to friction with the bench, involved its assessment of the defendant's intent . . . [which was] all the more [complicated] when juries brought to it powerful feelings about the defendant's personal worth and the justice of taking his life for the act he had committed."[75] Thus the law of homicide generally and the law of provocation specifically was a locus of conflict between the courts and juries, a topic likely to engage those (many?) men in Shakespeare's original audiences who were or might have been called upon to serve on juries.[76] Despite the law, audience members, like jurors, were likely to have felt that Othello was not guilty of murder—at least if he had been correct in his belief that Desdemona had committed adultery, and maybe even if he hadn't been since the killing was done "sincerely" and "without delight in the shedding of blood" (indeed without the shedding of blood) and he was of great "personal worth" and the victim of Iago's wicked and systematic manipulation.

All this legal framing ultimately directs our attention to the play's focus on Othello's mind and temper. The law of provocation imagines a simple dichotomy: hot blood *versus* cold. When one is initially enraged by some severe provocation, one is lost to the "transport of passion." The passion is "hot," but with time it "cools," and one is again capable of rational deliberation. But scholars of criminal law have pointed out that there is reason to doubt the simple hot/cold dichotomy.[77] We can see some of the reasons for this in *Othello*. For one thing, it is not obvious that Othello is more rational in his serene state at the beginning of the murder scene than during his hot-blooded moments. We reviewed above the ways in which his thinking is bizarre, as if he has been driven not back from anger but to some strange point beyond anger. We have also seen that when Desdemona awakes and denies the charges, Othello is at least on the verge of becoming angry again. It is obviously artificial to think that rage dissipates and deliberation strengthens in a linear fashion after the initial provocation. Even if it is true that, in the long term, emotional life generally works that way, in the short term, rage ebbs and flows. We see this in the scenes with Iago where Othello cannot fully sustain his rage, and we see it again in the final scene with Desdemona, where he cannot fully sustain his calm.[78] Like the "sword of Spain, the ice-brook's temper" that Othello recovers from his chamber (5.2.250–51), he too has been repeatedly heated and repeatedly cooled in the process of being, as he says, "wrought" (5.2.343). Neither heat nor cold alone could produce his condition. And Spain would have been seen by Shakespeare's audience not only as a source of fine swords and as the land of Sant'Iago the Moor-killer, but also as a locale where honor killings were accepted.[79]

In *Othello*, Shakespeare has presented, in detail and from the inside as well as the outside, a killing that does not possess, in any obvious or simple way, the identifying feature of murder (malice) or the identifying feature of manslaughter (hot blood). We can perhaps conclude that in this, as in his other Venetian play, Shakespeare is once again showing that one of the things that theater can do is present "cases" that reveal the limitations of the law.[80] The legal system could certainly have provided a serious punishment for Othello (had he not murdered [?] himself), but, however appropriate the punishment, it is not clear that the legal system could (or can?) adequately answer Lodovico's question or meditation: "O thou Othello, that wert once so good . . . What shall be said to thee?"[81]

NOTES

1. "Suitors" referred to tenants of a manor; the manorial or other local court could not proceed without their presence. See *Pill v. Towers*, 78 E.R. 1021 (1599): "[F]or a court-baron cannot be holden but before the suitors."

2. All quotations from *Othello* are from *The Arden Shakespeare, Third Series*, ed. E. A. J. Honigmann (Walton-on-Thames: Thomas Nelson and Sons, 1997), hereafter cited as Honigmann.

3. The term was used as early as the fourteenth century. See Anonymous, Jenkins, 127, 145 E.R. 89 (1340). For an overview see Sir Edward Coke, *The First Part of the Institutes of the Law of England* (London, 1628), section 208,138.

4. See, for example, John Ayliffe, *Parergon juris canonici Anglicani*, tit. "Of a cause, controversy, suit, instance, and the like" (London, 1726), 147. Courts used the term "cause of action" at least as far back as 1495. See Anonymous, Jenkins 183, 145 E.R. 121 (1495).

5. For the notion of "complex words," see William Empson, *The Structure of Complex Words* (London: Chatto and Windus, 1951).

6. On *Othello* as Shakespeare's version of *Paradise Lost*, see Richard Strier, "Excuses, Bepissing, and Non-being: Shakespearean Puzzles about Agency," in *Shakespeare and Moral Agency*, ed. Michael D. Bristol (London: Continuum, 2010), 55–68, esp. 63–66.

7. Honigmann, 217n.

8. See Richard McAdams, "Vengeance, Complicity, and Criminal Law in *Othello*," in *Shakespeare and the Law: A Conversation among Disciplines and Professions*, ed. Bradin Cormack, Martha C. Nussbaum, and Richard Strier (Chicago: University of Chicago Press, 2013), 133–39. For an argument that it is significant that this scene is not actually a formal legal one, see Richard Strier, "Shakespeare and Legal Systems: The Better the Worse (but Not *Vice Versa*)," 200 n65 in the same volume.

9. See Richard Cosin, *Apologie for Sundrie Proceedings by Jurisdiction Ecclesiastical* (London, 1593), part 1, chap. 2, p. 20; B. J. Sokol and Mary Sokol, *Shakespeare, Law, and Marriage* (Cambridge, UK: Cambridge University Press, 2003), 141–42. Adultery made possible divorce *a mensa et thoro*, which was not a complete legal termination of the marriage since the parties were not free to remarry.

10. It is possible to think that *Lear* does so too, but the killing of Cordelia is an execution on the basis of a military command and therefore not exactly a murder. Her death is important to the political situation (and, of course, to the ultimate meaning) of the play but is hardly "plot-determining" since the play is practically over when it happens—which is part of what makes it so awful. The one clear murder in the play, Goneril's poisoning of Regan, barely registers in the text.

11. Critics have been oddly unwilling to acknowledge the narratological weirdness of the supposed ghost of Hamlet Sr.'s narrative of his death. How does one make sense of an account someone gives of what happened (other than in dreams) when one was sound asleep? The assumption seems to be that the "ghost" somehow has retrospective access to this. For endorsement of the view that the speaking "thing" in question here is in fact a demon, see the comments by Strier in the "Roundtable" that concludes Cormack et al., *Shakespeare and the Law*, 304. For scholarly support of this view, see the Longer Notes in *Hamlet*, ed. Harold Jenkins (Methuen: London, 1982), 454, 483.

12. The Folio gives act and scene divisions.

13. Geoffrey Bullough, ed., *Narrative and Dramatic Sources of Shakespeare* (New York: Columbia University Press, 1978), 7: 250, 252.

14. The husband in Heywood's play, Master Frankford, does have "the ocular proof" (which he comes by rather easily, in sharp contrast to Iago's "It is impossible you should see this" [3.3.405]), yet Frankford simply banishes his wife *de menso e thoro* and leaves the seducer, his best friend, to the friend's own conscience. Frankford's reason for not killing the couple in (his) bed is parallel with that which Hamlet provides to himself for not killing Claudius at prayer: "I would not damn two precious souls" (xiii: 47). But how we are to think of this within the play is not clear. Frankford's wife thinks, "He cannot be so base as to forgive me" (xiii: 139), and when the wife's brother, an aristocrat (Sir Francis Acton), hears what has happened, he states that his "brother" (in-law) "showed too mild a spirit / In the revenge of such a loathèd crime" (xvii: 16–17). As the title of the play suggests, the wife is "killed" in any case (she dies of shame, sorrow, and self-starvation), and the seducer is "[p]ursued with horror of a guilty soul" (xvi: 38ff). The husband is certainly seen as a saintly figure, but perhaps a sort of holy fool. We are not sure what the early Jacobean audience would have made of all this, and Heywood, in his epilogue, seems unsure of this as well. He refers to five different opinions of the same wine. Whether there is any sense in which Heywood's play and Shakespeare's were actually in dialogue (one responding to the other) is unclear, though Honigmann thinks that Heywood's is a response to Shakespeare's (349). For the text see Martin Wiggins, ed., *A Woman Killed with Kindness and Other Domestic Plays* (New York: Oxford University Press, 2008), 70–128.

15. In a number of works Lorna Hutson has emphasized the importance of *narratio* in legal proceedings; see, for instance, *The Invention of Suspicion: Law and Mimesis in Shakespeare and Renaissance Drama* (Oxford: Oxford University Press, 2007), 121–45. For the importance of "hot blood" in the English legal context, see the section "The Mitigation to Manslaughter for Provoked, Hot-Blooded Killings" below; for its role in the sixteenth-century French legal context, see Natalie Zemon Davis, *Fiction in the Archives: Pardon Tales and Their Tellers in Sixteenth-Century France* (Stanford: Stanford University Press, 1087), ch. 2.

16. On Senecan rant, see Gordon Braden, *Renaissance Tragedy and the Senecan Tradition: Anger's Privilege* (New Haven, CT: Yale University Press, 1985).

17. On the nature and importance of Othello's grand style, see Reuben A. Brower, *Hero and Saint: Shakespeare and the Graeco-Roman Heroic Tradition* (New York: Oxford University Press, 1971), ch. 1; Richard Strier, "Paleness versus Eloquence: The Ideologies of Style in the English Renaissance," unpublished manuscript.

18. Earlier in the play Othello claimed a special relation to inner "hardness" ("I do agnize / A natural and prompt alacrity / I find in hardness" [1.3.231–33]), and this is probably related to his conception of his "perfect soul" (1.2.31); later in the play he imagines his heart literally "turned to stone": "I strike it and it hurts my hand" (4.1.79–80). The "solid virtue" of his public image was defined by its special hardness, which "[t]he shot of accident nor dart of chance / Could neither graze nor pierce" (4.1.266–67).

19. On the issue of "presumptive proof" in cases of adultery, see Gregory Kneidel, "Legal Evidence, Self-Betrayal, and the Case of John Donne's 'The Perfume,'" *Modern Philology* 112 (2014): 130–53. More generally see Michael Dalton, *The Countrey Justice* (1618; Norwood, NJ: Walter J. Johnson, 1975), 268: "[I]n cases of secret murthers . . . witchcraft, and the like secret

offenses, where open and evident proofes are seldome to be had, there (it seemeth) halfe proofes are to be allowed, and are good causes of suspition." For Iago as a "connoisseur of probabilities," see Joel Altman, *The Improbability of* Othello: *Rhetorical Anthropology and Shakespearean Selfhood* (Chicago: University of Chicago Press, 2010), 7.

20. This is not the first occasion on which Othello tells a fabulous whopper to Desdemona. In recapitulating for the council "the story" of his life, Othello includes, among realistic and what we are probably to believe were true events (being sold into slavery, etc.), a known traveler's fiction: the "men whose heads / Do grow beneath their shoulders" (1.3.145–46). Educated members of the audience would have recognized this as Herodotus via illustrated Marco Polo, Mandeville, and others. See Herodotus, *The Histories*, book 4, trans. Aubrey de Sélencourt, rev. A. R. Burns (Harmondsworth, Middlesex: Penguin, 1972), 334 (Herodotus doesn't "vouch for" this); Marco Polo, *El Libro de las Maravillas* (Madrid: Editorial Casariego, 2000), 74 (full-color illustration of "pueblos maravillosos . . . que no se trata en el texto"); *The Travels of Sir John Mandeville*, trans. C. W. R. D. Moseley (Harmondsworth, Middlesex: Penguin, 1983), 137. But the handkerchief moment must surely be seen as a much more sinister and calculated occasion.

21. On marking the face of a sexual malefactor, see Peter Spierenberg, *A History of Murder: Personal. Violence in Europe from the Middle Ages to the Present* (Malden, MA: Polity, 2008), 119; on the nose as phallic, see Spierenberg, and especially Peter Stallybrass, "Patriarchal Territories: The Body Enclosed," in *Rewriting the Renaissance: The Discourses of Sexual Difference in Early Modern Europe*, ed. Margaret Ferguson, Maureen Quilligan, and Nancy J. Vickers (Chicago: University of Chicago Press, 1986), 138–39. Shakespeare's general hatred of dogs (with the occasional exception of hunting hounds) is well-known. For a brilliant case study see Empson on "Timon's Dog" in *The Structure of Complex Words*, 175–84. In our play the dog imagery culminates in Othello's killing of himself as a "circumcised dog." On the bizarreness of this see Julia Lupton, *Citizen-Saints: Shakespeare and Political Theology* (Chicago: University of Chicago Press, 2005), 121–22.

22. For a legal reason why Iago suggests strangulation rather than poison, see McAdams, "Vengeance, Complicity, and Criminal Law in *Othello*."

23. In a production Desdemona and Bianca could be doubled—they never appear on stage together—so that there would not necessarily be any obvious way of telling them apart. We think that this would be a highly desirable ambiguity since the difference between these (fictional) women is not on the surface. For a study of a remarkable *cortegiana* and her context, see Margaret F. Rosenthal, *The Honest Courtesan: Veronica Franco, Citizen and Writer in Sixteenth-Century Venice* (Chicago: University of Chicago Press, 1992).

24. Stanley Cavell, "Othello and the Stake of the Other," in *Disowning Knowledge in Seven Plays of Shakespeare* (Cambridge, UK: Cambridge University Press, 2003), 125–42, esp. 136.

25. On the importance of the lack of specification here, see William Empson, *Seven Types of Ambiguity*, 3rd ed. (New York: Meridian Books, 1955), 209–11: "There is no primary meaning for lack of information. . . . We are listening to a mind withdrawn upon itself, and baffled by its own agonies" (210).

26. See Fred H. Crosley, *English Church Monuments AD 1150–1550* (New York: Scribner's, 1921). Empson notes that in the comparison here, Othello is "enjoying the straightforward relief of a Marlowan hyperbole," escaping "for a moment the clash between love and hatred . . . so that the effect is as if he thought her innocent" (*Seven Types of Ambiguity*, 211).

27. Honigmann, 306.

28. In this light Desdemona's claim that "nobody" killed her can, in a sense, be seen as true (5.2.122).

29. For a similar use of "pattern," see the final line and a half of Donne's lyric "The Canonization": "Beg from above / A pattern of your love."

30. In taking "Once more, once more" as indicating smelling rather than kissing, we are agreeing with Honigmann's note (306) and, as he points out, with the Quarto stage direction.

31. On the sweet "odor of sanctity," see Susan Ashbrook Harvey, *Scenting Salvation: Ancient Christianity and the Olfactory Imagination* (Berkeley: University of California Press, 2006) (with special reference to St. Teresa); Constance Classen, "The Breath of God: Sacred Histories of Scent," in *The Smell Culture Reader*, ed. Jim Drobnick (Oxford: Berg, 2006), 375–890.

32. See Hebrews 12:6, Revelation 3:19; echoing Deuteronomy 8:5, Proverbs 3:12.

33. On the confessor as having a judicial role, see *The Canons and Decrees of the Council of Trent*, trans. H. J. Schroeder (1941; Rockford, IL: Tan Books, 1978), Fourteenth Session, esp. chs. 6, 8 ("[I]t is not a bare ministry only . . . but is after the manner of a judicial act" [95]). Richard Helmholz has pointed out to us that "at the time, perjury had a broader scope than court proceedings; it meant false swearing (*mendacium juramento firmatum*), though the Common Law only punished it in legal proceedings" (private communication).

34. This is the second instance in the play of a male being pictured as pregnant with or in the process of giving birth to an idea. At the end of his first soliloquy, Iago says of his idea of using Cassio to make Othello jealous, "It is engendered," and he speaks of a "monstrous birth" in process (1.3.402–3). Shakespeare clearly wants to present this type of "conception" as monstrous.

35. On the "malice aforethought" formula, see the next section. Interestingly everyone in the play seems to have a specific definition of murder. On the set of distinctions about kinds of killing that Iago makes in his first speech to Othello, see the section "The Mitigation to Manslaughter for Provoked, Hot-Blooded Killings" below.

36. Spierenberg, *A History of Murder*, 188.

37. Diana Y. Vitoshka, "The Modern Face of Honor Killing: Factors, Legal Issues, and Policy Recommendations," *Berkeley Undergraduate Journal* 22 (2010): 17, 22.

38. See Joan Young Gregg, ed., *Devils, Women, and Jews: Reflections of the Other in Medieval Sermon Stories* (1906; Albany: State University of New York Press, 1997), 127–30. See the insightful discussion in Sara M. Butler, *Marital Violence in Later Medieval England* (Leiden: Brill 2007), 106–7.

39. See Melveena McKendrick, *Identities in Crisis: Essays on Honour, Gender and Women in the* Comedia (Kassel: Edition Reichenberger, 2002), *passim*; for the contrast with *Othello*, see 109. We owe our awareness of this important book to Strier's student Kathryn Swanton.

40. In *Shakespeare on Masculinity* (Cambridge, UK: Cambridge University Press, 2001), Robin Headlam Wells notes that violence in defense of honor "was a highly political issue in Elizabethan and Jacobean England," citing the Essex Rebellion (108). For a treatment of the Essex Rebellion as "the last honour revolt," see Mervyn James, "At the Crossroads of the Political Culture: The Essex Revolt, 1601," in *Society, Politics and Culture: Studies in Early Modern England* (Cambridge, UK: Cambridge University Press, 1986), 416–65. For an overview of honor and violence in the culture, with little focus on private honor, see James, "English Politics and the Concept of Honor, 1485–1642," 308–415, in the same volume.

41. "The Laws of Alfred," cap. 42 §7, in *The Laws of the Earliest English Kings*, trans. F. L. Attenborough (London: Cambridge University Press, 1922), 85. "Without becoming liable for

vendetta" is Attenborough's translation of the Old English word *orwige*. He explains, "The word *orwige* here evidently denotes a man who, having committed homicide (under the circumstances specified), is protected from vengeance at the hands of the relatives of the man he has slain" (198).

42. The Laws of King William the Conqueror, section 35, in *Ancient Laws and Institutes of England* (London: Eyre and Spottiswoode, 1840).

43. Sir Frederic William Maitland and Sir Frederick Pollock, *The History of English Law before the Time of Edward I*, 2nd edition (Cambridge, UK: Cambridge University Press, 1899), vol. 2, ch. 8, §2, p. 483. "[I]n 1212 King John orders that *A* who has emasculated *B* is to have his land restored to him, if an inquest finds that *B* committed adultery with *A*'s wife after being forbidden to visit her" (n135).

44. We stress that the mildness was relative. In the thirteenth century "the standard penalty for adultery . . . included being whipped while going around one's parish church or market." Richard H. Helmholz, *Marriage Litigation in Medieval England* (Cambridge, UK: Cambridge University Press, 2007), 182. By the fifteenth century some locales had abandoned whipping for the more lenient penance of walking the parish with a candle (182).

45. Maitland and Pollock, *History of English Law*, §4, 542.

46. 81 E.R. 534 (1616). We thank Kayla Gamin for an English translation of the medieval law-French.

47. Id., emphasis added.

48. Id. See J. Larkin and P. Hughes, eds., *Stuart Royal Proclamations, James I: 1603–1625*, nos. 132, 136, and 160. Proclamation 132 (November 5, 1613) forbids the publishing of reports of duels, noting that "no quarrel of any Subjects can be lawfull, except in defence of their Prince or their Countrey, the revenging of all private wrongs onely belonging to Us (under GOD,) into whose hand hee hath put the Sword for that purpose" (296). Reiterating the legal alternatives, the proclamation states, "And if a man should find himselfe grieved with any whisperings, or rumours spread abroad, misreporting the cariage of any such matter, he may resort to our Commissioners Marshall, who shall right him in his Reputation, if they finde he be wronged" (297). On the general place of honor in Tudor-Stuart English culture, see James, "English Politics and the Concept of Honor," esp. 322–25 (on dueling).

49. 173 E.R. 452 (1837).

50. See William Blackstone, *Commentaries on the Laws of England*, Book the Fourth (Oxford: Clarendon Press, 1769), ch. 14, pp. 182–85.

51. See John H. Baker, *An Introduction to English Legal History*, 4th ed. (Oxford: Oxford University Press, 2002), 513–15.

52. See "The Crime of Homicide and the Divisions into Which It Falls," Bracton Online, Harvard Law School Library, http://bracton.law.harvard.edu/Unframed/English/v2/340.htm#TITLE298, lines 25–31.

53. See William Lambard, *Eirenarcha, or the Office of the Justice of Peace, in foure Bookes* (London: Companie of Stationers, 1691 [1581]), second book, cap. 7, 233–34.

54. On this meaning of "sincerely," see *OED*, "sincere," adj., meanings 1a and c. A biblical example is "the sincere milk of the word" in 1 Peter 2:2 (AV and earlier). Interestingly the *OED* gives an example with regard to the law, from the *Dialogue of Pole and Lupset* (c. 1529): "The lawys, wyche be syncere & pure reson wythout any spot or blot of affectyon."

55. Francis Bowes Sayre, "*Mens Rea*," *Harvard Law Review* 45 (1932): 974, 997.

56. See *Raven's Case*, 84 E.R. 1065 (1661): "[M]anslaughter . . . in law is properly chance-medley, that is where one man upon a suddain occasion kills another without malice in fact, or malice implied by law" and "[I]f one man kill another, and no sudden quarrel appeareth, this is murder"; *John Royley's Case*, 79 E.R. 254 (1611): killing in a fight upon "sudden occasion" is manslaughter; *Rex v. Keate*, 90 E.R. 557 (1702): killing upon a "sudden affray" is manslaughter.

57. 84 E.R. 1065. The example given is this: "As if one called another son of a whore, and giveth him the lie, and upon those words the other kill him that gave the words, this not-withstanding those words, is murder." The explanation is that "such a provocation as must take off the killing of a man from murder to be but manslaughter, must be some open violence, or actual striving with, or striking one another."

58. 90 E.R. 1167.

59. Anonymous, 83 E.R. 112.

60. For evidence of the high frequency of adultery in an earlier period, see Butler, *Marital Violence in Later Medieval England*, 99–100.

61. Honigmann dates the play's composition as from mid-1601 to mid-1602 (appendix 1, 344–50), while noting that others argue for a date as late as 1604.

62. 173 E.R. 452 (1837), emphasis added.

63. See *The King v. Oneby*, 92 E.R. 465 (1727), for "transport of passion."

64. *Rowland Egerton v. Edward Morgan and Others*, 80 E.R. 770, 785 (1610), emphasis added. See also *Raven's Case*, 84 E.R. 1065 (1661), in which the judges agreed "that if two men fall out in the morning, and meet and fight in the afternoon, and one of them is slain, this is murder, for there was time to allay the heat, and their after-meeting is of malice."

65. 79 E.R. 254 (1611).

66. On the time problems in the play, see A. C. Bradley, *Shakespearean Tragedy* (1904; New York: Meridian Books, 1960), appendix 1, 338–44; and the discussion in Honigmann, 68–72.

67. In *The Invention of Suspicion*, referring to the last scene of *Titus Andronicus* and "Horatio's charge to tell Hamlet's story," Hutson observes that "the theatre audience assumes the position of the 'people' who are to be judges of all the circumstances that led to the [homicide] and, as such to participate in an act of critical judgment that has both moral and political dimensions" (70).

68. On the special legal status of poisoning in the period in England, see McAdams, "Vengeance, Complicity, and Criminal Law in *Othello*." For a general discussion of poison in the period literature, see Miranda Wilson, *Poison's Dark Works in Renaissance England* (Lewisburg: Bucknell University Press, 2014).

69. Butler, *Marital Violence in Medieval England*, 104 (discussing cases). See also Thomas A. Green, *Verdict According to Conscience: Perspectives on the English Criminal Trial Jury* (Chicago: University of Chicago Press, 1985), 42–43, reporting on a fourteenth-century case where the jury acquitted Robert Bousserman, who killed the adulterous partner of his wife, through the subterfuge of "alter[ing] the facts" to create a case of self-defense; Elizabeth Papp Kamali, "The Devil's Daughter of Hell Fire: The Role of Anger in Medieval English Felony Adjudication," unpublished manuscript, 2014, discussing the similar fourteenth-century case of Robert Mahen.

70. 78 E.R. 1009.

71. We see no significance in the similarity to Iago's attack on Cassio because the parallel attack in Shakespeare's main source, the Cinthio story, was also on the leg.

72. See Greene, *Verdict According to Conscience*, 140–43, discussing the evolution of the power of judges to coerce juries in their verdict.

73. 1 Jac. Ch. 8; 4 Statutes of the Realm, 1026.

74. See *Raven's Case*, 84 E.R. 1065, 1079–80 (1661), emphasis added. See also *Rowland Egerton v. Edward Morgan and Others*, 80 E.R. 770, 786 (1610). According to Chief Justice Flemming, stabbing was murder "at the common law" prior to the Statute of Stabbing. For a modern discussion, see J. M. Kaye, "The Early History of Murder and Manslaughter (pt. 2)," *Law Quarterly Review* 83 (1967): 569, 600–01, stating "it is probable that the judges who introduced the concept of the 'sudden occasion' did not realise that the perversity of juries would lead them to bring in verdicts of Manslaughter in cases where, although no premeditation had been shown to exist, the circumstances indicated Murder by 'implied malice.' It is one thing to make, as a point of law, a distinction between 'sudden killings accomplished when the blood was heated' and sudden killings done in cold blood, but it is another thing to get juries to take that point. . . . To remedy this the Statute of Stabbing was passed, in 1604."

75. Green, *Verdict According to Conscience*, 126.

76. For widespread civic participation as normal in the Elizabethan period, see Patrick Collinson, "The Monarchical Republic of Queen Elizabeth I," 1986, in *Elizabethan Essays* (London: Hambledon Press, 1994), 31–57. For a volume of essays on this thesis, see John F. McDiarmid, ed., *The Monarchical Republic of Early Modern England: Essays in Response to Patrick Collinson* (Aldershot: Ashgate, 2007).

77. See, for instance, Dan M. Kahan and Martha C. Nussbaum, "Two Conceptions of Emotion in Criminal Law," *Columbia Law Review* 96 (1996): 318: "It is not hard to imagine cases in which a defendant's smoldering or brooding anger seems morally appropriate or understandable, but in which a court might nonetheless be constrained as a matter of law, or even a jury as a matter of fact, to find 'cooling time.' "

78. The picture of "the vehement passions" that Philip Fisher presents in his book by that title (Princeton, NJ: Princeton University Press, 2002) is similar to the legal picture. It assumes the complete dominance of the relevant passion at the moment of its inception and the fading of the passion over time (see 43ff. on the "monarchical" quality of passion, and 72ff. on fading over time). Despite the fact that Fisher regularly includes *Othello* in his lists of works demonstrating his views, the way Othello enacts and experiences his jealousy does not conform to Fisher's picture.

79. One need not fully agree with Robert N. Watson on "*Othello* as Protestant Propaganda" to believe that Iago's Spanish name has some significance. See *Religion and Culture in Renaissance England*, ed. Claire McEachern and Debora Shuger (Cambridge: Cambridge University Press, 1997), 234–57.

80. For a reading of *The Merchant of Venice* along these lines (together with *2 Henry IV* and *Measure for Measure*), see Strier, "Shakespeare and Legal Systems."

81. Kahan and Nussbaum suggest that the reason for the "lingering imprecision" in the law about "hot" and "cold" blood is probably best attributed to "the inherent impossibility of devising legal rules that perfectly capture the relevant moral judgments in this setting" ("Two Conceptions of Emotion in Criminal Law," 318).

7

What's Love Got to Do with It?

SEXUAL EXPLOITATION IN *MEASURE FOR MEASURE*

Pamela Foa

THERE IS NO agreement about the meaning of *Measure for Measure*.[1] Is it a political description and critique of the rule of James I?[2] Is it a study of the exercise of absolute power implemented by the ruthless enforcement of the law?[3] Of the effect of power on character? Of the administration of law without equity or mercy?

The only apparent certainty about Shakespeare's *Measure for Measure* is that it is a difficult play, commonly described as a "problem" play.[4] It is difficult because there is disagreement about so much in the play: whether the character who triggers the events that will unfold over the course of the play, the Duke of Vienna, acts for good or evil and whether he intentionally uses and delegates his power to promote the lawful administration of law, to test the character of someone who is self-righteous, or to send Vienna to the brink of moral collapse to vindicate his own lax regime. At the simplest level there is no agreement about what motivates the duke at any stage of the play. It is a problem play because while it is nominally a Shakespearean comedy since an orgy of marriages ends the play, it reads like a tragedy: the marriages are imposed as punishments for sexual misconduct and generally portend lifetimes of dread and duty—worse even than a sentence of death (5.1.385).

M. C. Bradbrook has said that *Measure for Measure* is a highly analytic play about the interplay between law and justice, morality and mercy, and the risks of speaking truth to power.[5] Certainly Shakespeare encourages this view both with his title and with the play's opening. The title alludes to a passage from the "Sermon on the Mount," where Christ says, "Judge not, that ye be not judged. For with that judgment ye judge, ye shall be judged: and with what measure ye mete, it shall be meted, it shall be measured to you again" (Matthew 7:1–2). From the title alone we could conclude that at least one focus of the play is how we judge and punish others: the subject of criminal law. And the opening scene in the play reinforces that view, for the Duke of Vienna announces his imminent departure and his decision that Lord Angelo administer the law in his absence:

> In our remove be thou at full ourself.
> Morality and mercy in Vienna
> Live in thy tongue.
> ....
> Your scope is as mine own,
> So to enforce or qualify the laws
> As to your soul seems good. (1.1.43–44, 64–66).

So we know from Act 1, scene 1 that Lord Angelo's law enforcement will either be the central theme of the play or the impetus for what follows.[6] In fact it is both. And it is the application of the law that generates the dynamic conflicts between characters representing justice, mercy, revenge, and reason.

The laws are clear; it is their application that creates difficulty. In Shakespeare's Vienna it was for the magistrate to know the law and for the ruler, or his deputy in this case, to apply it—sometimes after hearing arguments on behalf of the lawbreaker, sometimes not. Indeed Bradbrook's discussion of the final act suggests that Isabella "is almost in the position of a prosecuting counsel" to the duke as judge, as she lyrically but emphatically describes the criminal conduct of Angelo during his term as the duke's deputy.[7]

If we view the play not simply as a discussion of whether there is justice in Angelo's administration of the law but more generally from the perspective of a prosecutor confronted with the facts of the play, then I believe that some of the problematic nature of the play can be resolved. To this end I propose that we proceed as I did when I was a federal prosecutor: let us start at the end and work our way backward in our search for understanding of the duke's actions in *Measure for Measure.*[8]

Prosecutors are faced with an awkward fact: they know that as a matter of law motive is never an element of the crimes that they must prove, and at the same time they know that it is human nature to want to know the impetus behind a defendant's actions—particularly when defendants' actions do not wear their rationales on their sleeves. If a prosecutor cannot explain the motive for the crime, then, no matter how strong the evidence, there is a real risk of a failed prosecution. We, the jury, want the world—both real and fictional—to make sense, to be something that we can understand and to which we can relate. That is what motive does for us.

Of course the motives for some acts are self-evident. We don't need a special explanation when someone who is poor steals money. But when the rich man steals or the successful doctor joins an insurance fraud scheme we want to know the motive, even when it is clear that the defendant is the guilty party and even when we know every detail of how the crime was done.

Shakespeare's Duke of Vienna shares one prominent feature with many defendants: he lies. He lies when he says that he is leaving Vienna; he lies when he says that he will be gone for so long that he needs to have a proxy stand in for him during his absence; he lies when he tells Angelo that he delegates to him all royal powers of law enforcement;[9] and he lies when he pretends to be a friar. People lie to hide the truth, often about their motives.

An analysis that explains the duke's motives will, I believe, explain the action of the play and, most important, reveal at the center of the play the duke's moral failure as a leader and as a man. Thus, on my analysis, *Measure for Measure* need not be viewed as a play about whether law enforcement should be stringent, humane, or lax or whether politics must inevitably bow to human sexual impulses and concomitant immorality or inhumanity. Rather it should be seen as a play about the Duke of Vienna's abuse of power and arbitrary enforcement of law to manipulate those who are subservient to him to achieve his desired end: marriage to Isabella.

This is not to say that the theme of whether and how mercy is to temper law to achieve justice is not present in *Measure for Measure*, or that such a discussion is not still relevant. The exercise of power and its expression in sexual demands by those who govern survive to this day as a social and political problem.[10] Should it matter to anyone's ability to govern how he conducts his personal life? Do our political leaders require moral centers in their personal life? Should we expect of them that in all aspects of their life they respect the Kantian duty to recognize the dignity of each person, or can they function as political leaders even when they shatter moral law in the pursuit of personal pleasure? These are broad and important questions that I believe are raised by Shakespeare in *Measure for Measure* and, if I am right in my analysis, answered—at least at the most fundamental level. But in my view the way these questions are raised is not, as may generally be thought, by showing us that the duke is the golden mean between the unachievable moral purity of Angelo and Isabella and the louche regent-defamer Lucio. To the contrary, on my analysis the duke is venal and knows no moral bound to achieve his desired end.

To create context for my argument I begin with a discussion of relevant portions of the play. The absolute monarch of Vienna, the duke, announces that he is leaving the country and that in his absence his power will be exercised by Lord Angelo, a man who is reputed to be incorruptible but who has little experience in law enforcement. To fill this lacuna, the duke names as Angelo's deputy and counselor Escalus, a wise and experienced magistrate who knows the law. So no sooner has the play begun than we have two questions that we should expect the play to answer: Why does the duke renounce his power? and Why does he delegate it to someone inexperienced when there is at hand someone whom the duke recognizes as wise and experienced?

Immediately upon the delegation and the duke's departure, we learn that the new man in charge, Angelo, has ordered a two-pronged attack against the sexual decay and promiscuity that the duke has let fester in Vienna. To show the citizenry that his regime will be different, that he will enforce the law, Angelo orders the arrest of Claudio, a young noble, for illegal sexual conduct, and the destruction of all brothels in and around Vienna. Claudio's offense was to fornicate—a capital crime.

But in the same scene in which we learn of Angelo's initiative to enforce the law against sexual promiscuity, we learn that for all his appearance of rectitude, Angelo is not above the most elemental Tammany Hall–type political persuasion: at the request of a rich constituent, a burgher, he has rescinded the directive to pull down Vienna's brothels; only those outside the city's limits will be subject to razing (1.2.89–90). So if there were any question about Angelo's rectitude, it is answered at the very start of the play, in Act 1, scene 2. Angelo can be had.

As for Claudio, his crime is indisputable: his fiancée, Juliet, is fairly bursting with child, days away from giving birth. But unlike the conduct that flourishes in brothels, Claudio's fornication was not wanton or random. He and Juliet were formally engaged, contracted to marry.[11] They slept together in the fullness of young love only when she had difficulty raising a dowry. If fornication can be innocent, then such was Claudio's. Nonetheless, against the advice of the wise and more moderate Escalus, Angelo orders Claudio's arrest and execution. In the context of all the louche sex in Vienna and Claudio's view of Juliet as his wife, Claudio's arrest and death sentence seem particularly harsh and arbitrary. Still, if an example is to be set, he is the only character in the play who is a candidate for the role. He is of high birth; he must be well known in Vienna, for he is humiliated by Angelo's direction that he be paraded through the city on his way to jail; and he admits his crime (1.2).

Claudio understands that a pardon is his best hope to live and that his best hope for a pardon lies with his sister Isabella. Isabella is a woman whose mere presence can "move men" (1.2.183). But Claudio must act quickly for his sister is to take her vows that very day to become a member of a cloistered community. Her vows will seclude her forever from the larger community. Claudio engages Lucio to persuade Isabella to delay her entry into the Order.[12] Only if she delays her vows will she be available to persuade Angelo to commute Claudio's death sentence. Once she takes her vows, her engagement with the outside world will be limited. She will not be able to leave the convent, and Angelo would have no reason to go there. Even were he to go, once she has taken her vows she will not be allowed to speak with any man except in the presence of the prioress, and even then she will be permitted only to speak to him or to look at him, but not both.[13] Lucio goes on his errand and is successful.

As Angelo's reign of terror against the sexually promiscuous of Vienna begins we learn that, contrary to his explicit representation, the duke has not left and does not intend to leave Vienna. Rather he will stay, he claims, to watch Angelo and his effort to enforce the law. He persuades a friar to give him the dress and teach him the manner of a friar so that he can roam the city unrecognized. But disguised as a friar, he does not merely observe; he intervenes in the lives of all the characters, along the way exercising the prerogatives of a friar.

Angelo orders that the execution of Claudio take place the day after his arrest. Nonetheless Angelo receives Isabella and hears her plea for mercy for her brother. He turns away her arguments but discovers that she sexually arouses him (2.3). He invites her to return in the morning.

When Isabella returns to plead her brother's case, Angelo, the man who has been chosen because he does not succumb to passion and is ruled by cold reason alone, propositions her: he will spare her brother's life if she sleeps with him (2.4). He even tells Isabella that he loves her (2.4.140). Isabella, the would-be nun, is horrified, defiant, and immediately aware of the incongruity: Angelo will pardon her brother if she does exactly what her brother has been condemned for doing. She refuses and tries a bit of blackmail herself: Release my brother, she says, or I will tell one and all of your crude attempt to seduce me. Angelo gives her one day to reconsider her refusal. As for her attempt at blackmail, he brushes it aside with the true observation that no one will believe her (2.4.154–69).

Isabella never waivers in her belief that the value of her chastity outweighs her brother's life. She goes to Claudio in jail to tell him that her efforts on his behalf have failed, that Angelo will spare him only for an immoral trade: her chastity, that is, her virtue and eternal soul, for Claudio's life.

After an initial reaction of disgust (3.1.103), and with the shadow of imminent death before him, Claudio tries in a brilliant but ultimately fruitless speech to persuade his sister to sleep with Angelo: Would God not forgive such an act? Is it a sin to give up one's chastity to save a loved one's life? Coercion, he argues, brings with it moral relief for what one does. No, Isabella, contends; nothing can justify, let alone sanctify the loss of her chastity. They would both be condemned to hell for such an act. Isabella tells her brother to prepare himself for death.

With each of the major characters acting from a sense of desperation, the duke, qua friar, intervenes. He tells Isabella that there is a way out of her dilemma: a woman named Mariana. Mariana was once the fiancée of Angelo, but when her dowry was lost at sea Angelo renounced his intent to marry her and, to cover the abruptness and cruelty of his rejection, spread false rumors about her sexual character. In the intervening years Mariana has become a recluse, but, oddly, she still loves and yearns for her erstwhile betrothed (3.1.206–8).

According to Northrop Frye, Mariana is introduced to create a parallel with Claudio and Juliet that shows the injustice of the law. It shows, Frye claims, that "the way the law works things out, Angelo's uncompleted engagement leaves him a person of the highest social eminence, whereas Claudio's uncompleted betrothal leaves him a condemned criminal. . . . Even if Angelo had remained as pure as the driven snow, the contrast in their fates would still be monstrous."[14] Enforcement of a law without regard to the possibility of its grossly inequitable consequences makes Angelo evil and suggests that the duke's laxity in enforcing the law is indeed benevolent. But if all the duke wants to do is show that his reign is not a failure for want of law enforcement, or that strict enforcement of the law is not necessarily just, surely he need not require that Isabella leave her cloister. To explain this we need a different understanding of the duke and his motives.

In any event, to save Claudio the duke proposes that Mariana save Isabella's chastity and Claudio's life by pretending to be Isabella and meeting Angelo's demand that Isabella sleep with him. If she does not speak Angelo will be fooled, and Mariana's erstwhile contract will be satisfied, her longing satisfied, and Claudio's life saved (3.2. 211–55, 267–70; 4.1.71–75).

The "bed trick," as this plot turn is called, is really quite vicious. Why should Mariana's chastity be sacrificed to Isabella's? Why is it morally permissible to fool Angelo into thinking he is sleeping with the woman he claimed to love when he is sleeping with one whose only value to him was the fortune that she lost? Given that they had been party to a marriage contract, this act may well have the legal effect of perfecting the contract. It raises as well deeper moral questions: How do we measure a man's life against a woman's chastity? Is Angelo so morally bankrupt that it does not matter that he is tricked into committing the act for which he has condemned another? Does it matter from a moral perspective with whom Angelo sleeps? Should he have married a woman who could not meet the conditions of the marriage contract through no fault of her own? If yes, then Angelo should have married Mariana and Claudio should have avoided at least capital punishment when he and Juliet delayed marriage to accumulate a dowry. If no, then Claudio's punishment is just and Angelo was right to reject Mariana.

All of these questions hang without resolution as the play continues. We are told that Isabella does indeed persuade Mariana to take her place in Angelo's bed. Angelo, however, cad that he is, and presumably afraid of anyone who might disclose his vicious act against Isabella, does not release Claudio but secretly condemns him to immediate death and orders that his head be brought to him to show that his order has been carried out (4.2.118–25). The duke, as friar, intervenes again to induce the warden to suspend the execution. He gives the warden a letter announcing that, although Angelo does not know it, the duke will return within two days (4.2.191–203). The friar directs the warden to kill another condemned man, Bernadine, in Claudio's place and to substitute his head for Claudio's. When Bernadine is unwilling to be the sacrificial lamb, another man who looks like Claudio conveniently dies, and his head is brought to Angelo. The duke intentionally keeps Isabella in the dark; he tells her that her brother has been executed, that the duke is returning the next day, and that if she can wait she will get her revenge (4.3.115–36).

Act 5, the final act, has just one scene; in my judgment it is structured as if it were a marriage ceremony. The duke orders his subjects to gather in a public square to greet him. In this setting he "returns" to resume his rightful powers and demands that anyone who has any complaint speak out or forever hold his peace. Isabella comes forward. She pleads for "justice, justice, justice, justice" (5.1.25). She accuses Angelo of the murder of her brother and fornication with her (5.1. 40–45).[15] Ultimately Angelo confesses to fornication with Isabella, the woman he thought he bedded; he still does not know with whom he slept. The friar briefly reappears to force Isabella to acknowledge that she has falsely accused Angelo; it is Mariana who was Angelo's sexual partner, not Isabella.

In this triangle of sex and blackmail no one can claim the high moral ground. Angelo *is* a fornicator, even if he does not know with whom. Mariana is as well and has tricked Angelo into sleeping with her, thus compromising not only her virtue but his chance to wed anyone else. Isabella is a liar and has participated in a conspiracy whose end was fornication.

In such a morass of moral failure in place of public shunning, all the sexual wrongs that have been committed or disclosed during the course of the play are rectified. The duke "condemns" Angelo to marry Mariana before he is executed.[16] Claudio, who wished to sacrifice his sister's virtue to save his own skin, is brought before the crowd and ordered to marry Juliet, who has just given birth to their child. Lucio is ordered to marry the prostitute mother of his out-of-wedlock child and assume its care.

Her brother free and Mariana married to Angelo, Isabella is now free to fulfill her ambition to become a cloistered nun. But can she take her vows? She has most uncharitably placed *her* virtue ahead of another's; she has let another take her place as fornicator to effect her brother's rescue. These are not trivial errors in judgment. Just at the moment when these questions might arise for the audience, the duke proposes marriage to her. The curtain falls, and the play ends without Isabella's response.

Really? Really. Crimes are forgiven; passion is excused and given its rightful place in marriage; the new law has not been vindicated, and the old law has not been enforced; nothing has changed except perhaps that the duke need no longer worry that his reign was too lax. Angelo's reign was even more corrupt and immoral than the duke's.

So is the duke a hero or a villain? Is the point of the play that law must be tempered with humanity, or that law cannot regulate sexuality? Are we to believe that coercion is an excuse for immoral activity? How can we maneuver in a world in which everyone with power is corrupt?[17]

There have been various answers to these questions. Frye would have us believe that the play ends without the resolution of any of these issues but with a regenerated society, "with forgiveness, reconciliation and the pursuit of happiness all over the place."[18] Marjorie Garber argues that the duke's inclination to test and tempt his subjects and thereby to regain his power is the only explanation available for what she calls his "puzzling" behavior and what I have called his lies.[19] G. Wilson Knight, on the other hand, sees in *Measure for Measure* an extended exposition of: "the moral nature of man in relation to the crudity of man's justice, especially in the matter of sexual vice."[20] Knight views the duke through a lens of Christian ethics. The imposition of judgment by people on people is doomed to failure since all people are sinners and therefore cannot stand in judgment of each other.[21] He sees the duke not as having failed in his administration of law but as someone who, upon self-reflection, sees that the legal process is a mockery because it does not take into account human nature. The duke, he claims, is like a kind father; all other characters in the play, his children. The plot, then, according to Knight, is a scheme, "a scientific experiment to see if extreme ascetic righteousness can stand the test of power."[22] He sees the final act of the play as the final judgment, where all problems are solved: the duke will teach by example human kindness and love; his marriage to Isabella is a blend of understanding, that is tolerance, and the imperatives of ethical purity. "Love asks no questions, sees no evil, transfiguring the just and unjust alike," writes Knight. He calls the play an ethical masterpiece.[23] I see no evidence to support this analysis.

In my view Harold C. Goddard hits closer to the mark when he claims that we see in *Measure for Measure* that the law is just a human instrument that may be used for good or evil and that we are mistaken when we confuse peace with the reign of law. When Isabella pleads that Angelo exercise mercy to save her brother from death, Angelo responds, "It is the law, not I, condemn your brother" (2.2.80). "The entire play," Goddard writes, "might be said to have been written just to italicize that lie."

What we see in Angelo and what the duke clearly suspects from the start is the truth of Lord Acton's observation almost three centuries later, that "power tends to corrupt and absolute power corrupts absolutely." That is why, Goddard observes, power pulls at the criminal element in all of us and is often "synonymous with crime."[24]

Certainly Angelo is guilty of the abuse of power when he, to whom the law has been entrusted, tries to trade his power of life and death over Claudio for Isabella's chastity. The question that I raise is whether the only other similarly situated character in the play, the duke, is similarly guilty of the criminal abuse of his power to the same end, to bed Isabella.

Contra Frye and Knight and others who may believe that the duke brings to his kingdom reconciliation, forgiveness, and peace, my experience with the law suggests that the play is as much as anything about the duke's manipulation of the law and of his subjects to secure the hand of Isabella.

What happens at the end of the play? Apparently out of nowhere the duke invites Isabella to marry him. Not any woman, but a young woman from a noble family on the cusp of permanently disappearing into the cloistered life of the convent of Saint Clare.[25] She has declared her intent to marry Jesus the very night the play begins.

The audience does not anticipate the duke's marriage proposal, which appears to the other characters to be without motivation, out of thin air. But that is unlikely, for it is not compatible with our understanding of how humans behave. We can and should assume that the end of the play is the culmination of the duke's intentional actions: events he initiated to fulfill a desire that has been building in him for some time and, more than that, that he has used his power in a way most likely to satisfy his ends, that is, to create success. This modest assumption gives us the first key to understanding the play. The duke lies to get the girl. He manipulates events to get the girl. And he is able to do this because he is smart about people and knows that he cannot do directly what he wants to do.

The duke is an absolute ruler. Why, then, does he not just propose to Isabella or order her to marry him in Act 1, scene 1? Perhaps the question has not been asked because the answer is so obvious: everything in the play tells us from the moment the curtain rises that Isabella would refuse any such proposal or order.[26] She is focused elsewhere and has made decisions contrary to those typical of the rest of "Vienna."[27] Her ideal life, the one she has chosen for herself, is that of a virgin who has decided to retreat as completely as possible from the vulgar and corrupt world in which she finds herself. She craves and seeks out in the cloister the most stringent limitations on her life (1.4.4). She seeks a life, it appears, deprived of sensual pleasure, of men, of contact with ordinary people, removed from the fleshly corruption and moral decay in which others wallow. Any marriage proposal to such a woman—even by an absolute ruler—would not succeed. Any order or direction to Isabella as the play begins that she is to marry the duke would be an invitation to her disobedience and martyrdom.

Once we make the reasonable assumption that the duke's idea to propose to Isabella does not arise on a whim, we can move on to the next issue: the lengths to which he will go to get the girl.

First, of course, the duke appears to abandon his power and leave town.[28] He says that he will stay in touch by writing from time to time (1.1.55). The clear implication is that he is about to leave for a sufficiently extended time that he must delegate his power (1.1.17–18, 43–44).[29] The state cannot exist with a vacuum at the top. He acknowledges that his departure is hasty; in Act 1, scene 1 we are witness to the few lines that are its entire preparation (1.1.53–55). What's the rush?

There is one immediate explanation. He has just learned or understood that Isabella is on the verge of taking her vows. Lusting after someone who is at the precipice of becoming permanently unattainable by becoming a cloistered nun is certainly a motive for immediate action. To achieve his end the duke must act quickly. And his longing for Isabella is not one that anyone, including the duke, might want to broadcast. Although Shakespeare will shortly tell us that he does not share the common view of the moral worth of the religious life,[30] any attempt to propose to, proposition, or seduce a novice or a nun might well be viewed by the duke himself and his subjects as not just an immoral pursuit but a depraved one. Thus the duke must act not only quickly but indirectly. He must find a way to bar Isabella from becoming a nun and to make it appear that what has made this happen is her own doing, an act of her own choice.

If we understand this to be the motivating impetus of the duke's actions, as I believe it is, much of the rest of the play falls into place.[31] To get the girl the duke engages in deceit and manipulation; he would use others as a means to his end, even unto their deaths, in violation of biblical law, Kantian first principles, and the natural sense in each of us that we should not use others as steppingstones to satisfy our sexual impulses. He abuses his power as regent to break laws and to violate the sanctity of the confessional, all to satisfy his passion against the explicit will of the object of his passion.

Shakespeare tells us two critical facts as the play begins: first, that virtue can flourish only in the public arena because virtue hidden (inside, say, a nunnery) is not really virtue; and second, that one's character is on one's face; that is, it cannot be hidden (1.1.27–39).

What comes of the first fact? The duke does not respect the life of a nun, a life in which virtue amounts to total withdrawal from society. What clearer example could there be of wasting virtue than a young woman about to take vows of chastity and retreat into a nunnery, never to be heard from again? And this young woman is one whom even her brother has noticed has "a prone [that is, ready] and speechless dialect such as move men" (1.2.182). That is, Isabella's manifest nature or character is that of a sexual being, a woman who is sexually charged, whether or not she knows it.

So the duke does not have any moral qualms about luring Isabella away from her chosen vocation. Such a commitment, in his eyes, would not be virtuous and would go against Isabella's very nature. The duke does not pause to worry about acting contrary to Isabella's express intent to join a nunnery. On his theory of goodness he is allowing her to become a moral creature.

To keep Isabella from taking her vows the duke must compromise her moral purity. To see how he does this, we must turn to the second fact: that one's character is on one's face. If this is true, then when the duke delegates his power to Angelo he knows both that Angelo will immediately move to enforce the laws against sexual misconduct and that Angelo will seek to satisfy his own sexual appetite (1.3.54). Both of these outcomes are necessary to the duke's plan.

With this understanding we can explain the first puzzle: why the duke delegates his power to someone who is neither wise nor experienced in law enforcement. Were the duke to delegate his power to Escalus, laws might well be enforced, but that enforcement would be tempered by a sense of proportion or justice and mercy. That is not what the duke wants. He wants someone to act so as to put Isabella in an untenable position and force her out of the nunnery. Angelo is perfect for this job. He can be counted on to enforce the laws without mercy. It is this characteristic, apparent to one and all, that secures him the position as the duke's stand-in. Lucio observes to Isabella after Claudio's arrest and death sentence that Angelo is "a man whose blood is very snow broth; one who never feels / The wanton strings and motions of the sense / But doth rebate and blunt his natural edge" (1.4.58–60). The duke acknowledges that he has not enforced Vienna's "strict statutes and most biting laws" (1.3.9), but Angelo, who does not appear to have blood in his veins or ordinary human appetites, renowned for his apparent imperviousness to sexual feelings, can be counted on to take a different course.

Many commentaries focus on the duke's observation "Hence we shall see / If power change purpose, what our seemers be" (1.3.53–54). On my account, however, this is something that the duke already knows about Angelo. Although the audience and readers learn this only later, from the outset the duke knows that Angelo's appearance that he is a "man of stricture and firm abstinence," that he is not to be moved by ordinary human emotions, is only that, an appearance (1.3.12). The duke, who believes that a person's character can be read on his face, already knows that Angelo will crack, that he will not be able to maintain his stance of emotional and sexual repression in the presence of a pleading Isabella. And how does he know this?

First, he knows that Isabella is a natural seductress; he has been seduced by her and understands the strength of that kind of power. Second, he is skilled at reading people's character—his own and others'. In Act 3 Escalus says, "Above all other strifes, [the duke] contended especially to know himself" (3.2.222), and in Act 4 the duke himself observes to the warden, "There is written in your brow provost, honesty and constancy. If I read it not truly, my ancient skill beguiles me" (4.2.152–53). He knows himself and he knows others.

With this understanding we can easily assume that the duke knows from the beginning that Angelo will strictly enforce the law, but that, at a human level, he is not as he appears, that in the right circumstance he is as subject to human sexual appetites and impulses as the next man. The duke is confident that with the authority he gives Angelo to enforce the law, Angelo will act to abate wanton sexual conduct, and to do this he will use Claudio, Isabella's brother, as an example. Acting against Claudio will bring Isabella into the action of the play and allow the duke to corrupt and compromise not only Angelo but, more important, Isabella.

It is a common practice in cracking down on rampant illegality to start enforcement in a way that makes clear the intent that what was allowed will no longer be tolerated. If one is looking to make an example of anyone, and Angelo can be predicted to be in search of such a person, Claudio is an inevitable choice. Once Angelo is in power and once he decides to make a priority the eradication of sexual misconduct, there is no other target for him. As I have said, Claudio is an admitted fornicator of high social status and known to the populace (see 1.6.66–68).[32] He is the only such character in the play.

My final assumption is that the duke knows not only that Angelo will act against Claudio but that he will impose a penalty severe enough to draw Isabella out of her cloister.[33]

With the condemnation of her brother assured by the duke's knowledge of Angelo, the duke begins his assault on Isabella. To wed Isabella he counts on two things: that she will fall for the bait he has created by putting Angelo in power, and that Angelo will out himself as a sexual being and use Claudio to seduce Isabella. We have no direct answer to how the duke knows these things; the evidence is circumstantial (a prosecutor's best friend) and cumulative.

First, as to Isabella, the duke counts on the fact that family ties will overcome religious scruples. Not a bad assumption: rare indeed is the family that puts principle ahead of the interests of its own, and Isabella, with her virtuous and sensual character apparent to the duke, is unlikely to be an exception. Had Isabella turned down Lucio's request in the opening act of the play that she plead her brother's case, the play would be over, the duke's hope of marriage destroyed. Given her claims to abhor fornication, were she as pious as she claims to be, had she the religious fervor and commitment she appears to have when she talks to the prioress about of the rules of the cloister, she might have slammed the door in Lucio's face. But she does not, as, I claim, the duke was betting.

Thus we know no later than the end of the first act that Angelo is corruptible (he has succumbed to the burgher's pleas to keep open Vienna's brothels) and early into the second that Isabella too can be compromised: she will abandon her principles when it concerns her brother; she will not live with the consequences of her own moral beliefs. On my analysis and the duke's calculation, she is morally lost as soon as she accedes to Lucio and goes to Angelo to plead Claudio's case. After all, she believes without question that Claudio has sinned and that if marriage, the simple solution, is not available to heal this wound, then it is just that he pay for his sin with his life. Isabella first says on meeting with Angelo that fornication is the

> vice that most I do abhor,
> And most desire should meet the blow of justice,
> For which I would not plead, but that I must,
> For which I must not plead, but that I am
> At war 'twixt will and will not. (2.2.29–33)

But whatever she says, she has left the convent to plead for her brother. With that action her fate is sealed. Neither of these two people are the moral stalwarts they declare themselves to be. That is what the duke needs for his manipulation. In different ways he is using their self-deceit to further his scheme to marry Isabella.

I do not claim that the duke knows in advance that he will use the bed trick to compromise Isabella. But I do claim that once she goes before Angelo, the duke knows that Angelo will succumb to Isabella and want to bed her. There are only two possible outcomes from this: she will be seduced by Angelo and be compromised, or she will resist him but succumb to the bed trick to save her brother and be compromised. In either event she is compromised, which is what the duke needs.

She is not seduced by Angelo but falls prey to the duke's morally invidious trick to spare Claudio. Replace one virgin for another in Angelo's bed; create fornicators who perfect their marriage contract, just like Claudio and Juliet. Deceive Angelo: substitute Mariana for Isabella.

It is certainly no later than this moment that Isabella loses her soul and with it her right to become a nun. For she has said about her brother that he has sinned. It is the moment for which the duke has waited.

With the bed trick the duke makes evident flaws in Isabella's character that leave her little choice but to give up the religious life. Once it is clear that she has made herself unworthy of that sanctuary, the duke's proposal of marriage is transformed from an nasty attempt to seduce an innocent bent on the religious life to the rescue of a woman who let another be corrupted to save her own virtue.

For this is what the duke must do to get the girl: save Isabella for himself and save her in a way that makes her both grateful to him and aware that she now has no alternative but to embrace society. The duke offers her the chance to do so as a reigning royal.

This theory explains as well why the duke's claims that he is acting in the best interests of the state are unpersuasive. His own explanation for his failures as a law enforcer (which he gives not to Angelo but to a friar he also corrupts by inducing him to help him hide in place) must be pretextual because it is so weak and implausible. When the friar who agrees to outfit and educate the duke as if he were a friar suggests that enforcement of law would be most effective when implemented by the duke, the duke protests that it would appear too dreadful (1.3.34), and he does not want to appear dreadful.

But this claim is undermined in that very conversation by other things that the duke says. He has already told Angelo that although he loves his subjects, he is uncomfortable with their enthusiastic admiration for him (1.1.67–70). Now he tells Friar Peter that it would hurt or anger his subjects if he, the man who let things go to wrack and ruin, were to enforce the letter of the law. So within the first act the duke has contradicted himself: he says he loves his people but is uncomfortable with their admiration and, at the same time, says that he cannot enforce the law for fear of losing the respect of his subjects. Hardly persuasive. The duke's explanation reeks of misdirection. Nor does it explain why the duke, having delegated his power to Angelo, will stay in Vienna to watch its implementation. On the other hand, on my analysis he must stay to maneuver the parties to his end.

And so we come to the end of the play. Isabella is now no longer the pure novice she was in Act 1; although still a virgin, she is morally corrupt. She has acceded to a plan to let another fornicate to save her brother—and as could have been predicted—to no avail. And she defamed Angelo by claiming that she slept with him to save her brother.

When the duke "returns" to resume power we see that the ploy of enticing Angelo to engage in the strict enforcement of the law has done nothing to promote the law and everything to demonstrate the duke's motive. After he has made lawful citizens of everyone else, the duke turns to Isabella with his marriage proposal. Her choices are limited: as the duke always knew, she is no longer fit to return to the cloister.

Her choices are to replace Mariana as a social outcast, perhaps to do penance in isolation for the rest of her life; to go to a less strict cloister to seek redemption; or to accept the duke's marriage proposal.[34] We know that Shakespeare does not value virtue in a vacuum. She really has only one choice, consistent with her sensual character and her hope to regain any moral footing. And so, silently, she must agree to the marriage.

The duke gets the girl, but only by having used the law to his own ends. He is the epitome of a hypocrite: appearing to use law enforcement to reestablish order when in fact he does nothing of the sort. He uses it to the end of getting his girl.

The manipulation of the enforcement of the law does nothing to bring respect to the lawmaker; it does nothing to make compliance with the law even an aspirational goal for his subjects.[35] Both Angelo and Isabella, who would favor law without mercy, who would preclude nonmarital sexual conduct on pain of death, are seen to create circumstances in which virtually all the duke's subjects would be subject to the death penalty.

Sexual longing and acts among the duke's subjects cannot be dismissed or precluded by law. That would be like making breathing illegal. Doing so would violate the impulse to life and have the effect of undermining the authority of the lawmaker. But the duke's malicious use of law to get the girl is morally bankrupt. Law is effective when it is not used tyrannically or for private gain, but when it respects and recognizes the equality of each of us within the context of shared moral values. None of this is present in *Measure for Measure.* There is no legal or moral guide for us in this play. There is no mercy or benevolence in the duke's marrying off all who have broken the law. There is only the cover of acts that make public Isabella's failures and the inevitability that her only future is with him. There is no model for us in how the duke deals with his responsibilities; there is only the haunting specter that the duke may some day be judged as he has judged, that he will be used as a means to someone else's greater glory. The unlawful and tyrannical use of power creates pity, contempt, anxiety, and fear. The duke's actions to the end of getting the girl are a lesson in power, not love. Love is the one human feeling that is not in play in *Measure for Measure*—not the love of God or a man's love for a woman. So vacuous is Angelo's claim of love to Isabella that it is said but once and never referred to again (2.2.140). Angelo, a novice at using power to achieve his ends, fails. While Shakespeare appears to leave the issue open, any prosecutor would conclude that with his experience in the exercise of power and his wisdom about people, the duke succeeds.

NOTES

I am grateful to Richard Hyland and Alexander Nehamas for their detailed and insightful comments on an earlier draft of this article.

1. All play citations are to William Shakespeare, *Measure for Measure*, ed. Jonathan Crewe New York: Penguin Books, 2000).

2. J. W. Lever, "The Disguised Ruler," in *Twentieth Century Interpretations of Measure for Measure*, ed. George L. Geckle Englewood Cliffs, NJ: Prentice-Hall, 1970).

3. Harold C. Goddard, *The Meaning of Shakespeare* (Chicago: University of Chicago Press, 1951), 2: 50–68.

4. For example, Marjorie Garber, *Shakespeare After All* New York: Pantheon, 2004), 563.

5. M. C. Bradbrook, "Authority, Truth and Justice in *Measure for Measure*," in *William Shakespeare's* Measure for Measure, ed. Harold Bloom (New York: Chelsea House, 1987).

6. In fact this conclusion is just an instance of Chekhov's oft-quoted direction to delete everything that has no relevance to the story. "If in Act I you have a pistol hanging on the wall, then it must fire in the last act." Donald Rayfield, *Anton Chekhov: A Life* (New York: Henry Holt, 1997), 203.

7. Bradbrook, "Authority, Truth and Justice in *Measure for Measure*," 20.

8. I served as a federal prosecutor for over twenty years in the Eastern District of Pennsylvania.

9. I would go so far as to argue that the duke acts illegally when he delegates his powers. Because he is the absolute regent he can abdicate, or he can rule, but he cannot lawfully turn his power over to another during a temporary absence. Since he vitiates all that Angelo does and attempts to do, there is also some question as to whether he *really* delegates his power to Angelo, or whether he just appears to do so in furtherance of a scheme of personal advancement that I describe in what follows.

10. We still struggle with the apparent indifference of the Clintons as to how President Clinton's power affected his ability to seduce and abandon a flirtatious intern, and several state governors have resigned when their sexual lives were disclosed.

11. That Claudio was a fornicator requires that we adopt conditions of marriage in the play's Vienna that were related to but not identical with those in England during Shakespeare's time. Then a marriage contract was legally binding once the parties publicly expressed their present intention to be husband and wife. Claudio and Juliet had a marriage contract but had not publicly expressed their intention to be husband and wife. They hid that intent and appeared instead to be betrothed. Betrothal was a commitment to be married in the future and was sometimes conditional on, for example, the receipt of a dowry. If the condition was not met, the engagement was nullified. In England, if a couple who were conditionally betrothed had sex, they were married, regardless of the fulfillment of the marriage or their public expression of the intent to be husband and wife. Claudio says that he and Juliet had a contract to be married, had not publicly announced their intention to be husband and wife, were waiting for their friends to fund a dowry, but nonetheless had sex. In the play their sexual relations, which Juliet's pregnancy made evident, was insufficient to consummate a marriage, and thus Claudio was a fornicator (1.2.144–54). Larry Weiss, "Common-Law Marriage in *Measure for Measure*," unpublished manuscript, 1966, Selected Works, http:// works.bepress.com/lawrence_weiss/1; Stuart Hampton-Reeves, *Measure for Measure* (Basingstoke: Palgrave Macmillan, 2007), 19–20.

12. Lucio is a friend of Claudio, but his primary function in the play is to demonstrate the state of debauchery and decay into which the society has fallen. In the course of the action we learn that he frequents brothels and prostitutes, is aware of Vienna's rampant plague (syphilis), and has fathered a child with a prostitute; abandoned the child, who is instead being raised by a madam. We see as well that he gossips irresponsibly and goes so far as to slander the regent—itself a capital crime.

13. Although not necessarily true, it is likely that if she could not see the man to whom she was speaking it was because she was speaking through a covering with only a few holes through which she could talk. If that is true, then the man could not have seen her either, and without such vision the de facto seduction that follows could not have occurred.

14. Northrop Frye, *Northrop Frye on Shakespeare*, ed. Robert Sandler (New Haven, CT: Yale University Press, 1986), 149.

15. Neither of these allegations is true. Even had Claudio been executed as Angelo directed, Angelo would not be responsible for a *murder*. Claudio committed the capital crime for which he was sentenced. And since Isabella did not sleep with Angelo, her claim that he induced her to sleep with him to save her brother's life is also false (5.1.102). At most, were Angelo to have had Claudio killed, Isabella could sue for breach of contract.

16. Mariana successfully pleads to save his life.

17. See, for example, Constance Jordan, "Interpreting Statute in *Measure for Measure*" and David Bevington, "Equity in *Measure for Measure*," both in *Shakespeare and the Law*, ed. Constance Braden, Martha C. Nussbaum, and Richard Strier (Chicago: University of Chicago Press, 2013); E. M. W. Tillyard, "*Measure for Measure*," in Geckle, *Twentieth Century Interpretations of Measure for Measure*.

18. Frye, *Northrop Frye on Shakespeare*, 155.

19. Garber, *Shakespeare After All*, 579.

20. G. Wilson Knight, "*Measure for Measure* and the Gospels," in Geckle, *Twentieth Century Interpretations of Measure for Measure*, 27.

21. Knight, "*Measure for Measure* and the Gospels," 29.

22. Knight, "*Measure for Measure* and the Gospels," 32.

23. Knight, "*Measure for Measure* and the Gospels," 48.

24. Goddard, *The Meaning of Shakespeare*, 2: 51, 59.

25. In an attempt to save Claudio's life, Escalus tells Angelo that Claudio and Isabella's father had a "most noble father" (2.2.6–7).

26. Isabella has made her decision against a background of an epidemic of syphilis and a general loss of moral rectitude among the duke's subjects. There is no passion that is not acted upon, no impulse controlled: life is licentious for one and all.

27. Vienna is a stand-in for London and is depicted as licentious and bawdy at every social level. Whether that is inevitable, as Lucio claims, or because of lax law enforcement, as the duke suggests, is a question that we still debate today.

28. I say "appears" because, as we have seen, with the exception of the arrest of Claudio, none of Angelo's orders is effected. Since on my calculation the duke "returns" after an absence of four days, there is no time to pull down all the suburban brothels. The duke intervenes to save Claudio from execution, and Bernadine saves himself from a similar fate. The exception has the duke's desired effect of keeping Isabella from taking her vows and bringing her back into the larger community.

29. In light of the duke's claims, which almost immediately follow, that the Viennese population has become lawless, lewd, and without conscience under his rule, this praise of his magistrate is extremely odd. He is lying to someone. As I discuss below, I believe his lie is not to Escalus but to the friar who equips him to execute his fraud scheme.

30. Virtue not played out among society is no virtue.

31. If we do not, nothing in the play makes sense and nothing appears true.

32. Escalus's attempt to plead for Claudio on the grounds that he comes from a good family is sufficient to establish that what will happen to Claudio will become known to one and all as an example. No one can escape Angelo's enforcement of the law. Angelo makes this point by directing that Claudio be paraded through town on his way to jail—not just to humiliate Claudio but also to educate the general public who see what has happened to him.

33. I owe this latter point to members of my Brown University class Sex and the Law: Strange Bedfellows (Fall 2013).

34. Tina Packer views the failure of Isabella to respond to the duke's proposal as a moment when the play shifts its foundation. It is at this moment, she claims, that the unconscious bursts forth with unexpected questions, new feelings are acknowledged, and "chaos of mind and body ensues." This moment "allow[s] the Duke to be the embodiment of the Higher Power, Isabella the suffering human being trying to reach him—and to symbolize the moment in a tableau like Michelangelo's picture on the ceiling of the Sistine Chapel, of God touching and giving Adam life. . . . Or men and women meeting so that together—and with the whole of themselves—they can meet and transform into a larger being which incorporates both the sexual and spiritual." Tina Packer, *Women of Will* (New York: Knopf, 2015), 211. While this is an optimistic view of the end of the play, as Packer admits, it is an interpretation not grounded in the play but in our contemporary understanding of psychosexual motives and expressions of our deepest selves. I see no need for such a reading when within the play we can find a clear answer to the duke's motivation, one that is consistent with the play and does not require us to shift at the last moment our fundamental understanding of the motives of the central characters.

35. On Justice Oliver Wendell Holmes's "bad man" theory of the law, the lesson of *Measure for Measure* is that all will be forgiven, except perhaps disrespect of the king himself. Oliver Wendell Holmes, "The Path of the Law," *Harvard Law Review* 10 (1897): 457.

PART II

Race and Crime

8

Justice Thomas and Bigger Thomas

Justin Driver

I

My Grandfather's Son, the book Justice Clarence Thomas wrote in 2007 chronicling his improbable ascent from poverty to power, is perhaps the most literary memoir a Supreme Court justice has ever written. The term *literary* here applies to Thomas's volume in at least two distinct senses. First, his engaging use of language far surpasses the mundane writing that typically appears in books by justices, allowing the finest passages in *My Grandfather's Son* to attain the status of literature. Beginning with Thomas's arresting first sentence, it is unmistakably clear that his book contains significant literary ambitions. "I was nine years old when I met my father," he begins.[1] This grim opening—composed of plain, almost exclusively monosyllabic words—succeeds in both transporting readers into Thomas's young mind and setting the stage for the familial and material privations that plagued his early childhood in Pinpoint, Georgia. The sentence's lone multisyllabic word (*father*) arrives at the very end, leaving the impression that Thomas uses it only because the informal, one-syllable counterpart (*dad*) would convey an inaccurate intimacy. Thomas did not, however, merely craft a first-rate overture as an effort to draw in browsing readers. More than two hundred pages later he offers a poetic account of the media's reaction when it became apparent that President George H. W. Bush had emerged from his vacation home in Kennebunkport, Maine, to nominate Thomas to the

Supreme Court in 1991: "At two o'clock we walked through the front door together. The press corps gasped. 'It's Thomas,' someone blurted out. The clicking of cameras sounded like summer rain falling on the tin roof of our hand-built house in Liberty County, the individual drops blurring together in a steady pitter-patter."[2] Apart from Thomas's concentrated use of onomatopoeia ("blurted," "gasped," "clicking," "pitter-patter"), this passage is notable for its deft comparison of two superficially incongruous events: the pomp of a Supreme Court nomination in privileged New England alongside a downpour in the decidedly unprivileged Old South. This inspired aural association, occurring toward the memoir's close, has the effect of bringing readers full circle, demanding contemplation of this ending's extreme unlikelihood given the author's exceptionally modest origins.

The second sense in which *My Grandfather's Son* is notably literary appears in its abundant references to fictional works. As befitting the former undergraduate English major, Thomas consistently cites—and periodically even quotes—several novelists who made an impression on him over the years. Some of these literary references are hardly revelations. Few knowledgeable readers, for instance, will be shocked to discover that Ayn Rand's *Atlas Shrugged* and *The Fountainhead* occupy positions of prominence on the Thomas bookshelf. But other references seem somewhat less predictable, including Franz Kafka's *The Trial*, Harper Lee's *To Kill a Mockingbird*, and Ralph Ellison's *Invisible Man*. From more recent decades Thomas briefly invokes John Berendt's depiction of Savannah, Georgia, in *Midnight in the Garden of Good and Evil* as a counterpoint to the Savannah that he knew during his youth. In addition to these novels Thomas also cites the poetry of Robert Frost and, by titling his final chapter "Going to Meet the Man," alludes to the short stories of James Baldwin.

No literary work, however, figures more conspicuously in Justice Thomas's memoir than *Native Son*, the Richard Wright novel from 1940 that introduced the world to his indelible creation, Bigger Thomas. In Justice Thomas's view, he and Bigger have considerably more in common than their surname. In a book that spans fewer than three hundred pages, Justice Thomas expressly identifies himself with Bigger on a few separate occasions. His reliance on *Native Son* merits sustained examination because it sheds significant light on how readers impose their own agendas on literary works, how particular historical moments shape those agendas, and how interpretations driven by those agendas can prove surprisingly durable. Examining Bigger Thomas through the eyes of Justice Thomas, moreover, appears to confound the notion that judges' opinions will reflect the most apparent lessons of the novels they hold dear.

Bigger Thomas, it would seem, is a man that only a mother could love. And given his mother's withering attitude toward him when the novel begins, that maternal love appears to have been no sure thing.[3] Even admirers of *Native Son* concede that its protagonist is basically unlikeable. As Arnold Rampersad has written, "[I]t is hard to think of a central character in all of literature who is less likeable than Bigger Thomas. With other blacks, Bigger is bullying, surly, treacherous, and cowardly; with whites—understandably, to be sure—he is wary and deceitful."[4] In a similar vein, some of *Native Son*'s most distinguished critics fault Wright's novel for selecting a protagonist with whom few readers would readily identify. In "Everybody's Protest Novel," James Baldwin in 1949 contended that *Native Son*, like *Uncle Tom's Cabin*, fails as literature because it is less interested in accurately depicting the human condition than in reducing actual people into abstract symbols of suffering: "The failure of the protest novel lies in its rejection of life, the human being, the denial of his beauty, dread, power, in its insistence that it is his categorization alone which is real and which cannot be transcended."[5] In 1963, Ralph Ellison echoed this critique of Bigger as a character lacking emotional depth and attributed the shortcoming to what he regarded as Wright's mistaken elevation of politics over art: "In *Native Son*, Wright began with the ideological proposition that what whites think of the Negro's reality is more important than what Negroes themselves know it to be. Hence Bigger Thomas was presented as a near-subhuman indictment of white oppression. He was designed to shock whites out of their apathy and end the circumstances out of which Wright insisted Bigger emerged."[6]

Given these persistent critiques that Wright's protagonist evinces little in the way of a likeable or relatable human being, Justice Thomas's close self-identification with Bigger Thomas is striking. Even many sympathetic readers would surely view Bigger as a particularly grotesque example of how racial oppression in the United States can disfigure its most vulnerable targets. On this account, Bigger presents a cautionary tale of the profound psychological damage that the nation inflicts on impoverished racial minorities who possess neither the education required to achieve even meager professional goals nor the socialization necessary to nurture mutually supportive interpersonal relationships. It should hardly be surprising that an individual growing up in Bigger's severely limited circumstances turned to lawlessness and violence. But comprehending the circumstances that shaped Bigger does not turn him into anything other than a charmless rogue. According to Wright's own account, Bigger is a man to be feared, not a man to befriend.[7] But where others might view Bigger as an antisocial menace, Justice Thomas appears largely to see himself.[8]

Justice Thomas has periodically entertained the distinct possibility that he could have ended up on the wrong side of the law instead of interpreting the law. During his Supreme Court confirmation hearings, before Anita Hill's allegations became public, then-Judge Thomas offered gripping testimony noting that he often confronted this possibility in his chambers at the D.C. Circuit. "[O]n my current court,

I have occasion to look out the window that faces C Street, and there are converted buses that bring in the criminal defendants to our criminal justice system, busload after busload," he explained. "And you look out, and you say to yourself, and I say to myself almost every day, But for the grace of God there go I."[9] In *My Grandfather's Son*, he briefly returns to this theme and details how his criminal potential could have materialized: "In Pinpoint I was a little Negro boy growing up among hard-working but uneducated people. From there I moved to the confusion and squalor of a run-down tenement in Savannah, where I led a life of being cold and not knowing when I would feel warmth again, of constant, gnawing hunger and not knowing when I would eat again, a life in which knowledge trickled in by the thimbleful when I yearned for floods of truth. To stay there would have doomed me to a dismal life of ignorance, perhaps even of crime—a life lost before it started."[10] Precious few other Supreme Court justices in the nation's history would be able to write those sentences or seriously envision their lives descending into criminality. One might be tempted to attribute Justice Thomas's identification with Bigger Thomas to his intimacy with a community where turning to a life of crime represents a familiar, well-traveled path. Yielding to that particular temptation, however, turns out to be incorrect. Justice Thomas identifies with Bigger Thomas not because he views him as a criminal, but precisely because he does not.

II

The first—and most significant—time *My Grandfather's Son* draws on *Native Son* occurs when Justice Thomas describes his rediscovery of the novel during the early 1970s. The passage merits quoting at length because it contains, I contend, a substantial misreading of the novel: "In the last semester of my senior year [in college], I took an independent-study course on black novelists. Richard Wright's *Native Son* had already made a deep impression when I'd read it in high school, but now it meant even more to me. As I reentered the nightmare world of Bigger Thomas, the innocent young black man who finds himself caught up in a chain of circumstances that spins out of control and causes him to commit an act of violence that leads inexorably to his own death, I envisioned myself slipping into a similar vortex of self-destructive behavior."[11] Here, Justice Thomas views Bigger Thomas as a fundamentally passive character, one whom events act upon and who holds little if any responsibility for the fate that befalls him. Justice Thomas's language captures this passivity well, as Bigger "finds himself" "caught up" "in a chain of circumstances." Those circumstances, in turn, "spin[] out of [Bigger's] control" and "cause[] him to commit" a violent act. On this account it seems less accurate to find "mistakes were made by Bigger" than "mistakes were visited upon Bigger." The subject of how much autonomy Bigger has is a central—perhaps *the* central—question *Native Son* poses.[12] That Justice Thomas sees Bigger as overwhelmingly a product of his environment may be at least somewhat surprising to those familiar with his generally austere treatment of criminal defendants at the Supreme Court. But many *Native Son* readers over the years have undoubtedly shared Justice Thomas's assessment of Bigger as a figure lacking any meaningful sense of autonomy. Although this fatalist analysis may encounter difficulty explaining why some individuals raised in circumstances similar to Bigger's (or conditions more dire still) lead lives that turn out very differently, it cannot be labeled a misreading, let alone a substantial misreading. Rather the quantum of Bigger's autonomy is an interpretive matter upon which reasonable readers can differ.

What seems far less open to interpretation in this passage, though, is Justice Thomas's classifying Bigger as "the innocent young black man" at the center of *Native Son*. While Bigger is undeniably a "young black man," Justice Thomas's description of him as "innocent" misses the mark. The beginning of *Native Son* establishes that Bigger is part of a crew that forcibly robs black shop owners with some regularity. When his crew conspires to commit a robbery against a white-owned business for the first time, Bigger becomes so overcome with dread at the prospect of robbing a white man that he scuttles the plan by physically assaulting Gus, one of his co-conspirators. Bigger brandishes his knife and humiliates Gus by forcing him to lick the blade in exchange for sparing him greater physical harm. When Bigger takes in a film at a local movie theater, he opts to supplement the visual experience with a tactile one, by—in his terminology— "polishing [his] nightstick."[13] Bigger spent some time in a reformatory school for the crime of stealing automobile tires. During his job interview with Mr. Dalton he asserts that he did not commit this particular crime. And it is certainly plausible that Bigger did not actually steal the tires, as racial minorities—then and now—are particularly susceptible to receiving sanctions for crimes they did not commit. But it is also quite plausible that Bigger's protestation to Dalton is simply one of the many lies that he utters throughout the novel.

Perhaps, though, Justice Thomas intends to suggest that Bigger is "innocent" in a narrower sense: innocent of the rape and first-degree murder of Mary Dalton, the crimes for which he is sentenced to die. Bigger did not, after all, rape Mary. Nor did he intend to kill Mary when he used a pillow to smother her; he sought merely to silence her so as to avoid having Mrs. Dalton detect his presence—a black man's presence—in the bedroom of a young white woman. On this view, Bigger's actions can be construed as stemming from a racialized panic that, as assessed by contemporaneous standards, was not only perfectly understandable but was downright sensible. Even if Bigger can accurately be viewed as committing some lesser homicide offense (say, manslaughter), it was not first-degree murder.

But if Justice Thomas views Bigger as "innocent" on this narrow understanding, his notion encounters serious analytical trouble when one steps back for a moment to contemplate what transpired immediately before Mary's death and what occurred in the days that followed. After Bigger drives Mary home, he notes that she is severely inebriated, verbally nonresponsive, and incapable of standing on her own two feet; she seems to have lost consciousness. Mary's incapacitated state does not prevent Bigger from repeatedly kissing her or from placing his hands firmly on her breasts after he has lifted her into bed. It seems impossible to understand his conduct as constituting anything other than sexual assault and anything but innocent. Indeed, after he places her in bed, his train of thought strongly suggests he is contemplating having sex with her—which is to say, given the context, raping her—before Mrs. Dalton enters the bedroom: "[Bigger] lifted her and laid her on the bed. Something urged him to leave at once, but he leaned over her, excited, looking at her face in the dim light, not wanting to take his hands from her breasts. She tossed and mumbled sleepily. He tightened his fingers on her breasts, kissing her again, feeling her move toward him. He was aware only of her body now; his lips trembled. Then he stiffened. The door behind him had creaked."[14] If this passage leaves some lingering doubt about his intentions, Bigger subsequently erases it, informing his attorney, Max, that he was preparing to rape Mary before Mrs. Dalton's interruption. Had Bigger actually followed through and raped Mary, it seems quite conceivable that he would have subsequently felt compelled to end her life. After Bigger entered Mary's bedroom, thus, it may have been a question only of *when* her corpse would enter the Dalton's furnace, not *whether* it would do so. In the cold light of the following day, it is true that Bigger regrets Mary's death. But his regret, alas, appears to stem principally, if not exclusively, from his failure to secure financial gain for the act—an oversight that he aims to remedy by concocting a kidnapping and ransom scheme.

There can be little question that Bigger possesses the capacity to rape and to murder because he rapes and murders his girlfriend Bessie when he is on the run from the police. After Bessie realizes the full extent of Bigger's involvement with the Dalton case, she clearly communicates both verbally and physically her aversion to having sex with him. But Bigger ignores her refusals because—in language recalling his feelings shortly before Mrs. Dalton intruded—"[h]e was conscious of nothing now but her and what he wanted."[15] Bessie howls in protest and tries to push Bigger away, and Wright continues, "He had to now. *don't Bigger don't* He was sorry, but he had to."[16] Almost immediately after Bigger climaxes, he begins plotting how best to kill Bessie because he concludes that he cannot take her on the lam with him: "He remembered that he had seen two bricks lying on the floor of the room as he had entered."[17] Bigger uses one of those bricks to strike Bessie in the head repeatedly, and then throws what he presumes is her dead body down an air-shaft. (Bigger would subsequently learn that Bessie died not from the blunt trauma but from hypothermia.) Thus, when Justice Thomas writes that Bigger committed "an act of violence," he conveniently disregards the brutally violent acts that Bigger inflicts on Bessie. Those crimes were neither accidental nor required to maintain his freedom. Whatever the range of words appropriate to describe Bigger Thomas, Justice Thomas's invocation of the term *innocent* is perplexing.

If Justice Thomas misreads Bigger Thomas, the question then becomes: Why did that misreading occur? No one other than Justice Thomas himself can know the precise answer to this question (and even he may not fully know the answer or be able to articulate it). It seems likely, though, that a good portion of his misleading portrayal of Wright's protagonist is attributable to the specific time and social milieu in which he had his most meaningful encounter with *Native Son*.

As Justice Thomas recounts in his memoir, when he reread *Native Son* as a college senior in the spring of 1971, he was in the midst of a period when he identified—however provisionally—with notions of Black Power: "[T]he more I read about the black power movement, the more I wanted to be a part of it."[18] As early as 1968, the year that witnessed the assassinations of Martin Luther King Jr. and Robert Kennedy, Thomas could at least in retrospect sum up his political identity with considerable ease: "I was an angry black man."[19]

During that same era, some prominent proponents of Black Power rediscovered *Native Son* and held up its protagonist as an early exemplar of black masculinity and black resistance in the face of white oppression. In 1966, Eldridge Cleaver wrote an essay for *Ramparts* that compares Baldwin's recent work unfavorably—and with unmistakable antigay sentiment—to *Native Son*. Referring to the gay Baldwin as "Sugar," Cleaver contends that "Rufus Scott, the weak, craven hearted ghost of *Another Country*," cannot hold a candle to "Bigger Thomas of *Native Son*, the black rebel of the ghetto and a man."[20] Inveighing against the civil rights movement's nonviolence, Cleaver asserts that black citizens should remember Bigger as "a man [engaged] in violent . . . rebellion against the stifling, murderous, totalitarian white world. There was no trace in Bigger of a Martin Luther King–type self-effacing love for his oppressors."[21] Cleaver further contends, almost wistfully, that "Bigger would have been completely baffled . . . at Baldwin's advice to his nephew (*The Fire Next Time*), concerning white people: 'You must accept them and accept them with love. For these innocent people have no other hope.' "[22]

The Black Power movement's veneration of Bigger would eventually find expositors within academia. Addison Gayle Jr.'s *The Way of the New World: The Black*

Novel in America offers an extended analysis of Bigger in a chapter called "The Black Rebel" that both resonates with Cleaver's interpretation and nicely anticipates Thomas's reading. Amplifying Cleaver's focus on black masculinity, Gayle suggests that within *Native Son* the white subordination of blacks serves to invert standard values, meaning "murder is not a mark of man's inhumanity, but of his humanity, not an act denoting the degenerate, but the hero, not an effort at self-destruction, but an attempt to validate manhood."[23] Gayle then summarizes: "In short, one must understand, that the murderer of Mary Dalton is a young man of great sensibility."[24] Preceding Justice Thomas's reading of Bigger Thomas as "innocent" by more than three decades, Gayle contends in similar (if more conceptual) language that Mary's death "move[d] Bigger from a state of innocence to one of maturity, that unleashed the man within the boy."[25] Yet Gayle arrives at this declaration of Bigger's innocence only after offering a severely sanitized account of the events in *Native Son* that precede Mary's death. "Everything before [Mary's death] is prelude," Gayle writes, the altercations between Bigger and his family; plotting robbery with neighborhood friends; the job as chauffeur to the Dalton family, where he is subjected to the obsequious behavior of Mary and her friend Jan."[26] Among the other incidents omitted from this account are Bigger's aggravated assault of Gus, Bigger's sexual assault of Mary, and Bigger's public masturbation. Indeed, Gayle's rendering almost manages to make "plotting robbery with neighborhood friends" sound like a wholesome afterschool activity. Never mind that Bigger and his pals do not typically stop with mere plotting. In order to elevate Bigger Thomas into a serviceable hero, it would seem that the Black Power movement needed to buff out some of his rougher edges and in the process transform the deeply flawed character that Wright actually delivered.

Justice Thomas's recollections of his views from this time demonstrate clear compatibility with the Black Power sensibilities that extolled Bigger Thomas as a model of racial resistance. After proclaiming his affinity with the Black Power movement in *My Grandfather's Son*, Thomas sounds much like Cleaver in allowing that he harbored serious reservations about the wisdom of nonviolent protest and the utility of "working within the system."[27] Echoing Gayle's doubts about using traditional values to confront racial injustice, Thomas notes that he viewed his relatives "and the millions of other compliant, self-deluded blacks who played by the rules" as naïve.[28] "Might it be that those rules were nothing more than a sinister invention devised by the white man to fool blacks into cooperating with the oppressive machinery of American life?" he asks.[29] For Justice Thomas this question could elicit only two valid responses: "Yes" and "Hell, yes!" Most pertinent of all, though, Justice Thomas discloses that, even when he worked in the Missouri attorney general's office during the mid-1970s, he was "bothered . . . that as a criminal-appeals attorney, [he] would have to argue in favor of keeping blacks in jail."[30] He found advancing such arguments troublesome: "I still thought of most imprisoned blacks as political prisoners. I had no facts to back up this opinion, a reflex response left over from my radical days, and didn't need any: I knew that anything 'the man' did to black people was oppression, pure and simple."[31] This statement vividly encapsulates the mindset with which Justice Thomas approached Bigger Thomas as an undergraduate and why he may have felt such kinship toward the character.

It is not exactly a secret that Justice Thomas no longer views most black inmates as political prisoners. Intriguingly, the triggering event that he identifies as prompting him to reject this view arose in one of his Missouri criminal cases that featured facts bearing at least passing resemblance to one aspect of Bigger Thomas's narrative. "What changed my mind [about black inmates] was the case of a black man convicted of raping and sodomizing a black woman in Kansas City after holding a sharp can opener at the throat of her small son," Justice Thomas explains. "He was no political prisoner—he was a vicious thug. Perhaps he and the woman he'd brutalized had both been victims of racism, but if that were so, then she'd been victimized twice, first by 'the man' and then by the thug."[32] Bigger's sexual violation of Bessie, of course, also involves a black man raping a black woman. Despite this significant overlap, Justice Thomas reaches starkly contrasting appraisals of the two figures. Where Bigger Thomas is an "innocent young black man," the unnamed criminal defendant is "a vicious thug." It is certainly true that the two narratives contain differences. But it is also far from clear that those differences redound to Bigger's benefit. Although Bigger did not threaten a small child with a kitchen tool before raping Bessie, the Kansas City rapist evidently did not bash in his victim's brains before leaving her for dead. Perhaps if the Kansas City rapist had the good sense to assault a white person first, he would have risen in Justice Thomas's estimation. Such a suggestion is nothing less than absurd, and Justice Thomas would certainly reject it. The suggestion does serve to highlight, though, how Justice Thomas arrives at his sanguine assessment of Bigger by effectively erasing the treatment of Bessie. It also underscores how the difference between "an innocent young black man" and "a vicious thug" sometimes lies in the eye of the beholder.

It hardly seems extravagant to maintain that if Justice Thomas somehow encountered Bigger Thomas today as a party in a Supreme Court case he would more readily see a vicious thug than an innocent man. That Justice Thomas continues to cling to his earlier reading of Bigger, long after he has abandoned the ideological commitments that yielded that reading, is a powerful testament to the durability of literary interpretations. After literary characters form deep impressions in readers' minds, those impressions harden and prove exceedingly difficult to dislodge. Many people alter their political attitudes quite dramatically during the course of their lives; attitudes toward characters from literature, however, remain remarkably constant. We change. Fictional characters seem to stay exactly the same.

III

Justice Thomas's frequent invocations of Bigger Thomas in his memoir succeed in complicating a central aspiration for the field of law and literature. If only judges had access to the correct creative works, this aspiration runs, their legal opinions would be improved because they would be grounded in the sorts of humanist considerations that dominate lasting literature.[33] Under this theory, great fiction leads to great law. Although scholars do not generally spell out the underlying premise that this literarily informed jurisprudence will be a more liberal jurisprudence, the implication is unmistakable. It would be truly astonishing, after all, if many professors writing in an overwhelmingly liberal field within the overwhelmingly liberal legal academy aimed to move the law in a more conservative direction.[34] Yet Justice Thomas's repeated appeals to *Native Son* make it quite clear that judges can simultaneously extol a literary work and prove impervious to the lessons that the work seems to propound. Novels, even more than most other types of written text, contain ample indeterminacy, and that is probably a good thing. (If you show me a novel featuring a clear thesis statement, I will show you a bad novel.) But the indeterminacy of novels allows readers with different normative commitments to walk away from the same book with starkly different conclusions.

Occasionally, readers even seem capable of deriving lessons from a novel that approach precisely the opposite of what the novelist likely would have intended. When *My Grandfather's Son* first invokes *Native Son*, for instance, Justice Thomas reflects upon a protest against the Vietnam War that he participated in as a college student. According to Justice Thomas, the protest spiraled out of control, with police firing tear gas into the crowd assembled in Harvard Square. That event led Justice Thomas to conclude that he needed to avoid future protests because, like Bigger Thomas, such events could "cause him to commit an act of violence" that resulted in his own death. "Something like that, I realized, could have happened to me in Harvard Square," Thomas writes. "I resolved to lead my life in such a way as to steer clear of such potentially deadly situations."[35] Had *Native Son*'s author been available to advise a young Clarence Thomas, it seems dubious that Wright would have encouraged him to drop antiwar protests. When Wright produced *Native Son* in 1940, after all, he was a member of the Communist Party, an organization that is not primarily known for its aversion to political protest or for its approval of America's military engagement in Vietnam.

It also merits contemplating whether Wright—and Bigger Thomas, for that matter—would find other invocations of *Native Son* in *My Grandfather's Son* availing. After discussing Anita Hill's allegations of sexual harassment, Justice Thomas invokes Bigger Thomas twice in rapid succession: "What had happened to Bigger Thomas, I knew, could happen to any black man, including me. 'To hint that he had committed a sex crime was to pronounce a death sentence. . . .' This was why I'd gone out of my way to avoid the very behavior of which I was now being accused."[36] A few pages later he describes feeling "wild-eyed and desperate" and "half crazed with fear" because, "[a]fter a lifetime of struggle and achievement, I'd been thrust back into Bigger Thomas's world, a dark, cramped hell devoid of hope."[37] Without diminishing the importance of a Supreme Court justiceship or the feelings of humiliation associated with Hill's allegations (regardless of their veracity), it seems highly implausible that Bigger Thomas would recognize Justice Thomas's world as bearing any meaningful relationship to his own. For Bigger Thomas, the question is life or death. For Clarence Thomas, the question is life on the Supreme Court or life on the D.C. Circuit. The inappositeness of these two existences is well captured by the sentence that appears immediately after Justice Thomas offers an extended, dreary quotation from *Native Son*: "I was spent by the time the U.S. marshals drove me home from the White House."[38] If this sentence captures even a small part of a "hell devoid of hope," Bigger Thomas would be only the first in a long line of people eager to sell their souls to the devil. In the heat of the moment, of course, we all tend to enlarge our problems out of proportion. But Justice Thomas wrote these lines more than fifteen years after the allegations became public and, not incidentally, more than fifteen years after he had won confirmation to the Supreme Court. The heat should have long since cooled, allowing him to appreciate that, even in his hour of desperation, he and Bigger occupied utterly distinct domains. At its best, literature affords readers a window onto a world that would otherwise remain unknown and in the process offers new insight into the lives of others. Here, however, Justice Thomas's appeals to literature do not illuminate reality; they obscure it.

If Justice Thomas's extractions from *Native Son* cannot be found among the novel's more pressing lessons, what can? Read today, perhaps the most striking legal lesson found in *Native Son* is its treatment of racial profiling. Although the novel recently marked its seventy-fifth anniversary, its depiction of police officers who view people with dark skin as criminals unless proven otherwise presents an all-too-familiar tale to modern readers. When Bigger arrives at the Dalton home for his job interview, Wright provides a vivid snapshot of the toll that profiling can impose on racial minorities.[39] Bigger is uncertain whether the Daltons would expect him to knock at the front door or the back door, and he walks along the house's perimeter to assess whether entering through the back is even an option. (He discovers it is not.) Wright presents Bigger's heartbreaking interior monologue as he returns to the front door: "Suppose a police saw him wandering in a white neighborhood like this? It would be thought that he was trying to rob or rape somebody. He grew angry. Why had he come to take this goddamn job? . . . This was not his world; he had been foolish in thinking that he would have liked it. He stood in the middle of the sidewalk with his jaws clamped tight; he wanted to strike something with his fist. . . . Goddamn!"[40] Bigger's rage at the police surveillance that accompanies his blackness is, of course, completely justifiable. The scene skillfully illustrates how black citizens are unable to escape the shadow of surveillance and the way that it breeds emotions (anger, resentment, defeatism) that are unlikely to be availing in a job interview and in many other settings besides.

A closely related lesson from *Native Son* that again contains some distressing modern echoes appears in the depiction of the propensity for using a single black person's guilt as an occasion to upend a city's entire black population.[41] When Bigger is on the run from authorities, the ensuing manhunt adversely touches Chicago's black citizenry as a whole and demonstrates scant respect for their individual rights. During the criminal trial, Bigger's lawyer Max emphasizes, "The hunt for Bigger Thomas served as an excuse to terrorize the entire Negro population."[42] This statement is not mere attorney bluster, as Max offers a bill of particulars, including "the hundreds of innocent Negro homes invaded, the scores of Negroes assaulted upon the streets, the dozens who were thrown out of their jobs, the barrage of lies poured out from every source against a defenseless people—all of this was something unheard of in democratic lands."[43] When he is on the lam, Bigger reads various newspaper articles about the search that support Max's claims. According to one report, "Police and vigilantes, armed with rifles, tear gas, flashlights, and photos of the killer, began at 18th Street this morning and are searching every Negro home under a blanket warrant from the Mayor."[44] Another article notes that "several Negro men were beaten in various North and West Side neighborhoods" and that Hyde Park and Englewood had also witnessed the formation of "vigilante groups" who were working in concert with the police.[45] This same article discloses that "several *hundred* Negroes resembling Bigger Thomas" had been "rounded up from South Side 'hot spots'" and were being held pending investigation.[46] That such indiscriminate searches, detentions, and even beatings occur on the basis of race is bad enough. That these tactics seem to have received the government's imprimatur is worse still, as the official support could encourage racial minorities to reject law's legitimacy.[47]

Justice Thomas's jurisprudence at the intersection of race and policing evinces little trace of these potential legal lessons from *Native Son*. There are many available cases that one could draw on to demonstrate that his jurisprudence pays insufficient attention to the hazards of racially inflammatory policing practices.[48] In the context of an essay analyzing *Native Son*, however, his dissenting opinion in *Chicago v. Morales* demands discussion.[49] After all, the Supreme Court in *Morales* entertained a constitutional challenge to an antigang ordinance, a measure that can helpfully be understood as targeting latter-day Bigger Thomases in his hometown of Chicago.

In response to persistent violence, the Chicago City Council in 1992 enacted the Gang Congregation Ordinance, a measure prohibiting "criminal street gang members" from "loitering."[50] The ordinance defined loitering as "remain[ing] in any one place with no apparent purpose."[51] The measure further empowered police officers to identify suspected gang members who were loitering and to instruct these individuals—and any other persons present, whether or not they were suspected gang members—to disperse and vacate the area.[52] Failure by anyone to heed the officer's dispersal instruction resulted in a criminal offense, punishable by a fine and up to six months' imprisonment.[53] In a 6–3 decision, the Court in *Morales* invalidated the ordinance, with various justices citing various constitutional infirmities, including its vague definition of loitering and its absence of any *mens rea* requirement.[54]

It requires no great insight into either modern racial realities or modern policing practices to apprehend that the weight of Chicago's ordinance would have fallen disproportionately on black and brown men. The measure afforded officers seemingly boundless discretion—to determine not only who looks like a gang member (and who does not) but also who possesses a sense of purpose when hanging out in public (and who does not). As William Stuntz emphasizes, (police) discretion and (racial) discrimination are constant traveling companions.[55] If Bigger and Gus and their buddies were hanging out on the South Side of Chicago during the early 1990s, it is exceptionally easy to envision police officers ordering them to disperse pursuant to the Gang Congregation Ordinance. A police officer would need to take only one glance at Bigger and his associates to conclude that they were up to no good. At least some percentage of the time, it seems essential to note, this officer's conclusion would be correct. Bigger and his friends appear to congregate on a semiregular basis to plan and then to execute robberies. Moreover, given the incredibly elastic way that authorities use the term *gang* today, officers would have no difficulty so designating Bigger's recurrent criminal enterprise. Yet other instances would surely exist when the officer's conclusion would prove unwarranted, when Bigger and his friends were not up to no good but instead were up to nothing at all. Police officers ordering young black men to disperse and vacate the area when they are doing nothing more sinister than shooting the breeze in their own neighborhood seems unlikely to inspire even the most reluctant and smalltime gangsters to mend their ways. If anything, those orders seem likely to send such people only further down the path of the crooked and broad.

Of even greater significance, though, police officers would on occasion—even if unintentionally—misidentify a law-abiding citizen as a gang member. Officers would, that is, look at Clarence Thomas but see Bigger Thomas. One might expect a student of *Native Son* to realize that the Gang Congregation Ordinance would in effect amount to a license to engage in racial profiling, as a number of upstanding black citizens would be drawn into unwanted interactions with police officers that could quickly grow acrimonious. The law-abiding black person who is informed by a police officer that he must vacate the area because he is suspected of gang affiliation might wonder—not without reason—whether following the law is pointless because police officers see him as a criminal. If the law disrespects me, the question might run, why should I respect the law? Chicago's antigang ordinance, in sum, seemed poised to take an already toxic relationship between racial minorities and police officers and make it worse.

Justice Thomas wrote a dissenting opinion in *Morales* voting to uphold the Chicago ordinance. That vote rests in evident tension with some of the more prominent legal lessons *Native Son* contains. Moreover, in contrast to the generous reading of the term *innocent* that Justice Thomas employs in *My Grandfather's Son* to describe Bigger, he displays a parsimonious understanding of the same term in *Morales*. Responding to the justices who expressed concern that the ordinance could inappropriately be used to prohibit "innocent conduct," Justice Thomas expressed sharp disagreement: "It is . . . anomalous to characterize loitering as 'innocent' conduct when it has been disfavored throughout American history. When a category of conduct has been consistently criminalized, it can hardly be considered 'innocent.'"[56]

Although Justice Thomas's opinion in *Morales* seems to clash with *Native Son*'s lessons, I am not suggesting that racial considerations played no role in his resolution of the case. To the contrary, concerns about race appear to have played a significant role in animating his thought in *Morales*. Unsophisticated and uncharitable critics may concede that his vote in *Morales* was racially motivated, but only in the sense that he enjoys casting votes that he believes will harm racial minorities. Such assessments, which disparage Justice Thomas as some sort of racial traitor, enjoy distressingly wide circulation in the press and in academia.[57] There is no reason to doubt, however, that Justice Thomas voted as he did in *Morales* at least in part because he believed doing so would help black citizens, not hurt them.[58] To be sure, his opinion carefully avoids appealing overtly to race, but he unmistakably seems to understand himself as articulating the views of law-abiding black people who live in poor urban areas that have been overrun by gang activity. "Today, the Court focuses extensively on the 'rights' of gang members and their companions," Justice Thomas writes. "It can safely do so—the people who will have to live with the consequences of today's opinion do not live in our neighborhoods. Rather, the people who will suffer from our lofty pronouncements are people like Ms. Susan Mary Jackson. . . ."[59] He identifies Jackson as an eighty-eight-year-old woman who testified in favor of the ordinance before the City Council by noting that she feared leaving her house during the day and saying, "At my age if they look at me real hard, I be ready to holler."[60] Justice Thomas explains that the Ms. Jacksons of the nation are "people who have seen their neighborhoods literally destroyed by gangs and violence and drugs. They are good, decent people who must struggle to overcome their desperate situation, against all odds, in order to raise their families, earn a living, and remain good citizens."[61] In addition to offering the quotation from Ms. Jackson, Justice Thomas proceeds to quote two other Chicagoans who expressed their support for the ordinance by noting the extreme measures that they either employed or contemplated employing in an effort to feel physically secure. The gang presence in Ms. D'Ivory Gordon's neighborhood left her terrified of commuting to work, prompting her to testify: "I have even come to the point now that I carry a meat cleaver to work with me. . . ."[62] Another fearful Chicago resident, whom Justice Thomas does not name, seriously entertained the question "Do I put my ax in my briefcase?"[63]

For close readers of *Native Son* these harrowing statements may bring to mind an earlier Chicagoan who carried a weapon to ensure that he arrived at a professional obligation unharmed. As Bigger prepares to travel to the Daltons for his interview, he decides to bring his firearm for personal safety reasons, as "[h]e was going among white people."[64] "[I]n order to get to the Dalton place," Wright explains, "he had to go through a white neighborhood. He had not heard of any Negroes being molested recently, but he felt that it was always possible."[65] At times, it would seem, the line separating the D'Ivory Gordons of the world from the Bigger Thomases may not be quite so bright as is commonly supposed.

IV

Native Son's opening line reproduces the sound of an alarm clock clanging in the cramped apartment that Bigger Thomas shares with his mother and two siblings: "*Brrrrrrriiiiiiiiiiiiiiiiiiinng!*"[66] Arnold Rampersad, along with many of the novel's interpreters, has suggested that this beginning contains significance quite apart from the plot: "The sound of the alarm that opens *Native Son* was Richard Wright's urgent call in 1940 to America to awaken from its self-induced slumber about the reality of race relations in the nation."[67] For his part, Irving Howe suggested that Wright's book realized its intended effect. "The day *Native Son* appeared, American culture was changed forever," Howe wrote. "It made impossible a repetition of the old lies [and] brought out into the open, as no one ever had before, the hatred, fear and violence that have crippled and may yet destroy our culture."[68] Since Wright published *Native Son*, the percentage of Americans who are either incarcerated or otherwise subjects of the criminal justice system has increased exponentially. A staggeringly large portion of those subjects, moreover, look something like Bigger Thomas. On few issues today is there greater need for a talented novelist to rouse a slumbering public than on mass incarceration and that system's woeful racial dimensions. If only it could be guaranteed that judges who read the novel would actually heed that wake-up call.

NOTES

I received helpful feedback on this project from William Baude, Emily Buss, Laura Ferry, Barry Friedman, Julius Getman, Pratheepan Gulasekaram, Daniel Hulsebosch, Randall Kennedy, Alison LaCroix, Daryl Levinson, Sanford Levinson, Saul Levmore, Jonathan Masur, Richard McAdams, Trevor Morrison, Martha C. Nussbaum, John Rappaport, Adam Samaha, Caleb Smith, Kenneth Warren, and Laura Weinrib. I also benefited from exemplary research assistance provided by Sarah David, Trevor Lovell, and Adam Weiner.

1. Clarence Thomas, *My Grandfather's Son: A Memoir* (New York: HarperCollins, 2007), 1.

2. Thomas, *My Grandfather's Son*, 214.

3. The preceding two sentences are meant to evoke B. B. King's essential blues number "Nobody Loves Me but My Mother." The relevant lyrics are "Nobody loves me, but my mother, / And she could me jivin' too." B. B. King, *Indianola Mississippi Seeds*, CD, D4-10677, MCA, 1970.

4. Arnold Rampersad, introduction to Richard Wright, *Native Son* (New York: Harper Perennial, 2005), xix.

5. James Baldwin, "Everybody's Protest Novel," in *The Price of the Ticket* (New York: St. Martin's Press, 1985), 33.

6. Ralph Ellison, "The World and the Jug," in *Shadow and Act* (New York: Vintage, 1995), 114.

7. Richard Wright, "How 'Bigger' Was Born," in *Native Son* (New York: Harper Perennial, 2005), 433, 434 (discussing the deep fear that Wright felt when he encountered one of the people on whom he modeled Bigger).

8. Justice Thomas is not alone in seeing parallels between his own life and Bigger Thomas's. For an elaborate argument in this vein, see Edith Efron, "Native Son: Why a Black Supreme Court Justice Has No Rights a White Man Need Respect," *Reason*, February 1992, 22–32.

9. U.S. Senate, *Nomination of Judge Clarence Thomas to be Associate Justice of the Supreme Court of the United States: Hearings before the Committee on the Judiciary*, 102nd Cong. 260 (1991).

10. Thomas, *My Grandfather's Son*, 27.

11. Ibid., 63.

12. For an insightful treatment of this central question, see Dan M. Kahan and Martha C. Nussbaum, "Two Conceptions of Emotion in Criminal Law," *Columbia Law Review* 96 (1996): 370–72.

13. Richard Wright, *Native Son* (New York: Harper Perennial, 2005), 30.

14. Ibid., 84–85.

15. Ibid., 234.

16. Ibid.

17. Ibid.

18. Thomas, *My Grandfather's Son*, 48. I have benefited immensely from several insightful pieces that analyze various intersections of Justice Thomas's judicial and racial identities. See, for example, Mark Tushnet, "Clarence Thomas's Black Nationalism," *Howard Law Journal* 47 (2004): 323; Angela Onwuachi-Willig, "Just Another Brother on the SCT? What Justice Clarence Thomas Teaches Us about the Influence of Racial Identity," *Iowa Law Review* 90 (2005): 931; Eric L. Muller, "Where, but for the Grace of God, Goes He? The Search for Empathy in the Criminal Jurisprudence of Clarence Thomas," *Constitutional Commentary* 47 (1998): 323; Stephen F. Smith, "Clarence X? The Black Nationalist behind Justice Thomas's Constitutionalism," *NYU Journal of Law & Liberty* 4 (2009): 583.

19. Thomas, *My Grandfather's Son*, 48.

20. Eldridge Cleaver, "Notes on a Native Son," *Ramparts*, June 1966, 55.

21. Ibid.

22. Ibid.

23. Addison Gayle Jr., *The Way of the New World: The Black Novel in America* (New York: Anchor Press/Doubleday, 1975), 169.

24. Ibid.

25. Ibid.

26. Ibid.

27. Thomas, *My Grandfather's Son*, 48.

28. Ibid.

29. Ibid.

30. Ibid., 94.

31. Ibid., 94–95.

32. Ibid., 95. Thomas proceeds to explain that this case awakened him to the realities of intra racial crime rates: "Until then I'd ignored the obvious implications of black-on-black crime rates. After I worked on that case, I knew better than to assume that whites were responsible for all the woes of blacks. . . . I also grew more wary of unsupported generalizations and conspiracy theories, both of which had become indispensable features of radical argument."

33. For an influential, sophisticated articulation of this idea, see Martha C. Nussbaum, *Poetic Justice: The Literary Imagination and the Public Life* (Boston: Beacon Press, 1997).

34. The field is not of course exclusively populated by liberals. See, for example, Richard A. Posner, *Law and Literature: A Misunderstood Relation* (Cambridge, MA: Harvard University Press, 1988). For a critique, see Robin West, "Law, Literature, and the Celebration of Authority," *Northwestern University Law Review* 83 (1989): 977.

35. Thomas, *My Grandfather's Son*, 63.

36. Ibid., 245 (ellipsis in original).

37. Ibid., 251.

38. Ibid., 252.

39. See Randall Kennedy, *Race, Crime, and the Law* (New York: Pantheon, 1997), 159 (contending that profiling is a sort of "racial tax").

40. Wright, *Native Son*, 44.

41. See *Brown v. City of Oneonta*, 221 F.3d 329 (2d Cir. 2000); R. Richard Banks, "The Story of *Brown v. City of Oneonta*: The Uncertain Meaning of Racially Discriminatory Policing under the Equal Protection Clause," in *Constitutional Law Stories*, ed. Michael C. Dorf (Eagen, MN: Foundation Press, 2004).

42. Wright, *Native Son*, 385.

43. Ibid.

44. Ibid., 244 (internal quotation marks omitted).

45. Ibid. (internal quotation marks omitted).

46. Ibid. (internal quotation marks omitted; emphasis added).

47. See Tom R. Tyler, *Why People Obey the Law* (Princeton, NJ: Princeton University Press, 1990).

48. Justice Thomas joined two opinions decided in 1996, *Whren v. United States*, 517 U.S. 806 and *United States v. Armstrong*, 517 U.S. 456, that made it extraordinarily difficult for an individual to prevail on a claim of racial profiling or racially selective prosecution. I believe that future generations will look back on the Court's opinions in those two cases as shameful. If that prediction is vindicated, Justice Thomas will have lots of colleagues with whom to share the blame; *Whren* was unanimous and *Armstrong* drew one solitary dissent.

49. *City of Chicago v. Morales*, 527 U.S. 41 (1999).

50. Ibid., 45–46.

51. Ibid., 47.

52. Ibid.

53. Ibid.

54. Ibid., 55.

55. See William J. Stuntz, *The Collapse of American Criminal Justice* (Cambridge, MA: Harvard University Press, 2011), 4 ("Discretion and discrimination travel together.").

56. *Morales*, 527 U.S., 113 (Thomas, J., dissenting).

57. See Randall Kennedy, *Sellout: The Politics of Racial Betrayal* (New York: Vintage, 2008), 87–90, 137 (collecting some of the more prominent articulations of such sentiments).

58. For an insightful treatment that ultimately rejects the charge that Justice Thomas is a racial traitor, see ibid., 87–143.

59. *Morales*, 527 U.S., 114–15 (Thomas, J., dissenting).

60. Ibid., 101 (Thomas, J., dissenting; internal quotation marks omitted).

61. Ibid., 115 (Thomas, J., dissenting).

62. Ibid., 100 (Thomas, J., dissenting; internal quotation marks omitted).

63. Ibid., 101 (Thomas, J., dissenting; internal quotation marks omitted).

64. Wright, *Native Son*, 43.

65. Ibid.

66. Ibid., 3.

67. Rampersad, introduction to *Native Son, ix*.

68. Quoted in ibid., xxii.

9

Reconciliation without Anger

PATON'S *CRY, THE BELOVED COUNTRY*

Martha C. Nussbaum

ON ITS FACE, Alan Paton's 1948 novel *Cry, the Beloved Country* is an intimate personal tragedy.[1] Two fathers lose their sons. One, James Jarvis, is rich and white. The other, Stephen Kumalo, is poor and black. One is the father of a murder victim, the other the father of his killer. That father too loses his son; in the novel's final scene Absalom Kumalo is executed in Johannesburg while his father, far away, watches the sun rise. But the personal is obviously political, and Paton's larger societal aims are announced in the title itself. The novel is at the same time a speech addressed to a nation by someone who loves it and hates its current path—in the mode of prophetic denunciation and, ultimately, prophetic hope.

Before he started writing novels Paton was an innovative juvenile corrections official whose proposals for reform as head of Diepkloof Reformatory were highly successful, promoting home leave and employment opportunities for (mostly black) juvenile offenders. As the climate of politics shifted, he lost his position. He wrote the novel while on an extended trip to a number of countries in Europe and North America to study juvenile corrections, finishing it in the United States in 1948, the year of the Nationalist victory that brought in the policy of apartheid. Seeing his country going down that doomed and hideous path, he invents a parable to call it to account, and he often addresses both readers and the nation itself directly, in the manner of Jeremiah or, perhaps more accurately—since the accent is ultimately on hope—of Isaiah.[2]

Here is a common view: The pursuit of justice, in a situation of great injustice, requires anger. People mobilize through their anger against injustice, and their anger is both a motivation and a creative force in the pursuit of justice. They will probably be met with anger and resentment on the other side, but if that happens they will just have to try to prevail. At the end of the struggle, if there is to be political reconciliation, it will require a process of public atonement on the part of the formerly unjust: they must acknowledge their wrongs, and if they ask humbly enough they may receive forgiveness, understood as a suspension of angry attitudes in response to an apology.[3] Desmond Tutu, for example, uses similar Christian ideas of atonement and contrition to argue that there is "no future without forgiveness."[4]

Such claims, however, may be doubted. Some great leaders, for example Mohandas Gandhi and Martin Luther King Jr., have been very suspicious of anger, feeling that it deforms the personality and impedes a future-directed search for reconciliation. I shall argue that Nelson Mandela was also such a leader. But if there is no anger, there is also no forgiveness, not of the classic anger-waiving sort.

What might the alternative be? We might say that it would have to lie beyond both anger and conditional forgiveness, both being oppositional and backward-looking attitudes. Paton's alternative, surprising in the narrative context, involves generosity, mutual respect and understanding, truth, and constructive work. Through the story of the restoration of Ndotsheni, the rural town that is home to both Stephen Kumalo and James Jarvis, he proposes a personal analogue of a public process in which a nation riven by injustice might possibly engage.

ABSALOM KUMALO: CRIME AND PUNISHMENT

The novel has two narrative arcs, intersecting but moving in opposite directions. Both end with the rising of the sun over Johannesburg and Ndotsheni. But sunrise has opposite meanings in the two different stories. The first narrative, the story of Absalom Kumalo, is the story of a murder during a burglary, followed by a trial, punishment dictated by a retributive mentality, and eventually the execution of one of the criminals. In this narrative sunrise has a literal meaning, and the meaning is death. At sunrise Absalom is to be executed, and his father, watching from the mountaintop, takes the sun's rise as a sign of his young son's death. We might call this the Johannesburg narrative. In the other narrative, which we might call the Ndotsheni narrative, the meaning of sunrise is hope and new life, but we must wait to see why that hope requires transcending the retributive impulses that generate the Johannesburg narrative.

Absalom Kumalo, though guilty of a crime, is also the victim of a criminal justice system that does not treat black Africans as full people. He did fire the shot that killed Jarvis's son Arthur during a burglary, so he would be technically guilty of murder under the felony murder rule, which still obtains in South Africa.[5] Since Paton appears ignorant of that rule, however, in the novel Absalom is very likely guilty not of murder but only of some lesser offense; the judge says that if he fired without intent to kill, he should not be convicted of murder (225). And Absalom did fire wildly in panic, with no intent to kill or even to commit serious bodily harm.[6] Clearly too he is a pliant dupe of older and more hardened criminals, one of them his cousin. It is they who planned the break-in, and it is one of them who assaults Jarvis's servant Richard Mpiring with an iron bar, clearly intending to cause grave bodily harm. Nonetheless because Absalom confesses truthfully and repeatedly, indeed volunteering a confession before he is even a suspect (198), he is convicted of murder, while the other two, with a different lawyer and denying that they were at the scene, are acquitted through clever legal maneuvers that cast doubt on Mpiring's visual identification. The reader feels that, despite the pro bono help of an excellent white lawyer, Absalom is never taken seriously as a person by the judge in the thoroughly racist system.

The issue of guilt is confused by the legal unclarity of Paton's presentation. But one thing that is reasonably clear is that Absalom deserves mercy and does not deserve the death penalty. He is not a hardened criminal but a confused boy. He carries a gun only because he is terrified of the city, and he has never fired it except once, in the woods, for practice.[7] He firmly asserts that it was his intention to use the gun only in self-defense (195). After he confesses, he leads the police to where he has buried the weapon—and immediately prays on the spot for forgiveness (197). He concludes his testimony before the court with another expression of remorse: "I shall not lie any more, all the rest of my days, nor do anything more that is evil" (199).

The court hears all of that and sees him for what he is, the dupe of others. The story of panic and wild firing that he consistently tells is utterly credible. And the corrections system knows him to be a promising young man, with an excellent work record in the work-release program devised by that imaginative juvenile justice official. He is a repeat offender, but he was doing very well at work until his cousin put pressure on him to participate in the burglary, and the entire burglary plan was initiated by the cousin. Certainly there are factors on the other side: his extreme passivity, the way he forfeits a fine opportunity of employment and reintegration, his irresponsible use of the gun. One could also doubt his determination not to commit any future crimes, for he immediately admits, under questioning, that he repented only "because I was in trouble" (199). So his plea for mercy is no open-and-shut case, but it is a serious plea that ought to be duly weighed at the highest level, with all the factors on both sides honestly set forth.

Absalom's plea for mercy, however, is brushed lightly aside by the court. "Nor is it for a judge to show mercy," the judge asserts (234), adding that the governor-general could show mercy if the judge were to make such a recommendation.[8] But he then refuses to show mercy or to recognize any grounds for it:

> I have given this long and serious thought, and I cannot find any extenuating circumstances. This is a young man, but he has reached the age of manhood. He goes to a house with two companions, and they take with them two dangerous weapons, either of which can encompass the death of a man. These two weapons are used, one with serious, the other with fatal results. This Court has a solemn duty to protect society against the murderous attacks of dangerous men, whether they be old or young, and to show clearly that it will punish fitly such offenders. Therefore I can make no recommendation to mercy. (236)

Given that his recommendation is all that the governor-general is likely to read of the case, the judge has simply deprived that official of any chance to ponder the pros and cons of mercy for Absalom. Whatever one thinks of the ultimate question, that omission seems grossly unjust.

Awaiting his only son's execution, the Anglican priest Stephen Kumalo has, in consequence, valid grounds for anger against white society.

On his side, James Jarvis has reasons for extreme anger against the killers, and perhaps too against a family who let their son move to Johannesburg with no supervision and without sufficiently preparing him for the lure of crime and bad companions. "I hope to God they get them. And string 'em all up," says Jarvis's friend Harrison, who lives in the city and is preoccupied with the crime (182).

But why has Absalom Kumalo left his home? The novel from the beginning draws attention to the lack of livelihood in Ndotsheni, as erosion dries up the river valley and causes everything to wither. Jarvis and other rich whites are aware of the problem and its causes (inefficient farming methods, too many cattle) and yet do nothing to address it. Indeed when Jarvis ponders the agricultural problem with an accurate diagnosis, he concludes that because "the people were ignorant, and knew nothing about farming methods . . . it was a problem almost beyond solution" (163). Somehow he "knows" that constructive work would be futile without trying, because he accepts a stereotype about the unscientific and unteachable nature of black people.

Why, furthermore, did Absalom fall into crime? Much blame attaches to the white minority's deliberate and highly successful attempt to fracture the traditional tribal system without replacing it with another source of moral authority, as both the urban Anglican priest Msimangu and the activist Arthur Jarvis observe. To Msimangu the fate of Absalom is part of a nationwide tragedy: "The tragedy is not that things are broken. The tragedy is that they are not mended again. The white man has broken the tribe. And it is my belief—and again I ask your pardon—that it cannot be mended again. . . . That is why children break the law, and old white people are robbed and beaten" (56). Arthur Jarvis concurs. In an untitled manuscript fragment his father finds on his table he observes, "The old tribal system was, for all its violence and savagery, for all its superstition and witchcraft, a moral system. Our natives today produce criminals and prostitutes and drunkards, not because it is their nature to do so, but because their simple system of order and tradition and convention has been destroyed. It was destroyed by the impact of our own civilization. Our civilization has therefore an inescapable duty to set up another system of order and tradition and convention" (179).[9] Blame no doubt attaches also to a racist society that has not educated Absalom or provided him with employment opportunities. Arthur wrote about that too in the manuscript on the causes of native crime that he was writing when he went downstairs to his death, as part of his indictment of the hypocrisy of supposedly Christian white society:

> We say we withhold education because the black child has not the intelligence to profit by it; we withhold opportunity to develop gifts because black people have no gifts. We justify our action by saying that it took us thousands of years to achieve our own advancement, and it would be foolish to suppose that it will take the black man any lesser time, and that therefore there is no need for hurry. We shift our ground again when a black man does achieve something remarkable, and feel deep pity for a man who is condemned to the loneliness of being remarkable, and decide that it is a Christian kindness not to let black men become remarkable. (187)

Arthur's argument (reminiscent of John Stuart Mill's argument in *The Subjection of Women*) makes evident the incoherence, as well as the viciousness, of white education policy. As Mill says, if it were really true that a certain group is not inclined to do or cannot do a certain thing, then it would not be necessary to deny them opportunities to do that thing. The sheer magnitude of white preventions (even before the passage of the Bantu Education Act in 1953, which limited blacks to substandard vocational schooling[10]) is evidence of a belief that blacks could do these things if they were allowed to do them. And the treatment of the extraordinary case betrays the fear of black achievement that prompts the entire policy, giving the lie to the ideology that God "created black men to hew wood and draw water for white men" (187).[11]

Absalom does encounter some good treatment from the white world, in particular from that reformist corrections officer, who takes a sincere interest in giving him useful work after he is sentenced for a prior theft. But he also encounters incentives to crime in the form of his hardened criminal cousin, and his sheer fear of the city and his reasonable mistrust of law make him a submissive accomplice. As he said at his trial, he would not have had a gun at all but for the fact that he is afraid of the city and decided that he needs to learn to defend himself.

So Absalom is a victim of circumstances and structures that are not peculiar to his own case but are endemic to white-dominated South Africa. And yet the Johannesburg narrative shows whites zealously pursuing the familiar crime-control device of "string 'em up," as if the judicial killing of a confused youth would somehow bring the dead to life or prevent other, similar deaths. The novel indicates throughout that this mentality is both futile and destructive.

At this point we should note that Paton's account of the origins of crime is primarily what is called an economic account, as distinct from a legitimacy account. That is, he suggests that the most important causes of crime are denial of education and economic opportunity, not the political exclusion of black South Africans per se. Although he himself strongly opposed that political exclusion, the novel does appear to suggest that economic and educational change might be sufficient to ameliorate the crime problem, without political change. This may be short-sighted, if Paton really means it. (It's hard to tell.) What we can see by now, however, is that the economic account remains powerful. Black South Africans have achieved political inclusion without sufficient economic and educational progress—and crime remains a huge national issue. Economic progress is surely necessary, even if not sufficient, for amelioration of the problem. So Paton is correct to focus on that issue.

THE BELOVED COUNTRY: FEAR AND HATE

The real problems of both Ndotsheni and Johannesburg are not caused by the ill will of a "criminal class." They are ecological, social, and economic, and they are made much worse by white negligence and prejudice. South Africa is a society in the grip of terrible fears and hatreds, which feed off one another. Fear of the black majority drives white society to favor ever escalating strategies of punitiveness and enforced separateness. The law is an expression of that fear, and its retributive zeal simply expresses the desire of the surrounding society to keep fear at bay through increasingly harsh treatment. On the side of the black majority there is also tremendous fear: fear of the dangers of the city, so alarmingly different from the familiar support structures of the tribal system; fear of the hatred and punitiveness of whites; fear of a closed future; fear of the law itself. Black crime is a desperate fear-inspired survival strategy, not an expression of hate, but the desire for payback is brewing. Msimangu fears "that one day when they are turned to loving, they will find we are turned to hating" (71). The fathers, like their communities, are apparently launched on a collision course of obduracy, fear, and hate that will not only prove counterproductive but will utterly fail to address the real social problems that need to be resolved if a nation is to prosper. The failure to think productively is, however, above all a failure of the white minority. Blacks would have a constructive role to play in thinking about the future of the nation, but they have not been permitted to speak.

I have said that this novel is written partly in the style of Old Testament prophecy. And indeed Paton does often address the nation directly, as in the urgent call for acknowledgment and genuine thought from which his title derives:[12] "Cry, the beloved country, for the unborn child that is the inheritor of our fear. Let him not love the earth too deeply. Let him not laugh too gladly when the water runs through his fingers, nor stand too silent when the setting sun makes red the veld with fire. Let him not be too moved when the birds of his land are singing, nor give too much of his heart to a mountain or a valley. For fear will rob him of all if he gives too much" (111). This agonized voice speaks from afar, yet with intense love for the near. Its message is that the fear and hate of the white minority are killing a beautiful country—and it really does not matter whether the unborn child is imagined as black or white, for all alike are going down a path of doom. Even if the white minority should relax its iron grip on power, the novel repeatedly emphasizes, it may be too late—if by that time the black majority has turned to vengeance and hate.

But prophecy is not the novel's only unusual formal device. Another that contributes to its allegorical reach is its frequent use of anonymous representative voices, "a hundred and a thousand voices crying" (110) like a Greek chorus of obtuseness and fear, representing the swirling and contradictory currents of white public opinion. (It is one of the subtler devices of the novel that black Africans appear only as individuals, and never as anonymous members of a type. Whites often appear as types, indicating Paton's view that through herdlike fear they have forfeited individuality.)

The primary characteristic of the voices is a short-term focus, a complete lack of useful forward-looking thought: "We do not know, we do not know. We shall live from day to day, and put more locks on the doors, and get a fine fierce dog when the fine fierce bitch next door has pups, and hold on to our handbags more tenaciously. . . . And our lives will shrink. . . . And the conscience shall be thrust down: the light of life shall not be extinguished, but be put under a bushel, to be preserved for a generation that will live by it again, in some day not yet come" (111). The voices speak but refuse to listen, opine but refuse to think. Fear narrows the compass of attention, and the voices live only "day to day," thinking that somehow the problem of the black majority can be kept at bay by more and more defenses, more and more punishments. The primary response to the killing of Arthur is to ask "for more police, and for heavier sentences for native housebreakers, and for the death penalty for all who carry weapons when they break in" (111).

The voices appear to have, and surely think of themselves as having, a deterrence or incapacitation theory of crime: locks, dogs, and prisons are all devices to protect the white community from criminal elements, and the threat of harsh treatment is a useful deterrent. However, a moment's thought would show that genuine deterrence would call for completely different strategies, including employment, education, and a reformist employment-oriented penology of the sort that Paton practiced, which did indeed deter many young men from crime by giving them gainful employment. If, then, the white majority fails to confront deterrence in a rational way and focuses narrowly on harsh punishments that inflict suffering, we are invited to conclude that their real theory of punishment is very different: it is retributive, paying with pain for the anxiety and pain that they believe they have suffered at black hands. Primitive fear and hatred are powerful sources of pain. For the pain of sharing a nation with people you fear and hate, the white community proposes payback: more and more punishment, more and more pain. That indeed is why whites are so cavalier about evidence and guilt: they would kill all blacks if they were not useful working bodies, but they can happily substitute lesser pains inflicted on a subset selected by more or less random procedures.

In effect blacks are being punished for being there, being superior in numbers, and being necessary, as workers, for the enrichment of the white community. The Johannesburg narrative is punctuated by gleeful enthusiasm about mining finds, which of course makes the problem yet more insoluble, compounding fear, since any concession to the majority would mean huge financial losses as well as the loss of cheap labor. So the voices simply give up on the task of creating a country: "Who knows how we shall fashion such a land of peace when black outnumbers white so greatly? . . . Who knows how we shall fashion such a land? For we fear not only the loss of our possessions, but the loss of our superiority and the loss of our whiteness" (110). So they just stop thinking and start punishing, as though payback (for what?) would accomplish what their impoverished thinking cannot. At times they excuse themselves by imagining that blacks must want payback just as they do, so if whites are even slightly less vigilant, they will be doomed.

The voices do not all agree, and some of them make more sense:

> I say we shall always have native crime to fear until the native people of this country have worthy purposes to inspire them and worthy goals to work for. For it is only because they see neither purpose nor goal that they turn to drink

> and crime and prostitution. Which do we prefer, a law-abiding, industrious and purposeful native people, or a lawless, idle and purposeless people? The truth is that we do not know, for we fear them both. And so long as we vacillate, so long will we pay dearly for the dubious pleasure of not having to make up our minds. And the answer does not lie, except temporarily, in more police and more protection. (107)

For every useful suggestion, however, whether about education or taxation or security, there is always someone who takes the question off the table, whether by saying it is too expensive or observing that "more schooling simply means cleverer criminals" (107). At the same time, absurd suggestions are taken seriously despite the objections of calmer voices pointing out why they won't work. Thus a female voice who feels disgust at sharing recreational space with blacks suggests that they should create large recreation centers at a great distance from where whites live and send all their live-in black servants there on free buses. "And how long will it take them to get there? And how long to get back? How many hours do you give your servants off on a Sunday?" "Oh, it's too hot to argue. Get your racquet, my dear, they're calling us. Look, it's Mrs. Harvey and Thelma. You've got to play like a demon, do you hear?" (109)

Fear leads to nonthought, and this vague pile-on-the-punishment style of retributivism (often masked as deterrence) is a prominent aspect of that nonthought. Indeed what is original in Paton's critique of criminal law retributivism is just this connection to fear. The powerful feel embattled, and, being unwilling or unable to think clearly about what would actually produce a decrease in crime going forward, they simply give up on serious thought about deterrence and, allowing their underlying hatred to take over, pile on more police, more punishments, harsher punishments, deluding themselves into thinking that they are thereby accomplishing something. So harsh punishment is seen as a useless and self-deluding response to fear, which, tragically, takes the place of constructive welfare-oriented political thought. Indeed the white community cannot stand to think because thought would demonstrate that they have to share power and lose superiority.

The black community is not given proportional blame since blame is not proportionate, but it is also not painted in rosy colors. There are indeed hardened criminals as well as confused youths. And there are also power-hungry politicians, such as Stephen Kumalo's brother John, a charismatic orator who has a way of stopping just short of what will really get him in trouble, getting power as a protest leader while lacking any useful conception of protest and what it might achieve. He has been corrupted by power and simply likes to enjoy the perquisites of power, not to do real good. It is no surprise that he rescues his own highly culpable son while throwing Absalom to the dogs of the white judicial system.

TWO FATHERS: THE TRANSITION

But the novel has another and more hopeful story to tell. The Ndotsheni narrative is a story of what might happen if people see the retributive mentality as the blind alley it is and decide to pursue a useful future, cooperating for the common good. "I see only one hope for our country," says Msimangu, "and that is when white men and black men, desiring neither power nor money, but desiring only the good of their country, come together to work for it" (71). The Ndotsheni story is a small-scale realization of that hope.

The Ndotsheni story, as I have said, also ends with sunrise, but this sunrise is speculative and metaphorical, a sign of hope and possibility for the nation. To understand this second narrative we need to explore what I call the Transition that the two grief-stricken fathers pursue, first separately and then together.

What do I mean by the Transition? In a related project I argue as follows.[13] Anger is an emotion that involves the thought that serious damage has been wrongfully inflicted on oneself or someone or something about which one cares deeply. The emotion itself contains as well a wish for some type of payback. The angry person does not necessarily wish to inflict harm on the perpetrator personally but would like to see some type of punishment, whether through the law, or by God, or just by having the perpetrator's life go badly somehow. Even in "civilized" anger one does find oneself wishing that the spouse who betrayed one will have an unhappy new marriage, and so forth. That anger contains a wish of this sort is not particularly controversial; all philosophical definitions of anger, as well as recent psychological inquiries, assert as much.

My more controversial argument, starting from that definition, is that anger is always normatively problematic in either one or the other of two possible ways. One possibility is that the person thinks payback really helps restore what was damaged, that punishing the murderer somehow makes the death of the victim less of a loss, that the misery of the betraying spouse lessens the loss of the betrayed. This is metaphysical thinking about balance, easy to fall into and possibly programmed in our evolutionary heritage, but just false and irrational. Serious goods that have been damaged are not restored by payback.[14]

The other possibility is that the person's focus is exclusively on relative status rather than on the serious item or person that was damaged, and the anger is a response to the injury seen as a status injury, or what Aristotle calls "down-ranking." I believe Aristotle is wrong to think that all anger is of this sort, but certainly it is a common type. In this case, where only relative status is the focus, payback suddenly works: humiliating or lowering the offender does change your status relative to him or her; putting the offender down does put you relatively up. So now there's no incoherence, but there is a different problem: focusing exclusively on normative status is morally objectionable.

A person determined to avoid these follies will still get angry, because human beings do, and he or she will very likely have brief thoughts of payback. Anger is often even useful as a signal that something is amiss and perhaps as a motivation to address it. But a reasonable person will quickly shift out of the payback thought to more productive ways of thinking, such as What shall I do to respond to the loss and go forward? What treatment of the offender will actually be useful for society? What measures would actually prove useful in reducing crime?

The Transition is that shift: from the irrational wishes of anger to constructive forward-looking thinking. (I also recognize a borderline case of anger that is rational from the start: Transition-Anger, as I call it, has as its entire content the thought, How outrageous! What's to be done about this? So, from the beginning, it looks forward constructively.)

It is a story of the Transition, I believe, that Paton wishes to tell us—not just as a personal story but as an allegory of a process in which South Africa itself, both white and black, might engage.

Both fathers, I have said, have reasons for anger. We learn early on, however, that neither man is prone to anger or to fruitless thoughts of payback. Stephen Kumalo has interpreted the job of a Christian priest as forgoing anger—so that when he finds himself yielding to anger against his corrupt brother John, who saves his own son but abandons Absalom, he criticizes himself relentlessly. As for Jarvis, when he hears that his son has been killed by a "native" housebreaker, he does ask, "Did they catch the native?"—but then immediately says, "What does that matter?" as tears fill his eyes (167). He understands that payback has no power to restore his son or assuage his own grief. Later, as he reads his son's manuscripts, he finds himself wishing that Arthur had not gone downstairs to investigate the noise of the break-in: "But these thoughts were unprofitable; it was not his habit to dwell on what might have been but what could never be" (186). He understands immediately that "it was the pain that did that, that compelled one to these unprofitable thoughts" (187).

Both fathers, then, are ripe for the Transition, and it is a Transition story that Paton wants to set before us as his prophecy of hope, scattering clues on the way: the generosity of a white motorist, who defies the police to give blacks an illegal lift during a bus boycott, saying cheerfully to the police officer, "Then take me to court!" (81–82); the productive experiment of that white corrections officer, which helped so many young criminals, even if not, ultimately, Absalom; the generous philosophy of the urban black priest Msimangu, "who had no hate for any man" (311), whose idea of a future of cooperative work gives Stephen Kumalo the glimpse of a new possibility (71).

For Jarvis the Transition begins in solitary meditation, as he sits for hours alone in his son's study, reading his son's manuscripts—first the manuscript on crime in South Africa on which he was working when he went down to his death, and then another unfinished manuscript entitled "Private Essay on the Evolution of a South African." He reads too the speeches of Abraham Lincoln that were Arthur's inspiration. The Second Inaugural Address, in particular, rivets him: "He read it through, and felt with a sudden lifting of the spirit that here was a secret unfolding . . . increasing knowledge of a stranger" (188). Paton does not quote the speech; he relies on readers to know that it contains a recipe for binding the wounds of a nation "with malice toward none, with charity for all." (The novel was written in the United States.) He begins to understand his son's hidden values and to see and know his son himself.

He might have become bogged down in guilt, realizing how little he had ever understood his own son. Instead he determines to get to know his son's values and to consider them seriously. When his wife tells him that he should not sit by himself, he smiles at her. " 'It's not my nature to brood,' he said. 'Then what have you been doing?' 'Thinking. Not brooding, thinking. And reading. This is what I have been reading.' " Jarvis is mildly disappointed by his wife's reaction to the manuscript for, instead of reading and thinking, she turns immediately to the last words, imagining her son's last moments: "He accepted that. Pain does not go away so quickly" (189).

Why does Lincoln's speech move him so, as it evidently moved his son? One obvious parallel is Lincoln's criticism of the hypocritical religion of the slaveholders. Lincoln's assertion "It may seem very strange that any men should dare to ask a just God's assistance in wringing their bread from the sweat of other men's faces" is the direct ancestor of Arthur's "We go so far as to credit Almighty God with having created black men to hew wood and draw water for white men." Another parallel is the recognition that financial interests have caused moral blindness: the "peculiar and powerful interest" of Lincoln's speech becomes the "fearful clutching of possessions" of Arthur's manuscript. Another clear parallel is Lincoln's insistence on "firmness in the right as God gives us to see the right"; Arthur's hidden manuscript (which Jarvis reads only later) expresses the same purpose: "I am moved by something that is not my own, that moves me to do what is right, at whatever cost it may be" (208).

Perhaps, though, Jarvis sees an even deeper similarity: the situation of South Africa is very like the "impending civil war" that Lincoln recalls as the U.S. situation when he was first inaugurated. As in the United States, a large proportion of the South African population (90 percent, not Lincoln's "one-eighth") have been completely deprived of rights and opportunities. As in the United States, so in South Africa it may turn out that one group of whites will "make war rather than let the nation survive," while another, along with blacks, "would accept war rather than let it perish." The war, however, was tragically costly and destructive. Lincoln's proposal to "bind up the nation's wounds" "with malice toward none, with charity for all," is an attempt to move beyond an appalling event. It is natural to ask whether the cataclysm in South Africa might be headed off by a little more "charity" and "firmness in the right" exercised sooner. Arthur is a man of determination and tenacious hope. He imagines how great it would be if his children grew up not hating anyone: "It would be unending joy . . . exciting, exhilarating, a matter for thanksgiving" (208).[15]

Shortly thereafter, by sheer chance, Jarvis meets Stephen Kumalo; visiting the home of his wife's niece, he opens the door when Kumalo comes to inquire about a neighbor's daughter who has been a servant there. Kumalo recognizes Jarvis and is appalled to be standing before the father of his son's victim. He nearly collapses. Gradually Jarvis, puzzled by Kumalo's consternation and grief, becomes aware of their relationship. "I understand what I did not understand," he says. "There is no anger in me" (214). From that moment on the fathers are joined in an uneasy but profound relationship; neither offers any apology, and neither asks for or grants forgiveness. They simply understand one another and share one another's grief.

The key to the Transition is that understanding, for they both know what it is to lose an only son, and each knows that the other knows that pain.

A primary agent in the Transition is a child—and this too is Paton's allegorical intention, indicating that a mental disposition free from rancor must guide policy. Jarvis's grandson, whose "brightness" reminds everyone of his dead father, visits Stephen Kumalo while out riding. He asks to be taught Xhosa words, but when he asks for a glass of milk, he learns that there is no milk in Ndotsheni because of the failed harvest and the dire effect on cattle and that many children are dying because they do not have milk (270). Not long after this, milk, "in shining cans," arrives at Kumalo's door with a message from Jarvis that it is for the children of the town. The (white) magistrate who is Jarvis's emissary, delighted by his mission, drives away in high good spirits. And Stephen Kumalo "laughed . . . that a grown man should play in such fashion, and he laughed again that [his neighbor] Kuluse's child might live, and he laughed again at the thought of the stern silent man at High Place. He turned into the house sore with laughing, and his wife watched him with wondering eyes" (272). Both fathers have started looking to the future rather than the past.

NDOTSHENI: THE FUTURE TAKES HOLD

What follows flows from that beginning. Jarvis and the magistrate come back again and take a survey of the land, with the permission of the chief. During this visit a downpour begins, and Jarvis and Kumalo take refuge in Kumalo's church. Jarvis quickly learns that the roof leaks "in many places" (278). Finding a spot where there is relative dryness, the two men sit together in silence while the heavens crackle and storm.

Next Jarvis hires a young, scientifically trained black engineer to come to Ndotsheni and make a plan for the rescue of its agriculture. With the cooperation of Stephen Kumalo and the tribal chief, they persuade the people to adopt new methods of farming, including keeping fewer cattle, despite the fact that cattle are a traditional mark of prestige. The black engineer is already the product of a new type of interracial cooperation: he credits his "love for truth" to a white professor, who also taught him that "we do not work for men, that we work for the land and its people" (303). A nascent freedom fighter, he brings the song "Nkosi Sikelel' iAfrica" to the village. But he listens too to Stephen Kumalo: "Hate no man, and desire power over no man. . . . For there is enough hating in our land already" (303). Msimangu had warned Stephen Kumalo "that one day when they turn to loving they will find we are turned to hating." Instead of hatred Ndotsheni gets hard work, rational planning, and hope.

Nor is there forgiveness in Ndotsheni. The two fathers never engage in any ritual exchange of confession, contrition, and apology. Each on his own has moved beyond anger, and neither extracts a humiliating gesture from the other. The relationship is founded on mutual respect, mutual empathy with the deep grief of the other, and a shared determination to do something for the country.

In its portrayal of the black Anglican bishop, the novel frowns at the dour penitential attitude toward wrongdoing that it associates with traditional Christianity. After Jarvis's wife dies of a long-term illness, Stephen Kumalo sends a careful letter of sympathy and arranges for the whole congregation to send a wreath of the sort white people appreciate. He even carefully inks the borders of the card that goes with the wreath, to show respect for white custom. Shortly thereafter the bishop arrives to tell Stephen Kumalo that it is his considered decision that Kumalo must give up the parish and go somewhere else as a mere assistant pastor because his continued presence in Ndotsheni would be too upsetting to Jarvis, and anyway, the church is in such disrepair that it cannot be used any longer. Kumalo protests that the people love him and that new things are just beginning in Ndotsheni. Moreover Jarvis has been their benefactor. But the bishop doesn't listen. He is adamant, and it's clear that he wants to extract penance.

Just then, however, a letter arrives, and the bishop urges Stephen Kumalo to read it:

> Umfundisi:[16]
>
> I thank you for your message of sympathy, and for the promise of the prayers of the church. You are right my wife knew of the things that are being

> done, and had the greatest part in it. These things we did in memory of our beloved son. It was one of her last wishes that a new church should be built at Ndotsheni, and I shall come to discuss it with you.
>
> Yours truly,
> James Jarvis
>
> You should know that my wife was suffering before we went to Johannesburg.

Kumalo "stood up, and he said in a voice that astonished the Bishop, this is from God, he said. It was a voice in which there was relief from anxiety, and laughter, and weeping" (296). When the bishop reads the letter, he sees fit for the first time to inquire about the new things that are being done in Ndotsheni. Kumalo describes them all, and all the bishop can do is blow his nose and say, "This is an extraordinary thing" (296). He has learned how to deal with atonement and penance but not with generosity. Kumalo then interprets the postscript to him, explaining how "these words were written out of understanding and compassion," attitudes for which it appears the bishop has a dull eye.

Cooperation, scientific planning, and generosity have outstripped the confessional. There is no need and no place for the bishop here, and he simply departs, trying to save face by saying, "I see that it is not God's will that you should leave Ndotsheni" (297). Paton's novel is suffused with biblical imagery, but it takes its stand with the Christianity of Msimangu and Stephen Kumalo, given to unconditional love and generosity, and against the hierarchical atonement procedures that Paton associates with established church hierarchy.[17]

And on the day when Stephen Kumalo climbs the mountain to be alone as his son is executed far away, Jarvis, passing him on the path, understands that too.

> Before he had spoken a word, the other had already spoken. I understand you, he said. I understand completely.
>
> And because he spoke with compassion, the old man wept, and Jarvis sat embarrassed on his horse. Indeed he might have come down from it, but such a thing is not lightly done. But he stretched his hand over the darkening valley, and he said, One thing is about to be finished, but here is something that is only begun. And while I live it will continue. Umfundisi, go well. (307)

Stephen Kumalo thanks Jarvis for the milk, the demonstrator, and the new church. Jarvis, in turn, thanks Stephen Kumalo: "I have seen a man . . . who was in darkness till you found him."

As the two fathers turn aside from anger to imagine, with generosity, a future of interracial cooperation and constructive work, they create, outside the corrupt legal order and outside the atonement-obsessed religious hierarchy, a vision or allegory of a new legal and political order, one committed to justice but generous and forward-looking in spirit and grounded in scientific and economic truth. As the novel ends, hope is real, but its time has not yet come: "The great valley of the Umzimkulu is still in darkness, but the light will come there. Ndotsheni is still in darkness, but the light will come there also. For it is the dawn that has come, as it has come for a thousand centuries, never failing. But when that dawn will come, of our emancipation, from the fear of bondage and the bondage of fear, why that is a secret" (312).

Alan Paton too turned to constructive political action, founding the anti-apartheid Liberal Party in 1953 and, when that party was banned because it contained both blacks and whites, helping the Progressive Party (the party of Helen Suzman).[18] From that time on he continued peaceful protests and was intermittently persecuted; his passport was taken away in 1960 and not returned until 1970.[19]

He died in 1988. So he did not live to see the fulfillment of his hope, but he certainly saw it edging closer. In 1982 Nelson Mandela was transferred from Robben Island to better conditions in Pollsmoor Prison. In the year of Paton's death, Mandela's seventieth birthday was celebrated with festivities around the world, and he was moved to Victor Verster Prison, where he lived in a warder's house, had a personal cook, and was allowed many visitors. In 1990 Mandela was released from prison, and in 1994 he became the first democratically elected president of South Africa.

In many respects Paton and Mandela were kindred spirits. Like Paton, Mandela always favored generosity and forward-looking strategies, eschewing anger and the fruitless idea of payback.[20] Like Msimangu, Mandela saw that hope for the nation required interracial work and cooperation, and with a genius for winning people over he set himself to create the conditions for that cooperation. Unlike his ally Desmond Tutu, Mandela did not use the language of apology, contrition, and forgiveness; instead, like Paton's two fathers, he preferred the language of understanding and friendship. Since 1989 the Alan Paton Award has been given annually by the *Sunday Times* of Johannesburg to a South African work of nonfiction that embodies "compassion; elegance of writing; illumination of truthfulness, especially those forms of it which are new, delicate, unfashionable and fly in the face of power; and intellectual and moral integrity." These are the same virtues that Mandela's life and writing embodied in a high degree. Mandela himself won the award in 1995 for *Long Walk to Freedom*, and Justice Albie Sachs, who did much to shift the direction of the judicial system toward these same values, has won it twice.[21]

It is the fate of any political fiction to end, leaving the future to alter the meaning of the text. Had South Africa become a scene of civil war and bloodletting, the novel's prophecy of hope would now be read with irony and sadness. It is Paton's good luck that his vision has been realized—though by human beings, and therefore incompletely.

NOTES

I am grateful to Douglas Baird, E. D. Hirsch Jr., Saul Levmore, Jonathan Masur, Melissa Murray, Saul Olyan, and participants in a Cogut seminar at Brown University for valuable comments.

1. All references to the novel are to the 1987 edition, published in New York by Scribner.

2. There is hope in Jeremiah 30–33, but on balance the emphasis is on denunciation.

3. See the canonical philosophical analysis in Charles Griswold, *Forgiveness: A Philosophical Exploration* (Cambridge, UK: Cambridge University Press, 2007). I discuss this and rival conceptions in Martha C. Nussbaum, *Anger and Forgiveness: Resentment, Generosity, Justice*, John Locke Lectures 2014, (Oxford: Oxford University Press, 2016).

4. Desmond Tutu, *No Future without Forgiveness* (New York: Doubleday, 1999). I discuss Tutu's view, and the difference between his view and the views of Nelson Mandela, in *Anger and Forgiveness*, ch. 7.

5. It was used recently in a very bizarre way, after police shot and killed thirty-four striking miners, to bring murder charges against 270 striking miners, since the strike was illegal. See "South Africa Mine Shooting: 270 Miners Charged," *Huffington Post*, August 30, 2012, http://www.huffingtonpost.ca/2012/08/30/south-africa-mine-shooting_n_1844145.html. South Africa has a mixed legal system, with elements of both the civil law system inherited from the Dutch and a common law system inherited from the British. The former predominates in private law, but the criminal law is predominantly British, and the felony murder rule has been part of the common law since medieval times.

6. Nonetheless some jurisdictions will convict a defendant of murder if he or she acted recklessly with "extreme indifference to the value of human life," and certainly Absalom's conduct fits this description.

7. The bad influence of the city on unprepared rural migrants is demonstrated in the story of Stephen Kumalo's sister Gertrude, who has turned to prostitution after moving there and ultimately refuses to return home, despite his offer of support for her and her child. She does, however, allow her child to go with him, and we feel that the child is likely to have a better life in Ndotsheni.

8. The novel thus raises, though it does not explore, the question of where mercy ought to reside in the system of criminal law. Should judges show mercy in sentencing? Executives through pardon or commutation? Or should mercy be shown by the laws themselves, for example by rejecting capital punishment?

9. Three manuscripts by Arthur are quoted in the novel. This first one, untitled and "obviously part of some larger whole," is found by James Jarvis among letters and other papers on his son's desk. The second, the manuscript on the causes of native crime that he was writing just before his death, is handed to Jarvis later by his friend Harrison (186). Presumably it was taken from Arthur's study by police investigating the death, with whom Harrison is in close touch. The third is found later by Jarvis in a "deep drawer" in Arthur's desk, among other articles,

including "The Need for Social Centres," "Birds of a Parkwold Garden," and "India and South Africa." It bears the title "Private Essay on the Evolution of a South African" (206–7).

10. Thirty percent of the schools reserved for blacks had no electricity; 25 percent had no running water; and less than 50 percent had toilets. In 1974 the Afrikaans Medium Act added to the impediments, requiring all black schools to give instruction in both Afrikaans and English. This led to the Soweto uprising, in which 575 people died, about one third of them under the age of eighteen.

11. From Arthur's manuscript on the causes of black crime.

12. The lament is even closer to the lament "Weep for Saul" in 2 Samuel 1, which is often included in prophetic materials but is not necessarily prophetic.

13. Nussbaum, *Anger and Forgiveness*.

14. One might also think in this connection of the unsatisfying attempt at restoration at the end of the Book of Job.

15. One might hazard a further conjecture. Lincoln and Nelson Mandela are in some ways kindred spirits, spirits of generosity and hope; Lincoln is said to have had the same type of graciousness and lack of status anxiety that Mandela owed, no doubt, to his royal tribal connections. See David Donald, *Lincoln* (New York: Simon and Schuster, 1996). Paton knew Mandela, of course, and may in part have thought of Lincoln as a forerunner—although perhaps Mandela's Lincolnesque characteristics were not fully apparent at that time.

16. This is a term of respect for a minister, similar to "Reverend." In his glossary Paton writes, "Means 'parson,' but is also a title and used with respect."

17. In chapter 3 of my Locke Lecture manuscript I contrast these two strands, both of which exist in both Christianity and Judaism.

18. So far as I have been able to discover, and subject to correction; all the leading members of the Progressive Party, at any rate, were white.

19. Meanwhile the novel was filmed in both 1951 and 1995 and was the basis for the Broadway musical *Lost in the Stars*, libretto by Maxwell Anderson and music by Kurt Weill.

20. I develop this theme, with references to Mandela's speeches and interviews, in my Locke Lectures.

21. In 1991 Sachs won for *Soft Vengeance of a Freedom Fighter*, and in 2010 for *The Strange Alchemy of Life and Law*.

PART III

Responsibility and Violence

10

Kidnap, Credibility, and *The Collector*

Saul Levmore

THE PRACTICE, AND then the criminal law, of kidnapping has a long history. There was bride kidnapping by those who sought not to pay or simply could not afford bride-prices. There have been abductions for the purpose of enslavement and impressment to military service or piracy, as well as some designed to put heirs and other rivals out of the way. Hostage taking by repeat players seeking political or commercial gain also has a long history. There is abduction for the purpose of rape or murder, in which case the kidnap label is usually dropped, as it is where the nabbing is by a parent dissatisfied with the law's award of child custody. And then there is ransom kidnapping, the crime that most comes to mind when the more general term is used. Kidnapping, and especially ransom kidnapping, imposes enormous costs on victims and potential victims, and yet, setting aside the case where the abducted party colludes with the kidnapper, the perpetrator is rarely successful. It is a difficult transaction to complete, and the crime carries a severe penalty.

Ransom kidnapping deprives the victim of liberty and is thus a kind of false imprisonment, itself a common law felony. But the ransom component adds a threat of something worse and thus resembles blackmail and extortion. Its infrequent success is best traced to the difficulty the kidnapper experiences in avoiding apprehension, not to the inherent incredibility of the threat. Nevertheless, because the crime imposes great costs, especially when it involves a child, it continues to capture popular as well as literary attention. It is not as common a subject of detective novels or literary classics as is murder or rape, perhaps because it is less often successful or, more likely, because it is especially unlikely to occur in serial fashion. Many murders and rapes are unsolved, and many perpetrators of these crimes need to be apprehended or they will strike again. The same cannot be said of kidnapping, where copycat crimes are probably more of a risk than are serial perpetrators. For these and other reasons kidnapping is undertheorized, and one goal of this essay is to think through the threat it represents.

Literature can play a role in reforming law, in developing public opinion about the operation of a legal system, and in exploring the real or imagined characteristics of wrongdoers and their victims. It has surely performed these roles with respect to murder, rape, and the treatment and punishment of those arrested and convicted of these crimes. Early novels about kidnapping focus on the struggles and eventual triumphs of characters abducted by competitors who wish them far out of the way.[1] The cornerstone of the present essay, in contrast, is John Fowles's chilling novel *The Collector*, about an abductor and kidnapper who seeks not distance but closeness and affection.[2] This 1963 British novel is about class, sex, and possession; love is entirely absent from the characters' lives. Inasmuch as the abductor seeks benefits that we associate with consensual relationships, the novel quickly focuses attention on the ways people control or even possess one another. In turn one wonders at the dividing line between the controlling behaviors and relationships that are criminalized and those that are enabled or even celebrated. Along the way and in uncanny fashion *The Collector* suggests many interesting features of threats, kidnapping, and wrongful imprisonment.

The Collector is not a detective novel. It describes a crime from the perspective of the wrongdoer, as narrator, and then from that of the victim, through her diary. The abductor, Frederick Clegg, stalks Miranda Grey, an art student, and regards her as he would a beautiful butterfly. Clegg collects butterflies, and is accustomed to collecting at the expense of his prey's freedom. He uses his winnings from a betting pool to buy a van and a secluded country house, and then abducts Miranda by force as well as deceit. She recognizes him because his picture was in the newspaper when he won the pool, and she sees through his claim that he is an agent of another. He seems surprised that she is an outraged captive rather than a willing guest in the cocoon he has prepared and whom he tries to please with small purchases. She categorizes him as a scientist who collects things and takes artless photographs, and herself as an artist who, the reader understands, would eventually be at the mercy of other collectors were she to pursue that line of work.

Miranda tries to escape by pretending to have appendicitis, by secreting a note to the outside world, and by digging her way out of thick walls and locked doors. These attempts fail. She bargains with Clegg,[3] securing a promise from him that he will release her after one month. On what was to be the last night of captivity, and armed with gifts, he proposes marriage. When she refuses, he reveals that he will not release her. She again tries to escape, and, after subduing her with chloroform, he photographs her in a state of undress. Subsequently, and now in desperation, she tries to kill him and, when that fails, seduce him. He takes the first in stride and is repulsed by the second. When she becomes ill, Clegg is afraid to call in a doctor and feels justified in his inaction.

We then read Miranda's diary, which tells of the captivity from her point of view and largely confirms what we know from Clegg's narration. The diary reveals some things the abductor does not know, including Miranda's past relationship with G.P., a painter, mentor, and sophisticate who is two decades older than she. He was critical of her family and her taste in art, and she was eager for his approval. Their relationship ended after he confessed a romantic interest in her, but now, if freed, she plans to rekindle the connection and marry him.

Clegg's narrative resumes in the novel's final sections. He realizes that Miranda is quite ill, but he is unable to obtain help from a pharmacist. He goes to a doctor whom he had earlier eschewed, but is frightened off by a police officer. Miranda dies after calling out in her delirium for G.P.; Clegg understands this to be a call for a doctor, or general practitioner. He thinks of suicide and fantasizes about a Romeo-and-Juliet conclusion. He arises the next day with a fresh view and decides that his error was in kidnapping someone from a higher social class. He knows better now, and, having disposed of Miranda, he has his eye on a more appropriate woman whom he has seen working in town behind the candy counter at a Woolworth's. She reminds him of Miranda, though she is not as pretty and, of course, is in his own social class. The novel ends with Clegg's musing, "This time it won't be for love, it would be just for the interest of the thing" (305).

Only at the very end of Miranda's captivity is Clegg under pressure. Although there are advertisements asking about the missing art student, there is no indication of a manhunt or of widespread concern about kidnap or sexual assault. Nor does Miranda wonder whether her family, G.P., or her other friends are out looking for her. When Clegg is in town, there is no evidence that citizens are in fear of a serial kidnapper. The reader feels greater urgency for a search than do Miranda's neighbors and fellow students. The reader's fears substitute for those unmentioned in the novel. *The Collector* is like most detective novels in its focus on the criminal and the victim, as it sets aside the costs imposed by criminals on those who fear becoming the victims of future crimes.[4] These precaution costs on the part of potential victims may well form the most important reason to criminalize theft and abduction and certainly to impose extreme punishments on many felons. The rapist and abductor not only traumatize their direct victims but also chill the behavior of many others who learn of the crimes and fear that they too will be victimized; indeed law might work harder to overcome the collective-action problem among potential victims who fear crime.[5] There is a good case to be made for calibrating the punishments meted out by criminal law to include consideration of these costs. For example, a street assault is not usually regarded as terribly serious, but if precaution costs were included in the calculus the assailant might receive a more severe penalty than an embezzler. Moreover the special circumstances that judges assess in determining the punishment for the convicted assailant do not include consideration of whether the crime was one that would cause others special fear. If precaution costs were taken more seriously, an assault on a stranger, for example, would be punished more severely than an assault on an acquaintance.

One of the interesting things about kidnapping is that publicized cases of child abduction, including the infamous Lindbergh kidnapping in 1932, generated change in the law. In the aftermath of the Lindbergh episode, kidnapping with an interstate element became a federal crime.[6] As a result there would be more federal participation in investigating kidnaps. There was, however, no sudden literary interest in kidnapping, although there are detective novels that were influenced by the sensational Lindbergh event.[7] It seems more likely that a spate of earlier kidnaps encouraged the Lindbergh crime itself. Authors who traded on crime were already aware of the mechanics and difficulties in carrying out and solving kidnaps. Somewhat similarly a serial murderer attracts attention and then stimulates investment by police departments in solving the crimes. It might also give ideas to potential murderers who lust to kill or crave the attention normally given to murders. The police might be motivated by the public relations attached to unsolved and solved crimes, but it is not a stretch to say that the level of enforcement rises with precaution costs.[8] These costs are often hidden, but in the extreme, as when a serial strangler is thought to be about, the increase in precaution costs is so great that political pressure is inevitable.

The Collector is a carefully constructed novel, and it is likely that the lack of any signs of widespread concern about Miranda's absence, and any hints that the police are closing in on Clegg's stronghold, is intentional. Precautions and investigation might distract from the focus on the protagonists' motives. They might also have detracted from the metaphor or reality of the title. Clegg is as free to capture and hold Miranda as he is to catch and pin one of "his" butterflies.[9] In neither case are there consequences to the collector or, for all we know, to the victim's peers.

The abductor who aims to benefit by putting some competitor out of the way or by collecting a ransom, gaining political advantage, or obtaining the release of prisoners seems rational to the normal observer, as does the murderer who wants his victim out of the way or stands to collect a sum for carrying out the crime. In each of these cases the motive is plain. In contrast the serial murderer who targets strangers captures our attention because the impulse is unfamiliar. Psychiatrists and police look for patterns in the choice of victims and the method of killing and expect to find some connection or cause in the criminal's personal life. Occasionally the serial killer keeps his victims alive for some time, enjoying his control over them in life as in death. The long-term kidnapper, who does not ask for a ransom, may share this motive. The abductor may want access to sex or simply someone over whom he can exercise power. In the process he objectifies his victim. It is difficult to know whether *The Collector* presents a typical kidnapper of this sort or an unusual specimen. Clegg wants and expects Miranda to like him. He tells himself, and then her, that he has no chance with her in London, where she would surely ignore him in favor of members of her own social class (39). He abducts her so that she can get to know him. She responds in a manner that mirrors basic tenets of criminal law, which is to say she has been forcibly abducted and cannot possibly develop affection for her abductor. At times she tries to understand him, and occasionally she pities him (108), but mostly and understandably she loathes him. There are, to be sure, cases in which an abducted victim develops an attachment to her captor, but there is no indication that Clegg is motivated by an expectation of "capture bonding," a psychological and perhaps adaptive behavior that became known as Stockholm Syndrome a decade after *The Collector* appeared.[10]

The Collector is disturbing in part because Clegg is not a particularly violent or cruel captor, though of course he uses force (not to mention chloroform) to abduct and maintain control over Miranda. He claims to want affection and to win her over, and he is eager to be respectable and to respect his hostage, at least in his own mind. He announces himself before entering her room, gives her time to dress, keeps himself clean, dresses for dinner with her, cooks for her, responds to her needs and desires, converses with her, buys gifts for her, and makes no attempt to force himself on her sexually. There are times when she is in control of the relationship—setting aside the obvious fact that she is there against her will and that he can gag, bind, and knock her out when he pleases. The novel is known and titled to emphasize the analogy between Clegg's capture of his precious butterflies and his treatment of Miranda, but it is plain and far more disturbing to observe the similarity between their relationship and those experienced within the confines of many perfectly legal relationships. He keeps her and controls her, even as he thinks he treats her well, and he occasionally loses small battles. These are words that could be used to describe many relationships, including marriages.

The point is not that *The Collector*'s theme is marriage-as-kidnap. For one thing, the "problem" of control in relationships is hardly limited to marriage. Parents kidnap their children, in a manner of speaking, and virtually all of us try to control our friends and family (as well as employees, if any) on occasion. Criminal law is not unaware of the danger of a broad definition of kidnap, and no legal system criminalizes power struggles or tries to define and criminalize "excessive control over others," though this forms the core of most understandings of kidnap, rape, bullying, discrimination, and enslavement. Miranda insists that she was forced to Clegg's place and is forced to remain there; the law takes these facts as reason to regard him as a criminal and her as a victim. But it is also plain that many other victims do not meaningfully consent to the control exercised over them by others. They too are like butterflies in a collection, though the law offers them no help, which is to say about as much help as it offers the butterflies.

The Collector goes much further when it reveals Miranda's diary. From the perspective of control her report is nearly as unsettling as Clegg's narration. Her view of love and her reasons for seeking a relationship with G.P. are not just shallow but comparable to Clegg's pursuit of her.[11] Each wants a specimen from a higher social class; each separates sex from love; each is a collector. To be sure, the parallel has its limits, much as most controlling men do not go so far as to chloroform "their" women or the objects of their desire.

Miranda, like Clegg, wants approval, but hers must come from G.P., who disapproves of everything about her, until slowly she changes her own tastes one at a time until he wants her. Of course she never told G.P. that she finds him ugly and old. She is now willing to have sex with G.P., and even to marry him, but only for instrumental reasons. "I will give myself to G.P. He can have me. And whatever he does to me I shall still have my woman-me he can never touch" (267). At first it is absurd to think of Miranda's interest in G.P., or his for her, as anything like Clegg's for hers. There must be a huge gap between manipulative seduction and forcible abduction. But is there? Clegg uses force on a number of occasions, but like Miranda he is only occasionally dishonest. He lies about a dog in need of help in order to get her to look into his van so that he might abduct her. Later he lies about mailing a contribution that she has urged. Of course he also breaks his promise to limit the captivity to one month, though he might have intended to keep his word on that matter.

Remarkably Clegg's abduction of Miranda might not rise beyond wrongful imprisonment to the level of kidnap. He demands no ransom and intends no other felonies. It is arguable that he does her bodily harm, with his gags and chloroform, but with a little lawyerly and poetic license it is also arguable that his methods fall short of that requirement of some kidnap statutes and definitions.[12] Thus a nightclub hypnotist who draws a mark onto the stage with false pretenses or without full disclosure, and then blindfolds her and causes her to stumble out of the room, only to return in a daze at the end of the show with an undergarment on her head, would hardly be guilty of kidnap. Clegg is certainly guilty of wrongful imprisonment, and while we have no doubt that he would be convicted of kidnapping (and perhaps felony murder) and that Miranda would face no legal sanction if she escaped by maiming him, his actions come close enough to the line to be interesting in this regard. In turn the courtship between Miranda and G.P. comes close to criminal fraud. She will profess love and offer sex, and we can be confident that he would reject these offers if he knew how unattractive she found him. Her behavior will hardly be out of the ordinary because most relationships involve some fraud, as the controlling party seeks to acquire admiration, sex, parenting skills, housework, and much more. Clegg's aims are chaste and his means are wrongful, whether or not they amount to kidnapping, at least during the early days of captivity. Miranda's intentions are far more manipulative, and yet the tools she would deploy would never lead to a fraud conviction. The lesson is not that Clegg's behavior is normal and undeserving of criminalization, but rather that many relationships involve control over another through wrongful means—but we simply and unthinkingly regard those means as normal and, certainly, as noncriminal.

Unlike terrorism, assassination, many murders, and perhaps political kidnaps,[13] ransom kidnapping is a crime that the perpetrator is unlikely to regard as successful if he or she is apprehended. Professional ransom kidnappers are virtually unknown in Britain and in the United States.[14] However well executed the abduction, the kidnapper faces the difficult task of convincing someone to pay a ransom and then the more difficult task of obtaining the ransom in a way that does not lead to apprehension, especially if the target has involved the police. In films the kidnapper sometimes instructs that the ransom be flung from a moving train at a particular spot (to be communicated while the target is in motion) or left in a public park in a trashcan to be identified by a caller to a public telephone, but in most of these cases the plot is flawed. The target must find the kidnapper's threat credible at several levels, and then must either face a separate credible threat that serves to keep the police out of the picture or participate in an untraceable payment scheme. There are ways to make threats more credible, but the problem of ransom collection is usually insurmountable. Moreover the two intersect. The kidnapper can try to solve the second problem by holding the hostage until payment is safely received and found to be in untraceable form, but this weakens the credibility of the promise to release the hostage once payment is made. It should be noted that most threat-makers need to build primary credibility ("Comply with my demand or I will carry out an act injurious to you") and also develop secondary credibility ("If you capitulate I can be relied upon not to injure you anyway, and also not to repeat the threat for further gain, now that you reveal that you are a complying type").[15] In the case of kidnapping, primary credibility is in doubt until the kidnap actually takes place. A criminal could demand money by threatening to kidnap if no money is transferred, but apparently most victims will prefer to take precautions and not give in to this threat. The threat of harming the hostage is much greater, or simply more credible, once the nabbing is accomplished or it is established that the kidnapper has abducted and proved credible on previous occasions. At this point it is secondary credibility that is in doubt; the target needs to believe that the hostage will be safe if the target complies—knowing that capitulation will be complicated by the kidnapper's need to avoid apprehension.

The Collector deals with these matters brilliantly. From the outset Clegg does not abduct and imprison for money but rather to gain affection, insight, love, or a specimen. There will be no ransom for the police to track. Indeed it becomes clear, to the reader and then to Miranda, that there will be a tragic ending. After failing to convince Clegg that if he simply lets her go she will tell no one and will be his friend (35, 38), Miranda bargains with her abductor; he promises that he will let her go after one month, but it is plain that he cannot keep his word. The fact that the parties bargain over the period of captivity is itself interesting. When the abductor seeks affection such bargaining is plausible; the parties can be understood as earning one another's trust. If they "agree" on a time period, then perhaps each appears more trustworthy; negotiators and hostage-takers often try just such a step, establishing some small exchange so that each can see that the other is in control of events on one side and then the other. The subbargain also promotes trust—to a degree. Clegg might think that Miranda has implicitly agreed to be cooperative and even to see whether she can feel affection for him in return for the promise that if she does not like him within the month, the experiment is over. He thinks that abducting her "was the best thing I ever did in my life" (28) and "I wasn't really worried, I knew my love was worthy of her" (27). When, for example, she asks to be allowed out of her cellar room to bathe upstairs and says, "If I gave you my word, I wouldn't break it," he responds, "I'm sure. . . . So that was that" (48).

Bargaining is more difficult when the kidnapper threatens death unless a ransom or other favor is received. The target might say explicitly or implicitly, lower your demand from $3 million to $1 million, and I will gather the funds and not go to the police. At the higher price I will take my chances with the police. Miranda's bargain over the period of captivity is just such a bargain. It is not like one where the kidnapper demands $1 million, the target accedes, and then the kidnapper raises the demand to $2 million. Nor is it like one where the parties agree on $1 million, and then the target tries to reduce the ransom. These last two maneuvers lead to distrust as the parties can see that reopening the terms after apparent agreement destabilizes whatever bargain they reach.[16] Miranda's one-month bargain precedes any quasi-agreement to cooperate.

Any promise that Miranda makes not to go to the police is incredible, and she has no extra hostage to leave behind. This is especially clear once Clegg finds out that Miranda recognizes him. It will be difficult to relocate and escape detection. Clegg might imagine a happy ending even after he is identified. He might reason that if Miranda comes to know him and love him, as would be most unlikely in London, where their class differences would keep them apart, she will no longer seek to escape. He might imagine that she will truly accept his proposal of marriage, and then, after some time, they can rejoin the world and say that she ran off with him so they could spend time together; their elopement would seem romantic rather than criminal. In turn his implied threat is that she must fall in love with him or be his prisoner forever, unless death intervenes, as of course it does. He knows he will not kill her and that having her is like "catching a specimen you wanted . . . coming up slowly behind and you had it, but you had to nip the thorax, and it would be quivering there. It wasn't easy like it was with a killing-bottle. And it was twice as difficult with her, because I didn't want to kill her, that was the last thing I wanted" (39). On the other hand, once he proposes marriage and she explains or frustrates him by saying that marriage, to her, requires mutual possession and that she could never give herself to him, the bargaining atmosphere changes. "I said, that changes everything then, doesn't it. I stood up, my head was throbbing. She knew what I meant at once, I could see it in her face, but she pretended not to understand" (89). And then, having understood that she will never be released, she gives it a try: "I'll marry you. I'll marry you as soon as you like" (89). But he responds, "I don't trust you half an inch, I said. The way she was looking at me really made me sick" (90). A month has now passed, and she sees that she is doomed. It is too late to feign love or willingness to marry.

The secondary credibility problem inherent in ransom kidnapping is not avoided by the novel's lepidopterist device. The butterfly collector wants a new specimen or even affection rather than ransom, but in true law-and-economics fashion the reader might imagine that every collector has a price at which he can be induced to part with his catch. We learn that Miranda's father is a doctor, but there is otherwise no indication of the Grey family's ability to pay an amount sufficient to cause Clegg to change course. In any event Clegg has acquired funds through gambling, and no modest ransom will appeal to him, inasmuch as he has rather simple tastes. When he plans his next kidnap it is, again, of someone who will not command a significant ransom.

Miranda reasons that Clegg may want sex rather than money. She is willing to trade sex for her freedom (99). Some abductors aim for sex of course; we penalize them as rapists. Their strategy is usually to hide their identity, to vanish after the crime, or to frighten the victim so much that she will choose not to report the crime or not to assist in the rapist's capture. The last strategy seems most effective with minors and family members; most victims will feel more threatened by a rapist on the loose. Clegg is repulsed by Miranda's offer, and more horrified still when she tries to seduce him (105). He never sought loveless sex and now regards her as inferior to the woman he fantasized about and stalked. More generally it is not credible for a victim of kidnapping to offer sex in exchange for freedom. If the abductor wanted sex, there would likely have been a rape and an attempt at anonymity. If not anonymous, the kidnapper-rapist anticipates a long period of captivity. Once the kidnapper is recognized, the victim has no way of making a credible promise to refrain from turning him in for the crimes of kidnap and rape.

Clegg's negative reaction to Miranda's sex-for-freedom offer is made more interesting by the fact that it follows closely on the heels of his complimenting a drawing she rendered, and then offering to buy it (60–61, 131). She finds this mad, and it is, to be sure, strange. If Clegg thinks of her as a guest on the way to a mutually affectionate relationship, he should ask politely for the creation but not offer to pay. Moreover why would an abductor ever pay a victim for an asset when both are in his control? Clegg may be trying to convince her that he expects that she will have a life after this captivity. Miranda toys with him and then refuses his offer and tears up the artwork. When he is repulsed by her offer of sex, it is clearer why she was similarly put off by his offer for the drawing. Each sought to commodify something the other regarded as precious and beyond trade. And, of course, the horror and criminality of abduction itself reflects the view that human life and liberty are beyond commercial exchange.

As Miranda comprehends that Clegg wants neither money nor sex, she resorts to the interesting, if unspoken, threat that she will starve herself to death (110). It is not simply that she threatens her abductor with a murder conviction if the felonious abduction leads to her death, but also that she understands his need for company, affection, or collection. Presuming that he wants a live specimen, she reasons that as she diminishes her value as his hostage, he will be more inclined to end the hostage-keeping, inasmuch as it is costly for him to continue. Miranda's tactic is of the scorched-earth kind, and it is clever. The novel has us wondering why kidnap victims do not try this strategy. Perhaps this is why many kidnappers choose children, who can be counted on to eat rather than starve themselves in the interest of short-term preservation or other goals. When the kidnapping is of an adult it is often to extract ransom or other benefit from a company or government, so that the person who is abducted has an incentive to improve rather than lessen his or her value as a hostage. In the case of hostages taken in order to compel the target to undertake some action, the abductor is often a professional agent of a sophisticated organization capable of force-feeding the hostage. Clegg is unlikely to have the means and knowledge to do the same. If kidnap victims tried this scorched-earth strategy, kidnappers would probably plan to feed them by force. Why, then, does Miranda end the starvation plan? Perhaps she has thought of using violence against Clegg, as she will soon do; in a weakened state she is less likely to succeed and escape. Perhaps she has already planned to offer sex or marriage in return for freedom. Miranda must understand Clegg's dilemma; if she does not develop affection for him, she cannot live, unless he loves her enough to suffer the consequences or end his own life. The latter possibility might have been viable in the early days of captivity, but once she repulses him with foul language and later with the offer of loveless sex, it is clear that he does not like her enough to sacrifice his life or liberty for hers.

How else might the captivity end if there is to be neither love nor ransom? Clegg has the idea of holding another threat over her, so that if he releases her, or even if she escapes, she will not turn him in. His notion is to take obscene photos. "I got to protect myself. I want some photos of you what you would be ashamed to let anyone else see" (113). She recoils at his suggestion that she reenact her attempted seduction. Although Clegg is more prudish than Miranda, he can reason that the existence of these photos, even if she were to pose or he were to force her into a suitable position, would not prevent her from going to the authorities if she escapes or is freed. Perhaps he understands enough about university students, worldly enough to keep up with artistic trends, to know that a few pictures will hardly keep her quiet. Miranda might have tried to convince Clegg that pictures would indeed be enough to keep her from turning him in. She might, for example, have tried to outsmart her captor by writing in her diary that the photos frightened her and that she hoped Clegg did not realize this because she would do anything in return for his promise not to release them. She could then allow him to discover her diary. Similarly she might have written that she was wanted for murder in another jurisdiction and so could not go to the police even if she escaped. When Clegg found the diary with this planted information, it is possible that he would think he had a way out of the situation. Similarly if she had written about some medical condition and later feigned appropriate symptoms, she might have gained the upper hand. Miranda shows no such creativity, though she is "clever" and won prizes in school and sees right through Clegg's opening yarn about his working for someone else (33). In any event the medical-condition gambit is difficult to deploy; Clegg would head into town for the necessary medicine and likely find some holes in her story.

Clegg likes the photos he takes of her seated and dressed in their early days together. But when he gets around to taking the sort of photos she refused, he likes them better after he cuts her head from them (118). Might this make her more like a butterfly specimen? Might the gag visible on her mouth make the lack of consent apparent and the threat less valuable? Could he think that headless photos will be less valuable evidence against him in the future? Each of these is plausible and provocative. Each suggests the connection between kidnap and blackmail and suffers from problems of secondary credibility.

The Collector is on to something when it toys with the idea of putting a second threat in the kidnapper's hands. There is the implicit threat of death, and then the threat of releasing photos or terrorizing her in London after her release. It happens that none of these threats is especially credible. The first suffers from secondary incredibility. Clegg says he wants her to get to know him and possibly to love him, but she cannot convincingly offer that. He might have imagined that once she loved him, the kidnapping would be successful because she would become his companion and have no interest in turning on him. But as he begins to see that love is out of reach, whether because there is too much of a class division between them or for some other reason, he cannot trust any claim of affection. If she dies and he disposes of the body, it is possible that the disappearance will never be solved. If she escapes or is released, there is the danger that she will report the crime, lead the police to him, and end his life as a collector. The photographs form an insufficient threat. Even if she could act as if the prospect of their release would be enough to keep her quiet, Clegg must recognize that she will fear that he will demand more in the future and that she will never be safe. He has already broken his word about the one-month limit on her captivity, and they both understand that neither can trust the other. Similarly she hints at the possibility that from time to time he could see her in London after her release, but they both perceive that she could use such occasions to have him apprehended. Both parties suffer from secondary incredibility.

The idea of a backup threat does not seem to appeal to kidnappers. Imagine a creative kidnapper who abducts two siblings. The criminal demands a ransom and promises to release one hostage upon receipt of the ransom and the other some time later, when it is clear that the ransom is safely received and that the target has not involved the police. The kidnapper could be long gone and simply send a message regarding the second hostage's location. In theory the plan does not require two hostages, but the release of the first hostage surely adds to the kidnapper's credibility. Indeed the kidnapper might repeat the crime with other targets and suggest they inquire of the previous target in order to learn that the kidnapper was reliable in releasing the first and then the second hostage. Of course nabbing and holding two hostages requires more effort on the kidnapper's part. *The Collector* twice hints at such a credibility-enhancing strategy, though not at the double-kidnapping strategy. First, in an inept opening gambit, Clegg tells Miranda that he works for someone who is a serial kidnapper (29–31). As the novel ends we can imagine Clegg asking his next victim whether she remembers reading about a missing art student. He might even show her evidence of his earlier crime. With each new specimen the collector becomes more credible. Second, when Clegg contemplates acquiring a new specimen, we recall that when first stalking Miranda he observed that "she and her younger sister used to go in and out a lot" (3). There is a moment when one wonders whether he will move on to the sister, until it is apparent that inasmuch as he attributes his failure to social class divisions, the sister is probably safe.

The Collector is a haunting novel from two perspectives. At its unsettling best, it suggests that the lower-class man's forcible crime, that collector of butterflies who treats a woman like an insect or pet, may not be so very different from the educated person's deceits. Miranda is as much a collector as Clegg. The perspective is more provocative than convincing, and unfortunately few readers seem to remember Miranda's relationship with and plans for G.P.[17] Perhaps we readers are too quick to take comfort in the dividing line constructed of chloroform and gags. It is Clegg's narrative in *The Collector* that is iconic, though I have suggested that Miranda's diary is yet more provocative. The second perspective emphasizes the mechanics of a successful kidnap. It is not an easy crime and, once begun, its threats and counter-threats spin out of control. In this respect the novel succeeds the moment the reader understands that a happy ending is impossible.

NOTES

I am grateful for discussions with Martha C. Nussbaum and Richard McAdams and for excellent research by Lingfeng Li.

1. The best known of these are Robert Louis Stevenson, *Kidnapped* (1886) and Alexandre Dumas, *The Count of Monte Cristo* (1844). Nathaniel Hawthorne, *Fanshawe* (1828) is about bride kidnapping and monetary gain, and not about rival clans where bride kidnapping might amount to repeat trading.

2. I use the terms *abductor* and *kidnapper* interchangeably, though the discussion quickly attends to the line separating false imprisonment, sometimes a misdemeanor, from kidnapping. See note 11 and accompanying text.

3. I refer to him by his surname (and yet the victim by her given name) because Clegg alters his given name, perhaps to obscure his identity. John Fowles, *The Collector* (Boston: Little, Brown, 1963), 37. Citations are to the Back Bay paperback edition.

4. Detective novels have been grouped in three categories. Lawrence M. Friedman and Issachar Rosen-Zvi, "Illegal Fictions: Mystery Novels and the Popular Image of Crime," 48 *UCLA Law Review* 1411 (2001). There are those with clues, in which the reader joins Sherlock Holmes, Jane Marple, or another sleuth in a process of elimination; those that reflect a darker and grittier urban

existence (as in the work of Dashiell Hammett); and those that bring forensic science into the mix. The last subset, extended to include film and television, often involves serial killers, and these stories might be said to reflect the fear and precaution costs that such criminals impose.

5. For an excellent discussion of precaution costs, and how they ought to be calculated and then reduced, see Jim Shliferstein, "Fear Itself: Secondary Mischief and its Policy Implications" (unpublished manuscript, 2011) (on file with author).

6. 18 U.S.C. §1201 (a)(1) (Federal Kidnapping Act). The law originally provided for capital punishment and enabled federal authorities to step in once a kidnapper crossed state lines with a victim.

7. In Agatha Christie, *Murder on the Orient Express* (1934), Hercule Poirot deduces that twelve persons on a train cooperated to murder the true kidnapper of a child. The kidnapper had avoided justice in the United States. The kidnapping was plainly modeled on the Lindbergh kidnapping, and the plot reflected general concern at the time about the evidence that had been mustered to convict Bruno Hauptmann.

8. See, for example, Susan Kelly, *The Boston Stranglers* (2002) (amassing evidence that infamous murders in 1962–63 were likely committed by as many as eight separate killers and that police and politicians were pressured to find a single strangler).

9. Some commentators have compared *The Collector* to Vladimir Nabokov's *Lolita* (1955). See, for example, Bavjola Shatro, "'The Collector' as Experience of Eros and Sexuality in Vladimir Nabokov's 'Lolita' and John Fowles' 'The Collector,'" 8 *European Scientific Journal* 64–78 (2012). Nabokov was a butterfly expert, but that seems beside the point unless Fowles, who had an amateur interest in the insect, was inspired by this fact or inclined to make a joke of it. *Lolita* also involves an abduction, though in other respects the novels are quite different. In any event *The Collector* is a superior vehicle for thinking about threats and the difference between criminal kidnapping and other relationships.

10. Capture bonding is not rare. See G. Dwayne Fuselier, "Placing the Stockholm Syndrome in Perspective," *FBI Law Enforcement Bulletin*, July 1999, http://www.au.af.mil/au/awc/awcgate/fbi/stockholm_syndrome.pdf (FBI estimates it develops in 8 percent of kidnappings). In an environment in which women were abducted and brought into rival and violent groups, it may have been adaptive to develop empathy for the captors rather than to fight. See Azar Gat, *War in Human Civilization* (2006).

11. The symmetry point is advanced in Perry Nodelman, "John Fowles's Variations in *The Collector*," 28 *Contemporary Literature* 332–46 (1987). Nodelman notes that "Miranda's obsession with G.P. strangely parallels Clegg's obsession with her. . . . Miranda is herself a variation on Clegg. . . . Miranda is as offended by G.P.'s interest in sex—'his one horrid weakness' (150)—as Clegg is offended by her sexuality." Nodelman observes that Miranda and Clegg both hate dirt and both collect. Despite her claim that she is no collector of men (266), she says, "I hated it when he [G.P.] went off to Italy like that, without telling me. Not because I was seriously in love with him, but because he was vaguely mine, and didn't get permission from me" (146).

12. Kidnapping in the United States is usually defined by forcible confinement for one of several purposes, including ransom, the commission of another felony, and the infliction of bodily harm upon or intent to terrorize the victim or another person. Thus in Minnesota M.S.A. §609.25:

> Kidnapping.
> Subdivision 1. Acts constituting. Whoever, for any of the following purposes, confines or removes from one place to another, any person without the person's consent or, if

the person is under the age of 16 years, without the consent of the person's parents or other legal custodian, is guilty of kidnapping and may be sentenced as provided in subdivision 2:

(1) to hold for ransom or reward for release, or as shield or hostage; or
(2) to facilitate commission of any felony or flight thereafter; or
(3) to commit great bodily harm or to terrorize the victim or another; or
(4) to hold in involuntary servitude.

Clegg can hardly be said to have intended to terrorize Miranda, and a lawyer might note that gags and chloroform do not themselves inflict great or lasting bodily harm. Ironically a prosecutor could argue that Miranda's worsening cold or flu must have been transmitted by him. Involuntary servitude is even more of a stretch inasmuch as it was Clegg who tended to Miranda and saw to the preparation of meals and cleaning. If Clegg had taken Miranda across U.S. state lines, the broader Federal Kidnapping Act would reach him with "whoever unlawfully seizes, confines, inveigles, decoys, kidnaps, abducts, or carries away and holds for ransom or reward *or otherwise* any person" (18 U.S.C.A. § 1201; italics added).

In *The Collector*'s home jurisdiction, kidnapping is defined at common law as the "taking or carrying away of one person by another, by force or fraud, without the consent of the person taken or carried away and without lawful excuse. It must involve an attack on or loss of that person's liberty." It is thus an aggravated form of false imprisonment, which includes every wrongful deprivation of a person's liberty. Both are common law offenses with no limits on imprisonment. See Law Commission, "Simplification of Criminal Law: Kidnapping," Consultation Paper 200, http://lawcommission.justice.gov.uk/docs/cp200_kidnapping_consultation.pdf. Under this overbroad law Clegg can be convicted of the more serious offense, kidnapping, but so could a driver who deceived someone into an excursion for a surprise birthday party.

13. Politically motivated kidnappings are easier to execute because they do not involve a transfer of ransom to the kidnapper. The authorities cannot track the kidnappers by following the ransom. The kidnappers might want prisoners released or the government to agree to halt some policy, and none of these payoffs gives the government something to follow in order to find the wrongdoers. On the other hand, political kidnappings suffer from secondary credibility; the government can see that if it complies with the demand, there will be more demands and hostages in the future.

14. They are known in a few countries where they abduct corporate executives and collect ransoms from employers and, sometimes, from families. This crime often involves collusion, either with victims or with police, and I set it aside here.

15. Credibility is explored in Saul Levmore and Ariel Porat, "Criminal Deterrence in Multiple Dimensions" (available on SSRN (2016)).

16. See Levmore & Porat, note 15.

17. Unsurprisingly, but unfortunately, the prize-winning film version of *The Collector* (1965) includes nothing of Miranda's plans for other men and none of her narration. There are too many other adaptation decisions to detail, but it is noteworthy that the film has Miranda quickly "accepting" Clegg's marriage proposal, and then Clegg backing off because he lacks the witnesses necessary for a legal marriage ceremony and, presumably, because he knows her promise is not credible.

11

Premeditation and Responsibility in *The Stranger*

Jonathan Masur

INTRODUCTION

The title of Albert Camus's 1942 novel *L'Etranger* is usually translated literally as *The Stranger*. However, the term is better understood as "the foreigner" or "the outsider"—one who is a stranger to his community and his culture.[1] The title describes Camus's narrator and protagonist Meursault. Meursault is the existentialist ideal personified: he moves blithely through life, nearly emotionless, acting on little more than whim and caprice and following the easiest path available to him. Camus's objective is to show how French society, even French Algerian society, cannot tolerate someone so alien to their ways of life and even their notions of humanity. He turns Meursault into a victim, persecuted and ultimately executed as much for his differentness as for his crimes.

The first half of the novel is Camus's exploration of Meursault's character. It opens with the death of Meursault's mother, whom he had earlier placed in a state-run home for the elderly. Meursault famously does not cry at his mother's funeral. He shows little emotion at all, treating the event as another typical moment in his life, no more or less meaningful than the ones that precede or follow it. The novel's first half closes with Meursault's killing of an Arab—identified only as "an Arab"—who had fought and injured Meursault's friend Raymond earlier that day. Camus portrays the killing as a great deal more emotionally fraught for Meursault than the death of his mother, but in a peculiar way. Meursault is blinded by the sun and oppressed by its heat. When the Arab draws his knife, Meursault thinks, "The scorching blade slashed at my eyelashes and stabbed at my stinging eyes," though he is describing only the light glinting off of the blade. The Arab is still many steps away. Then, as the sky seems to "split open from one end to the other to rain down fire," Meursault points his gun at the Arab and pulls the trigger.[2]

The second half of the novel describes Meursault's trial and eventual execution for the murder. The trial is Camus's vehicle for demonstrating French intolerance of Meursault's manner of being. The centerpiece of the trial is not Meursault's shooting of the Arab, its apparently unprovoked nature, or Meursault's inability to justify his actions or even account for them. Rather the trial focuses on Meursault's failure to show emotion at his mother's funeral. This, more than the senseless killing, funnels the outrage of the judge, jury, and vengeful prosecutor toward Meursault. Meursault is eventually convicted largely based upon testimony concerning this failure to cry and a variety of similar personal episodes. The prosecutor alleges that Meursault's conduct—at his mother's funeral and afterward—demonstrates his cold, unfeeling heart. But his behavior is simply Camus's existentialist ideal sprung to life.

In his portrayal of Meursault's trial and execution, Camus's objective is to depict Meursault's expurgation from French Algerian society on the basis of his otherness. For the French, that someone might not cry at his mother's funeral is so incomprehensible, and so repugnant, that the individual must be banished (or worse). Camus thus builds the trial around evidence of Meursault's status as an outsider and rests Meursault's conviction on that evidence. The reader, having been privy to Meursault's inner thoughts throughout the novel, is meant to understand the injustice and outrageousness of Meursault's conviction on the basis of these facts.[3] As the reader understands (but the judge and jury do not), Meursault's failure to cry at his mother's funeral and the killing of the Arab are evidence of his general indifference, not his depravity.

Accordingly most scholarly commentary has focused on the funeral and the emphasis placed upon Meursault's lack of emotion at his trial.[4] Scholars have pointed to the use of those facts at trial as the apotheosis of French rejection of Meursault's otherness. They have documented the unfairness perpetrated against Meursault and the injustice of his conviction.[5] Judge Richard Posner has written that the facts about Meursault's mother's death would never have been allowed into evidence had his trial been held in the United States. (Interestingly such evidence might well have been admissible in a French court of the time, where testimony as to the defendant's "character and morals" was permitted.) Nonetheless, as Posner notes, Camus's point is not so much to criticize French criminal procedure as to attack the society that has judged Meursault's attitude as unacceptable.[6] Meursault's lack of emotion at his mother's death is the touchstone for Camus's message, and thus for the critical response to the novel.

Yet it is not enough that Meursault be convicted on spurious and irrelevant facts. If he is in fact guilty of murder, and if death is the appropriate penalty, then Camus's depiction loses much of its force. The judge, jury, and prosecutor would have arrived at the right result, if for the wrong reason. What reader would have followed Camus down the path he hoped to tread? Humans have a well-known tendency to trust and seek out evidence that confirms the outcomes they believe to be correct. This confirmation bias would have made it difficult for Camus to maintain with any force that the (correct) prosecution of Meursault—albeit for the wrong reasons—demonstrates the antipathy of French society. It is thus necessary for Camus to demonstrate that Meursault should not have been convicted and executed and that he would not have been convicted had it not been for the irrelevant evidence from his mother's funeral. Indeed the verdict of death must come as something of a shock, a final betrayal of Meursault's humanity, for it to have the desired effect. To some degree Camus is successful; the casual reader may feel great sympathy for Meursault and view him as mistreated to an uncommon degree. As Kamel Daoud put it in *The Meursault Investigation*, a retelling of *The Stranger* from the perspective of the Arab, "The original guy was such a good storyteller, he managed to make people forget his crime."[7] But close scrutiny of the circumstances of Meursault's crime, and the law that governs it, compels a different conclusion as to his criminality.

While this legal analysis has ramifications for how a reader understands Camus's novel, the novel and Camus's portrayal of the trial should affect our understanding of the role of law. Criminal trials, as adjudicated by neutral judges and juries, are meant to function as bulwarks against emotion, bias, and the impetuous rush to judgment. Camus describes Meursault's trial as if it has failed: Meursault has been convicted because of the unrelenting bias and hostility of the other parties to the proceeding. Camus paints the French legal system as a slave to its own prejudices. But if Camus's intimations are wrong, and the trial has reached the correct outcome, then his pessimism about the law and its role in the adjudication of guilt is similarly misguided.

PERCEPTIONS OF GUILT

The tip of the spear in Camus's effort to convince the reader of the trial's injustice are Meursault's lawyer and his girlfriend Marie. The lawyer, who plays a central (if often silent) role in Meursault's life for the second half of the novel, is Camus's primary vehicle. We are introduced to the lawyer almost immediately following Meursault's arrest, just a few pages into part 2. The initial portrait of the lawyer—who is never named, referred to only as "a lawyer"—is relatively positive and bespeaks confidence. The no-nonsense lawyer has already reviewed Meursault's file and recognizes that the case is not straightforward.[8] He immediately grasps the significance of Meursault's mother's funeral and asks Meursault whether he "had felt any sadness that day."[9] This is the first explicit indication that Meursault's behavior at the funeral will play a central role in his trial. By allowing the lawyer to deliver this news rather than having the prosecutor blindside the defense Camus instills within the reader a sense of confidence that the lawyer is competent and able.

At the same time, Camus suggests that the lawyer finds Meursault's attitude distasteful, much as the judge, prosecutors, and jurors soon will. After Meursault denies that he "held back [his] natural feelings" in not crying at his mother's funeral, the lawyer gives him "a strange look, as if he found [him] slightly disgusting." He warns Meursault that "things could get very nasty" when this story is revealed at trial. He then fails to appear at Meursault's interview with the examining magistrate later that day "due to unforeseen circumstances," as the magistrate reports.[10] One cannot help but wonder if the lawyer's disgust toward Meursault has caused him to distance himself from Meursault and the case, or whether this is merely the well-worn policeman's trick (perhaps even in Algeria?) of informing the suspect that his lawyer hasn't yet arrived in order to prolong the questioning outside of the presence of counsel. If so, the tactic is successful, as Meursault reveals several self-incriminating details at this interview. In any event it is clear that the lawyer has no particular interest in sheltering Meursault from the truth of his actions or the likely consequences.

Yet once the trial begins, Meursault's attorney is all optimism. In the midst of witness testimony that appears damaging to Meursault, his lawyer tells him that "everything is working out for the best." After closing arguments the lawyer thinks that he will be sentenced to at most a few years of prison or hard labor. By this point the reader may have come to doubt the defense attorney's ability, as the prosecutor lets fly one rhetorical salvo after another and seems to encounter only feeble resistance from Meursault's attorney. But Camus continues to reassure the reader that the lawyer is actually performing well. Following the closing argument Meursault explains, "His colleagues came over to shake his hand. I heard: 'That was brilliant!' One of them even appealed to me as a witness. 'Wasn't it?' he said."[11]

Camus also enlists Meursault's girlfriend Marie in an effort to suggest that Meursault is unlikely to be convicted of a serious crime. During her one and only visit to Meursault in prison, she twice proclaims that he is likely to be acquitted.[12] Marie is not a lawyer, and these remarks must be understood in context as the hopeful exhortations of someone trying to raise the defendant's spirits. Nonetheless they come before the prosecutor has made his case, and even before Meursault has appeared to be in any grave jeopardy. It is only natural, then, for Marie's words to boost the spirits of concerned readers, just as they are meant to improve Meursault's.

MEURSAULT'S CONVICTION

Those are the impressions that Camus endeavors to create in the mind of the reader. But what of the law behind Meursault's actions? From the French conquest in 1848 until Algerian independence in 1962, France administered Algeria as a *département*, a status above mere colony. As such, French law applied in Algeria just as it did in France.[13] The relevant French criminal law was the Code Pénal of 1810, which was not substantially amended until 1959, well after *L'Etranger* was published.

In order for Meursault to have been put to death, he must have been convicted not merely of murder but of *assassinat*—assassination. Murder under the French Penal Code was defined as a "willful" killing, by which the French meant that it must be intentional. However, murder could be punished with death only when it "preceded, accompanied, or followed any other crime or delict." (This is much like a U.S. felony murder statute, which turns ordinary murder—or less—into first-degree murder that in many states is punishable by death.) Absent such an aggravating factor, murder was punishable at most by "perpetual hard labour," that is, life imprisonment.[14] Meursault's homicide was not accompanied by any other crime, and so his sentence cannot be based upon a conviction for "only" murder.

Rather Meursault was found guilty of assassination. The French defined assassination as a murder "committed with premeditation, or with lying in wait."[15] The prosecutor suggests several times that Meursault acted with premeditation, though Camus does not explicate this point.[16] Assassination was punishable under all circumstances by death. On its face the French Penal Code provides no flexibility in sentencing a criminal convicted of assassination. The Code states that anyone found guilty of assassination "shall be punished with death" and provides an exception only in special instances not relevant to Meursault. In practice, however, judges retained discretion to lessen a criminal's sentence where mitigating circumstances existed.[17] The Code does not define the types of mitigating circumstances that a judge may take into account, but one treatise writer suggests that a defense attorney should raise the repentance of her client, his illnesses, his brilliant military service, laudatory certifications from his employers (if such exist), and so forth. If such mitigating factors were present, Meursault's punishment could conceivably have been reduced by as much as two "degrees"— first, from death to life at hard labor and, second, from life at hard labor to a fixed period of years, possibly as few as five.[18] Nonetheless it seems unlikely that Meursault would have been able to take advantage of any opportunity for mitigation. Not a single traditional mitigating factor exists, and even Meursault himself is unable to conjure one. If he is convicted, he is likely facing the maximum penalty.

The fact that Meursault was convicted of assassination helps make sense of what might seem to modern audiences a peculiar aspect of the trial. Just before his trial begins, Meursault's lawyer mentions that his case "isn't the most important case of the session. Right after you, there's a parricide coming up." Similarly, at the conclusion of the trial the prosecutor mentions in court that the next case on the docket involves "the most monstrous of crimes: the murder of a father." As a means of impressing upon the judge and jury the heinousness of the crime he goes on to add that Meursault's offense "inspired in him a horror nearly greater than that which he felt at the crime of parricide".[19] This might strike the modern reader as odd: Why is a case of parricide the appropriate comparison? It turns out, however, that under French law *parricide*, the killing of a father or mother, is similarly punishable by death as a type of aggravated murder.[20] A French reader in 1942 would undoubtedly have understood parricide as a particularly odious crime, and its repeated invocation in connection with Meursault's own trial is meant to suggest the perceived gravity of Meursault's offense.

DEFENSE AND EXCUSE

The extreme nature of Meursault's punishment, coupled with what would seem to be his more limited moral responsibility, is the foundation upon which Camus builds his case. The question that Camus never confronts directly but addresses only in passing is the crime for which Meursault should properly have been convicted had his trial been fair and confined to the relevant facts. There are a number of possibilities of varying degrees of plausibility.

The first possibility, suggested at various points by Marie and Meursault's lawyer, is that he might have been acquitted entirely on the ground that he was acting in self-defense.[21] The Arab had recently slashed Meursault's friend Raymond with a knife, and before the shooting he drew his knife again and pointed it (perhaps menacingly) toward Meursault.

But self-defense is not a real option. At the time of the killing the Arab is nearly lying on his back, having "sat up a little" from a prone position. Even drawing his knife does not cause him to stand up. Also, Meursault is quite a distance from the Arab; the encounter begins with Meursault approximately ten meters away, and he advances only a few paces before he pulls the trigger.[22] In essentially every jurisdiction in the world much more is required before a defendant can argue that he acted in self-defense. For instance, the Model Penal Code, which has been highly influential in the United States, provides that an individual may not use deadly force in self-defense "unless the actor believes that such force is necessary to protect himself against death, serious bodily injury, kidnapping or sexual intercourse compelled by force or threat." That necessity must also be "immediate,"and the defendant must not have "provoked the use of force against himself."[23]

French law of 1942 was largely in accord. Before a right to self-defense could exist, the threat must be severe, unjust, and irreparable, such that the defendant's actions were driven by necessity. The harm must be immediate as well.[24]

Meursault meets none of these conditions. He is not in serious danger, to say nothing of "immediate" danger. The Arab has not even stood up, much less moved to attack him. And it is Meursault who has happened upon the Arab and is advancing toward him, not the other way around. If anyone has provoked the confrontation, it is Meursault. There have been jurisdictions in which a subjective fear of bodily harm, even one that is objectively unreasonable, can form the basis for a valid claim of self-defense. But here the reader, in a privileged position of omniscience, knows that Meursault does not fear for his life. Nor would there be any reason for a judge or jury to believe that he did.

The Model Penal Code contains a further limitation on the use of deadly force: the individual whose life or health is threatened must not be able to "avoid the necessity of using such force with complete safety by retreating."[25] This "duty to retreat" is now a minority position in U.S. jurisdictions, but it was the law in France in 1942: a criminal defendant could not claim that he had acted in self-defense if he could have escaped the danger by means other than violence.[26] There can be little doubt that Meursault could have retreated from the prone Arab rather than shooting him, had he so chosen. This is yet another insuperable barrier to any claim of self-defense that Meursault might offer.

In the absence of a claim to self-defense Meursault might have attempted to argue that his murder of the Arab was provoked and therefore "excusable."[27] The French use the term in much the same way it is employed in U.S. criminal law, though the usage is contrary to both colloquial English and French. Under the law of provocation, "excusable" means that an offense is mitigated, though not entirely forgiven, due to the circumstances under which it was committed. A claim of excuse by virtue of provocation can never be a complete defense, only an argument that the defendant should be convicted of a lesser crime.

Under French law, murder was excusable if it had been "provoked by blows, or grievous personal violence."[28] Perhaps Meursault could claim that he was provoked to kill by the Arab's earlier assault on his friend Raymond, an assault that left Raymond bloodied and in need of medical attention.

In his closing arguments Meursault's lawyer seems to argue for precisely this result. He pleads first that Meursault is guilty, but "with an explanation," by which he means that the crime is excusable.[29] (The original text reads, "L'avocat levait les bras et plaidait coupable, mais avec excuses."[30]) The prosecutor responds by arguing that Meursault is guilty with no explanation. Later, in the same closing argument, Meursault's attorney argues again that the jury should find that there had been "extenuating circumstances."[31] This would be a potentially significant defense for Meursault were it available. The penalty for murder, or even assassination, if excused is only one to five years in prison, a far cry from the life of hard labor (or death) that Meursault would otherwise face.[32]

There is an interesting threshold question as to whether a defense of provocation is available in a case of premeditated murder. Most U.S. jurisdictions will allow a defendant to mitigate even premeditated murder down to manslaughter if the defendant can demonstrate that he was provoked. But French commentators have recognized the inherent contradiction between a provoked killing (unthinking and irrational) and premeditation (deliberate and contemplated). Two separate treatises conclude that it would be internally inconsistent for a jury to convict a defendant of premeditated murder but excuse it for provocation. They argue that such a verdict should, as a matter of logic, be annulled by the presiding judge.[33] One of the two treatises notes, however, that the Court of Cassation, France's highest criminal appeals court, had in fact allowed such mitigation; a conviction for premeditated murder can be "excused."[34] The Court of Cassation's ruling is consistent with the language of the French Penal Code, if not the logic of the law. Assassination is a type of murder, and murder can be excused if provoked. The Penal Code also states explicitly that parricide is never excusable, but it says nothing about premeditated murder.[35] So it would seem as though Meursault could surmount at least this initial hurdle.

Yet Meursault is nearly as far from being able to demonstrate that he was provoked as he is from demonstrating that he acted in self-defense. First, the fact of the matter is that *he was not provoked*, in the sense that his actions were not driven by any heightened emotional response to the assault that had taken place earlier. He goes walking on the beach and eventually encounters the Arab with the same attitude of disengagement that pervades all of his other activities. Before he begins the walk he thinks to himself, "To stay or to go, it amounted to the same thing." When he eventually experiences some emotional upheaval, it is due to the heat and the blazing sun, not to the Arab and certainly not to the earlier combat. Before he even encounters the Arab, he is nearly overwhelmed by the heat: "All that heat was pressing down on me and making it hard for me to go on. And every time I felt a blast of its hot breath strike my face, I gritted my teeth, clenched my fists in my trouser pockets, and strained every nerve in order to overcome the sun and the thick drunkenness it was spilling over me."[36] Criminal juries are rarely privy to a killer's true thoughts in the moments before a homicide, and so the reader here finds herself in a privileged position. But if the question is whether a conviction for excusable homicide would be the "correct" result of Meursault's trial, the unequivocal answer is that it would not.

Could Meursault's attorney nonetheless have made out a plausible case for provocation? Such a defense immediately runs into a number of hurdles. The first is that none of Meursault's conduct before or after the killing would support a claim that he was provoked or excited. An argument for provocation would likely be stillborn. Moreover Meursault would have great difficulty in satisfying several of the other elements typically required to make out a claim of mitigation by provocation. Many—though not all—criminal jurisdictions do not permit a defendant to argue that he was provoked if "cooling time" has elapsed between the provoking incident and the crime. The theory behind a standard provocation defense is that the situation (and possibly the victim), not just the defendant, bear some responsibility for the crime. That is, in some cases it may be that even a "reasonable" person would lose his temper and commit a violent act. If an otherwise reasonable person might behave in such a fashion, then perhaps the defendant should not be punished as harshly as someone who transgresses all boundaries of reasonable behavior. Yet if cooling time has passed and the defendant still has not been able to calm himself, this is an indication that the resultant crime is less attributable to the context and more attributable to the defendant himself.[37]

Like the law in most U.S. jurisdictions, French law of 1942 required that the provocation and the crime that followed it be proximate in time for the crime to be excused.[38] If there were an opportunity for the criminal to reflect upon his actions, that reflection would exacerbate the crime rather than excusing it. In addition most U.S. jurisdictions judge the question of cooling time objectively rather than subjectively. That is, it does not matter whether the defendant *actually* reflected or cooled; it matters only that sufficient time passed to have made such cooling possible.[39] The French Penal Code followed the same rule, focusing specifically on the time interval between provocation and crime.[40]

Here there can be no doubt that abundant cooling time existed. After the initial confrontation between Raymond and the Arab, Meursault has time to accompany his friend home, attend to him, and then head back to the beach for another walk.

Courts have regularly viewed even a much shorter passage of time as an adequate cooling period.

In addition, many jurisdictions would bar Meursault from offering a provocation defense because it was his friend who initiated the combat that underlies the claim.[41] Again the theory that underlies mitigation through provocation is that the situation or the victim is partly to blame. It is difficult to hold the Arab responsible for Meursault's crime when the Arab was attacked and acted in self-defense. Similarly, one cannot attribute some of the moral responsibility to the situation in which Meursault found himself when that situation was created by Meursault and his friend, whose injury is the source of the alleged provocation.

Finally, courts generally hold that an individual can be provoked only by violence against certain people, not just anyone under the sun. Jurisdictions typically restrict the defense of provocation to violence against the defendant himself or against the defendant's family and loved ones. It is unclear if Meursault has any remaining family or any loved ones at all; indeed that is part of his problem. Regardless, no one involved in the combat with the Arab could conceivably qualify. Meursault's closest friend (and I use that term advisedly) among the individuals involved is Raymond. He is merely a casual friend of Meursault's, not someone with whom Meursault has any type of close connection. (Again, it is unclear whether any such person exists.)

Surprisingly, the French law of 1942 appears to be much more lenient than U.S. law on this score. The Penal Code states that murder is excusable if provoked by violence "envers les personnes"—literally, toward one or more persons. This indicates that the violence need not be directed at the individual who commits the murder or anyone close (in relational terms). One commentator notes, "The law does not demand that the violence has been against the accused. The excuse might exist either if the perpetrator of the crime or the offense has himself been attacked, or if the violence has been exercised against his relatives or against third persons who are unknown to him." It suffices that the provoking blows be delivered against *people.* In an excess of completeness French scholars have noted that violence against *property* or *domestic animals* is not adequate.[42]

For an existentialist there is partial justice in this result. It is central to Meursault's personality—and Camus's notion of existentialism—that he would lack the type of close connections necessary to give rise to a claim for provocation in U.S. jurisdictions. French law is notably more solicitous, yet this applies only to the need for a personal connection. The emotional response necessary to make out a defense of provocation is equally foreign to the existentialist archetype. Camus must believe that by privileging emotion and anger the law does not deal fairly with individuals such as Meursault. And indeed there is some force to that objection. But it can provide no succor to Meursault, given the many hurdles he faces in mounting a provocation defense.

PREMEDITATION AND RESPONSIBILITY

For Meursault this leaves only two possibilities: conviction for murder or for assassination by premeditation. Regardless of the eventual outcome, he is facing an extremely stiff penalty: death or a life of hard labor. Already this casts his trial and conviction in a very different light. Had his mother's funeral never been made part of the discussion, Meursault should nonetheless have been convicted of an extremely serious crime.[43] The remaining question is which of those very serious crimes it would have been.

The standard for premeditation has varied from jurisdiction to jurisdiction over time, with some jurisdictions adopting positions notable for their outlandishness. For a time the state of Pennsylvania held that "no time is too short" for a defendant to premeditate a murder.[44] An appeals court in Alabama expressed the same approach more colorfully, holding that "[p]remeditation and deliberation may be formed while the killer is 'pressing the trigger that fired the fatal shot.' "[45] However, most jurisdictions have recognized that such a stance would risk entirely collapsing the distinction between premeditation and intentional but unpremeditated murder. In the majority of jurisdictions a killer must have "considered and weighed his decision to kill" if the government is to establish that he acted with premeditation.[46]

French law accords with this general consensus. Section 297 of the French Code Pénal specifies that "[p]remeditation consists in a design formed, *before the action*, of attacking the person of any particular individual."[47]

What, then, of Meursault? If one adopts an internal perspective it is clear that he did not premeditate the killing. When he heads back for his fateful walk along the beach, he does so for no particular reason: "To stay, or to make a move—it came to much the same. After a moment I returned to the beach, and started walking."[48] He does not form the intention to shoot the Arab until the instant before he pulls the trigger. Indeed it would be wholly inconsistent with his personality and state of being to have "considered and weighed" his decision to kill.[49] An existentialist does not premeditate! If Meursault is a reliable narrator, then he cannot be guilty of premeditated murder.

Let us suppose that we do not have the advantage of bearing witness to Meursault's innermost thoughts and consider what evidence might have been adduced against him at trial. Because it is generally impossible outside of the literary context to know the defendant's state of mind directly, courts have identified particular types of evidence that are especially probative of premeditation. In *People v. Anderson*, an influential California case, the California Court of Appeals classified relevant evidence into three categories: "(1) facts regarding the defendant's behavior prior to the killing which might indicate a design to take life ('planning activity'); (2) facts about the defendant's prior relationship with the victim which might indicate a reason to kill ('motive'); and (3) evidence that 'the *manner* of killing was so particular and exacting that the defendant must have intentionally killed according to a "preconceived design." ' "[50]

As others, including Richard Posner, have written, there is a great deal of evidence introduced at Meursault's trial that is irrelevant to his guilt and would never have been permitted in a U.S. trial.[51] Chief among this evidence is Meursault's failure to cry at his mother's funeral, but there is also the fact that he is not Christian and does not believe in god, as well as his affair with Marie, which began the day after he buried his mother.

Yet there is also significant evidence that bears directly on the question of whether Meursault premeditated the killing. Posner focuses on the fact that Meursault fired once at the Arab and then, after a pause, fired four more shots. Posner states that "those four shots fired after a pause are highly indicative of premeditation."[52] Posner's view is perhaps influenced by the examining magistrate in Meursault's trial, who latches onto the same fact. In the course of their second conversation the magistrate repeatedly asks Meursault why he fired four additional times after the first shot seemed to have killed the Arab. "But why, *why* did you go on firing at a prostrate man?" he demands. And later, "I ask you '*Why?*' I insist on your telling me."[53]

Meursault's conduct is certainly peculiar for an existentialist. Yet it is difficult to see how it could be probative of premeditation as Posner suggests. A killer acting in the heat of passion or on the spur of the moment might easily squeeze the trigger multiple times, even after the first shot seems to have found its mark. Continuing to fire "at a prostrate man" is more indicative of Meursault's having lost his head than of cold, calculating behavior associated with premeditation. It should come as no surprise that there are legions of cases in which killers have been convicted of murder—but not premeditated murder—despite firing multiple shots at their victims.[54] To be sure, Meursault's multiple shots are evidence that the killing was intentional rather than accidental.[55] But that is not the question.

However, there is other evidence that is far more probative of premeditation. The victim had cut Raymond with a knife just hours earlier, in a fight Meursault witnessed but did not participate in. Raymond and Meursault had then come across the same individual again, just a few minutes before the killing. Raymond had contemplated renewing the combat or simply shooting the Arab. Meursault convinced Raymond not to shoot and then persuaded Raymond to hand him his gun.

And these are not chance encounters. The victim is the brother of a girl Raymond had assaulted several days earlier.[56] A confrontation had been brewing ever since. Thus there is both planning activity and a prior relationship which might indicate motive. On the basis of these facts alone there is a plausible case for premeditation.

It is impossible to predict with any certainty whether a properly instructed jury would have convicted Meursault of assassination or murder. But the difference is largely immaterial. Meursault is guilty of a very serious crime, one that will carry a protracted jail sentence. Although his trial was infected by discussion of his mother and Marie and his lack of Christian faith, the judge and jury arrive at the correct outcome, or close to it. Camus succeeds in convincing the reader of Meursault's essential innocence—victimhood, even—only by leveraging the reader's unfamiliarity with French criminal law. Similarly, he convinces the reader of the justice system's fundamental unfairness only by obscuring the truth of Meursault's guilt. Camus deploys Marie and the lawyer to smuggle in the idea that Meursault's homicide was justifiable or at least excusable. But there is little truth in their words.

Camus's objective in *The Stranger* is to demonstrate the fundamental illegitimacy of French intolerance for the existentialist ideal. One can hardly indict an entire philosophical movement on the basis of one murder. And yet here at least it is difficult not to side with the French.

NOTES

I thank Eva Bornstein, Saul Levmore, Richard McAdams, Martha C. Nussbaum, and participants in the Conference on Crime in Law and Literature for helpful comments; Kate Long, L. T. Edwards, Morgan Yates, Margaret Schilt, and Lyonette Louis-Jacque for superb research assistance; and the David and Celia Hilliard Fund for research support.

1. Some more modern translations use "The Outsider" as the title. See, for example, Albert Camus, *The Outsider* (Joseph Laredo trans., Penguin Books 1983) (hereinafter "Camus (Laredo trans.)").

2. Albert Camus, *The Stranger* 59 (Matthew Ward trans., Vintage International 1989) (hereinafter "Camus (Ward trans.)").

3. Robert R. Brock, "Meursault the Straw Man," 25 *Studies in the Novel* 92, 99 (1993) ("Had Meursault gotten even an impossible five years in prison instead of the guillotine, can anyone seriously believe that this slim book would have had a second printing?"); René Girard, "Camus's Stranger Retried," 79 *PMLA* 519, 531 (1964) ("The secretly provocative nature of the murder is never acknowledged, and the reprisals of society are presented as unprovoked aggression.").

4. See, for example, Richard A. Posner, *Law and Literature* 42 (1998); Girard, at 519.

5. See, for example, Louis Hudon, "The Stranger and the Critics," 25 *Yale French Studies* 59, 61 (1960).

6. Posner, *Law and Literature* 42, 43.

7. Kamel Daoud, *The Meursault Investigation* 1 (2015) (Cullen trans.).

8. Camus (Ward trans.), at 64 ("My case was a tricky one, but he had no doubts we'd win, if I trusted him.").

9. *Id.* at 65.

10. *Id. at 65–66.*

11. *Id.* at 91, 106, 105.

12. *Id.* at 75.

13. Dahmène Touchent, "Algerian Law Guide," GlobaLex, January 2006, http://www.nyulawglobal.org/globalex/algeria.htm.

14. French Penal Code, Book the Third, Title II, Chapter I, §§295, 304 (1810).

15. *Id.* at §296.

16. Camus (Ward trans.), at 99.

17. Penal Code §§302, 463; Roger Merle, *Droit Pénal Général: Complémentaire* 305 (Presses Universitaires de France 1957).

18. Merle, at 309–10; Penal Code §463.

19. Camus (Ward trans.), at 82, 101.

20. Penal Code §§299, 302.

21. *Id.* at §328.

22. Camus (Ward trans.), at 58–59.

23. Model Penal Code (MPC) §3.04 (2)(b), (1), (2)(b)(ii).

24. Garraud, at 211–12, 216.

25. MPC §3.04(2)(b)(ii)(A).

26. Garraud, at 216.

27. Penal Code §321.

28. *Id.*

29. Camus (Ward trans.), at 98.

30. Albert Camus, *L'Etranger* 116 (Prentice-Hall 1955).

31. Camus (Ward trans.), at 105.

32. Penal Code §326.

33. R. Garraud, *Précis De Droit Criminel* 326 (Librairie de la Société du Recueil Générale de Lois et des Arrêts 18ème éd. 1903); Merle, at 302.

34. Merle, at 302 (citing Crim. 6 août 1898, D. (P.), 99.1.95; Crim. 12 juill. 1907, D. (P.), 1909.1.279.).

35. Penal Code §§296, 321, 323.

36. Camus (Ward trans.), at 57.

37. To be clear, the law of provocation, including the requirement that there be no cooling time, has received withering criticism on a number of different grounds. I do not mean to endorse existing doctrine, only to describe it.

38. Garraud, at 326.

39. See United States v. Bordeaux, 980 F.2d 534 (8th Cir. 1992); Sanford H. Kadish et al., *Criminal Law and its Processes*, 9th edition (Alphen aan den Rijn: Wolters Kluwer, 2012), 450–51.

40. Garraud, at 326.

41. See, for example, Or. Rev. Stat. § 163.135(1) (prohibiting a defendant from offering a provocation defense when the provocation stems originally from a criminal act on the defendant's part).

42. 2 R. Garraud, *Traité Théorique Et Pratique Du Droit Pénal Français* 740–41 (Librairie de Recueil Sirey 3ème éd. 1914).

43. There is some suggestion in *The Stranger* that Meursault would escape serious punishment because he is a Frenchman living in Algeria and has killed an Arab, a person of lower status. As a descriptive matter this is certainly possible; the French were notorious for their poor treatment of the indigenous Arab population of Algeria, particularly in comparison to persons of European descent. See Brock, at 92, 96. But if this is Camus's point, it is a peculiar one. He is unlikely to garner much sympathy either from modern audiences or from contemporary French ones by arguing that Meursault should have been treated more leniently because he killed "only" an Arab. If his claim is that French society should tolerate the existentialist ideal, it is especially unconvincing to argue that this tolerance should be manifest through continued institutionalized racism.

44. Commonwealth v. Carroll, 412 Pa. 525 (1963); see also State v. Berhanu, 724 N.W.2d 181, 186 (S.D. 2006) (adopting the same approach).

45. Young v. State, 428 So. 2d 155, 158 (Ala. Crim. App. 1982).

46. State v. Guthrie, 194 W. Va. 657 (1995). See generally Kadish et al., at 427–37.

47. Penal Code §297 (emphasis added).

48. Albert Camus, *The Stranger* 73 (Stuart Gilbert trans., Alfred A. Knopf, 1946) (hereinafter "Camus (Gilbert trans.)").

49. See René Girard, "Camus's Stranger Retried," in *Albert Camus* 84 (Harold Bloom ed. 1989) ("How could Meursault premeditate murder, since he cannot premeditate a successful career in Paris or marriage with his mistress?").

50. Kadish et al., at 435 (citing People v. Anderson, 447 P.2d 942 (Cal. 1968)).

51. Posner, at 43.

52. *Id.*

53. Camus (Gilbert trans.), at 84.

54. Perhaps Posner believes that Meursault premeditated the killing between the first shot and the remaining four. But that would have been an extraordinarily short time for him to have formed a design of attacking the Arab. It would also require segmenting "the attack" into a first phase (the first shot) and a second phase, as French law requires that the defendant have formed a design before beginning the attack. And this is not to mention the fact that the Arab most likely dies after the first shot. One translation describes the Arab's body as "lifeless" (Camus (Laredo trans.), at 60); another as "inert" (Camus (Gilbert trans.), at 76); and a third as "motionless" (Camus (Ward trans.), at 59). "Lifeless" would seem to indicate that the Arab dies after the first shot; "inert" and "motionless" are more ambiguous. The original French is "inerte." Albert Camus, *L'Etranger* 88 (Gallimard 1941). I conducted my own informal survey of native French speakers, most of whom agreed that "lifeless" is the best interpretation of what Camus wrote. By the time Meursault squeezes the trigger a second time, there may have been no murder to premeditate.

55. This is contra Hudon, at 61, who contends that Meursault's homicide was accidental. That contention is untenable on the facts.

56. *Id.* at 71, 51.

12

Walking Away

LESSONS FROM "OMELAS"

Saira Mohamed and Melissa Murray

INTRODUCTION

Written in 1973, Ursula K. Le Guin's "The Ones Who Walk Away from Omelas" is a stalwart of the science fiction genre.[1] Spare and abstract, the short story invites the reader to consider a utopian paradise—and the horrifying bargain that is required to maintain it. As Le Guin describes it, Omelas is a picturesque city of profound beauty. Arising along the seashore and half-encircled by mountains, it boasts a harbor "sparkl[ing] with flags," "moss-grown gardens," "broad green meadows," and grand "avenues of trees." The morning air hums with the "snap and flutter" of the banners that bedeck the city's racecourse, the "shimmering of gong and tambourine" from the city's procession of street performers, and "the joyous clanging of the bells."

As might be expected of those who live their lives in the midst of this explosion of sensorial delights, the citizens of Omelas are deeply contented—if not a bit self-satisfied—with their "fairy tale" existence. But, as Le Guin reveals, their happiness is contingent. "In a basement under one of the beautiful public buildings . . . is a room." Within this close, fetid space lives a child, "a boy or a girl," who "looks about six, but actually is nearly ten." Locked away from the rest of Omelas, the child is "feebleminded"—perhaps as an accident of birth or perhaps because of "fear, malnutrition, and neglect." Either way, the child is utterly alone in its abjection. Those Omelans who do visit either "kick the child to make it stand up" or "peer in at it with frightened, disgusted eyes." As Le Guin recounts, the people of Omelas "all understand that their happiness, the beauty of their city, the tenderness of their friendships, the health of their children, the wisdom of their scholars, the skill of their makers, even the abundance of their harvest and the kindly weathers of their skies, depend wholly on this child's abominable misery."

The happiness of all in exchange for the misery of a single child.[2] As Le Guin explains, most Omelans submit to this horrifying bargain with a sense of resignation. Although they once might have been outraged by the child's mistreatment, they now realize that "there is nothing they can do." They all understand that if the child were freed and raised in better conditions, "all the prosperity and beauty and delight of Omelas would wither and be destroyed." "To throw away the happiness of thousands for the chance of the happiness of one" is unthinkable.

But there are a few who, upon seeing the child in its wretched state, can no longer tolerate the terms of the bargain. Some Omelans do not submit to the sense of resignation and futility that pervades the town around them. Upon seeing the child these Omelans do not retreat to the safety and comfort of their homes and happy lives. Instead they "leave Omelas, they walk ahead into the darkness, and they do not come back."

Le Guin does not offer an obvious moral lesson in "Omelas." Her description of those who walk away is not a simple account of the triumph of these unnamed persons over their weaker brothers and sisters who remain. Instead the moral space that the defectors occupy is complex. Are they defiant objectors? Or are they cowardly deserters, too weak or scared or selfish to relieve the child's suffering? The structure of the story suggests that the hideous bargain that sustains Omelas continues forever; the few who leave the town do not inspire revolution or the liberation of the child. What are we to make of the fact that the ones who walk away never return to right the wrong they fled? These questions merit exploration, and they have generated discussions worthy of their complexity.[3] In this essay, however, we turn to a different question, one equally complex but neglected in discussions of the story: what the criminal law would say about "Omelas."

Scholars and students of criminal law may not readily think of "Omelas" as a meditation on the culpability or innocence of the defectors; indeed, Le Guin directs the reader to view the story as a reflection of the "dilemma of the American conscience."[4] But reading "Omelas" through the lens of the criminal law is illuminating. In our view this exercise reveals the troubling ways in which autonomy is and is not credited in the criminal law's account of what it means to walk away from a criminal enterprise.

We examine the law of withdrawal, renunciation, or abandonment—in Omelan terms, the law of walking away. After briefly reviewing these doctrines, we explore their rationales. As we explain, although the criminal law offers those engaged in a collective criminal enterprise an opportunity to withdraw from the enterprise (and thus be relieved of liability for any subsequent crimes undertaken in pursuit of the enterprise's objectives), the terms of withdrawal are strict. They require affirmative action on the part of the individual seeking to withdraw. Indeed, the primary justification for the strict requirements for withdrawal is a concern for the particular dangers associated with group criminality.

But in seeking to stanch the particular threat of group criminality, do we discredit and discount exercises of individual agency? Using "Omelas" as a point of entry we explore the law of walking away and consider whether its requirements ask too much of the individual. In doing so we are principally preoccupied with the law's approach to individual agency in the context of withdrawing from situations where criminality is both endemic and normalized. Although the criminal law generally honors autonomy, it undervalues the extraordinary exercise of will required to extract oneself from an environment of pervasive wrongdoing. In this way "Omelas" powerfully illustrates what criminal law overlooks: that it is incredibly difficult to walk away from situations in which everyone insists that wrongdoing is the right thing to do. In the context of Omelas, where the abuse of the child has become naturalized and inevitable, the titular Omelans' decision to walk away is the ultimate exercise of agency and autonomy. We thus find in this short story a compelling lens through which to consider not only the gravity and meaning of the act of walking way, but also the law's incomplete and impoverished understanding of those who do so.

THE LAW OF WALKING AWAY

"Omelas" draws our attention to a set of individuals who walk away from a world of wrongdoing. As compared with the townspeople who continue to enjoy their hideous bargain and let the child suffer, the ones who walk away from Omelas might seem relatively blameless. Nonetheless, in the eyes of the criminal law they would not be readily forgiven. Traditionally Anglo-American criminal law has not allowed a defense based on abandonment of a crime. A change of heart after a crime is completed could be taken into account at sentencing as mitigation, but typically abandonment of one's crime is irrelevant as to guilt or innocence. In recent years, however, states have begun to embrace abandonment and withdrawal defenses for inchoate crimes like attempt and conspiracy and for complicity. The availability of the defense, however, varies according to the crime. For attempt crimes the defense is usually patterned along the lines of the Model Penal Code (MPC), which provides an affirmative defense where the defendant "abandon[s] his effort to commit the crime or otherwise prevent[s] its commission, under circumstances manifesting a complete and voluntary renunciation of his criminal purpose."[5] Reflecting the MPC drafters' interest in excluding from criminal liability only those actors who prove themselves no longer dangerous or culpable based on their change of heart, the defense is not available to those who abandon their criminal attempt because they find that the crime is more difficult to accomplish than initially anticipated or because they hear the call of police sirens in the distance.[6] It is likewise not available to those who simply decide to postpone the act until a better time or a better victim comes along.[7]

These same requirements of a complete and voluntary renunciation of the crime have appeared in abandonment defenses for conspiracy and complicity, and the same goal—to encourage individuals to withdraw from crimes before they are completed—animates the defense in those contexts.[8] For conspiracy and complicity, however, the defense differs somewhat from the abandonment defense for attempt in light of the social aspects of group criminality.[9] Unlike attempt, abandonment or withdrawal in the context of conspiracy requires the actor to take some affirmative act to communicate her withdrawal to all co-conspirators. Some jurisdictions require the withdrawing actor to go further to persuade her co-conspirators to abandon their criminal plan or to actively thwart the plan themselves by, say, contacting authorities.[10]

Notably, under the common law tradition withdrawal or abandonment typically is not a complete defense to conspiracy, if the conspiracy itself is complete—usually once the overt act is committed. In that case withdrawal provides only a defense to subsequent crimes committed by co-conspirators. By contrast the MPC drafters believed that a defector should have a defense to the conspiracy itself, provided that she can thwart the success of the conspiracy. In this way the Code's "renunciation" defense, adopted in several states,[11] is more generous to those who walk away. Unlike the common law defense it not only relieves the individual of liability for subsequent crimes undertaken in furtherance of the conspiracy; it also relieves the individual of liability for the conspiracy itself.

The Code's requirements for renunciation, however, are so rigorous as to make the defense very difficult to deploy successfully.[12] The individual not only must withdraw from the enterprise; she also must thwart its success. The drafters settled on this compromise—a generous defense coupled with quite exacting requirements—in recognition of the unique harms of conspiracy. As they acknowledged, even though the act of agreement is not so dangerous as to "warrant punishment in spite of subsequent withdrawal," the underlying crime will most often continue, despite the renunciation of a single co-conspirator, therefore requiring the withdrawing co-conspirator to thwart the crime at the heart of the conspiracy.[13]

The requirements for abandonment and withdrawal in the context of complicity reflect the same concern for the social dynamics of group criminality that we see in the doctrine of conspiratorial withdrawal. In order to successfully claim abandonment or withdrawal as a defense to complicity, it is not enough for the actor to simply withdraw her aid. She must actually neutralize the aid that she furnished, and must do so before the crime is unstoppable—that is, while the principal actors still have an opportunity to terminate the crime. This might mean retrieving the materials that were provided or vocally negating prior encouragement. In most jurisdictions that offer a withdrawal or abandonment defense for complicity (admittedly a small number), the defector could warn the police about the impending offense or otherwise make an effort to prevent the crime, regardless of whether the crime is actually prevented.[14] As in conspiracy and attempt, jurisdictions typically require that the withdrawal be complete, not simply postponed to another time or another act, and voluntary, not motivated by the probability of detection.

Thus while abandonment for an attempt crime offers a defense because of a belief that the actor's change of heart proves that she is not sufficiently culpable or dangerous so as to merit punishment, the availability of the defense in the context of group criminality is structured around an impulse to reward the defector for taking some action that might affect or influence her partners in crime, whether by convincing them to abandon their criminal plans entirely or at least by enabling law enforcement to apprehend them before they accomplish their objectives.

"OMELAS" THROUGH THE LENS OF THE CRIMINAL LAW, OR THE CRIMINAL LAW THROUGH THE LENS OF "OMELAS"?

What is particularly striking about the criminal law's approach to withdrawal and abandonment is how much it requires of the individual. In the contexts of conspiracy and complicity, walking away does not relieve the actor of any criminal liability unless and until she goes the extra mile to negate her actions or otherwise stop the criminal enterprise before it is completed. Indeed, the law requires the individual defector not only to modify her own behavior, but also to at least attempt to directly change the behavior of others. But why should this be?

The requirements of withdrawal, abandonment, and renunciation reflect an attempt to balance respect for individual agency with recognition of the dynamics of collective criminality. Anglo-American criminal law is based on the concept of an individual actor who is capable of free will and rational thought. Consider, for example, the *actus reus* requirement. As any first-year law student will attest, every criminal offense must result from an individual's voluntary act. This emphasis on volition underscores the centrality of the individual actor's agency and autonomy to criminal responsibility. Criminal acts are not the product of reflexive, uncontrollable urges but rather the result of individual decision making—choices that are within the actor's control. When this capacity for individual decision making is impaired, relief from criminal liability for the act may be available to the actor. For example, the provocation defense rests on the understanding that in certain limited circumstances an individual acting in the heat of passion is unable to engage in reasoned decision making and thus may be less blameworthy.[15] When this capacity for reasoned decision making is completely absent—as in the case of the criminally insane—the law offers a complete defense, recognizing the injustice of holding an individual accountable for actions undertaken when she was incapable of exercising reasoned agency. On this account, when the individual's act is the product of rational thought, the state may fairly impose punishment, condemning the individual's poor choices and bad acts.

Even as the foundation of criminal law depends on the concept of the autonomous individual making good (or bad) choices, the criminal law is also concerned with the social or communal aspects of criminal wrongdoing. In particular the unique dangers and risks associated with group criminality have drawn considerable attention. The law of conspiracy is instructive on this point. The basic structure of the legal doctrine surrounding conspiracy stems in large part from the assumption that group criminality poses greater dangers than the single criminal actor working in isolation. According to this logic, although the individual engaged in a criminal act is obviously dangerous, that danger is amplified when the individual combines with others to accomplish some bad act. Having a partner in crime may strengthen one's resolve to actually complete the act in question. And if one actor falters, there are others willing and able to see the act through to completion.[16]

This concern for the dangers inherent in group criminality is also reflected in criminal law's treatment of complicity. The person who counsels, encourages, or otherwise assists the principal in the completion of the criminal act assumes the principal's liability for those acts by virtue of her role as the principal's agent.[17] Criminal liability attaches to the agent simply because of her efforts to aid the principal, even if her actions ultimately have no effect on the principal or the completion of the bad act. The mere fact of the agent's efforts to encourage, facilitate, or assist is sufficient to render her criminally liable.[18]

Because of concern with the all-consuming threat of groupthink, it is perhaps unsurprising that, in the context of group criminality, the criminal law requires more for withdrawal than simply walking away. In order to be relieved of criminal liability for conspiracy or complicity, the individual must display a herculean degree of agency and autonomy. She may not merely walk away; she must actually disrupt and extinguish the criminal threat that the group poses.

Scholars have noted how difficult these requirements are to fulfill.[19] How does one adequately withdraw from a wide-ranging drug conspiracy that spans states, even continents, especially in cases when not all participants are known? Why should a person who has long been imprisoned be held accountable for a conspiracy that continues after she is no longer active in the enterprise or, for that matter, no longer even enjoying her liberty? These accounts acknowledge the logistical difficulties of walking away, but they are less attentive to the other social and moral challenges that present themselves for individuals who know nothing but the world of the criminal enterprise or for those who have reason to question the relevance of the world outside it.

The act of walking away can require a feat of faith and an exercise of unique moral imagination. Consider those individuals in Nazi Germany, Rwanda, Cambodia, or Bosnia who chose to risk serious harm and even death in order to separate themselves from a system of normalized violence. The criminal law would view their acts of walking away with an eye toward the effects on others: whether they communicated their withdrawal, whether they disrupted the enterprise, whether they alerted authorities in a timely manner. Of course it is true that the criminal law generally plays a limited role in prosecuting individuals who have participated in large-scale acts of violence, like genocide. Criminal trials of participants in mass-atrocity crimes are few and far between, and prosecutors typically do not pursue charges against those who ultimately renounce their earlier participation in the criminal acts and relinquish their allegiances to the criminal regime. But common perceptions of these individuals, as much as the criminal law, reflect society's views of what is creditable and what is condemnable. On occasion we recognize the individuals who have forsworn their past bad acts as heroes. But more often we scarcely acknowledge the sheer force of will it takes to leave behind a situation of all-consuming violence, just as the criminal law ignores the awful and awesome exercise of agency and choice demonstrated in these acts of walking away. Some who renounce their past acts and walk away from a criminal regime are characterized as individuals fleeing their former lives—vulnerable victims in need of stability, security, and often public resources—rather than as individuals who valiantly refused to abide a corrupt and criminal system. Some are more generously characterized as defectors from the regime, acknowledging their resistance to the regime's policies. But even in these circumstances we do not acknowledge the enormity of their decision to walk away. More often defectors from a criminal regime are viewed with suspicion because of their former involvement in or tolerance of the regime's wrongdoing. Less attention is paid to what it took for them to leave that life behind. Within and outside of the criminal law we do not recognize the exercise of will and choice undertaken by individuals who break away from normalized wrongdoing. In these difficult circumstances we fail to acknowledge the real meaning of walking away.

The difficulty of walking away may also be glimpsed in the circumstances of those who become enmeshed in criminality because of familial or family-like connections. For example, the Mafia famously has functioned as a criminal enterprise that has strong familial associations for its members. In this regard one's co-conspirators may be not only one's partners in crime; they might be neighbors, friends, or even actual family members as well. How does one successfully withdraw from the enterprise in these circumstances? Upon being released from prison and returning to his old neighborhood, Joseph Lombardo sought to publicly declare his withdrawal from the Calabrese Street Crew, a neighborhood criminal collective associated with various racketeering schemes. To do so he placed ads "in the *Chicago Tribune* and two other Chicago newspapers," explaining that he had just been paroled and adding, "If anyone hears my name used in connection with any criminal activity please notify the F.B.I., local police and my parole officer, Ron Kumke."[20]

In placing these ads Lombardo sought to distance himself from the criminal enterprise with which he was previously associated, even as he tried to reintegrate into the community in which that criminal enterprise flourished. His statement of withdrawal, published and distributed throughout the community, no doubt took courage and conviction. The government, however, found this attempt at withdrawal to be ineffective; indeed, the government considered it a "stunt." The intermediate appellate court reviewing the denial of Lombardo's withdrawal defense agreed: "One cannot avoid liability for conspiracy simply by ceasing to participate." Although "an unequivocal statement of resignation communicated to one's conspirators can . . . constitute withdrawal," it was unclear that Lombardo's newspaper ads were sufficient to accomplish these ends. With this in mind the intermediate appellate court held that Lombardo's jury reasonably could have agreed that the ads were merely a "stunt" rather than a good-faith effort to proclaim his withdrawal to the relevant parties.[21]

Membership in street gangs poses similar problems with regard to withdrawal. Sociologists have often noted the degree to which street gangs may function as fictive families for their members, deeply enmeshing the individual in a criminogenic culture from which it can be difficult to extricate oneself. In this context what does it mean to withdraw from a criminal enterprise that is deeply entangled with group membership? May one renounce the crime while continuing to live and socialize among those who are like family members? Critically, a number of U.S. courts have considered this question, maintaining the high standards for withdrawal or abandonment. The Tenth Circuit's approach in *United States v. Harris* is illustrative. Tracy Harris, along with numerous other members of the Wichita Crips, was convicted of various offenses related to a wide-ranging drugs and wire fraud conspiracy. Harris appealed his conviction, arguing that he had effectively withdrawn from the conspiracy, as evidenced by the fact that he had "become a Muslim and rejected the gang lifestyle as antithetical to his faith." Further Harris "cooperated with police after a 2007 search of his house and told a police detective that he used to be a member of the Insane Crips, but that he had left the organization in the early 1990s." All of this, Harris argued, established his withdrawal from the conspiracy, relieving him of liability for any offenses committed by former co-conspirators in furtherance of the conspiracy. The Tenth Circuit disagreed, concluding that Harris "fail[ed] to establish that he either reported to law enforcement about the conspiracy with particularity or adequately communicated his withdrawal to his co-conspirators."[22]

Harris's claim echoed those of Timothy Kevin Duke, a defendant in *United States v. Starrett*. Duke, along with six other members of the Outlaw Motorcycle Club, had been convicted of federal conspiracy charges. On appeal Duke claimed that he had presented evidence sufficient to establish his withdrawal from the conspiracy. In particular he noted that more than five years before he was indicted he had "added [an] 'out date' to his [gang] tattoo; he sold his motorcycle; he joined a church and got a job; and he moved out of Florida and 'cut off virtually all contact' with the Outlaws." Although the Eleventh Circuit conceded that these actions were sufficient to establish that Duke "took affirmative steps to disavow the conspiracy," they were "insufficient to satisfy the second requirement," as nothing indicated that Duke "made a reasonable effort to communicate his withdrawal to his co-conspirators, or that he disclosed the Outlaws' criminal schemes to law enforcement."[23]

As these three cases illustrate, under the criminal law, simply walking away does not absolve the actor of his sins. Animated by the concerns associated with group criminality, criminal law requires more in order to qualify for the defense of abandonment or withdrawal. But these cases might also suggest that, in requiring so much, the law may expect too much of the individual. Indeed, the law does not register how difficult it might be to simply walk away in these circumstances, where one's life and identity are completely enmeshed in a criminal world and those who inhabit it. In this regard the law may undervalue the fact that, in these circumstances, walking away—by itself—might be the ultimate act of agency and autonomy.

So too with the ones who walk away from Omelas. If we view the walkers as complicit in the town's crimes, then criminal law offers little in the way of absolution or a defense to these defectors. They never announce their departure; they make no effort to stop the criminal acts of those they leave behind. If we believe that criminal law reflects society's views about which behavior is (or should be) condemned and which behavior is (or should be) credited, then we would expect to condemn those who walk away from Omelas because they have failed to stop the townspeople, or at least failed to announce to their brethren that they will no longer stand for the child's mistreatment.

At the same time we might admire their bravery and the difficulty of their decision. Instead of seeing the walkers as mired in the groupthink that makes collective criminality especially troubling and challenging, we might understand their decision to walk away as an effort to recuperate their agency as individuals. We might recognize their decision as the ultimate expression of autonomy and a powerful denunciation of the group dynamics that makes the child's torment possible. The criminal law, however, offers no opportunity to value these aspects of their decision in determining criminal liability.[24] It offers no opportunity to give legal significance to the difficult circumstances that may undergird withdrawal and abandonment of a group criminal enterprise.

In this regard the structure of abandonment doctrine does not account for the nuance of human behavior, the allure of the status quo, and the challenge of walking away when everyone else is content to go along with the group. In "Omelas," Le Guin captures this complexity in her depiction of the solitude of the defectors and the burdens they continue to bear long after they leave. The ones who walk away from Omelas do so on their own, one by one. They do not rise up en masse; they do not organize; they do not take comfort in the resistance of their family or friends or leaders.

In this way "Omelas" reveals some of the shortcomings of criminal law's approach to abandonment and withdrawal in the context of group criminality. The criminal law of withdrawal for conspiracy and complicity is purportedly structured around the social dynamics of those acts. The defenses require the withdrawing person to exert influence on her former partners in crime in order to neutralize the criminogenic nature of groups. But despite this recognition of the role that groups may play in fostering crime, there is little acknowledgment of the role that groups may play in impeding an individual's efforts to walk away.[25] In environments of pervasive wrongdoing, individuals who otherwise would not engage in harmful acts may be driven to do so by pressure to conform or to obey authority.[26] In such circumstances they may question their own instincts; they may go along with the group. The individual is affected—even transformed—by the collective, and walking away becomes, for many, and impossible task.

In any environment of pervasive wrongdoing is it not impossible to walk away? Consider the example of Paul Rusesabagina, the hotel manager who risked his life to protect more than one thousand individuals during the Rwandan genocide and whose experience was brought to Western audiences in the film *Hotel Rwanda*. There is also the example of Aleksander Jevtic, a Serb who saved the lives of several Croatians who would otherwise have been tortured or murdered during the Yugoslav civil war and who is profiled in Eyal Press's *Beautiful Souls*. But such examples are hard to come by. Indeed, the fact that these individuals and their brave acts have been memorialized in film and literature suggests the degree to which their actions were indeed rare and extraordinary.

Mass atrocities like those in Rwanda and the former Yugoslavia are of course distinct from the criminal enterprises of the Calabrese Street Crew or the Wichita Crips. Mass atrocity is sweeping in its scope and encompasses not merely street-level criminal acts but the kinds of systematic crimes perpetrated by complex organizations and states. Nonetheless, although the wrongdoing differs in scope and kind, certain commonalities link mass atrocities and the kinds of "ordinary" offenses with which the criminal law typically is concerned. Both contexts are marked by the normalization of deviance and violence, whether in a small community or throughout an entire state. In both contexts what was once deviant and abnormal comes to be seen as typical; it is understood and experienced as an acceptable and expected part of life in the community. And in both the wrongdoing may be viewed not merely as typical, but as important, good, necessary to achieve particular objectives deemed desirable and even admirable—the protection of one's survival, one's family, one's people.[27]

Omelas is in many ways no different from Rwanda, Yugoslavia, Chicago, or Daytona. Like these other places Omelas is a town in which deviance has become normalized. The entire community participates in the torment and torture of the child: no one is ignorant of it; they all recognize their part in it. But still they all turn a blind eye, allowing it to continue and reaping the benefits that flow from it. And yet even in the face of the overwhelming acceptance of this "hideous" bargain, something rare and extraordinary happens: a few manage to see through the clouded judgment of the masses and manage to resist the pressure to conform.

CONCLUSION

What can the criminal law learn from Le Guin and "Omelas"? Withdrawal from a criminal *act* is distinct from withdrawal from a criminal *world*. It may take some conscience to abandon one's own plans to commit a criminal offense, but to abandon a society, a family, or a gang in which criminality is pervasive, normalized, and routine takes not merely conscience but fortitude, imagination, and an ability to deviate from conformity that, according to social science research, does not come naturally. On this account the Omelans who walk away perhaps deserve more than their lonely defections. And those who remain likely do not deserve the peace that they enjoy.

What could Le Guin have learned from the criminal law? While her story grasps the challenges of breaking away from a group, it does not contemplate the impact that individual defection may have on collective wrongdoing. The law seeks to incentivize withdrawal in part because the abandonment of one actor can affect the decisions of the rest.[28] The departure of one may cause the others not only to fear detection as a result of the defection but also to question the wisdom, propriety, or necessity of their actions.

In imagining the ones who walk away as solitary creatures, and in suggesting that the abuse of the child—and the happiness of the town—continue indefinitely, Le Guin does not consider that the defectors' acts may actually inspire others in the town to themselves walk away or even to intervene to protect the child. After all, as the criminal law recognizes, in group settings the acts of one may impact the thinking and conduct of others. To imagine that the ones who walk away inspire those who remain to abandon their hideous bargain is, of course, a wildly optimistic reading of the story, and perhaps one that is unrealistic, but it is one for which the criminal law encourages us to hope.

NOTES

1. Ursula K. Le Guin, "The Ones Who Walk Away from Omelas," *in The Wind's Twelve Quarters* 275 (1987). As the published story is only four pages long we do not cite page numbers of quotations.

2. Le Guin is not the first to depict the sacrifice of an innocent for the greater good. Perhaps the earliest iteration of this theme occurs in *Agamemnon*, the first play in the *Oresteia* trilogy. Agamemnon, King of Argos, must sacrifice his daughter Iphigenia in order for his ships to have safe passage to Troy. See Aeschylus, *The Oresteia*, trans. A. Shapiro and P. Burian (New York: Oxford University Press, 2003). The classic short story "The Lottery" describes a town's annual forced sacrifice of one of its residents. Shirley Jackson, "The Lottery," *New Yorker*, June 26, 1948, at 25. More recently Lois Lowry's *The Giver* (1993) depicts a dystopian society where, in an effort to maintain order and equality among residents, a single child is forced to absorb and retain the community's pain and strife.

3. See, for example, Kenneth M. Roemer, "The Talking Porcupine Liberates Utopia: Le Guin's 'Omelas' as Pretext to the Dance," 2 *Utopian Stud.* 6, 13–14 (1991) (arguing that those who leave Omelas "may look even less villain-like" than those who remain); Elizabeth Cummins, "'Praise Then Creation Unfinished': Response to Kenneth M. Roemer," 2 *Utopian Stud.* 19, 19–22 (1991) (disagreeing with Roemer's interpretation).

4. Le Guin, at 275.

5. Model Penal Code §5.01(4) [hereinafter MPC]. See Paul R. Hoeber, "The Abandonment Defense to Criminal Attempt and Other Problems of Temporal Individuation," 74 *Calif. L. Rev.* 377, 382 (1986) ("Today approximately one-half of American jurisdictions recognize the abandonment defense."). For discussion of the refusal to provide an abandonment defense at common law, see Hoeber, at 380–81; Paul Marcus, "Joint Criminal Participation: Establishing Responsibility, Abandonment," 34 *Am. J. Comp. L. Supp.* 479, 487–88 (1986); Rollin M. Perkins, "Criminal Attempt and Related Problems," 2 *UCLA L. Rev.* 319, 354 (1955).

6. *See* MPC §5.01(4) cmt. at 359 (1985); *Commonwealth v. McCloskey*, 341 A.2d 500 (Pa. Super. Ct. 1975) ("The defense of complete and permanent abandonment should be allowed because voluntary abandonment negates the conclusion that the accused continues to be dangerous; and, the knowledge that voluntary abandonment exonerates one from criminal liability provides a motive to desist prior to completion of the crime."). The other motivation for allowing an abandonment defense for attempt is to incentivize would-be offenders to stop their acts before the crime is complete. See Hoeber, at 397.

MPC §5.01(4) ("Within the meaning of this Article, renunciation of criminal purpose is not voluntary if it is motivated, in whole or in part, by circumstances, not present or apparent at the inception of the actor's course of conduct, that increase the probability of detection or apprehension or which make more difficult the accomplishment of the criminal purpose.").

7. *Id.* ("Renunciation is not complete if it is motivated by a decision to postpone the criminal conduct until a more advantageous time or to transfer the criminal effort to another but similar objective or victim.").

8. Marcus, at 488.

9. See Neil Kumar Katyal, "Conspiracy Theory," 112 *Yale L.J.* 1307, 1378–79 (2003).

10. See Hyde v. United States, 225 U.S. 347 (1912); Eldredge v. United States, 62 F.2d 449 (10th Cir. 1932).

11. See R. Michael Cassidy and Gregory I. Massing, "The Model Penal Code's Wrong Turn: Renunciation as a Defense to Criminal Conspiracy," 64 *Fla. L. Rev.* 353, 366–70 (2012) (discussing state defenses of withdrawal and renunciation).

12. MPC §5.03(6). Some of the modern rewrites of the law have taken this same position, but others have softened it to allow the defense when the actor gives timely warning to law enforcement or makes some substantial effort to prevent the crime. Wayne R. LaFave, *Criminal Law* 689 (5th ed. 2010).

13. MPC §5.03(6), cmt. at 458 (1985).

14. See Daniel Moriarty, "Extending the Defense of Renunciation," 62 *Temple L. Rev.* 1 (1989); see also Paul H. Robinson, *Criminal Law Defenses*, §81(e), at 363–64 (1984) (commenting that the requirement of "'proper effort' to prevent the offense" is "clearly more lenient than the 'actual prevention' standard" that governs the conventional renunciation defenses for conspiracy).

15. See Joshua Dressler, "Provocation: Partial Justification or Partial Excuse?," 51 *Mod. L. Rev.* 467 (1988).

16. See MPC §5.03 cmt. (1985) ("The act of combining with another is significant both psychologically and practically, the former because it crosses a clear threshold in arousing expectations, the latter because it increases the likelihood that the offense will be committed. Sharing lends fortitude to purpose. The actor knows, moreover, that the future is no longer governed by

his will alone; others may complete what he has had a hand in starting, even if he has a change of heart.").

17. See Sanford H. Kadish, "Complicity, Cause and Blame: A Study in the Interpretation of Doctrine," 73 *Calif. L. Rev.* 323, 353–55 (1985).

18. Joshua Dressler, "Reassessing the Theoretical Underpinnings of Accomplice Liability: New Solutions to an Old Problem," 37 *Hastings L.J.* 91, 102 (1985).

19. See, for example, Katyal, at 1378; "Developments in the Law—Criminal Conspiracy," 72 *Harv. L. Rev.* 920, 959 (1959).

20. United States v. Schiro, 679 F.3d 521, 528 (7th Cir. 2012).

21. *Id.* at 521, 528, 529.

22. United States v. Harris, 695 F.3d 1125, 1137–38 (10th Cir. 2012).

23. United States v. Starrett, 55 F.3d 1525, 1550 (11th Cir. 1995).

24. The decision to walk away may, however, be considered as mitigation at sentencing.

25. See Jens David Ohlin, "Group Think: The Law of Conspiracy and Collective Reason," 98 *J. Crim. L. & Criminology* 147, 186 (2007) (considering how individuals manage to withdraw from conspiracies).

26. See Lee Ross and Richard E. Nesbitt, *The Person and the Situation: Perspectives on Social Psychology* (2011); see also Katyal, at 1317–18.

27. See Saira Mohamed, "Deviance, Aspiration, and the Stories We Tell: Reconciling Mass Atrocity and the Criminal Law," 124 *Yale L.J.* 1628, 1642–43, 1679–82 (2015) (discussing normalization of violence in mass-atrocity situations and international criminal courts' understandings of categories of deviance and normalcy).

28. Critically, however, the requirement of some jurisdictions that the withdrawing conspirator *thwart* the completion of the crime itself underestimates the degree to which the withdrawal of any of the group's participants may disrupt the actual perpetration of the crime.

13

Before the Law

IMAGINING CRIMES AGAINST TREES

Mark Payne

IN "DOES THE Climate Have Standing?" Christopher Stone revisits the discussion of how advocacy on behalf of nonhuman natural entities might take shape that is advanced in his earlier, seminal "Should Trees Have Standing?" With the prospect of rapidly escalating climate change in mind, he returns to his earlier discussion in order to imagine how legal representation in such cases as a stand of trees threatened by global warming might start with "the advocate seeking appointment of himself as the object's legal guardian."[1] In "Trees," the extension of legal standing to plants is envisaged as a continuation of the history of human ethical progress that granted such standing to women, other races, children, and animals. Stone understands these groups' prior condition of rightlessness as a failure on the part of right holders to see right worthiness in things that are of use value to them that was remedied by a more capacious moral imagination on the part of their advocates.[2] The advocate seeking appointment on behalf of a stand of trees in the present would therefore be taking up the same task of expanding his society's moral imagination on behalf of a still rightless, but right-worthy, class of beings that was shouldered by antislavery organizers, feminists, and animal rights activists in the past. As Stone envisages it, this turn to advocacy will likely be occasioned by a perceived threat to some particular member of this class of beings to which the would-be guardian has a prior attachment that is strong enough to elicit a commitment to acting on its behalf.

One might question the idea that right holders who opposed the extension of legal standing to women, other races, children, and animals simply did not see the particular members of the class of beings to which they belonged otherwise than as things for instrumental use. But it must surely be true nonetheless that arguments for right extension that appeal to the imagination have a significant role to play in overcoming the bad faith involved in refusing to see such beings as anything other than use objects.[3] It is this relationship between the educative function of criminal law and our "real thinking" about plants and animals—which is not fully represented by the law—that Stone emphasizes in "Climate." Environmental law should not distort what we actually feel about the right of plants and animals to legal standing in order to accommodate the fact that it is easier at present to bring a suit in the name of a human being who has suffered aesthetic impoverishment as a secondary consequence of the damage done to a plant or animal than it is to bring a suit for immediate harm in the name of the plant or animal itself. We want legal action in the name of plants and animals themselves because "suits on behalf of Nature are better suited to moral development."[4]

From the perspective of the educative function of criminal law, one potential benefit of legal action in the name of complex natural entities of the kind Stone envisages is that such suits would have the capacity to provoke reflection on the intertwining of ontological, ethical, and aesthetic commitments that inform legal standing:

> If the court permits a spokesperson for [a stand of] trees [threatened by global warming], need she grant a guardianship to hear the beetles out [beetles that have heretofore been eliminated by freezing temperatures]? And looking ahead, if standing is granted to both petitioners, how will a court possibly come down on one side or the other, for the trees or the beetles? These are extraordinarily difficult questions nested in ontological quandaries: Is the proper judicial person a particular tree, the stand, the species, tree DNA, or the ecosystem of which the tree is a part (which we presume includes the beetles)?[5]

Stone is agnostic as to how such questions might be resolved. However, while he acknowledges that he can provide "no ultimately convincing reason why marine mammals should be preferred to cod" and that he would not expect a court to be able to do so either, he continues to link the possibility of such a decision to the larger ethical narrative invoked in "Trees": "The fact that we can bring a suit on behalf of loggerheads and leatherbacks is an affirmation of who we are as a people" (76).

In Stone's view the difficulty in making the first-person commitments that would induce a person to become the advocate of a turtle or a tree morally binding upon those who do not share them points to the wisdom of "entrusting the crucial determinations to legislatures and administrative agencies" so that "when courts are confronted with a motion for guardianship or suit on the merits, they at least have some orientation as to the appropriate ontology and prioritizations."[6] The possession of an appropriate ontology is to be the basis for decisions about legal standing, and this possession is located outside the domain of first-personal conviction in the discourse of experts. But is it not doubt as to whether one's society possesses an appropriate ontology that leads the would-be guardian to seek appointment by the court in the first place? It is difficult to see how this conflict between the "psychic and socio-psychic aspects" of being a right holder and the "legal-operational aspects" of right extension is to be resolved within the existing legal mechanisms that Stone has in mind here.

Before I think about how this encounter between first-personal conviction and third-personal authority might be worked out in practice, I would like to take a step back and point to the fact that Stone's conception of an advocate of Nature who emerges from his people in the role of Nature's guardian echoes quite precisely a certain Romantic conception of the poet. In "On Naïve and Sentimental Poetry," Schiller formulates the idea that the poet represents Nature in periods of history when humanity loses touch with its own naturalness: "By virtue of the very notion of a poet, poets are everywhere the *guardians* of nature. Where they can no longer completely be this, and where they have already experienced within themselves the destructive influence of arbitrary and artificial forms or have had to contend with them, they will appear as nature's *witnesses* and *avengers*. They will either *be* nature or *seek* the lost nature."[7] This idea would prove attractive to poets in the century to come. In "A Defence of Poetry," Shelley goes further and argues that poets' representation of Nature has a proto-institutional character. Because poets are "mirrors of the gigantic shadows which futurity casts upon the present," they nudge humanity along the path of moral improvement that Stone has in mind; poetry thereby retains its archaic character as legislation and prophecy even in modernity. Insofar as they are poets and allow their imaginative capacity to operate as a faculty distinct from their quotidian moral commitments, poets are ahead of their time, and because they are ahead of their time they are outside history as such. What poetry wills as "the great instrument of moral good" and "institutor of human life" has a quasi-institutional character as representative, in both a literary and a legal sense, of a society to come, with moral sentiments that are more capacious than the society in which the poet finds himself and, as such, more truly reflective of the "real thinking" that takes place in the moral imagination of humanity at large than the parochial laws of his own time and place: "Poets are the unacknowledged legislators of the world."[8]

In developing this argument, Shelley reiterates the conflation of legal roles in Schiller's conception of poets as "nature's *witnesses* and *avengers*" within a society that has lost touch with human naturalness. Shelley, however, displaces the conflation of legal roles from the presentation of the poet's quasi-legal authority within such a society to a second-order reflection on how a third party might judge a poet's right to speak for what is rightless: "Let us for a moment stoop to the arbitration of popular breath, and usurping and uniting in our own persons the incompatible characters of accuser, witness, judge, and executioner, let us decide without trial, testimony, or form, that certain motives of those who are 'there sitting where we dare not soar,' are reprehensible."[9]

Shelley takes upon himself the task of negotiating between first-personal conviction and third-personal jurisdiction that is the obvious practical impediment to Stone's vision of the progress from vocational advocacy to authoritative legal representation in standing for natural entities. The obstacle becomes a moment in the total drama of the poetic representation of Nature as Shelley enacts it for his readers in the "Defence." Once the question of Nature casts the poet within the legal imaginary, the full spectrum of juridical roles becomes available for first-person appropriation. The first-personal character of poetic representation of Nature is not limited to the roles of witness and avenger: the poet wishes to enact in imagination the future justice of which he is the distant mirror, but his awareness that, as one of the "unacknowledged legislators of the world," he has no actual juridical power displaces this enactment to a fictional stage trial of his fitness for the task that he would like to accomplish on Nature's behalf.

In his representation of Nature, the poet experiences the uprooting from history that Levinas has characterized as one aspect of the priority of ethics to ontology that emerges in a transformative encounter with the Other.[10] Justice and injustice offer "primordial access to the Other beyond all ontology," such that, in a relationship to Nature that is enacted in the modality of justice or injustice, there can be no reduction of our involvement in the lives of particular nonhuman beings to an ontology of Nature conceived as a matrix of impersonal entities with whom one maintains a relationship of universal, impartial disinterest. In a relationship of justice, nonhuman beings retain the personal character they assume when we enter into the kind of face-to-face relationship with them from which obligation emerges: their appearance as entities with whom we have a personal relationship exceeds the idea we have of them prior to our entering into such a relationship with them.[11]

I want therefore to examine how such an idea of a personal relationship with a nonhuman Other might entwine itself with the idea of a guardianship of Nature envisaged by Stone and the Romantic poets, insofar as both ideas involve a kind of vocation to act on Nature's behalf that is evoked by nonhuman entities themselves. Because this vocation is accepted as the anticipation of a history to come, it is experienced as access to a legal imaginary outside history as such, where the institutional function of the imagination in an imaginary past and an imaginary future converge. If Schiller is correct, however, this vocation is experienced with particular intensity in historical periods in which poets find themselves members of societies that have lost the capacity to enact their relationship with other living beings in ways that realistically instantiate their relationship to one another as natural beings. I begin therefore with a Greek poet of the Hellenistic period, for it is this moment in the Greek cultural imaginary that, according to Schiller, is the moment at which Greek culture lost touch with its own naturalness, and so has a special capacity to disclose the loss of naturalness that casts poets into their role as guardians and avengers of Nature to such periods in the future.[12]

The "Hymn to Demeter" by the third-century BCE Alexandrian poet Callimachus tells the story of Erysichthon, a figure from the heroic age, who one day gathers his gigantic henchmen and sets off to cut down a poplar tree in a grove that the goddess Demeter loves. In this grove fruit trees and wild trees grow together in a primeval forest so dense you can hardly shoot an arrow between their trunks (ll. 31–36). The tree that Erysichthon chooses to fell is so tall it reaches to the sky, and, when struck with the axe, it cries aloud to the other trees. Demeter hears and hurries to the scene in disguise, but Erysichthon will not heed her warnings. He threatens to cut her down too, as he is intent on making a mead hall for his comrades, and at this point Demeter manifests her divinity. Her feet remain rooted to the ground, but her head, like the top of her tree, reaches all the way to Olympus. She lets Erysichthon finish his work but punishes him with insatiable hunger.

The poem now changes character. We leave behind the world of primeval forests, magical trees, and half-human giant men for Erysichthon's home, which is where his punishment is enacted. Callers come to seek him out for civic and social events, and his parents experience an all too human embarrassment in the face of his hunger. The excuses with which they try to conceal it (and him) from visitors—he can't come to a party, for example, because "he fell out of his chariot" (86)—map a human world whose forms of relationality are drastically limited in comparison to the scene of Erysichthon's crime. As Erysichthon's body withers away in hunger, the human world shrinks to human beings alone, and their relationships with one another appear stultifying and claustrophobic in comparison to the open horizons of relationality in which the story began.

Erysichthon is punished for harming what is sacred to a god, but it is the form of his punishment that reveals why what he harmed was sacred to a god in the first place. Erysichthon consumes all his family's domestic animals, which include mules they keep for transportation, an ox awaiting sacrifice, horses for racing and for war, and a cat for catching mice. These animals are at hand for Erysichthon to eat because they have already been instrumentalized for human use, and their distribution throughout the household—apart from one another in places assigned to them according to their operationalization by human intelligence—contrasts with the consociality of the fruit trees and wild trees in Demeter's grove. Growing together and at random, the trees are interesting to the goddess as entities that exist through self-care, and it is as such that Erysichthon's victim is allowed to fall: the goddess warns, but she does not intervene, for to intervene would be to domesticate the trees, to own them like the animals of a human household.

When Erysichthon refuses Demeter's plea for her tree, he looks at her "more fiercely than a lioness in the mountains of Tmarus looks at a hunter when she has just given birth" (50–52). This ferocity is his last moment of wildness before he becomes completely dependent on others as a result of Demeter's punishment. The insatiable hunger that requires his household's nonstop devotion to the task of feeding him is a hypertrophic condition of dependence that ends only when he is finally ejected from his house to become a homeless beggar in the streets, outside all forms of relationality other than momentary occasions of charity. In Erysichthon's Gregor Samsa story, it is the failure to honor what exists through self-care that exposes the emptiness of need-based forms of relationality: the use relations with domestic animals that are immediately fungible as food, and the mutual dependence of the human household whose care is exhausted with the food supply. What is talionic about Erysichthon's punishment is not simply that it is a life for a life but that it obliges him to recognize that, in the extremity of his suffering, he too is a being who exists through self-care, who may or may not be of interest to others as such.

In the "Hymn to Demeter," Erysichthon's story is framed by a ritual celebration of Demeter as an agricultural deity. Erysichthon is thus a kind of culture hero in negative: he is punished for the harm he does to primordial nature, but on the other side of his crime lie the normative forms of relationality to nonhuman beings in the society within which his story is told, and it is only by reimagining his ancient crime that access is gained to the expanded forms of relationality that are imagined to have been available in a deep past that lies behind his crime. Other Hellenistic poets echo Callimachus in this respect. In Theocritus's *Idyll* 7, imaginative reenactment of the violence done to the centaurs by Heracles and to the Cyclops by Odysseus gives cognitive access to primordial life and its open horizons of relationality. In Apollonius's *Argonautica*, Heracles's killing of the chthonic serpent Ladon, who kept watch over the garden of the Hesperides, is the gateway to understanding the early world that existed "until yesterday,"[13] which is about to be replaced by historical life as such as the poem comes to an end. The life of centaurs, Cylopses, and chthonic beings is grove-like: they are of interest to the gods but not dependent on them, any more than they are dependent on one another, and it is this condition that provokes the violence toward them that is to be reimagined by the reader in the present.

The dramatization of self-care versus dependence in these Hellenistic poems nuances the dichotomy between the wild and the domesticated that structures so much Greek thought about the relative merits of different forms of life. As opposed to the idea that civilization is the natural outcome of human beings' incapacity for self-sufficiency,[14] Hellenistic poets imagine a primordial way of being together with nonhuman life from which human beings are propelled into civilization by the violence occasioned by what lives though self-care. In some absolutely primordial before-time, human beings lived alongside nonhuman life in relationships that were not predicated upon the binary of the wild and the domesticated, but the very indefiniteness of the human vis-à-vis the nonhuman in this primordial time provoked the violence toward the nonhuman that brought the era of open relationality to an end. Killing is the refusal of the faciality of nonhuman life that results in the ordinary forms of human being together with trees and animals in the present, whereas the poet encounters the Other outside history in the space of a fictional juridicality where the roles of criminal, witness, judge, and avenger are all in his power to inhabit as poet and to dispose as he sees fit among characters of his own choosing as the author of such fictional juridical narratives.

I would call the primordial way of being together with nonhuman life that the Hellenistic poets imagine choric consociality: the way human life is consocial with other forms of life whose principles of aggregation in the world around it can be intuited but are not readily available for the self-understanding of human sociality. The resources of myth and narrativity of which Callimachus avails himself in order to make choric consociality available for readerly understanding indicate the purchase that crime gives on the apprehension of this intuitive awareness as it lingers as a mode of our real thinking about nonhuman beings that is backgrounded by normative forms of relationality. In Levinas's terms justice and injustice disclose a primordial relationship to the nonhuman Other that is occluded by normative ontologies.

For Callimachus chorality is instantiated first in the grove itself and the consociality of its trees, both among themselves and with respect to humanity, and second in Demeter, both willing and unwilling to intervene on their behalf. It looks like injustice for Demeter to punish Erysichthon for a crime he did not know he was committing, but punishment in the absence of a law points to the costs of legislating the open relationality that occasions Erysichthon's violence. Laws to protect the nonhuman entities that instantiate choric consociality can only bring about the disappearance of the relationality they are meant to protect because they transform an undefined, discoverable possibility for relationality into a normative kind of relationship—in this case one of dependence—in which the partial apprehensibility of the other form of life as such is replaced by the transparency of a humanly authored relationship whose terms are determined in advance. Demeter's noninterventionist appearance reveals the conditions that must obtain for choric consociality to be available for human understanding.

When Demeter appears to Erysichthon with his axe in his hand, she says to him, "My child, you who are cutting down trees sacred to the gods, stop, my child, child of parents who prayed for you dearly," to which Erysichthon replies, "Get lost, or I'll stick my big axe in *your* skin" (ll. 46–53). Demeter points to the relationships of the human family in the hope that they will allow Erysichthon to grasp the relationship in which the trees stand to herself as god: a maternal attachment whose responsibilities cannot be systematically calculated and totalized. Erysichthon's response is to restate Demeter's nonexplicit analogy between the relationships of care that bind human beings to one another and the relationship of care that binds her to the trees as a license to harm both her and her trees. Beyond this point Demeter is not prepared to go: she will not turn almost-sacrilege into sacrilege by according it the status of crime as such. The entailments have the irremediality of tragedy: destructiveness is a predictable outcome of the indistinction of the human and the nonhuman in open relationality, but open relationality can be legislated only at the cost of its discoverability, so the preservation of what exists through self-care means risking the very lives that embody it.

Is there any way out of this tragic bind in which to value something for the freedom of being wild means being unable to intervene on its behalf should it be threatened with harm? As a way of approaching this possibility, I want to turn now to a modern discovery of personhood in trees in which the relationship between choric consociality and sacrilege can be seen to emerge spontaneously from an encounter with the faciality of living trees. The year is 1842, and Nathaniel Hawthorne is living an idyll of early married life with his wife, Sophia, at the Old Manse in Concord. One form of the expansion of Nathaniel's imagination that Sophia produced was sensitivity to household relationality, as this extended not just to the inhabitants of their house but also its garden, which Nathaniel had under cultivation in a modest fashion. In a notebook entry of August 8, 1842, he expresses the wish that he "could give a description of [their] house; for it really has a character of its own."[15] In giving expression to this wish, he focuses not on his own inhabitation of it but on its previous inhabitant, the clergyman Dr. Ripley, and his relationship to its orchard:

> It pleases me to think of the good minister, walking in the shadow of these old, fantastically shaped apple-trees, here plucking some of the fruit to taste, there pruning away a too luxuriant branch, and all the while computing how many barrels will be filled, and how large a sum will be added to his stipend, by the

> sale. And the same trees offer their fruit to me, as freely as they did to him—their old branches, like withered hands and arms, holding out apples of the same flavor as they held out to Dr. Ripley, in his life-time. Thus the trees, as living existences, form a peculiar link between the dead and the living. My fancy has always found something very interesting in an orchard—especially an old orchard. Apple-trees, and all fruit-trees, have a domestic character, which brings them into relationship with man; they have lost, in a great measure, the wild nature of the forest-tree, and have grown humanized, by receiving the care of man, and by contributing to his wants. They have become part of the family; and their individual characters are as well understood and appreciated as those of the human members. One tree is harsh and crabbed—another mild—one is churlish and illiberal—another exhausts itself with its free-hearted bounties. Even the shapes of apple-trees have great individuality, into such strange postures do they put themselves, and thrust their contorted branches so grotesquely in all directions. And when they have stood around a house for many years, and held converse with successive dynasties of occupants, and gladdened their hearts so often in the fruitful autumn, then it would seem almost sacrilege to cut them down.[16]

Whereas in Demeter's grove fruit trees and wild trees grow together, Hawthorne acknowledges the presence of the wild and the domesticated in a single kind of tree. The apple trees have a domestic character, "which brings them into relationship with man," and they have lost, "in a great measure, the wild nature of the forest-tree." They have not lost it entirely, however, and it is because their form of life is wild and domesticated at once that they manifest themselves to Hawthorne as distinctive individuals. They enact possibilities of their form of life in distinctive ways rather than standing for wildness or domestication as reified ideas of life.[17]

Because they are individuals the apple trees become a choric presence around the household and hold converse with the successive dynasties of its human inhabitants. Their talk is of subsistence and finitude. As each generation enjoys the same flavor of fruit as those who come before and after them, it experiences the succession of human generations through the mediation of the trees, the "living existences" that form "a peculiar link between the dead and the living" among the human beings that live with them. The apple trees tell us what our own death will feel like when it becomes part of the world of the trees, but they do so in a way that does not provoke resentment at their longevity. By both giving care to and receiving care from human beings they obviate the different kinds of resentment provoked by the wild and the domesticated: the hatred of the wild because it makes us think of our own domesticity as domestication, and the hatred of the domesticated as a form of life that does not understand what it is living.

The fruit of the apple trees gladdens the heart because their form of life is akin to our own—not identical to it, but not entirely other either. It is for this reason that "it would seem almost sacrilege to cut them down." Hawthorne might look like he is hedging with this "seem almost," but the apple trees are not an equivalent of ourselves, and to legislate the relationality they offer would preempt discovering it in the first place. The genius of Hawthorne's care is to be content with the accuracy of reserve, the "would seem almost sacrilege" that is as close as we can get to giving the discovered form of relationality juridical expression.

Hawthorne gets outside the reification of the wild and the domesticated not by attempting to strike down the difference between the two or attempting to do away with it as a structure of relationality; his access to the succession of generations—the particular form of the historicity of human life that he is interested in—depends upon it, just as much as the Hellenistic poets depend on it for access to the primordial form that interests them. Instead he tries to inhabit the binarism differently, through interpersonal encounters with the uncanny individual trees that express it in different ways: one manifests it in a form of life that is "harsh and crabbed," another is "mild," another "churlish and illiberal," and so forth.

Hawthorne's way of inhabiting the binarism of the wild and the domesticated puts pressure on the way this binarism informs the binarism of the free and the owned. Apple trees are property, yet they also appear to him as instantiations of spirit, and it is the irreducibility of this hybrid appearing that seems to provoke the impulse to harm them—the sacrilege of cutting them down—that Hawthorne imagines arising in their owner.[18] The uncanniness of the apple trees at the Old Manse holds both danger and the possibility of salvation for the trees themselves. Insofar as they hybridize the wild and the domesticated, the free and the owned, in an expressive form of appearing, they risk provoking violence toward themselves as the outcome of the desire to be rid of the threats to self-certainty that expanded relationality offers. Insofar as they constrain the imagination toward an intelligibility in human finitude that is available through their mediation of it, they instantiate choric consociality as an available good. Like the gods, the apple trees embody a possibility for human self-understanding that we could not have without them.[19]

Hawthorne's apple trees instantiate choric consociality in measures that accord with human time scales. But there are trees that instantiate it on the scale of Demeter and the Olympian gods. Bristlecone pines are capable of such negligible senescence that they do not need to die.[20] The oldest known individuals are five thousand years old, predating the Greek immortals by several millennia. At the high elevations in California and Nevada where they live the longest, the largest of these ancient trees are no more than thirty feet tall. They live in sparse groves just below the tree line, niche environments where cold temperatures, poor soils, and high winds prevent other trees from gaining a foothold. To spend time with them is to extrapolate one's understanding of organismic ambition to mineral durations and to try to grasp how such massively extended life articulates itself in the minuscule extensions of a single organism living in conditions of highly circumscribed sociality.

Despite their potential for organismic immortality, most bristlecone pines are now dying, from a combination of climate-related maladies that include blister rust, pine bark beetles, and the acceleration of their growth rate induced by high-elevation warming. Over the past fifty years the trees have grown 30 percent faster than in any other fifty-year period in their lives, and they are now at risk of "burning themselves out."[21] They are becoming mortal, like the vegetation gods of Frazer's *The Golden Bough*, but only because human beings have made them mortal by foreclosing the organismic immortality that is one form of life available to them.

The bristlecone pine groves instantiate just the kind of ontological dilemmas to which Stone refers in "Climate," when he imagines how advocacy and guardianship might take shape in the case of a stand of trees threatened by global warming.[22] And we are now in a position to ask what it is that the literature of crimes against trees can tell us about the death sentence we have imposed on bristlecone pines that we miss when we explain their death as an accidental outcome of the life we live alongside them. Before answering this question, however, I want to pause for a moment and consider once again what Stone calls our "real thinking" about plants and animals—what emerges in a face-to-face encounter with them, and which, as such, is both the foundation of advocacy on their behalf and the very thing that is most liable to be distorted by environmental law that is not enacted in the name of this face-to-face experience.

In August 2012 I visited two groves of bristlecone pines at two very different sites in eastern Nevada: Wheeler Peak in Great Basin National Park and the Table in Mount Moriah Wilderness. Wheeler Peak is reached by a well-maintained National Parks trail from a readily accessible parking lot, and the grove itself has a signposted, interpretive trail that leads visitors through the trees and points out various things about them. I entered the grove with the age of the trees on my mind, especially the fact that some of them antedate classical Greek culture by a millennium and are still alive. This prior orientation of my viewing experience was confirmed by the interpretive trail, which assigns birth and death dates to individual trees so as to foreground a contrast between living bodies that are more ancient than culture yet still part of life, and the cultures these bodies have outlived. Culture, from this perspective, has the being of ruins; it belongs to the inanimate, like the rocky mountainside on which the trees somehow find a purchase, whereas one encounters the trees as one living being face-to-face with another. The lifelessness of culture and rock is what stages the meeting of precarious living bodies, human and bristlecone.

But it isn't just their life span that demands recognition for the trees as individuals. The trees grow apart from one another, even as they are together in a grove, and particular sites afford distinct possibilities for growth: "complacent" sites result in faster growth and softer wood, whose consequences are coarse grain and center rot, whereas "sensitive" sites result in slower growth and finer grain, which are the keys to extreme longevity. The largest of these millennial trees are no more than thirty feet tall, and the modest extension of their side branches makes them look like tiny arms compared to the trunk, as if they were the expression of a will to live that can express itself only in minuscule increments.

When I visited them for a second time on the morning after my arrival, I saw one tree with a gaping hole through its main trunk and a side trunk that was almost detached where its connection to the main trunk had rotted out. Large pieces of stone had collected in the hollow bole, but it was green above, with fully formed cones. Another was just a diagonal spar lying on the ground but flourishing along its leeward side. The smaller trees have rounded trunks covered with tight auburn bark, but the trunks of the older ones have split open, exposing a striated interior, as if they had opened themselves up as they grew. Almost all of them are blackened, often from top to bottom, where they have been hit by lightning, burned, and yet lived. While the site of any kind of tree may foster a particular kind of growth, the long life and infinitesimally slow growth of the bristlecone pines gives a special character of individuality to the way each of them has grown. Their form bespeaks a life and a life history. On my way back down from the glacier above the grove, I yielded to the urge I had felt on the way up to touch them. This was the moment of departure, and I said to one of the younger ones, "I hope you are well, I hope you survive, I hope you don't grow too fast."

Getting to the second grove in Mount Moriah Wilderness required a ten-mile hike up a mountain creek from an obscure trailhead that is accessible only by unpaved Forest Service roads. After an exhausting three-hour hike up Hendrys Creek on my second day in the wilderness, I made it to the Table, a vast mesa just below the elevation of the rounded, forested mountains that surround it. (I had turned back an hour short with dusk approaching on the evening of the first day.) The Table is covered with yellow grass and gray stones with orange lichen. There are no trees or shrubs in sight, and it is just like being on a table lifted into the mountains. Storm clouds ring it, and ravens fly at its edge. As I walk across the tundra surface that crunches underfoot, my ears are full of the sound of grasshoppers, dozens to the square foot, whose hopping is like the pattering of raindrops. At the far edge of the Table is a grove of bristlecone pines in their natural estate. On a couple I see dark blue first-year cones that look almost like fruit, as well as older second- and third-year cones. It is a grove, although the trees grow some forty to fifty feet apart from one another.

In my mind it seems like an image of the place rather than the place itself: the flat table of land slightly inclined with ridges so that there is no uninterrupted line of sight; the ring of rounded peaks; the dark clouds that promise lightning and hail; the swarms of grasshoppers everywhere underfoot, their pattering at some threshold of hearing that attracts my attention only when I move; the discordant bright orange of the lichens. I recall the difficulty of the ascent—six thousand feet in ten miles—such that I named every stage of it: ponderosa flat, where I pitched my tent under two ponderosa pines that have grown together facing another, magnificently straight tree that took my breath away when I first saw it; aspen meadow 1, barely a meadow at all, really, but a thin wood stretched out along the trail with tall grass among the thickly clustering aspen poles whose spindliness expresses their character as clones; aspen meadow 2, this one a real meadow, steep, and looking up at the rock face of the mountain, opening a vista onto it, but also where its snows descend in winter; bee meadow, where I stopped the first day, thick with yellow owlsclaw and buzzing loudly with bees and wasps in the afternoon, a spring emerging from the left side of the trail about halfway through it (the next morning there was a different kind of insect in huge abundance, a kind of long-bodied wasp or hornet that made for anxious passage); then the final ascent through stunted poplars and limber pines, where I saw the antlered elk on the way down, until only a small valley separated me from the rim of the Table and its sudden expanse.

Mount Moriah is a more rigorous way to experience a grove of bristlecone pines than the interpretive trail at Wheeler Peak. The woods of Mount Moriah offer little in the way of protective enclosure, and the sheer steepness of the climb, in the constant presence of thunderheads that in the afternoon pour soaking showers and hailstones that accumulate to a depth of several inches, make it less like a place one is fully inside, or could ever be inside, and more like an experience of pure exteriority, that encounter with the outside for the sake of which one seeks the outside. But what the grove at the end of the journey proves is that the interpretive trail at Wheeler Peak is not wrong to present the bristlecone pines in the way it does. The signage that draws out what is inherent in the encounter with the trees and makes of it an itinerary through biographies and obituaries of individual, nonhuman lives is an attempt to give narrative shape to the "real thinking" about these lives that is, or, as Stone argues, should be, the lived, and living, basis of environmental law, as it is the lived and living basis of other kinds of law.

From the perspective of poetic narratives of crimes against trees, the poetizing gestures of the interpretive trail are readily interpretable. They memorialize in advance of every visitor's arrival the essence of the face-to-face encounter with lived particularity that, when it claims us for relationality, makes that ethical relationship our access to a value ontology, the insuperable sense that what has an individual life has rights because it realizes a will to live in an expression of life that is like our own. Gerard Manley Hopkins's sonnet "As kingfishers catch fire, dragonflies draw flame" takes us to the heart of this intuition in our encounter with animal life:

> Each mortal thing does one thing and the same:
> Deals out that being indoors each one dwells;
> Selves—goes itself; *myself* it speaks and spells,
> Crying *Whát I dó is me: for that I came.*

An intuition of grove life takes us even deeper than this, however, for it lets us discern this brightly lit foreground of appreciative attention to individual life against the background of other forms of sociality from which it emerges. Adumbration of this background is the after-gift of the foreground encounter, an intuitive understanding of the primordial way of being together that I have called the choric consociality of nonhuman life. It is an intuition of the way human life is consocial with other forms of life whose principles of aggregation can be sensed but are not readily available for the self-understanding of human sociality.

As we have seen, Hellenistic Greek poetry offers a gateway to this primordial consociality through narratives of crime against nonhuman life, and, for Schiller, these narratives emerge within a horizon of human life that has lost touch with its own naturalness. But in a larger perspective, earlier Greek efforts to articulate human relationship to the nonhuman in terms other than the mythology of epic poetry and its divine persons also afford their readers an adumbration of this primordial consociality. Heraclitus offers this example: "Immortals mortals, mortals immortals, living their death, dying their life" (Heraclitus DK B 62). θνητός, "mortal," is often contrasted with its opposite, ἀθάνατος, "deathless," in poetic and ritual contexts in which the plural, ἀθάνατοι, is a customary designation of the gods. Here, however, the contrast expresses a relationality between mortals and immortals for which there is no syntax and which is figured instead as an emblematic arrangement of their way of being together. Immortals are disposed as a choric presence around human life, and from within this horizon of consociality an attempt to bridge the inapprehensibility of one form of life to the other emerges: immortals live the death of mortals; mortals die their life.

Here is a "real thinking" of consociality that is willing to accept the embarrassment that such advocacy entails. Its language is "strained," "silly," and "ingenious" in just the ways such efforts to acknowledge the real are likely to strike people on any occasion when they make their first appearance as efforts to expand the capacities of the ethical imagination.[23] But acknowledging any being whose expressivity is enacted in temporal horizons drastically different from our own—a bristlecone pine or the goddess Demeter—requires a certain amount of humility. For it is to be uprooted from history and replanted in time, where we draw near to those "mirrors of the gigantic shadows which futurity casts upon the present" that Shelley calls poets.

NOTES

1. Stone (2010) 66.

2. Stone (2010) 3: "Until the rightless thing receives its rights, we cannot see it as anything but a thing for the use of 'us'—those who are holding rights at the time."

3. What Stone (2010) 4 calls the "psychic and socio-psychic aspects" of being a right holder, as opposed to the "legal-operational aspects."

4. Stone (2010) 65.

5. Stone (2010) 67.

6. Stone (2010) 67, 76.

7. Schiller (1998) 196.

8. Shelley (2003) 677, 682, 699–701. Compare Hölderlin's claim in "Andenken": "Was bleibet aber, stiften die Dichter."

9. Shelley (2003) 699.

10. Levinas (1969) 52: "When man truly approaches the Other he is uprooted from history."

11. Levinas (1969) 46–50, 89. Cf. 302–4: "The relation with the face is produced as goodness. The exteriority of being is morality itself. . . . The ethical, beyond vision and certitude, delineates the structure of exteriority as such."

12. Schiller (1998) 196.

13. εἰσέτι που χθιζόν, *Argonautica* 4.1397. I have not been able to reproduce the pun on χθόνιος, "of the earth," and χθιζόν, "yesterday." All translations are my own.

14. As in, for example, the famous account of the naturalness of the *polis* in Aristotle, *Politics* 1253a.

15. Hawthorne (1991) 323.

16. Hawthorne (1991) 326–27, August 9, 1842.

17. On Wittgenstein's "form of life" as the set of possibilities available for enactment in a given situation, see Kishik (2008) 24: "You misunderstand the expression 'form of life' if you see it as a method to categorize living beings into different classes. In fact, a formal concept enables you to see a difference within the form itself." The idea has vegetable origins: Kishik cites the opening of Goethe's *Die Metamorphose der Pflanzen* as a spur to Wittgenstein's thinking: "Dich verwirret, Geliebte, die tausendfältige Mischung / Diese Blumengewühls über den Garten umher."

18. It is instructive to compare his feelings on this occasion with his acerbic letter to Caroline Tappan, the owner of the cottage in the Berkshires where he wrote *The House of the Seven Gables*,

over the right to dispose of the produce from the garden that came with his rented house. On that occasion he wrote, "The right of purchase is the only safe one. This is a world of bargain and sale and no absurdity is more certain to be exposed than the attempt to make it anything else" (Hawthorne [2002] 155). As Hawthorne imagines the situation here, no laws, written or unwritten, impinge upon an owner's prerogatives with respect to things like apple trees, and his uncharacteristic harshness is perhaps best explained as a defensive reaction: the desire not to expose himself with an account of the forms of relationality that manifest themselves to nonowners.

19. The companion species already has a substantial history in animal studies, and, in extensions of the concept to plants that are now beginning to emerge, much of the emphasis is on articulating forms of interspecies relationality that move beyond the reification of relationality in the binary of the domesticated and the wild. Kirksey and Helmreich (2010), in their introduction to multispecies ethnography, address a number of efforts to move beyond the logic of domestication, particularly insofar as this logic maps on to a history of private property, and highlight Anna Tsing's work on mushrooms, for which see "Unruly Edges: Mushrooms as Companion Species," *Party Writing for Donna Haraway!*, http://tsingmushrooms.blogspot.com/2010/11/anna-tsing-anthropology-university-of.html. Here there is a concerted effort to move beyond a mere reversal of the logic of domestication—"cereals domesticated humans"—to the specificities of being with particular kinds of nonhuman life, as in her elaboration of what is entailed in the fact that "the mushrooms we eat congregate at edges."

20. Seymour and Doncaster (2007).

21. According to Matthew Salzer, a researcher at the Laboratory of Tree-Ring Research at the University of Arizona, quoted in Jim Robbins, "Old Trees May Soon Meet Their Match," *New York Times*, September 27, 2010, http://www.nytimes.com/2010/09/28/science/28pines.html?pagewanted=all&_r=0.

22. Stone (2010) 67.

23. Cf. Stone (2010) 65.

WORKS CITED

Hawthorne, N. 1991. *The American Notebooks*. Columbus: Ohio State University Press.

———. 2002. *Selected Letters*. Columbus: Ohio State University Press.

Kirksey, S. E., and Helmreich, S. 2010. "The Emergence of Multispecies Ethnography." *Cultural Anthropology* 25.4: 545–76. doi: 10.1111/j.1548-1360.2010.01069.x.

Kishik, D. 2008. *Wittgenstein's Form of Life (To Imagine a Form of Life, I)*. London: Continuum.

Levinas, E. 1969. *Totality and Infinity*. Pittsburgh: Duquesne University Press.

Schiller, F. 1998. *Essays*. New York: Continuum.

Seymour, R. M., and Doncaster, C. P. 2007. "Density Dependence Triggers Runaway Selection of Reduced Senescence." *PLoS Computational Biology* 3.12: e256. doi:10.1371/journal.pcbi.0030256.

Shelley, P. B. 2003. *The Major Works*. Oxford: Oxford University Press.

Stone, C. D. 2010. *Should Trees Have Standing? Law, Morality, and the Environment*. Oxford: Oxford University Press.

PART IV

Suspicion and Investigation

14

Crime Scenes

FICTIONS OF SECURITY IN THE ANTEBELLUM AMERICAN BORDERLANDS

Caleb Smith

"A CONSPICUOUS LAND-MARK": LAW, LITERATURE, AND LANDSCAPE

In an early episode from John Rollin Ridge's 1854 narrative, *The Life and Adventures of Joaquín Murieta, the Celebrated California Bandit*, three Mexican outlaws ambush the sheriff of Yuba County, firing a shot that strikes him near the spine. Afterward they disappear into the hills:

> The bandits did not remain long in the vicinity of Marysville after this occurrence but rode off into the coast range of mountains to the west of Mount Shasta, a conspicuous land-mark in the northern portion of the State, which rears its white shaft at all seasons of the year high above every other peak, and serves at a distance of two hundred miles to direct the course of the mountain-traveler, being to him as the polar star to the mariner. Gazing at it from the Sacramento Valley at a distance of one hundred and fifty miles, it rises in its garments of snow like some mighty archangel, filling the heavens with his solemn presence.[1]

As the narrator's eye comes to rest on this white shaft, mapping the surrounding territory with reference to its fixed point, setting aside fictional characters to introduce the suppositional figures called the "mountain-traveler" and the "mariner," shifting from the simple past of storytelling to a present tense that emphasizes permanence, imagining the mountain as an austere and pacifying angel—as the story pauses to introduce this strange tableau, it reminds us that crime literature does not only traffic in sensational plots. It also develops pictures of solemn order: images of security.

In this chapter I consider crime fiction by Ridge and one of his contemporaries, William Gilmore Simms, to explore how popular literature took up the legal history of the southern and southwestern borderlands between the Jacksonian era and the Civil War. It was a time of profound legal transformations. A conflict over lands in Georgia ended with Indian "removal" and the Cherokee diaspora. The United States annexed California and much of the Southwest in the wake of the Mexican-American War. More slowly but no less significantly, local customs in the South and elsewhere were displaced by a stronger, more centralized and homogenized state law. The signs of all these changes can be discovered in the sensational fictions of Ridge and Simms.

Ridge was the son of the Cherokee leader John Ridge, who signed the removal treaties. Also known as Yellow Bird, John Rollin Ridge was living as a fugitive in California when he wrote *Joaquín Murieta*, sometimes called the first Native American novel. Simms was arguably the most prominent man of letters in the South in his time, an attorney, legislator, and editor who opposed nullification for strategic reasons before he eventually supported secession. These two writers stood on opposite sides of some political questions, especially the question of removal. I'll suggest that they also developed different styles of literary sensationalism. Simms tried to elevate crime fiction to the status of the romance, a genre that, he fancied, could be to modern South Carolina what the epic had been in ancient Greece: a communal form, mediating a sense of collective identity. Ridge saw crime fiction as a degraded form, a symptom of legal and political disorder in a society that was not yet ready for the nobler genres of history and poetry. Yet there are intriguing similarities too, and these are my topic. Despite their political antagonisms, both Simms and Ridge used crime fiction to generate an image of the state—not the local authorities and not the imperial nation—as the legitimate enforcer of the peace and guardian of rights.

In this way Simms and Ridge adapted the resources of crime literature to the project of institutional and ideological reorganization that the legal historian Laura F. Edwards analyzes in *The People and Their Peace*. Focusing on the Carolinas, Edwards traces deep shifts in the legal system in the 1820s, 1830s, and 1840s, when state law expanded its reach into matters of security—or keeping the public peace, as it was called—which had previously been left to local authorities. In the postrevolutionary system of the 1780s, Edwards argues, "local legal practice was not some quaint, folksy exception to a formalized, rational body of state law"; rather "local decisions officially shared space with legislation and appellate decisions as central components of state law."[2] Local authorities around the turn of the nineteenth century were operating as part of a coordinated system. They were not acting arbitrarily, in the absence of norms and traditions. That view, which took hold after the 1820s, was a retrospective distortion, promoted by state authorities who depicted the consolidation of their own power in the usual, mystifying ways: as an ascent from petty vengeance to dispassionate reason, from private interests to the public good, from barbarism to civilization, from chaos to order. The process tightened the state's grip on small-scale communities, but some citizens understood it as an extension of their own authority. A growing swath of the white population came to identify with the state, imagining that its institutions embodied their sovereign will and protected their civil rights. Thus the jurisdictional reorganizations of the period can be seen as the background of the strong commitment to state power that animated the nullification and secession movements.

I would like to show how Simms and Ridge contributed, each in his way, to this transformation, figuring the state as the ideal horizon of collective identity and of legal administration. I don't think this will turn out to be a very controversial claim; it is right on the surface of the works, even in the subtitle of Simms's *Guy Rivers: A Tale of Georgia* and Ridge's *The Life and Adventures of Joaquín Murieta, the Celebrated California Bandit.* Yet the role of the state in these narratives has gone more or less unnoticed by scholars of American literature because of our fixation on the frameworks of nation and empire. A certain method, allegorical reading coordinated with the reconstruction of national-political context, was central to the reflexive turn in American literary studies in the 1980s, when our field began to investigate the relations between literature and ideology; a key question was how literature had served to justify state power and cultivate national fantasy, convoking publics into what Benedict Anderson famously called the "imagined community" of the nation.[3] The recovery of Ridge's work has been undertaken by New Americanists and Native Americanists working in this vein. John Carlos Rowe, for example, describes *Joaquín Murieta* as a text "of little intrinsic aesthetic interest that nevertheless brings into sharp relief historical and ideological issues crucial to the formation of dominant cultural values."[4] And Mark Rifkin calls Ridge's book "an allegory of U.S. expansion."[5] As for Simms, he has tended to languish or to be read only within the confines of a conservative southern studies, probably because he was a Carolina secessionist who launched the wrong kind of resistance against the nation. Edwards's legal history, with its focus on the displacement of local authorities, gives literary scholars a clearer view of how the state became the specific kind of imagined community that could matter most to these two antebellum southerners.

What happened in the Carolinas (and elsewhere) was a reordering and homogenization of law; it changed the horizons of belonging according to which justice claims were made and contested. In other words, it was a slow revolution in *jurisdiction*. In *A Power to Do Justice*, Bradin Cormack shows how much this legal concept can do for literary studies. Cormack works on a different context, England in the century leading up to 1625, but like Edwards he tells a story of centralization and normalization, one in which local customs are absorbed into or displaced by a more uniform common law. Along the way Cormack develops a theory of jurisdiction, which, he argues, "amounts to the delimitation of a sphere . . . that is the precondition for the juridical as such, for the very capacity of the law to come into effect." When matters of jurisdiction are at stake, the question is not, How might a just decision be reached in this or that particular case? It is, Who will decide, and what other normative communities, what other claims to jurisdiction, will have to be excluded so that this one power can secure its authority to speak the law into being? An ordering of conceptual and territorial space that is the precondition for legitimate legal practice, jurisdiction, Cormack writes, "often comes to function invisibly, under the legal conceptual maps that help order experience."[6] Ordinarily operating beneath consciousness, imperceptibly ordering the social world, it emerges into visibility in periods of crisis and transition. Following the path marked out by Cormack's work, I argue that the question of sovereignty, so central to our understanding of imperial expansion and crisis in nineteenth-century America, should be complemented and expanded by the question of jurisdiction—of which power has the authority to ensure the people's security within a bounded territory.

From the broad reach of empire to the states within it. From the politics of sovereignty to the law's jurisdictions. Having made these two turns, I experiment with a critical method that makes a third: from allegorical reading to an analysis of crime fiction's maps of space. The usual assumption, among law-and-literature critics, has been that literature engages with law mainly by plotting allegories of justice and injustice; that it endows power with authority through justification; or, on the contrary, that literature's different norms and modes allow for critiques of legal logics, institutions, and so on. Attending to the deep, often invisible structures of jurisdiction, however, involves looking beneath the more spectacular dramas of justification to the conditions of acceptability of an entire system. I think this other method might be especially suited to our own era, when transformations in the penal system—most spectacularly the rise of mass incarceration—are showing how that system concerns itself less with justice than with *security*. While we critics of crime fiction have usually taken an interest in the exceptional case, especially with the controversial trial, it is everyday policing that keeps the prisons full. While we analyze the motives and reasons of the one who chooses to break the law, the state identifies whole social classes for surveillance, exclusion, and control. While we think about vengeance and mercy, the criminal justice system imposes mere incapacitation. While we consider justice and injustice, it operates on logics of security.[7]

What kind of reading practice might be brought to bear on the cultural history of security? The challenge, I think, would be to shift our attention away from character, where we become preoccupied with the diagnosis of the criminal mind, away even from plot, where we concern ourselves with allegories of justice or the miscarriage of justice, and toward setting, where space is imagined as either secure or insecure. Steven Wilf's chapter in this volume shows how detective stories frame and reframe the time of action. More generally crime is usually associated with plot, with a certain sensationalism that keeps the action moving. But I find that crime fiction often arrests motion. From the bedrooms of Poe's Rue Morgue to the alleyways of Chandler's hardboiled noirs, crime scenes appear as frozen tableaux. Experimenting with a critical method that might grasp these conditions, then, I set aside such basic narrative concepts as character and plot and the practice of allegorical reading that has conventionally been brought to bear on them. I attend instead to crime fiction's spatial imaginary—its ways of depicting certain territories as either generative of violence or conducive to security. The crime fictions of Simms and Ridge dreamed of the state as a coldly rational, impersonal and dispassionate force; they called their publics to adore this image of a solemn order, to love this frigid angel.

BARREN LANDS: *GUY RIVERS*

Simms's *Guy Rivers: A Tale of Georgia* was written in Charleston and published in New York in 1834; it was a big commercial success by the standards of the time, and a revised version was issued in 1855.[8] Simms called it "the first of [his] regular novels," marking the beginning of his literary career.[9] Simms scholars class the book among the author's "border romances," a series of fictions set in the frontier zones of Georgia, Mississippi, and the further Southwest. But Simms had a peculiar vision of the borderlands. Contrary to the conventional reading of American "frontier" fiction, where such literature is thought to concern itself with the emergence of new legal orders within empty, primitive, and uncivilized zones, I argue that Simms sees the borderlands as a zone of too much law, not too little; he depicts, with a certain anxiety, the proliferation of legal forms and practices, and he anticipates the arrival of state jurisdiction as the imposition of clarity and unity. Thus Simms plays his part in the retroactive mystification by which a functioning, localized legal system is made to seem illegitimate and incompetent.

Guy Rivers tells the story of Ralph Colleton, the son of South Carolina planters who wanders into northern Georgia during the gold rush of the 1830s. There he encounters the title character, Rivers, a fugitive from justice who heads a notorious band of outlaws called the Pony Gang; his own past crimes include the murder of a judge. Rivers plots against Colleton, who is wrongfully arrested and convicted of a crime he did not commit, but the miscarriage of justice is corrected in the end. Colleton is vindicated and returns to South Carolina. Rivers is apprehended and jailed; he curses those who offer him redemption, stabs himself in the heart, and dies in his jail cell.

Between sensational tales of crime and adventure, Simms takes the time to investigate the dynamics of his villain's psychology, probing "those influences and tendencies, which have made him a criminal" (443). The novel belongs to the history of popular crime literature in the period of its secularization; by the 1830s Christian genres like the execution sermon, which identified crime with sin, had given way to romances and novels that offered quasi-scientific, forensic investigations of motive and method.[10] Indeed Rivers gets involved in his own diagnosis. He is a Byronic antihero who justifies his crime as the expression of a gifted character frustrated by a lack of prospects in a stagnant economy: "How could I, the petty lawyer of a county court, in the midst of a wilderness, appropriate time, find means and opportunities even for travel? I was poor, and profits are few to a small lawyer, whose best cases are paid for by a bale of cotton or a negro, when both of them are down in the market. In vain, and repeatedly, did I struggle with circumstances that for ever failed me in my desires; until, in a rash and accursed hour when chance, and you, and the devil, threw the opportunity for crime in my path!" (245).

Part of Rivers's explanation for his crimes is the claim that all men have an appetite for violence. "The best heroes and the best poets" have the courage to pursue their desires, and thus "they are always great criminals" (244). But in Rivers's view everyone else also cherishes, in secret, the same impulses. His example is the crowd that gathers in the public square on execution day. What brings them there, the murderer argues, is not the pious wish to see justice done: "It is the morbid appetite, which sometimes grows to madness" (244). The spectators want "to gape and gaze upon the last agonizing pangs and paroxysms of a fellow-creature" (244). Their curiosity betrays their deep kinship with the felon on the gallows. Such passages are rich material for law-and-literature scholarship, and a recent essay by John Cyril Barton has shown how Simms drew from the popular antigallows rhetorics of the

1830s to develop a "literary aesthetics of crime and capital punishment" in the border romances.[11]

Guy Rivers has been read, reasonably enough, in two ways that seem almost irreconcilable: as serving to legitimate the state's power to punish crime by providing a new, secular theory of the deviant mind, and as taking part in a broader movement of protest against the excesses of state violence. Either of these interpretations might be true, in its way, to Simms's depiction of his antihero. To get at Simms's imagery of jurisdiction, though, requires a shift of focus away from the title character to the "tale of Georgia" where, from the opening pages, Simms is mapping the landscape of the borderlands. Here another kind of cultural work is getting done: "Our scene lies in the upper part of the state of Georgia, a region at this time fruitful of dispute, as being within the Cherokee territories. The route to which we now address our attention, lies at nearly equal distances between the main trunk of the Chatahoochie and that branch of it which bears the name of the Chestatee, after a once formidable, but now almost forgotten tribe. Here, the wayfarer finds himself lost in a long reach of comparatively barren lands" (1). Nothing has happened yet. No plot is in motion, and there is only the faintest suggestion of a character—the unnamed "wayfarer" who might be anyone or no one. There is only a setting.

Yet the novel has already entangled itself in one of the great legal crises of its time, the struggle over Cherokee removal. The land, Simms writes, is "comparatively barren." But it does bear a kind of fruit: the controversy over jurisdiction. As Timothy Sweet has demonstrated, the landscape in *Guy Rivers* has an ideological design: opponents of removal had emphasized the Cherokees' agricultural practices, taking them for signs of civilization and of the people's rightful claim to the land. By the 1820s many Cherokee farmers had established agricultural concerns on the southern model; Ridge spent his early boyhood on a 419-acre plantation, where his family and their eighteen slaves grew staple crops, raised livestock, and tended an orchard. His grandfather, Major Ridge, had his own plantation nearby.[12] In composing his "tale of Georgia," Simms simply erased such farms from the region, seeing only the wilderness and the gold that white speculators had begun to mine from the hills. In the process he consigned the Cherokees to the oblivion of the Chestatees, "a once formidable, but now almost forgotten tribe" (1).[13]

What Sweet says of the landscape is also true of the lawscape: the state of Georgia in the Jacksonian period was in a fierce jurisdictional struggle over the question of whose law would apply in Cherokee lands. The Cherokees kept the peace through a combination of formalized and customary legal practices, and they adopted a written constitution in 1827. Two years later, in December 1829, the Georgia legislature passed a statute asserting jurisdiction in civil and criminal matters, extending the reach of its police power and its courts into the Cherokee territories. According to the legal scholars Vine Deloria Jr. and Clifford M. Little, the act "had the effect of abolishing the Cherokee laws."[14] Soon afterward, in 1830, the federal Congress passed the Indian Removal Act. Yet Simms's tale of Georgia recalls no such histories of erasure and displacement; it seems almost entirely to repress the memory of the violence. Simms devoted several works of fiction, poetry, and nonfiction to thinking about the native peoples of the Americas, but he made no more mention of the Cherokees in *Guy Rivers*—as if he had invoked them only to enact their disappearance from memory.

Thanks to Simms's near-total repression of the history of jurisdictional crisis, John Caldwell Guilds, the leading scholar of the author's life and work, is able to approach *Guy Rivers* as a frontier novel about a zone beyond the reach of civilized law and order: "In *Guy Rivers* for the first time in our literature the ugliness, the lawlessness, the brutality of the early nineteenth-century American frontier were fully exposed."[15] Although Simms did not acknowledge the legal system that had exercised jurisdiction in Cherokee lands, however, his tale of Georgia remains preoccupied by problems of jurisdiction. The state government, not yet holding a clear power over the northern territories, comes into conflict with outlaws and fugitives, but it also encounters local vigilantes exercising improvised forms of law and order. Thus the spokesman for a group calling itself the Regulators explains how the peace is kept: "The regilators are jest then, you see, our own people. We hain't got much law and justice in these pairts, and when the rascals git too sassy and plentiful, we all turn out, few or many, and make a business of cleaning out the stables. We turn justices, and sheriffs, and lawyers, and settle scores with the growing sinners. We jine, hand in hand. . . . It's a regular court, though we make it up ourselves, and app'ints our own judges and juries, and pass judgment 'cordin' to the case" (53). Although they conduct their business without "much law and justice," the regulators have a system. They operate a court; they appoint judges and juries. They impose penalties based on the norms of the community. Here Simms does not represent the borderlands as mere natural landscapes or primitive zones without law. He does something like the opposite; he depicts a border zone overcrowded by the forms of law but lacking the dignity and impersonality associated with the formal procedures of the higher courts. Improvising the business of passing judgment, this local community confronts the state with a parodic and uncanny reflection of its own system.

Part of the parody is the regulator's backwoods dialect. As David W. Newton observes, in Simms the frontier is a zone of contact and conflict among diverse kinds of speaking voices: "It is the chaotic interaction of voices along the frontier—the struggle between different voices to speak and to be heard—that most powerfully evokes the frontier's social instability." The cacophony of irreconcilable voices lets us know that we have entered a borderland "where social institutions—such as education, religion, and the law—have very little power."[16] In his treatment of the Georgia Regulators, Simms makes the most of the contrast between two registers: the self-consciously literary register of the exposition and the strongly marked dialect of the Regulators' spoken English. *Guy Rivers* uses this difference to stake a boundary between a rationalized and impersonal legal order and its uncanny other, the fully embodied and locally interested code of the Regulators. This semiliterate community, the novel implies, has no law; it awaits the arrival of the state.

In a study of the politics of Simms's fiction, Colin D. Pearce has discerned a "metaphysical federalism." By siding with the secessionists, Pearce argues, Simms depicted the United States as a "parchment entity," a political fiction without human substance. Simms viewed the state of South Carolina, by contrast, as a "historical community," organic rather than artificial, whose spirit found expression in its government and laws. Simms's South Carolina, Pearce writes, "is local enough to provide each citizen a home or extended family precisely because it is more historical in its character than the United States."[17] The distinction is useful, as far as it goes, but it names the interpretive problem rather than resolving it. Simms did contribute to something like the spatial and linguistic imaginary of federalism, but this federalism was not simply a reactionary embrace of local institutions; it was actually produced through the discrediting and dislocation, by the state, of other, smaller-scale distributions of legal authority.

To understand the place of the state in the legal and political imagination that Simms helped to shape, we have to see how it defined itself not only against the federal government but also against those internal jurisdictions that, through the 1820s, had been able to make a stronger claim to the "local" attachments of the people. As Edwards shows, the planters who cultivated the ideology of states' rights in the 1830s "offered a distinctive vision" of the state as the people's true home; "they made the state, an altogether abstract entity, so compelling a concept that ordinary white South Carolinians could identify with it." And this effort meant not only standing in opposition to Andrew Jackson in Washington but also "elevating the state [over local courts] as a primary locus of law and government."[18] South Carolina state law in Simms's era was expanding its own reach precisely by absorbing and displacing local customs, especially in matters of criminal justice. Simms's crime fiction generated, for his readers and perhaps for himself, an image of state power that appeared not to impose itself but to emanate from the community under its jurisdiction.

"PURE ADMINISTRATION": *JOAQUÍN MURIETA*

The Life and Adventures of Joaquín Murieta was published in San Francisco in 1854 by W. B. Cook and Company. One of the few surviving copies, held at Yale

University's Beinecke Rare Book Library, is a poorly edited text, bound in yellow paper, not in cloth or boards. *Joaquín Murieta* is an early example of the genre that would come to be known as the dime novel—industrially produced fantasies of rural conflict, designed especially for mass sales in urban markets.[19] Murieta did become a legend, largely thanks to pirated editions and retellings, but the book did not bring Ridge the money he hoped it would.

Ridge's romance tells the story of a Sonoran-born immigrant to California in the era of the gold rush, just after U.S. annexation of the territory in the aftermath of the Mexican-American War. Murieta is peaceable and proud by nature, but he encounters rough treatment at the hands of racist Americans who harass him and his mistress, drive him from his property, and lynch his half-brother. Murieta devotes himself to revenge in the form of banditry and violence against the Americans. In time he plots a full-scale war: "I intend to kill the Americans by 'wholesale,' burn their ranchos, and run off their property," he announces to his men. "When I do this, I shall wind up my career. My brothers, then we will be revenged for our wrongs, and some little, too, for the wrongs of our poor, bleeding country" (75). Since the republication of *Joaquín Murieta* in 1955, some readers have approached the text as Ridge's own revenge fantasy for the dishonored Cherokees, as offering a coded critique of U.S. imperial power in the drama of an outlaw's heroic resistance.[20] The text, Cheryl Walker argues, "can be read as a novel about the law, for by representing its protagonist as an outlaw but as a figure designed to engage our sympathies, Ridge continually puts pressure on the question of what is 'lawful.' Opposing a concept of natural law to mere legalisms, at times making law the opposite of justice . . . Yellow Bird speaks as much as an Indian as he does as a voice of white culture."[21] Like many other tales of transgression and martyrdom in the antebellum period, Ridge's novel depicts a world where the letter of law is out of sync with the spirit of justice, where the outlaw has a claim on the reader's sympathies.

Still Walker and other critics also find deep contradictions in Ridge's own politics. Although he and his family had attempted to defend the rights of the Cherokees against Georgia's incursions, in the end they assented to removal; Ridge's father signed the Treaty of New Echota, and the family fought a bloody factional war against the more radical Cherokee nationalists under John Ross. The Ridges were no antiracists; they were slave-owning opponents of abolition, and Ridge's novel indulges in grotesque caricatures of California's Indians. In one notorious passage the narrator describes Sapatarra, the chief of the Tejon Nation, as an absurd savage, "seated upon his haunches in all the grandeur of 'naked majesty,' enjoying a very luxurious repast of roasted acorns and dried angle-worms. His swarthy subjects were scattered in various directions around him, engaged for the most part in the very arduous task of doing nothing. The little smoky-looking children were sporting, like a black species of water-fowl, in the creek" (36). The satirical viciousness and elitism of Ridge's style, the cruel irony of phrases like "very luxurious" and "very arduous," corrode the passage from beginning to end. We are in the company of an author who, to borrow Walker's gentle phrasing, "upheld views repugnant to those who wished to maintain traditional Indian cultural practices."[22]

At least some of the contradictions that scholars have identified in Ridge's work, however, can be understood as products of our own commitment to reading him within the frameworks of sovereignty and the nation. Timothy Powell, for instance, finds in *Joaquín Murieta* Ridge's "conflicting feelings of a deep-seated racial rage at white society and an equally powerful desire to be included into 'America.' "[23] But there would have been no paradox here for Ridge himself. He laid out his position in an 1849 article for the *Clarksville* (Texas) *Northern Standard*, "The Cherokees: Their History—Present Condition and Future Prospects." Ridge began with the story of the Cherokees in Georgia, who, he wrote, had "abandoned their savage customs and habits for the conditions of civilized life; creating for themselves a simple but wise form of government" (49). The Cherokees, in other words, were not living in a state of nature but in the social state, under a formal code of laws. These opening sections rehearsed the arguments against removal that had been made in the *Cherokee Phoenix* and elsewhere in the 1830s; in *Worcester v. Georgia* (1832), the U.S. Supreme Court under John Marshall had acknowledged the Cherokees as a community "having institutions of their own, and governing themselves by their own laws," with a right of jurisdiction over their own territory that could not legitimately be abridged by the state.[24] Ridge indicted Georgia's appropriation of Cherokee lands as an act of aggression, carried out in defiance of the law and justified by the weakest of jurisdictional claims: "The meager, but fatal pretensions of Georgia . . . on the miserable ground that it lay within their 'chartered limits,' are well known" (49).

But the heart of Ridge's article was dedicated to the condition of the Cherokees after they had been driven west, toward Arkansas and Oklahoma. By the 1840s, at the end of the Trail of Tears, the Ridge faction was a despised minority, and the power rested with Ross's followers. This bitter division, Ridge argued, made it impossible for the Cherokee legal system to do justice, especially when the accused belonged to what was known as the Ridge or Treaty Party. "I believe that confusion must reign amongst them; one faction must tyrannize over another—a furious banditti must exist, defying law and order, and all the miserable consequences, which flow from such a state of things, must surround and oppress the Cherokee people, until a strong arm is extended over them—I mean the laws of the United States." Up to this point, perhaps, we really are caught in a contradiction between loyalty to the Cherokees and longing for inclusion in the nation. But Ridge explains himself immediately: "I would advocate a measure therefore which looks to the event of making the Cherokee nation an integral part of the united States . . . possessing all the attributes, first of a territorial government, and then of a sovereign state." Living under domestic dependency, Ridge argued, was a "useless peculiarity": "Let [the Cherokee nation] change this nominal sovereignty for a real one. Let her attach herself to the Union as one of its members, and rise with the fair sisters of the Republic to a position which is truly lofty and rationally independent."[25]

Ridge's argument for Cherokee statehood was forged out of bitter personal experience. He had seen his own father dragged from the house and murdered by members of the Ross faction. He had seen his mother abandon the family farm, afraid for her safety and her children's lives. When Ridge himself killed a man in the ongoing feud, he lit out for California to avoid arrest and trial under the Cherokee courts.[26] In the study of jurisdiction the task is not to reconstruct Ridge's political position-taking but to understand how his fiction projects a certain horizon for the resolution of the crises it stages. Yet the two problems turn out to be related, since Ridge made it clear in his journalism that in his view the proper horizon is not, as most ideological readings have assumed, a multicultural nation or empire. It is a strong, sovereign state, "rationally independent," in Ridge's vision, and "truly lofty," a little like Mount Shasta. In his outlaw romance Ridge would extend the same federalist map to the California of the early 1850s.

On the opening page of *Joaquín Murieta*, Ridge reflects on the task of composing his work of crime fiction. He offers his title character as a product of a distinctive environment: "I do this, not for the purpose of ministering to any depraved taste for the dark and horrible in human action, but rather to contribute my mite to those subtle materials out of which the early history of California shall one day be composed. The character of this truly wonderful man was nothing more than a natural production of the social and moral condition of the country in which he lived, acting upon certain peculiar circumstances favorable to such a result, and, consequently, his individual history is a part of the most valuable history of the State" (7). Twice in these two sentences Ridge identifies the state of California as the horizon of his tale. He does refer to Murieta as a "natural production . . . of the country," but *country* here does not refer to the nation as a political unit; it refers to a stretch of landscape, a territory that has not yet been brought under the unifying jurisdiction of the state. Already too Ridge is connecting the legal problem of jurisdiction to the literary problem of genre. The history of California is yet to be written because California in 1854 remains the mere notion of a state, lacking the ordering rule of law. Ridge's narrative is a contribution to a future history; the sensational tale forecasts its own absorption into a higher genre.

Joaquín Murieta continues to suggest the impossibility of composing itself as a proper history. Toward the end of the book, when vigilantes are pursuing

Murieta and his band, Ridge describes the disorder in California, a territory (like the Cherokee lands under Ross's leadership, in Ridge's account), where confusion reigns: "Thus was the whole country alive with armed parties, whose separate movements it would be impossible, without much unnecessary labor, to trace. Arrests were continually being made; popular tribunals established in the woods, Judge Lynch installed upon the bench; criminals arraigned, tried, and executed upon the limb of a tree; pursuits, flights, skirmishes, and a topsy-turvy, hurly-burly mass of events that set narration at defiance" (135–36). The boundary between law and violence has broken down. But here, as in Simms's depiction of the Georgia Regulators, the unauthorized use of force is most menacing to any prospect of legitimate order precisely when it parodies the forms and usages of law. The problem is not merely that murders and thefts are rampant. It is that private persons are going through the ceremonies of establishing tribunals, that lynch mobs are conducting arraignments, trials, and executions. This is a spectacular crisis of jurisdiction. It is also, for Ridge, a problem in narration. He cannot accomplish the work of mapping the territory or of telling the story. The confusion is so generalized that it has become "impossible . . . to trace," and the events "set narration at defiance." The incoherence of Ridge's narrative is a symptom of the legal crisis whose contours it describes. The violence in California baffles literary form.

Murieta first swears his oath of revenge after local vigilantes, accusing him and his half-brother of stealing a horse, "listened to no explanation, but bound him to a tree, and publicly disgraced him with the lash. They then proceeded to the house of his half-brother and hung him without judge or jury" (12). For most of the rest of the book, though, Ridge imagines postannexation California not as a lawless frontier but as a territory plagued by *too much law*, by a bewildering proliferation of legal rituals. In one of the narrative's most troubling episodes, Murieta and his men are captured by the Tejon Indians and subjected to a grotesque penal ceremony, presided over by the absurd chief: "Sapatarra made a long speech upon the merits of the important transaction which was about to occur, enlarging upon the enormity of the crime which had been committed . . . and went off into extreme glorification over the magnanimity which would allow such great rascals to escape with their lives. He then gave orders to have them whipped." Afterward "Sapatarra . . . declared the ends of justice satisfied" (39). Once again we are not in a territory of lawlessness but of the uncanny and illegitimate reproduction of legal forms—a "hurly-burly" proliferation of law. Until this "topsy-turvy" society is brought into a coherent, properly hierarchical legal order, the country is not yet a state, and the history of California cannot be written. In many ways *Joaquín Murieta* reflects on its own sensational form as a kind of primitive literature, not yet able to achieve the dignity or grace of higher genres. It can foresee a California literature only as a prospect in the future

Ridge introduces this prospect with an abrupt shift in genre, as the narrative pauses to introduce the poem "Mount Shasta, Seen from a Distance." The opening lines are an address to the reader, who is asked to picture a landscape:

> Behold the dread Mount Shasta, where it stands,
> Imperial midst the lesser hight [*sic*],
> and like some mighty, unimpassioned mind, companionless
> And cold.

The mountain is distinguished by its loftiness and its cold rationality, its detachment from human passions and sentimental attachments. We have left behind the sensational world of the dime novel; we have ascended to a sphere where such feelings have no place. At the end of the poem, a few dozen lines later, it becomes clear that Mount Shasta is a figure for the possibility of a future legal order. These are the concluding lines:

> And well this Golden State shall thrive, if, like
> Its own Mount Shasta, sovereign law shall lift
> Itself in purer atmosphere—so high
> That human feeling, human passion, at its base
> Shall lie subdued; e'en pity's tears shall on
> Its summit freeze; to warm it, e'en the sunlight
> Of deep sympathy shall fail—
> Its pure administration shall be like
> The snow, immaculate upon that mountain's brow!

In Simms's treatment of the Regulators in *Guy Rivers*, a passage of dialect is framed by the dominant register of literary exposition. In Ridge the relation is inverted. The entire narrative in prose identifies itself as degraded stuff, far beneath the formal grandeur of the two-page poem. In this utopian interruption in verse, Ridge halts the topsy-turvy movement of his sensational plot and suspends the affective action of the romance. The fantasy of a purified legal order under the administration of state authorities finds its clearest expression in a poem that halts the narrative and surveys the territory of jurisdiction from a position of lofty and impersonal detachment. The heart turns to ice in this solemn atmosphere.

NOTES

1. Yellow Bird (John Rollin Ridge), *The Life and Adventures of Joaquín Murieta, the Celebrated California Bandit* (1854; Norman: University of Oklahoma, 1955), 23.

2. Laura F. Edwards, *The People and Their Peace: Legal Culture and the Transformation of Inequality in the Post-Revolutionary South* (Chapel Hill: University of North Carolina Press, 2009), 5.

3. Benedict Anderson, *Imagined Communities: Reflections on the Origin and Spread of Nationalism* (London: Verso, 1983); Sacvan Bercovich and Myra Jehlen, eds., *Ideology and Classic American Literature* (Cambridge, UK: Cambridge University Press, 1986); Lauren Berlant, *The Anatomy of National Fantasy: Hawthorne, Utopia, and Everyday Life* (Chicago: University of Chicago Press, 1991).

4. John Carlos Rowe, "Highway Robbery: 'Indian Removal,' the Mexican-American War, and *The Life and Adventures of Joaquín Murieta*," *NOVEL: A Forum on Fiction* 31.2 (1998): 149–73, quote on 150.

5. Mark Rifkin, "'For the Wrongs of Our Poor Bleeding Country: Sensation, Class, and Empire in Ridge's *Joaquin Murieta*," *Arizona Quarterly* 65.2 (2009): 27–56, quote on 29. An exception to the general rule of national and imperial readings is Timothy Mark Donohue's dissertation chapter on Ridge (Columbia University, in progress).

6. Bradin Cormack, *A Power to Do Justice: Jurisdiction, English Literature, and the Rise of Common Law* (Chicago: University of Chicago Press, 2008), 3, 11.

7. My account of the contemporary criminal justice system is informed especially by Malcolm M. Feeley and Jonathan Simon, "The New Penology: Notes on the Emerging Strategy of Corrections and Its Implications," *Criminology* 30 (1992): 449–74.

8. W. Gilmore Simms, *Guy Rivers: A Tale of Georgia* (1834), ed. John Caldwell Guilds (Fayetteville: University of Arkansas Press, 1993).

9. See John Caldwell Guilds, introduction to ibid., xvii.

10. On the secularization of crime fiction, see David Brion Davis, *Homicide in American Fiction, 1798–1860: A Study in Social Values* (Ithaca, NY: Cornell University Press, 1957); Daniel A. Cohen, *Pillars of Salt, Monuments of Grace: New England Crime Literature and the Origins of American Popular Culture, 1674–1860* (Amherst: University of Massachusetts Press, 1993); Daniel E. Williams, *Pillars of Salt: An Anthology of Early American Criminal Narratives* (Madison, WI: Madison House, 1992); Karen Halttunen, *Murder Most Foul: The Killer and the American Gothic Imagination* (Cambridge, MA: Harvard University Press, 1998).

11. John Cyril Barton, "William Gilmore Simms and the Literary Aesthetics of Crime and Capital Punishment," *Law and Literature* 22.2 (2010): 220–43.

12. James W. Parins, *John Rollin Ridge: His Life and Works* (Lincoln: University of Nebraska Press, 1991), 13.

13. See Timothy Sweet, *American Georgics: Economy and Environment in Early American Literature* (Philadelphia: University of Pennsylvania Press, 2002), 145–47.

14. Vine Deloria Jr. and Clifford M. Little, *American Indians, American Justice* (Austin: University of Texas Press, 1983), 28.

15. Guilds, introduction to Simms, *Guy Rivers*, xv–xxi, xx. Citing Guilds's account with approval, Rayburn S. Moore describes the setting this way: "Such country . . . is wild in that

nature has not yet been tamed by the settlers and law and order have not yet been firmly established." Rayburn S. Moore, "William Gilmore Simms's *Guy Rivers* and the Frontier," in *William Gilmore Simms and the American Frontier*, ed. John Caldwell Guilds and Caroline Collins (Athens: University of Georgia Press, 1997), 55–63, quote on 55.

16. David W. Newton, "Voices along the Border: Language and the Southern Frontier in *Guy Rivers: A Tale of Georgia*," in Guilds and Collins, *William Gilmore Simms and the American Frontier*, 118–44, quote on 124.

17. Colin D. Pearce, "The Metaphysical Federalism of William Gilmore Simms," *Studies in the Literary Imagination* 42.1 (2009): 121–82, quote on 125.

18. Edwards, *The People and Their Peace*, 263.

19. See Bill Brown, ed., *Reading the West: An Anthology of Dime Novels* (New York: Bedford, 1997).

20. As David Farmer and Rennard Strickland argued in 1981, *Joaquín Murieta* is "a novel of the Mexican in California into which Ridge poured the frustrations of his Cherokee life." David Farmer and Rennard Strickland, introduction to *A Trumpet of Our Own: Yellow Bird's Essays on the North American Indian: Selections from the Writings of the Noted Cherokee Author John Rollin Ridge*, ed. David Farmer and Rennard Strickland (San Francisco: Book Club of California, 1981), 24–25.

21. Cheryl Walker, *Indian Nation: Native American Literature and Nineteenth-Century Nationalisms* (Durham, NC: Duke University Press, 1997), 112.

22. Ibid., 111. Similarly Rowe reads *Joaquín Murieta* as a defense of "possessive individualism, a crucial part of dominant cultural values in the United States in the 1850s" ("Highway Robbery," 150), and Rifkin emphasizes Ridge's elitist reaction against collective forms of popular resistance while reading the novel as "an allegory of U.S. expansionism" ("'For the Wrongs of Our Poor, Bleeding Country,'" 29).

23. Timothy Powell, "Historical Multiculturalism," quoted in Rifkin, "'For the Wrongs of Our Poor, Bleeding Country,'" 28.

24. *Samuel A. Worcester v. The State of Georgia*, 31 U.S. (6 Pet.) 515 (1852), reprinted in Jill Norgren, *The Cherokee Cases: Two Landmark Federal Decisions in the Fight for Sovereignty* (Norman: University of Oklahoma Press, 2004), 171.

25. John Rollin Ridge, "The Cherokees," in Farmer and Strickland, *A Trumpet of Our Own*, 49–53.

26. See Parins, *John Rollin Ridge*.

15

Sleuthing toward Bethlehem

OXFORD'S TAMAR, JERUSALEM'S OHAYON, AND HISTORICAL DEVICES IN DETECTIVE FICTION

Steven Wilf

NO METHODOLOGICAL DIFFERENCE has animated legal historical scholarship more than the competing approaches of understanding law within its social landscape versus drilling deep down into legal texts. On one side, legal scholars such as Lawrence Friedman have described legal institutions as a social phenomenon that remains deeply embedded in the broader culture, economics, and politics of surrounding organized social units and have identified legal actors as integral parts of society. On the other side, law has been seen as encompassing its own internal logic; its autonomous structures, its historical genealogies rooted in precedent, and its independent institutions constitute a historical subject that must be scrutinized on its particular terms. This disagreement—so fundamental and so unresolvable—has been a constant of legal historical scholarship for nearly a century.[1]

Much late nineteenth-century legal historical scholarship was internal, cordoned off by the well-defined boundaries of legal texts. Fin-de-siècle scholars such as F. W. Maitland and other practitioners of historical jurisprudence widened the aperture of legal study to include the development of social institutions such as marriage and inheritance. By the early twentieth century legal realists, influenced by Progressive Era historians, critiqued those relying on historical precedent for their overly internalist approach. Closer to our own time historians influenced by critical legal studies reinvigorated the understanding of legal texts by sharply identifying the possibilities and contradictions inherent in law's claims to be an autonomous framework. In contrast historical work within the compass of the law-and-society movement continued the dispute by arguing that law can be interpreted *only* as a response to social forces.

This essay examines two mystery novel series, one British and one Israeli, whose protagonists are legal historians. Sarah Caudwell's Hilary Tamar and Batya Gur's Michael Ohayon are not the only fictional historian detectives.[2] But the fact that they employ historical methods radically at odds with each other serves as a striking representation of these two quite different historical approaches. Tamar is the master of the telling error embedded in text. Such microcosmic historical details capture the past—like insects caught in amber—so as to view the shifting motives of an individual criminal. Ohayon, on the other hand, constructs historical narratives describing underlying tensions in the particular social milieu where the crime takes place. He views the historian's role as dynamic excavation across a broad expanse of time—to uncover the structure of what the historian and mystery novelist Fred Vargas calls the "histoire de plaques qui dèconnent dans tous les sens á la surface de la terre—impossible de tenir en place [shifting time as tectonic plates sliding in all directions across the earth, unable to stay in one place]."[3]

In other words, detective novels not only provide optics for examining the character of different societies, from Henning Mankell's Ystad to Paul Auster's Brooklyn, logical puzzles—a form of Rubik's cube with a dash of blood, glimpses of the criminal justice system, and an uncovering of the psychological underpinnings of violence. The detective novel—*all* detective novels—are procedural. And by their procedural nature they probe questions of method. This essay is about one particular technique, historical practices, and how these might be simultaneously deployed, altered, and reconceived within the compass of detective fiction. The thin man does *on occasion* utilize historical thick description.

Although concerned with historical time, Caudwell's and Gur's novels remain deeply rooted in their local settings, Britain and Israel. Drawing upon her background as a Chancery barrister, Caudwell's four books portrays Tamar as the quintessential Oxford don: waspish, pompous, and a bit dithering. [4] A member of the law faculty at St. George's College, Tamar is "happy to confess that I am an historian rather than a lawyer, and there is little in the English law of taxation after the year 1660 which I find of absorbing interest."[5] Endlessly procrastinating, the character claims to be writing a study of *causa* in medieval common law. Yet Tamar's real métier seems to be snooping: "I am an historian. My profession largely consists of speaking ill of the dead."[6] A literary critic for *Haaretz* newspaper, Gur has written six novels featuring Ohayon, a Sephardic detective uncovering webs of deception in various corners of Israeli society.[7] Ohayon had intended to complete his history doctorate in the structure of medieval guilds. But, as we learn in scattered passages throughout Gur's novels, was sidetracked by his personal life.

The parallels—and differences—of these two crime fiction series are striking. Both are closed oeuvres. Caudwell and Gur died of cancer at comparatively young ages, and their last novels created a kind of thematic ending to their series. Both identify their fictional epicenter as a major city. Caudwell begins her books with Tamar's visit to the London chambers inhabited by former students in Lincoln's Inn. Tamar's London revolves around high culture and high finance where navigating tax and trust issues emerge in a chaotic world of economic exuberance. Ohayon's Jerusalem is a "withdrawn, austere, provincial place" that had been transformed into a "city pretending to be a metropolis."[8] Gur idealizes this lost city in an extended essay, *Requiem for Humility or Living in Jerusalem*. Her novels are constructed with political events—war and intifada—drawing a circle of violence around the core narratives.[9]

Caudwell was the sister of the well-known political essayist Alexander Cockburn and the daughter of Jean Ross, who was said to have been Christopher Isherwood's model for Sally Bowles in the Berlin stories[10] Raised by a communist single mother, Caudwell (a pseudonym; her original name was Sarah Cockburn) had a peripatetic upbringing. After reading classics at Aberdeen University, she studied law at Oxford. Her writing is sharply plotted, irreverent, jocular, and nonchalantly witt, and her novels—*Thus Was Adonis Murdered, The Shortest Way to Hades, The Sirens Sang of Murder,* and *The Sybil in Her Grave*—are crammed with classical literary allusions. Gur's writing is much more somber. Her central character, Ohayon, dwells in a fragile society and was intended to be a social critic with a conscience as much as a literary sleuth.

In her 1935 Oxford lecture, "Aristotle on Detective Fiction," Dorothy Sayers stressed the formulaic aspect of the genre. It begins with a murder, "the middle is occupied with the detection of the crime and the various . . . reversals of fortune arising out of this, and the end is the discovery."[11] Caudwell and Gur are examples of this Aristotelian poetics of mystery fiction since their novels remain tightly bound by convention. But I argue that two contrapuntal formulae are employed by the legal historians in these novels. Tamar is a textual scholar who utilizes the techniques of close reading to uncover inconsistencies. Stepping beyond the ordinary deductive reasoning of Hercule Poirot's little gray cells, Tamar sees life as experience transmuted through some strange alchemy into text. By rigorously employing academic textual analysis, it is possible to expose the traces of concealment—the clues left behind in the aftermath of murder's immense disruptive power.

Gur's novels are equally fixed in their approach. Each identifies a closed society and asks what deeply held norms particular to that society have been violated, damaging such fundamental norms as to provoke murder. The closed societies vary—a psychoanalytic institute, the Literature Department at Hebrew University, a kibbutz, the symphony orchestra, a tightly knit community in Jerusalem, a public television station—but the formula is always the same. By immersing himself in the historical *mentalité* of each society, Ohayon interrogates what "different laws apply here." Seeking to understand "parshat ruach ha-devarim [the essence of things]", Ohayon must become part of the environment he is investigating to sense "the subtle nuances of the murdered person's world."[12] This is the historian's métier, tracing closed societies over decades, from their beginning to the troubled period when the homicide occurred. If Caudwell's Tamar is all about making a textual problem legible in order to uncover what might be lost in time, Gur's Ohayon frames an extended narrative arc when exploring the social historical context.

I interrogate this difference by focusing attention on the literary sleuths themselves, for their particular postures of text and context are deeply rooted in their character, and by providing examples of their methods at work. Mystery novels rely upon a variety of conventions as technologies of detection, from logical deduction to forensics. The historian's gaze will be analyzed within this broader framework.

Finally, I look more closely at the concluding novels of both authors. At the end of their lives, I argue, Caudwell and Gur unsettled their own deployment of historical method. Caudwell's sleuth comes to recognize the limits of relying upon a rational practice such as textual analysis to probe the makings of a crime of passion. Behind the traces of past actions—the accretions of life transmuted into text—Tamar reluctantly uncovers an irrational, emotionally volatile character that eludes hermeneutic analysis. Gur's police detective finds that closed societies are never truly closed. He must look at the social context as a fabular text, a cultural narrative constructed through interactions with a complex and frightening larger world. In their ultimate novels these two arch-formulaic writers abandon convention, which results in the uncanny convergence of text and context. However, I do not intend this essay simply to be an exploration of how two well-regarded detective fiction writers mined legal history in order to expand their genre beyond predictable police procedurals.

Legal historians, as I have suggested, use text and context as formulaic conventions. Their formulae, tropes, and narrative framing conventions can be as two-dimensional as those employed in crime fiction. I argue—at the conclusion of the essay—that these conventions inevitably break down. Other understandings of history as charged with redemptive meaning exist beyond text and context: *Heilsgeschichte* (seeking to identify divine salvation operating within the compass of human history), Marxist historical dialectics, utopian conjuring, and various eschatological musings represented by Jewish messianism and Christian formulations of *Parousia* (Christ's return as the culmination of history). These alternative narratives, wildly imaginary, unruly conceptions of the past ultimately come to unravel more formulaic historical methods.

I therefore conclude by examining more closely how prophetic readings of history unsettle Caudwell's and Gur's last novels. Text and context—the traditional jousting partners of legal history—ultimately disappoint as methods. Caudwell's sleuth, Tamar, comes to recognize the limits of relying only upon reason when employing textual analysis to probe the makings of a crime of passion. Behind the traces of past actions—the accretions of life transmuted into text—Tamar reluctantly uncovers an irrational, emotionally volatile character who eludes hermeneutic analysis. Ohayon, Gur's police detective, finds that closed societies are never truly closed. He must look at the social context—especially in his Israeli setting—as a fabular text imbricated with utopianism and constructed in the midst of a threatening larger world. In their final novels, these two arch-formulaic writers abandon their methodological convention—which results in an uncanny overturning of text and context.

THE ANXIETY OF INVESTIGATION

At the beginning of *The Sybil in Her Grave*, Tamar drops a playful tease. Although "some of my readers, it is true, have been kind enough to say that they would like to know more about me—what I look like, how I dress, how I spend my leisure hours, and other details of a personal and sometime even intimate nature," Tamar chooses to maintain the "modest reticence which I think becoming to the historian."[13] However, more is at work than mere diffidence. In Caudwell's quartet of novels, Tamar's gender is never revealed. This might partly explain why the books are written in the gender-neutral first person. What do we know about Tamar? He or she is fussy, sponges off friends—especially at the pub near chambers called the Corkscrew—pedantic, sighs about the burdens imposed by college life, and drops a bit of Ciceronian rhetoric ("O Tempora, O Mores," he or she exclaims about those failing to learn classical tongues).[14] But is Tamar a man or woman?

Caudwell avoids descriptions of dress, gestures, and attractions for these might reveal her character's sex. It is as if Caudwell is taking to the point of absurdity Sayers's claim that detective fiction might have episodes without character.[15] What does it mean to go one step beyond Virginia Woolf's gender-shifting Orlando or Jeffrey Eugenides's hermaphrodite Cal Stephanides and devise a character completely lacking an ascribed gender? Occupying social terrain apart from kin relationships he or she cannot be classified as a lover or parent or significant other. Instead Tamar appears self-invented purely through professional identity. Hilary Tamar's epicene, gender-bending first name might be a gesture referring to Oxford's

Hilary Term (January to March) or a division of England's court calendar, which has four quarters: Hilary, Easter, Trinity, and Michaelmas. Such a Christian name underscores how Tamar's relationships are circumscribed by the college Commons Room and the Inns of Court.

Being ungendered also means being unsexed. Not even the hint of a romantic relationship appears in any of Caudwell's mysteries; Somerset Maugham claimed that romance has no place in detective fiction since the main purpose is solving a murder. "To introduce a pretty love story in the unraveling of a mystery," wrote Maugham, "is an error of taste for which there is no excuse. Marriage bells have no place in a detective story."[16] Sayers tried to prove him wrong in her novel *Gaudy Night* (1935), which features an extended romance between her sleuth Lord Peter Wimsey and the Oxonian mystery writer Harriet Vane. She sought "to bring the love problem in line with the detective-problem so that the same key should unlock both at once."[17] Tamar's textual detective key, the capacity to view existence as disembodied text, neatly fits his or her particularly sexless existence.

Tamar's sexual ambiguity is not simply a matter of disembodiment, a gaping omission in a gendered world. Tamar decenters commonplaces about authority in detective literature. Crime fiction has often been riven by gender. Male protagonists dominate hardboiled genres such as those featuring private investigators or police procedurals; they do not mind the occasional brush with violence. Women—from St. Mary Mead's Miss Marple to Melbourne's Phryne Fisher—pry, gossip, and seduce, often relying largely upon psychological insight when solving crimes. Male deduction and female intuition, male forensics and female gossip, male forthright interventions into the plot's action and female shaping situations from the periphery form alternative, deeply divided claims to authority. Tamar's scholarly persona borrows a bit from both gender stereotypes. Not surprisingly Tamar is curiously ignored, belittled, and rendered powerless even by his or her closest friends. "Shifting to and fro between libraries and senior commons rooms, and giving the odd lecture or two on novel disseisin," one character remarks, "isn't exactly training in the tough school of life."[18] Julia Lathrop says she could explain Tamar's awkward presence by introducing him or her as a distinguished academic lawyer whose advice we have found useful. After all, "she added in a tone of surprise, 'there is a sense in which one could say that's actually true.' "[19]

Tamar nevertheless deploys this vexed ungendered status as a source of strength, wryly noting that "character is a myth invented by novelists for the sake of adding interest to the narrative. Human beings are not so different from one another as the authors of fiction would have us believe."[20] Writing of the golden age of detective fiction (the interwar period) in general and Sayers in particular, Raymond Chandler criticized the thin creation of character: "Her kind of detective story was an arid formula which could not even satisfy its own implications. If it started out to be about real people . . . they must very soon do unreal things in order to form the artificial pattern required by the plot. When they did unreal things, they ceased to be real themselves. They became puppets and cardboard lovers and papier-mâché villains and detectives of exquisite and impossible gentility."[21] Mysteries, in Aristotelian terms, favor plot (*mythos*) over character (*ethos*). Caudwell does not deny this fundamental prescription by fattening up characters to make them ever more rounded with nuances, complexities, and psychological dimensions that might surprise the reader. Instead she accentuates their caricature-like quality.

If detective fiction would use character as mere vehicles for transporting the plot from one point to another, then Caudwell creates the ultimate protagonist, who, by lacking a gendered embodiment, *transcends* sex. De-gendering also speaks to a historian's professional myth: the idealization of historical objectivity. Leopold von Ranke identified the historian's main duty as reporting the past "wie es eigentlich gewesen [as it actually happened]."[22] Tudor historian Geoffrey Elton's *Practice of History* (1967) might be the most assertive claim to a professional model of objective history. Elton distinguishes the historian's role as an empiricist eschewing reified theory, partisan ideology, and—does this deny the historian a body?—personal identity politics. Caudwell simultaneously mocks the concept of thin character exemplified by detective fiction and perhaps the equally emaciated notion of the objective historian.

All Caudwell's novels begin—again formulaically in the style of Greek epics—with an invocation. Take, for example, the first few lines of *Thus Was Adonis Murdered*: "Scholarship asks, thank God, no recompense but truth. It is not for the sake of material reward that she (Scholarship) pursues her (Truth) through the undergrowth of ignorance, shining on Obscurity the bright torch of Reason and clearing aside the tangled thorns of Error with the keen secateurs of Intellect. Nor is it for the sake of public glory and the applause of the multitude: the scholar is indifferent to vulgar acclaim."[23] Despite such protestations, Tamar quickly puts aside his or her research on the monograph *Causa in the Early Common Law* and is inevitably quickly drawn into a murder investigation at the urging of a somewhat rowdy crowd of barristers in Lincoln's Inn.

In *The Sirens Sang of Murder*, Caudwell burlesques formulaic character construction through the contrivance of Cantrip and Julia, two members of Lincoln's Inn, coauthoring a steamy novel about life at the bar entitled (what else?) *Chancery*. Drawing upon the chamber's lovely new temporary typist as the model for the novel's romantic interest and idealized portrayals of themselves, the novel has as much to do with everyday legal practice as the British detective cozy might have to do with real murder. By transforming the typist into a mere sketch of a figure, Caudwell suggests a counterpoint to Sayers's invention of the Cattery, an unofficial investigative agency staffed by typists whose prowess at gossip, snooping, and emotional intuition makes them more than mere attractive women.[24] Yet the write-by-the-numbers approach to character is *Chancery*'s most striking feature. Cantrip and Julia determine that some novels have "heroines who are sort of fragile and waiflike . . . and some of them have heroines who are more sort of regal and imperious. . . . So to be on the safe side we're going to have one of each."[25]

Julia Lathrop is a gendered reverse-image of Tamar. Tamar's student, she read classics in Oxford, but in her case the study of Athenian texts led to a fatal attraction to comely Greek youths. Julia spends much of her adult life slipping in and out of bed in her quest for Adonis. She employs classical texts as part of her art of seduction. Incredibly absent-minded, Julia is the antithesis of the orderly Tamar and ultimately resembles "one of the more disheveled heroines of Greek tragedy."[26] Although an expert on tax law, she is hounded by Inland Revenue for her disregard of income tax payments. Her "strategy for dealing with real life, on those rare occasions when she came across it, was to keep very quiet and hope it would go away."[27] Hopelessly impractical, Julia breaks the boundaries of space by constantly scattering books, papers, and her ample body. Her clothes, like her erotic practices, are described as "dégagé."[28] If Tamar is ungendered, Julia is oversexed. Selecting erotic partners purely on the basis of their Praxitelean physique, she decenters gender categories by (like so many men) objectifying the opposite gender in pursuit of casual sex.

Gur's Ohayon, on the other hand, is a soft-boiled detective. Endowed with Dalglieshian interiority, he is "tall, polite, quiet, with that sadness, and those eyes" that prove irresistible to women.[29] Ohayon is ill at ease with others. When, P. D. James has asked, do we find a well-adjusted fictional detective?[30] Ohayon's own past is slowly revealed through the novels. Born in Morocco and coming to Israel as a young child, Ohayon experienced the dislocation of being sent to a northern moshav after his father's death. No place ever felt like home. His mother's abode "radiated strangeness and alienation."[31] Sent to a boarding school in Jerusalem as an adolescent, he underwent an erotic and cultural initiation under the tutelage of a classmate's sophisticated Ashkenazi mother. His love of classical music and literature comes from their being intermingled with a sexual awakening during these trysts.

Ohayon experiences dislocation as a Sephardic Jew in an Ashkenazi world. His brief marriage to the only daughter of a Polish-born diamond dealer—who blackmailed him into the commitment by becoming pregnant—proved disastrous.[32] New family responsibilities cost him a scholarship to study history at Cambridge.[33] While at the ever so Germanic Hebrew University his Moroccan background stood out, he also never fit within the largely Sephardic, working-class police force. Detectives are idealists, Ohayon tells us, "who believe there's a world with laws, a nearly utopian world." And this leads to detachment, what a colleague of Ohayon would call "your preference for solitude, your withdrawal, your perfectionism."[34] But it also provides the distance needed for a participant-observer in culturally dissimilar worlds.

Gur playfully underscores the importance of interiority. She describes Ohayon telling a social worker that he does not read detective fiction: "They seem completely unreal to me. . . . It's all so contrived. What is interesting is not the whodunit. It is what is going on in the murderer's mind. How can Raskolnikov live with himself after what he has done—the remainder of his life. . . . When everything serves the plot there is no room to breathe, no beauty. No digressions from the central concern. . . . A conversation like this, between us now, couldn't take place in a detective story because it's not functional."[35]

Indeed much of the plot in *Murder Duet* has little to do with the homicide. It involves Ohayon's attempt to construct a peculiarly assembled family—including a needy neighbor and a foundling infant—as he grapples with his own emotional detachment from his troubled adolescent son. When a child is unexpectedly left on his doorstep, Ohayon turns to the young single mother upstairs to help care for the infant. It is a purely instrumental relationship intended to share child care duties and without—at least so he claims—a romantic dimension. Can Ohayon, whose postdivorce life has been so well insulated (an occasional affair with a married woman, rented apartments), take all this human driftwood and build something more closely resembling a permanent home? "A man needs a framework," Ohayon would say. "It's human nature." But the child welfare investigator assigned to his case insists that he is acting just like a fictional detective. He has embraced his loneliness: "Detectives hardly ever have intimate relationships—they lack basic trust." They cannot create bonds of affection. Parenting, she tells him, requires the anxious anticipation of the possible loss of a partner.[36] Accusing Ohayon of trying to create an instant family absent emotional complications, the welfare investigator denies him custody.

This story of Ohayon's bloodless failed ménage is the counterpoint to the central plot in *Murder Duet*, which traces the intense (and lethal) sibling rivalry within a musical family as two brothers contend for their violin teacher's affection. Duets have particular emotional intensity. Ohayon discovers how musicians locate their own place within an expressive spectrum that extends from untrammeled romanticism to restrained period instrumentation in early music. Reared in a musical household, his single-mother neighbor struggles with such a powerful emotional legacy. Ohayon, who often fails to answer his cell phone, prefers disconnection. Although capable of reconstructing a history of sentiment among musicians through a close examination of the normsand taboos of the past, he ultimately finds the passions of others overwhelming. Ohayon retreats into solitude. The duet—both dangerously impassioned and alluring—proves elusive.

FATAL FICTIONS, LITERARY CONVENTIONS, AND HISTORICAL METHOD

When in *Thus Was Adonis Murdered* Tamar tries to save Julia from a false accusation of murder that lands her in a Venice prison, he or she encounters an Italian investigator who explains the case: an intellectual woman falling in love for the first time turns to unyielding, violent fury when she discovers that she has been deceived. It seems that the *questore* suffers from the same malady common to so many of Caudwell's characters: thinking in Mandarin cultural terms. On this occasion the world is all rather operatic.[37] A lover murdered in Venice, especially if the death occurs in a hotel named the Cytherea (Aphrodite), requires only a bit of bel canto to explain the motives behind the homicide. Tamar dismisses this sort of psychological explanation and instead shows how textual analysis can assist in recognizing a case of false identification. Resorting to text, of course, is Tamar's specialty. "For the scholar," Tamar elsewhere explains, "the reasoning was very simple. When one finds that two manuscripts have a curious number of features in common, one is disposed to conclude that one is a copy of the other, or that they are copies of the same original."[38]

All this comes naturally to Tamar for life imitates books. Why do people kill out of jealousy? Is there a hot-blooded temperament? No, Tamar answers. It is less a matter of temperament than literary traditions of honor: "People do what books have taught them to do and feel what books have taught them to feel."[39] Tamar blames the English bar's *Guide to Professional Conduct* for making barristers believe that every ethical issue places them in the sort of existential dilemma faced by Sir Thomas More. Tamar's deep-seated attachment to text comes at the expense of any sort of contextual argument. Not surprisingly Tamar announces to chambers that he or she is a "refugee from a gathering of sociologists."[40] Caudwell, of course, underscores the vexed relationship between a set of rules, which are created in the abstract, and their quite tangible though fraught application to a less-ordered set of real-life circumstances.

Caudwell's *The Shortest Way to Hades* provides perhaps the best example of Tamar's unlocking past motives by identifying a textual discrepancy. The method he or she employs is haplography, writing once what should have been copied twice—a common problem found among copyists. In this case a last will was drafted with the wrong name. Caudwell utilizes a classic device of detective fiction: the investigator deploys his or her gaze in an explanatory fashion that remains inexplicable to others until revealed at the opportune moment. Yet Tamar's interpretive strategies are different; he or she does not rely upon the customary modes of detection from classic works of detective fiction writing: observational skills (Sherlock Holmes), the stitching together of gossip in pursuit of the puzzle (Miss Marple), straightforward deductive logic (Hercule Poirot), or the psychological quarrying of motivation (Inspector Maigret). Tamar examines a document and notices what is known in textual criticism as *dictation interne*: when a copyist reads a document but mentally repeats the words and writes what is mistakenly heard.[41] Caudwell's Tamar is radically focused on hermeneutic clues; as Freud famously observes in *Moses and Monotheism*, "The distortion of the text is not unlike a murder. The difficulty lies not in the execution of the deed, but in the doing away of the traces."[42]

In *The Sirens Sang of Murder*, Julia is scandalized by the introduction of a monogrammed fountain pen at a murder site: "On the subject of the pen, Julia became indignant." She had never heard of such a thing,

> at any rate not in any respectable crime fiction published since the beginning of the Second World War. A physical object, forsooth, with the initials of a suspect engraved on it—why, it was worse than a fingerprint. If we must have a clue of a physical nature—and in Julia's experience the best authors nowadays wholly eschewed such vulgarities—then let it at least be one invisible to the naked eye and identifiable only by the most sophisticated techniques of modern pathology. If the progress of the past half-century was to count for nothing, then one might as well go back, said Julia scathingly, to murders committed by means of arsenic or for motives of matrimonial jealousy.[43]

Forensic technology permits the body to serve as a legible text through fingerprint analysis, fragments of DNA, or a study of the pattern of wounds. In contrast, Tamar largely ignores the presence of the corporal forensic subject in much the same way as he or she denies a sexual embodiment.

Throughout the novels Caudwell plays on a central theme: the contrast between the practical, hard-nosed world of British money-making and the odd, surreal spheres of toff-inflected literary and legal culture. At one point, Greek classicism influences sexual conduct when Julia takes the Alcibiades approach to seduction: let the man know you are willing rather than take the initiative. Tamar's quotidian experiences are cast in epic form. Arriving at Victoria Station to set off by train for Sussex, Tamar sounds as if he or she is embarking on the Trojan War: "Victoria—ah, Victoria, starting-point of all true journeys, all southward voyages of pleasure or exploration, all escapes, all elopements, all flights from financial and emotional creditors. At the thought of her infinite possibilities what pulse could fail to beat faster?"[44] Legal texts are similarly portrayed as a kind elite literary gesture. Impenetrable statutes are strewn across the pages of Caudwell's novels: the Variation of Trusts Act, the Finance Act, and the Inland Revenue Act (which Julia unfortunately leaves by the bedside of a murdered lover). When Cantrip's loony uncle wreaks havoc in chambers, Ragwort (one of the younger barristers) considers suing under the classic tort case *Rylands v. Fletcher* (1868), which concerns damages for a wild beast.[45]

With its opaque legal English and claims to be a separate sphere unmoored from immediate self-interest, legal culture has become superstructure in much the same way as has a culture of taste, with its *Bildungsreise* (Julia travels in *Thus Was Adonis Murdered* to Italy with an art lovers group), classical allusions, and Oxbridgian affectations. Law's anomalous relationship to a sordid underworld forms a recurring trope in Caudwell's novels. As legal adviser to the tabloid *Daily Scuttle*, Cantrip is tasked with reading each issue before it goes to press. He explains that the publishers are "subject to the endearing superstition that they will protect themselves, by this ritual, against all claims and proceedings for libel, blasphemy, obscenity, sedition, contempt of court, *scandalum magnatum*, or any other crime or civil wrong known to English law."[46] Law indeed balances the apparent contradiction of claiming legitimacy through its ancient traditions and serving as an instrument for modern corporations. A rather lengthy subplot in *A Sybil in Her Grave* involves the building of new bookcases in chambers. Basil Ptarmigan (the name comes from a particularly sedentary species of bird), QC, "the most silken of Chancery silks," opposes modernization. He demands woodwork that looks like a "set of Chambers where Lord Nottingham just invented the Rule against Perpetuities."[47] Cantrip's solution is simply to hide computer terminals and all sorts of practical devices behind the bookcases. Is law, Caudwell seems to be asking, simply an instance of creative carpentry?

While Caudwell emphasizes the tug of war between British notions of the actual (market economy) and the ideal (valorizing common law), Gur focuses on Israel's social diversity as a patchwork of microsocieties. She discovers normative pluralism grounded in the diverse origins of Jewish citizens—ethnic and political—as well as their unsettling capacity to set themselves apart. In Gur's first novel, *The Saturday Morning Murder*, Ohayon investigates a killing in Jerusalem's psychoanalytic institute. His first intuition is that "the institute had something in common with the guilds of the middle ages": its ceremonies, setting high barriers to entry through training analysis, and its peculiar sense of custom. A professor of literature is murdered in another novel, and Ohayon, discovering that the man's graduate student and acolyte had tacitly agreed to his wife's affair with the professor, observes "Different laws apply here."[48]

Gur's closed societies trace their lineage to the locked room of the British cozy detective story. In his classic study of British detective fiction, *Snobbery with Violence*, Colin Watson describes constructing this sort of hedged-off setting for crime stories, "what we might call the Mayhem Parva school," as a "cross between a village and a commuters' dormitory in the South of England, self-contained and largely self-sufficient. It would have a well-attended church, an inn with reasonable accommodation for itinerant detective-inspectors, a village institute, library and shops—including a chemist's where weed killer and hair dye might be bought. The district would be rural, but not uncompromisingly so—there would be a good bus service for the keeping of suspicious appointments in the nearby town—but its general character would be sufficiently picturesque to chime with the English suburb dweller's sadly uninformed hankering after retirement to the country."[49]

A kibbutz, a psychoanalytic institute, and a symphony orchestra provide Gur's plots with a hermetic milieu much like a remote country house in Yorkshire or a steamship slowly making its way down the Nile. Reflecting the idea of a closed society (and a well-defended psyche), her novel about the psychoanalytic institute begins with images of locks and keys. There is a ritual unlocking of the main door in the morning, training analysts are granted keys as a sign of status, and even the telephone is locked. The gates of the kibbutz make it difficult for a lover from the outside to enter without detection; it is sealed off by large bales of hay that had been stacked into a "broad, high golden wall."[50] But there are fundamental differences between the conventional English mystery taking place in an isolated manor house and Gur's sealed Israeli locations. The barriers constructing the boundaries of Gur's world are not accidents of geography; they are purposeful cultural constructions. Nothing closes off the Literature Department at Hebrew University except its own reified academic culture. Nor are Gur's closed societies mere artifacts of emplotment intended to limit the collection of suspects to those who can fit within an ample drawing room. Particular cultural milieux construct their own hermeneutics establishing a truth test for social facts and fabrications. The historian Wilhelm Dilthey distinguished between empathy, the immediate recognition of the other, and understanding (*Verstehen*), which is a mediated process taking into account the history, language, and episteme of the *other*.[51] Ohayon slowly slips into the character of these different social settings, but more to follow its rhetoric and logical measure of authenticity than to create a connection with his interlocutor. Indeed the insiders in these closed societies often find Ohayon's chameleon-like use of their cultural capital disconcerting. He urges a psychoanalyst to free-associate; at the Literature Department his speech is peppered with literary references. Psychoanalysis and literary interpretation obviously have their own particular hermeneutics, but in *Murder on the Kibbutz,* Ohayon discovers that the kibbutz too bases its authenticity upon a reading of individual actions: the commitment to collective work as expressing redemption through labor (*kiddush ha-avodah*).

Ohayon's insistence upon knowing the "inner life" of the closed society shapes his particular approach to interrogation:[52]

> The only way to get into the wavelength of the person sitting opposite him and pick up the ostensibly trivial thing, the things people said between the lines and sometimes never said at all, that in the last analysis provided the master key solving the mystery. He privately referred to this as "my historical need." In other words, the historian's need to see everything concerning human beings . . . as part of an overall process like a historical process possessing laws on its own, which—he repeatedly explained—if we only were able to grasp their meanings—provide us with the tools for going right to the heart of the problem.[53]

Ohayon detests usual modes of interrogation: the covert threats, grilling a suspect with the Punch and Judy figures of the good and bad cops, the alternative reality of a sealed room with bright lights. He is angered when a Palestinian is questioned alone, for fear undermines understanding.

Instead Ohayon's method of interrogation is to prod suspects into justifying themselves to the interrogator. In order to create trust Ohayon reveals details from his own personal life. Perhaps his interest in psychoanalysis, and in the issue of transference, in *The Saturday Morning Murder* connects to his interrogation practice. The detective questioning must succeed in "becoming a figure with moral authority. One capable of granting absolution. People have a great need for moral justification in general. And sometimes, with some luck, the interrogator can turn into someone who in the suspect's mind's eye can insure forgiveness, pardon, or moral legitimization. He becomes an authority figure."[54] In part this trust rests upon an understanding of the context, the particular norms of the society—and therefore it is also necessary to know the past. What is the genealogical connection between Freud's disciples and Jerusalem's community of psychoanalytic believers? And what fractures have existed in this small world even from the beginning?

In a famous essay published in 1972, "Under This Blazing Light," novelist Amos Oz argues that as a new society Israel lacked the "attic"—the repository of past strata—that makes for a truly great literature.[55] Yet Gur's Ohayon uncovers precisely those sorts of earlier secrets, desires, and transgressions that can be discovered only by rummaging in the past. Not surprisingly this sort of Freudian stripping away of earlier palimpsestic layers might most easily be found in Gur's novel about Jerusalem's psychoanalytic institute, *The Saturday Morning Murder*. Eva Neidorf, a well-respected psychoanalyst of a certain age, is killed before she delivering a lecture on ethical dilemmas encountered during analytic treatment. She has been shot in the temple (does this have psychological significance?), and drafts of her lecture are missing. In order to solve this mystery Ohayon needs to unpack in the mportmanteau fashion the movement's roots in Vienna, the construction of a clinical chronicle from case histories, the narrative of how a band of cultivated Central European émigrés purchased a large house in the Bukharin quarter of Jerusalem—the predecessor to the psychoanalytic institute—in order to create a Freudian community, and what it means to establish a pedigree through training analysis passed down from Freud to leading disciples from his inner circle to a younger, Israel-born generation with very different, decidedly non-Germanic cultural norms.

Yet the novel has its own past, its own attic, that must be excavated (as Ohayon might) in order to understand why homicide could come to a quiet institute in a corner of the upscale Jerusalem neighborhood of Talbieh. Gur never mentions the fact in her novel—and not in any other of her writings that I have seen—but there was a remarkable historical tale, perhaps true or perhaps untrue, linking the founder of the actual institute, Max Eitingon, to murder. In 1988 Stephen Schwartz published a sensational accusation: Eitingon was part of special unit established by Moscow to assassinate anti-Bolshevik exiles in the West. Born to wealthy East European Jews, Eitingon was a trusted and devoted apostle of Freud's in Vienna and the leading psychoanalytic figure in interwar Berlin. Yet Schwartz charges him with serving the Soviet secret police in conjunction with other émigré intellectuals such as the anthropologist Mark Zbrowski and, possibly, working with his close relative Leonid Eitingon, who was the architect of Trotsky's murder in Mexico City.[56]

In *Murder on a Kibbutz*, Ohayon again finds himself confronting the historical transformation of a hermetic place. The Hebrew title, *Linah Meshutefet* [*Shared Sleeping Quarters*], refers to the collective sleeping arrangements for kibbutz children. But the contemporary kibbutz is wrenched in new directions: parents want their offspring to stay at home overnight; meetings held to run the kibbutz, now televised for the benefit of older members, are being watched in living rooms by those disinclined to attend in person; and a clubhouse has replaced the old dining hall. Quotas and bonuses for work supplant an ethos of volunteerism. Pro-privatization members speak of the "new concept." But what really seems to have transpired is a kind of comfortable materialism. Buses now transport kibbutzniks to concerts in town. For the first time members find themselves locking their rooms to prevent burglaries. The kibbutz is suffering from "the curse of affluence." Violent crime is quite rare in kibbutz society, and in the past the kibbutz has survived both profiteering and romantic entanglements. However, in this case embezzlement leads to homicide because it ruptures the entire mythology of the kibbutz at a moment when its cultural fabric is most vulnerable. An old-timer explains to Ohayon what the kibbutz means to those who experienced its founding fifty years earlier: "Those were different times, hard times. . . . It's difficult to transmit what the first contact with the land was like. The hardship, the dryness, the water, the hunger. Especially, the hunger and the hard work. Twelve hours at a stretch sometimes, clearing and plowing, and gradually building. And the heat in summer, the cold in winter, the poverty and the hunger. The men were weak with hunger and hard labor, all of us were. There were days . . . when all we had to eat were two slices of bread and half an egg a day for a pregnant woman, and a few olives."[57]

Such chronicles become the warp and woof of norms. There is no objective history, as Elton suggested, but instead a deeply embraced set of beliefs about an inherited past's character. The homicide in *The Bethlehem Road Murder* is grounded in the claim of Yemenite Jews that in the course of their mass migration to Israel (1948–54) thousands of their young children disappeared from absorption camps and were subsequently adopted by Ashkenazi parents. Gur never examines the validity of this accusation. Nevertheless three commissions of inquiry—the Bahlul-Minkowski Committee (1967), the Shalgi Committee (1988), and the State Commission of Inquiry (1995)—determined that in almost all cases the children had died of natural causes and there was little basis for the allegations. Yet for the purposes of solving the murder, and for understanding the profound ethnographic rifts in a Jerusalem neighborhood, the truth, even if it can be determined conclusively, is less important than the perceived past.

Ohayon employs what Dilthey identifies as *Verstehen* and Atticus Finch would call standing in the shoes of another. Part of *The Saturday Morning Murder* involves digressive conversations about the nature of analysis. In other novels Ohayon immerses himself in various subcultures: in *Murder Duet* he attends a master class by a musician; in *Murder on a Kibbutz* he reads the extensive, tedious kibbutz debates found in crumbling movement journals; he carefully studies the bookcase of a homicide victim in *A Literary Murder*. In *The Saturday Morning Murder* he scrutinizes the row of photographs of the founding generation of psychoanalysts for its genealogical significance. "It's important to us," Ohayon tells a colleague, "because it's important to them. You have to try and enter their world."[58] Accessing the past of another often means uncertainty about what matters: "Only in retrospect is it possible to know whether something is pertinent or not. And, in fact, as an historian, you should realize this. . . . If you go digging around in documents, you don't always know what you are going to find . . . and sometimes you find something completely unexpected which turns out to be the most important thing of all."[59]

A different sort of forensics applies when sleuthing mental worlds. The fundamental principle is that "every contact leaves a trace."[60] Ohayon explains his technique to a skeptical colleague: "I sense the person, I get inside his mind, I think like him, I hear him speak, and then I know. Not the fact, perhaps, but the principle."[61]

Every closed society has its norms, every society its own violations. But to understand these it is necessary to recognize that closed societies are not static. In each of Gur's novels the hermetic world stands at the cusp of a social transformation. In *The Saturday Morning Murder* the rigid, somewhat Germanic notion of the training analyst who would not attend social functions of analysands crumbles as Israelis shift to more informal, personal relationships. The kibbutz is becoming more individualistic, undergoing economic privatization, and embracing family sleeping arrangements rather than collective children's sleeping quarters. In *Murder Duet* a member of a musical family breaches a taboo by advocating the performance of Wagner's music in Israel. And in *The Bethlehem Road Murder* the old Capulet and Montague–style feud between Yemenite and Ashkenazi Jews on this crowded Jerusalem street might be turned topsy-turvy by a younger, romantically adventurous generation.

Dissension and the breakdown of mechanisms to deal with it, such as the *sicha* (the collective debate) in the kibbutz, create the fissures in these closed societies. Yet it is still necessary to know what norms are so powerful as to lead to murder. The commonplace equation in detective fiction is Eros plus Mammon leads to Thanatos. But in Gur's psychoanalytic institute sex becomes explosive *only* when it takes place in the midst of analytic transference and countertransference. Greed prompts homicide when it completely undermines the collective ethos of self-sacrifice in a kibbutz. A young lecturer can subjugate himself to a literary mentor, even acquiescing to his wife's serving as a mistress, until his cherished notions of art are violated by the older man's plagiarism. Violations of sexual taboos and the betrayal of trust in the pursuit of riches have existed in almost every time and place, mostly without recourse to homicide. Gur's norms are more than simple social customs or legal frameworks. Breaching potent cultural norms infused with almost sacred meaning—for love or for money—can lead to defilement, a rupture so powerful than a character is compelled to turn to murder.

PARADIGMS LOST

It comes as no surprise that two detective fiction series should see text and context as the identifying features of the historical method. What else are hallmarks of modern historiography? Throughout their mysteries Caudwell and Gur sharpen their focus on legal textual hermeneutics and social analysis as mechanisms of detection. What is striking, however, is the way these approaches fail the protagonists in Caudwell's and Gur's last novels. Sayers's Aristotelian conventions for the mystery novel underscore the psychological importance of closure. A world shattered by violence must be restored to justice. Detection is a return of the rational, of the moral, of the setting aside of the fundamental fear that we ourselves might be a potential victim or, still worse, a murderer. Why do these authors cast aside their formulae and set up their investor protagonists for failure? What happens when we press forward in time and the trauma is not healed? Are there secrets impenetrable to the historian's gaze?

Caudwell's final novel, *The Sybil in Her Grave*, is the mystery Tamar cannot seem to solve. Robert Renfrew, an aging, respected private banker, faces a problem with inheritance: he has two possible successors as head of the bank. Edgar Albany is a member of the family by both blood and marriage, with Eton and Cambridge pedigrees (a gentleman's third-class degree in history). By contrast Edgar Bolton is said to come from Lancashire, to have a red-brick university education, and to have been influenced by American business culture while living in New York. Albany, of course, is the conservative choice. Bolton's claim to being heir rests upon his tremendous energy. Nothing, however, is as it first appears. It turns out that Bolton actually was educated at an elite public school and received a first at Oxford in philosophy, politics, and economics, but he discovered that he was trusted more if he employed a midlands brogue than if he spoke with a posh accent.[62] And Renfrew suspects one of his potential heirs might be leaking confidential information to traders.

Moreover there are a string of deaths in the small town of Parsons Haver. Isabella Del Comino, a psychic who lived in the Old Rectory, mysteriously turns up dead. A stranger from elsewhere, a craftsman who seems overly interested in the church's stained-glass windows, suddenly appears for her funeral. It turns out he uses an assumed name. There is an ancient book employed by the psychic to prophesy, and possibly the object of burglary. Another villager is struck down by an unknown automobile. Has Parsons Haver suddenly become the crime capital of West Sussex? The local parson in his white robe ascends the pulpit, delivers an odd sermon on Virgil as a prophet citing the Fourth Eclogue (which refers—for readers who do not have their *Oxford Classical Dictionary* handy—to the fact that even in the Apollonian age "old crimes will remain"), and then collapses, dying under suspicious circumstances. He leaves his entire estate to the craftsman. The psychic's niece, Daphne, who has taken upon herself the role of succeeding her aunt as a soothsayer and healer, is found dead in her home. And, finally, a black Mercedes had been spotted in Parsons Haver. Who might be the owner? What is the connection to these recent occurrences?

It sounds like we have a classic British cozy: a remote village with a limited list of suspects, two sets of stories that intertwine: Renfrew (we later discover) is the owner of the Mercedes. Textual analysis leads Tamar to the person guilty of revealing intelligence about pending mergers and acquisitions involving a private London bank. Indeed, with a customary Caudwell touch, Tamar confronts the person beneath a statue of Hermes (god of thieves and tricksters) in London's Sir John Soane's Museum. But the person responsible for the suspicious string of deaths among those connected to this insider training proves elusive. It is only when Tamar understands that the psychic believed in her powers that Tamar determines that there have been no actual murders. Instead a series of accidental fatalities were simply linked in the psychic's mind. The burglary was bogus and the hit-and-run accidental, though the medium believed her spiritualist intervention caused the death. *The Sybil in Her Grave* is a detective novel without a homicide. By desperately seeking to be a psychic healer like her aunt, the niece employs hemlock as a healing potion and brings about the death of the people to whom she is most devoted. Cantrip, who plays a role in all of Caudwell's stories, expresses his dissatisfaction with the story's denouement. Have we "been all wasting our time," he asks disappointingly, since "nothing sinister is going on?"[63]

Like all of Caudwell's mysteries, *The Sybil in Her Grave* has a major epistolary component. The letters shape the texts that Tamar can parse. But the truth embedded in them does not demand fancy textual footwork. Rather it requires understanding the *mentalité* of an oracular figure. Partly the problem is that Tamar, notably lacking personal attachments, misses the niece's, the Sybil's, psychological longing to be an irreplaceable caregiver. More striking, however, is the oversight within the ambit of Tamar's expertise as a medievalist. The person who most believes the Sybil is the Sybil herself. "In order to deceive others, it is necessary also to deceive oneself. The actor playing Hamlet must believe that he is indeed the Prince of Denmark, though when he leaves the stage he will usually remember who he really is. On the other hand, when someone's entire life is based upon pretense, they will seldom if ever return to reality."[64] How could a young clairvoyant in West Sussex see herself as if she spoke prophecies in Delphi or Erythrae? Tamar's tardiness in unraveling the mystery is ironic. The noted medievalist S. D. Goitein asked whether a secular scholar could completely understand a person from the Middle Ages for whom religion is the overriding concern in life.[65] Tamar understands the hermeneutic of medieval texts but remains utterly baffled by the social context and psychological posture of those who lived in earlier ages.

At the end of *A Sybil in Her Grave*, Tamar receives as a gift the mysterious book that was used by the medium for oracular purposes. But now it is disenchanted, and Tamar describes the volume as a "pleasing addition to my modest personal library."[66]

Has Tamar learned anything from this methodological comeuppance? Despite her jocular tone, Caudwell may have left us one final clue. Virgil's Fourth Eclogue represents the prophecy of the last Sybil, the Cumaean Sybil. It is this Sybil who Aeneas consults in book 6 before he descends into Hell, and it is this Sybil whom Virgil presents as foretelling the coming of a messianic savior (who is identified by later Christians as Jesus). The Eclogue begins with an invocation: "Born of time, a great new cycle of centuries begins. Justice returns to earth."[67] Moral choices take place in context. All the psychological perturbations, the passions, the desperate desire to be essential to another embodied by the prophetic Sybil in Caudwell's novel echo the alternatives posed by Virgil's Sybil: leading either to a netherworld or to salvation. Tamar cannot and will not ever learn how to identify these directions. He or she remains unprophetic as well as ungendered.

Gur's final novel, *Murder in Jerusalem*, looks at the microcosm of state-sponsored television. There are all the usual fracture points: politics, religion, lust, and the egotism of those working in a dramatic milieu. But the real problem is the tension between reality and representation. This is reflected in Gur's original Hebrew title, *Retzah, Metsalmim*, which might be loosely translated as "Murder, Photographing." The killing itself is directly linked to the camera as a technology for (personal and collective) self-fashioning. By recording images the camera dangerously serves as an ocular presence for recording a past that will be too candid, too threatening. Alternatively the photographic record is a contrived artifact and therefore can be rehabilitated to create an idealized representation. The title also refers to the first murder, which occurs during the filming of a production of Nobel Prize author S. Y. Agnon's *Ido and Enam* when the actress Tirzah, who played the female lead role, was murdered on the set.

Agnon's enigmatic story—itself a kind of sibylline tale—revolves around prophecy. It describes the possession of Gemulah, the young wife of an antiquarian bookseller who was brought from a distant land to Jerusalem. She remains attached to Dr. Ginath, a mysterious philologist, who somehow compels her to set forth on mysterious nightly journeys across the city, especially when there is a full moon. While her wanderings are prompted by erotic urges, Ginath also seeks to draw from her lips a lost book written in a distant tongue. Yet the expression of that mythic language leads to an uncontrollable somnambulism, and ultimately both moonstruck lovers plummet from a rooftop and die.[68]

Ginath is obsessed with recovering a pure, absolutely complete text of a missing book, *Enamite Hymns*, a "new-found link in a chain that bound the beginnings of recorded history to the ages before."[69] The philologist shares Ohayon's remorseless need to uncover the past, but in his case the impulse is so great that he wishes to destroy the flawed, partial record of the *Hymns* that he has within his possession.

In the end he creates a new text of sorts after compelling Gemulah's moonlit recital of the verse chronicle—not the lost book, of course, but the record of destruction wrought on the rooftops of Jerusalem.

This is a disquieting tale. Does the unrelenting desire for a perfect text (or a perfect historical narrative of an idealized past) bring about cataclysmic results? Is photography, when pressed to assume a relentless truth-telling role, simply a modern-day version of Ginath's mania? It is clear that Gemulah's death is the *ur*-murder in *A Death in Jerusalem*, much as Eitingon's alleged killing serves that unspoken role in *The Saturday Morning Murder*. At play are norms for journalists, such as transparency and responsibility to the public, and these norms are conflicted throughout Gur's novel. Gur tosses out the usual red herrings: professional jealousies and a love triangle involving Tirzah. The real story is more ominous. It emerges that a handful of ex-soldiers kept a painful secret. During the 1973 Yom Kippur War a platoon of Israeli soldiers brutally killed prisoners who had surrendered. They agreed to keep silent, convinced of the damage such a disclosure might inflict on the fragile peace with Egypt. But mostly the problem lies in the trauma of the past event itself, for to cover up this war crime a member of the platoon was willing to murder even those closest to him, Tirzah and other fellow secret bearers.

Murder in Jerusalem is Gur's most overtly political novel. It is also her most psychological. The mythological parents of a generation were Holocaust survivors, refugees from Arab pogroms, heirs to ideologies of collective purity such as the kibbutz movement—the enemies of violence. Purity, it turns out, was a "constructive lie." The slaughtering of prisoners in cold blood therefore implied the symbolic murder of these parents. "My whole life, our whole lives," confessed the killer," are a cover-up for the murder of our mother and father, and for the murder we committed. It wasn't exactly a lie; the fig leaf was not a lie, but a culture, a way of life. It was all that we had."[70]

Tirzah, the actress performing in the enigmatic Agnon tale, does not consider decades of atonement after the War of Atonement sufficient. Believing in the purity of the mythological past, she refuses to keep silent and instead accuses a member of the platoon of committing this ultimate patricide. But Tirzah too, like Agnon's protagonist, finds that mythic speech leads to death. What about Ohayon? At the conclusion of the novel he has a heartfelt discussion with his deeply critical adolescent son about Israel's future. Ohayon finds himself defending the very notion of a homeland. Connection, national narratives, and commitment are raised as crucial to the process of making a society. In the end truth may not be his highest value. The foundational myths, the very core values of self-contained realms such as psychoanalysis, kibbutz collectivism, music and literature, journalism and, perhaps even modern Israel, which was conceived as part of a utopian project, might in the end lead to murder. But they also form the fabric of society. After solving the homicide in the television studio, Ohayon remains troubled by the consequences. The truth threatens to corrode idealistic impulses. "What's so disagreeable about myths?" Ohayon asks.[71]

Text and context turn back on themselves in Möbius fashion. In the end Caudwell's Tamar understands that text must take into account the particular cultural context (even if it is irrational) of individuals. The past, with its peculiar *mentalité*, resurfaces as a dense cultural matrix shaping a person's choices. Gur's Ohayon discovers that closed societies are not set apart simply by guild rituals or segregated space, such as he found at the psychoanalytic institute and the kibbutz. Israel's distinct mythos seals the country off in a certain fashion. Its distinctive narrative as a utopian-refugee state and its sense of being under siege by hostile neighbors not only have provided the sinews for a new society but have also served to construct barriers. These myths, Gur's last novel tells us, demand to be read as texts.

Neither of these two last novels leaves us with a neatly packaged conclusion. There are no homicides in Caudwell's novel, simply the bringing to light of a medium's worldview as she claims the oracular power to shape matters of life and death. Gur's Ohayon does apprehend the murderer, but he harbors lingering doubts about the destructive legacy of uncovering truth. Most important, both Caudwell and Gur abandon the historical forensics they established in their earlier books. While Aristotelian principles might work to establish a *poetics* of sleuthing, historical method can never be mechanistic or conventional.

Neither text nor context alone can truly explain a phenomenon as complex as the past—its endless labyrinth of "cunning passages, contrived corridors."[72] But beyond situating legal history in its familiar dichotomy—text and context, sleuthing amid the sophisticated rhetorical architecture of legal language and rule or, alternatively, situating law in a complex social ecosystem—what other possibilities might there be? In these concluding novels a third, destabilizing historical voice is added: prophecy. How might historians react when their own comfortable formulae are shattered by those whose episteme includes the unreal, the apocalyptic, or the utopian? A distant, mythic disruptive prophetic past—evoked by both the Virgilian Sybil and Agnon's Gemulah—unsettles even the most adroit historian's craft.

NOTES

1. Kunal Parker, *Common Law: History and Democracy in America 1790–1900* (Cambridge University Press, 2013); Steven Wilf, "Law/Text/Past," 1 *U.C. Irvine L. Rev.* 543 (2011).

2. Dorothy Sayer's protagonist, Lord Peter Wimsey, received a first in history from Balliol College. Alfred Alexander Gordon Clark, a British judge trained in history and law at Oxford,

wrote under the pseudonym Cyril Hare a particularly well-crafted mystery, *An English Murder* (1951) (reprinted Faber and Faber, 2009), centered upon a Jewish Central European émigré historian. Most notably Fred Vargas (the pseudonym of a renowned French archaeologist who specializes in the bubonic plague and is the sister of an equally well-regarded historian of World War I) authored a series of *roman-policier*, or *polar*, books about a threesome of underemployed historians known as the three evangelists, who inhabit a ramshackle house in Paris. See *Debout les morts* (Viviane Hamy, 1995), *Un peu plus loin sur la droite* (Éditions J'ai Lu, 2000), and *Sans feu ni lieu* (Éditions J'ai Lu, 2001). More generally see Guillaume Lebeau, *Le Mystère Fred Vargas* (Éditions Gutenberg, 2009).

3. Vargas, *Debout les morts*, 109.

4. Sarah Caudwell, *Thus Was Adonis Murdered* (Scribner, 1981), *The Shortest Way to Hades* (Dell, 1985), *The Sirens Sang of Murder* (William Collins Sons, 1989), *The Sybil in Her Grave* (Delacorte Press, 2001).

5. Caudwell, *The Sirens Sang of Murder*, 5.

6. Caudwell, *The Shortest Way to Hades*, 81.

7. Batya Gur, *The Saturday Morning Murder: A Psychoanalytic Case* (HarperCollins, 1992), *Literary Murder: A Critical Case* (HarperCollins 1993), *Murder on a Kibbutz: A Communal Case* (HarperCollins, 1994), *Murder Duet: A Musical Case* (HarperCollins, 2000), *Bethlehem Road Murder: A Michael Ohayon Mystery* (HarperCollins 2004), *Murder in Jerusalem: A Michael Ohayon Mystery* (HarperCollins 2006).

8. Gur, *Murder Duet*, 1.

9. Gur approaches Jerusalem with a sense of loss, mourning the quiet, intimate academic community built by Jewish refugees in the early and mid-twentieth century. See Batya Gur, *In Jerusalem leben: Ein Requiem auf die Bescheidenheit* (Schöffling, 2000).

10. "Sarah Caudwell Cockburn," *Oxford Dictionary of National Biography*, http://www.oxforddnb.com/view/printable/73725.

11. Dorothy L. Sayers, "Aristotle on Detective Fiction," in *Unpopular Opinions: Twenty-One Essays* (Harcourt, Brace, 1947), 225.

12. Gur, *Literary Murder*, 152, 71, 99.

13. Caudwell, *The Sybil in Her Grave*, 2.

14. Caudwell, *The Shortest Way to Hades*, 69.

15. Sayers, "Aristotle on Detective Fiction," 225.

16. W. Somerset Maugham, "The Decline and Fall of the Detective Novel," in *The Vagrant Mood: Six Essays* (Doubleday Press, 1952), 117.

17. Cushing Strout, "Romance and the Literary Detective: The Legacy of Dorothy Sayers," 109 *Sewanee Review* (2001): 423–436, quote on 426.

18. Caudwell, *The Sirens Sang of Murder*, 145.

19. Caudwell, *The Sybil in Her Grave*, 203.

20. Ibid., 236.

21. Raymond Chandler, "The Simple Art of Murder (1944)," in *Chandler: Later Novels and Other Writings* (Library of America, 1995), 977, 990.

22. Quoted in Peter Gay, *Style in History* (Basic Books, 1974), 57–94.

23. Caudwell, *Thus Was Adonis Murdered*, 1.

24. Dorothy L. Sayers, *Unnatural Death* (Golancz, 1937).

25. Caudwell, *The Sirens Sang of Murder*, 11.

26. Caudwell, *Thus Was Adonis Murdered*, 7.

27. Caudwell, *The Shortest Way to Hades*, 18.

28. Caudwell, *Thus Was Adonis Murdered*, 37.

29. Gur, *Murder Duet*, 8.

30. P. D. James, *Talking about Detective Fiction* (Bodleian Library, 2009), 154.

31. Gur, *Bethlehem Road Murder*, 93, 96.

32. Gur, *The Saturday Morning Murder*, 152.

33. Gur, *Murder in a Kibbutz*, 85; Gur, *The Saturday Morning Murder*, 190.

34. Gur, *Murder Duet*, 241.

35. Ibid., 242.

36. Ibid., 11, 245.

37. Caudwell, *Thus Was Adonis Murdered*, 160–61.

38. Caudwell, *The Sirens Sang of Murder*, 152.

39. Ibid., 175.

40. Caudwell, *The Shortest Way to Hades*, 48–49, 7.

41. Caudwell, *The Shortest Way to Hades*, 106.

42. Sigmund Freud, *Moses and Monotheism*, trans. Katherine Jones (Vintage, 1939), 32.

43. Caudwell, *The Sirens Sang of Murder*, 97.

44. Caudwell, *The Shortest Way to Hades*, 75.

45. Caudwell, *The Sirens Sang of Murder*, 75; *Rylands v. Fletcher*, [1868] UKHL 1.

46. Caudwell, *Thus Was Adonis Murdered*, 27.

47. Caudwell, *The Sybil in Her Grave*, 25.

48. Gur, *Literary Murder*, 152.

49. Colin Watson, *Snobbery with Violence: English Crime Stories and Their Audience* (1971), revised ed. (Methuen 1987), 169–70.

50. Gur, *Murder on a Kibbutz*, 1.

51. Dilthey, "The Understanding of Other Persons and Their Manifestations of Life" (1910). In selected works: vol. 3, Wilhelm Dilthey, "The Understanding of Other Persons and Their Manifestations of Life," in *The Formation of the Historical World in the Human Sciences*, trans. Rudolf A. Makkreel and John Scanlon (Princeton University Press, 2002 [1910]), 226.

52. Gur, *The Saturday Morning Murder*, 50.

53. Ibid., 51.

54. Gur, *Murder Duet*, 420.

55. Amos Oz, "Under This Blazing Light," in *Under This Blazing Light* (Cambridge University Press, 1995), 19–35.

56. Stephen Schwartz, "Intellectuals and Assassins—Annals of Stalin's Killerati," *New York Times Book Review*, January 24, 1988. See the following responses: Theodore H. Draper, "The Mystery of Max Eitingon," *New York Review of Books*, April 14, 1988, which argues that Schwartz's accusations are false and that he is engaged in character assassination. Robert Conquest, "Max Eitingon: Another View," *New York Times*, July 3, 1988. Mary-Kay Wilmers, the founding editor of the *London Review of Books* and a member of the Eitingon family, was prompted by this controversy to write an investigative memoir of her family, *The Eitingons: A Twentieth-Century Story* (London: Faber and Faber, 2009).

57. Gur, *Murder on a Kibbutz*, 22–23, 49, 151, 169.

58. Gur, *Literary Murder*, 183.

59. Gur, *Bethlehem Road Murder*, 126.

60. Gur, *Murder Duet*, 138.

61. Gur, *Literary Murder*, 245.

62. Caudwell, *The Sybil in Her Grave*, 323.

63. Ibid., 270.

64. Ibid., 293.

65. Shlomo Dov Goitein, "Religion in Everyday Life as Reflected in the Documents of the Cairo Geniza," in *Religion in a Religious Age*, ed. Shlomo Dov Goitein (Association for Jewish Studies, 1974), 3–4.

66. Caudwell, *The Sybil in Her Grave*, 296.

67. Virgil, "The Eclogues," in *The Eclogues, Georgics, and Aeneid of Virgil*, trans. C. Day Lewis (Oxford University Press, 1979), 18.

68. On Agnon's *Ido and Enam*, see Ilana Pardes, *Agnon's Moonstruck Lovers: The Song of Songs in Israeli Culture* (University of Washington Press, 2013), 98–119; Yaniv Hagbi, *Language, Absence, Play: Judaism and Superstructuralism in the Poetics of S. Y. Agnon* (Syracuse University Press, 2009), 89–91.

69. S. Y. Agnon, *Two Tales: Betrothed and Edo and Enam*, trans. Walter Lever (Schocken, 1966), 152.

70. Gur, *Murder in Jerusalem*, 373.

71. Ibid., 385.

72. T. S. Eliot, *Gerontion*, in *The Complete Poems and Plays 1909–1950* (Harcourt, Brace, and World, 1971), 22.

Index